Creating Heritage for

What does 'heritage' mean in the twenty-first century? Traditional ideas of heritage involve places where objects, landscapes, people and ideas are venerated and reproduced over time as an inheritance for future generations. To speak of heritage is to speak of a relationship between the past, the present and the future. However, it is a past recreated for economic gain, hence sectors such as culinary tourism, ecotourism, cultural tourism and film tourism have employed the heritage label to attract visitors.

This interdisciplinary book furthers understanding on how heritage is socially constructed, interpreted and experienced within different geographic and cultural contexts, in both Western and non-Western settings. Subjects discussed include Welsh linguistic heritage, tango, mushroom tourism, Turkish coffee, literary tourism and the techniques employed to construct tourist accommodation. By focusing upon heritage *creation* in the context of tourism, the book moves beyond traditional debates about 'authentic heritage' to focus on how something *becomes* heritage for use in the present.

This timely volume will be of interest to students and researchers in tourism, heritage studies, geography, museum studies and cultural studies.

Catherine Palmer, PhD, is an anthropologist, University of Brighton, UK, and a Fellow of the Royal Anthropological Institute. Her research focuses on identity, heritage and materiality; post-conflict/memorial landscapes; embodiment, tourism; and the coast/seaside. She is the joint book series editor for 'Routledge Advances in Tourism Anthropology' (with Jo-Anne Lester), and the author of the 2018 Routledge monograph *Being and Dwelling Through Tourism: An Anthropological Perspective*. She is the editor of *Tourism Research Methods: Integrating Theory and Practice* (with Pete Burns and Brent Ritchie) and *Tourism and Visual Culture: Volume 1 Theories and Concepts* (with Pete Burns and Jo-Anne Lester).

Jacqueline Tivers, PhD, is an honorary research associate in geography at Oxford Brookes University, UK, and a previous Chair of the Geography of Leisure and Tourism Research Group of the Royal Geographical Society–Institute of British Geographers. She has published several books, contributions to edited collections, and journal articles during her long career as a lecturer and researcher in geography. She is joint editor (with Tijana Rakic) of *Narratives of Travel and Tourism*, a previously published book within the 'Geographies of Leisure and Tourism Research Group (GLTRG)' series.

Current Developments in the Geographies of Leisure and Tourism

Tourism and leisure exist within an inherently dynamic, fluid and complex world and are therefore inherently interdisciplinary. Recognising the role of tourism and leisure in advancing debates within the social sciences, this book series is open to contributions from cognate social science disciplines that inform geographical thought about tourism and leisure. Produced in association with the Geographies of Leisure and Tourism Research Group of the Royal Geographical Society (with the Institute of British Geographers), this series highlights and promotes cutting-edge developments and research in this field. Contributions are of a high international standard and provide theoretically informed empirical content to facilitate the development of new research agendas in the field of tourism and leisure research. In general, the series seeks to promote academic contributions that advance contemporary debates that challenge and stimulate further discussion and research both within the fields of tourism and leisure and the wider realms of the social sciences.

Series Editors: Jan Mosedale and Caroline Scarles

Other titles in the series:

Moral Encounters in Tourism
Edited by Mary Mostafanezhad and Kevin Hannam

Travel and Imagination
Edited by Garth Lean, Russell Staiff and Emma Waterton

Neoliberalism and the Political Economy of Tourism
Edited by Jan Mosedale

Creating Heritage for Tourism
Edited by Catherine Palmer and Jacqueline Tivers

For more information about this series, please visit www.routledge.com/ Current-Developments-in-the-Geographies-of-Leisure-and-Tourism/book-series/ ASHSER1372

Creating Heritage for Tourism

**Edited by
Catherine Palmer and
Jacqueline Tivers**

Routledge
Taylor & Francis Group

LONDON AND NEW YORK

First published 2019
by Routledge

2 Park Square, Milton Park, Abingdon, Oxfordshire OX14 4RN
52 Vanderbilt Avenue, New York, NY 10017

Routledge is an imprint of the Taylor & Francis Group, an informa business

First issued in paperback 2020

British Library Cataloguing-in-Publication Data
A catalogue record for this book is available from the British Library

Library of Congress Cataloging-in-Publication Data
A catalog record has been requested for this book

ISBN: 978-1-138-57271-3 (hbk)
ISBN: 978-0-367-66591-3 (pbk)

Typeset in Times New Roman
by Swales & Willis Ltd, Exeter, Devon, UK

Contents

Illustrations

Figures

Tables

Contributors

Julia Nina Albrecht, PhD, is a senior lecturer at the University of Otago (New Zealand). Her research interests include tourism management and strategy, visitor management, guiding and interpretation, and nature-based tourism.

Kimberly Berg is a doctoral candidate at the State University of New York at Albany, and studies identity and tourism through the lenses of linguistic revitalisation, nationalism, and transnational heritage production. Kimberly has conducted research in Wales, Argentina, and with the Welsh descendant communities of North America by exploring the ways in which language ideologies influence individual actors to participate in Welsh cultural heritage revitalisation efforts. Kimberly's research uses qualitative social network analysis to understand how heritage networks, as influenced by homeland institutions, mediate what it means to be Welsh in the context of Welsh diaspora communities.

Giovanna Bertella, PhD, is associate professor at the School of Business and Economics, UiT The Arctic University of Norway. She received her PhD on learning and networking in tourism from the Department of Sociology, Political Science and Community Planning at UiT. Her research interests are: small-scale tourism, food tourism, rural tourism, nature-based tourism, animal-based tourism, active tourism, entrepreneurship, experience design, event management, knowledge and networks. She has published and reviewed several papers in international journals and is a member of the editorial board of *Gastronomy and Tourism*.

Maurizio Droli, PhD, is an economic sociologist with a PhD in rural and business economics, 'Doctor Europaeus' certified. He is a research fellow at the University of Udine, Italy, serving in the fields of sustainable food tourism, rural, health and wellness tourism. His research fields include: economic potentials of UE-USA business-to-business markets, business model innovation ('albergo diffuso'), public–private partnering processes innovation and 'health and wellness' ecosystem services innovation.

Michael Fagence, PhD, is Honorary Research Fellow at the University of Queensland and is first and foremost a geographer. Excursions into town planning, tourism planning, history and heritage have all drawn on the toolkit of a deeply-ingrained undergraduate training in geography. Recently, interest in historical geography and history-linked and heritage-based tourism has aligned his application of the processes of 'thinking geographically' with others from semiotics to forge a particular form of epistemological pluralism with which to investigate historical and heritage landscapes.

Duccio Gasparri is a PhD candidate in social anthropology at the social sciences department of Oxford Brookes University, funded by a joint scholarship from the University and the Sasakawa Foundation. He graduated in anthropology at Venice University in Italy, with a thesis on representation aesthetics of contemporary Japanese fake-food models (*shokuhin sanpuru*). He is currently conducting fieldwork on the social and commercial roles of local food in post-disaster Miyagi Prefecture, north-eastern Japan. His interests include post-disaster studies, social change, Japanese food, media, photography, and domestic tourism. He hosts a weekly broadcast on Japanese news and culture with an Italian radio station.

Penny Grennan, PhD, is an artist and researcher. She gained her PhD in fine art practice on the value of souvenirs in 2015 and she continues to research, make work and explore this area of study. She has given papers, shown films and exhibited at conferences on: travel writing, objects in literature, archiving, literary form and visual culture, on memory, commemoration and memorial and at the International Conference of Art Historians. She has exhibited in Newcastle, Oxford, London, Boston Spa and Japan and has taught at Newcastle and Northumbria Universities. She is currently researching the narrative content of mantelpieces.

Ilkay Tas Gursoy, PhD, is assistant professor in the Tourism Management Department, Reha Midilli Foca Faculty of Tourism, Dokuz Eylul University. She is acting as the co-head of the European Union Department at the Graduate School of Social Sciences, Dokuz Eylul University. Her research interests include cultural heritage, sustainable tourism, health tourism and tourism policies of the EU. She is a member of the executive team in the Jean Monnet Chair in European Social Policy Project and Heart of Anatolia Jean Monnet Center of Excellence Project.

James Higham, PhD, is a professor of tourism at the University of Otago (New Zealand) and visiting professor of sustainable tourism at the University of Stavanger (Norway). He serves at the co-editor of the *Journal of Sustainable Tourism*.

Alan Hooper is a qualified architect with over twenty years' teaching experience, leading the BArch (Hons) Programme at the Mackintosh School of Architecture since 2008. Alan represented Scotland at the 2014 Venice Biennale leading a team from The Glasgow School of Art and Strathclyde University presenting research on the impact of twentieth-century modernism on Glasgow's nineteenth-century urban grid. Alan's research interests originate from his lifelong relationship with the city of Glasgow. His interest in the impact of geology, architecture's hidden landscape, originated from observation of the rich interplay between Glasgow's urban grid overlying an undulating landscape hewn by glaciers.

George S. Jaramillo, PhD, is a research associate/lecturer for The Glasgow School of Art in its Highlands and Islands campus in Forres. As part of the Innovation School, his main focus is on challenging Historical Highland Romantic perceptions and acknowledging contemporary Hebridean realities. In understanding these ideas, new industries and innovation can be developed to create the future heritage of the region. His interests also include cultural geographic themes of deindustrialised landscapes focusing on the intersection between material phenomenologies, performative politics, social entities and labour that goes into making those landscapes.

Venetia Johannes, PhD, completed her doctorate in anthropology at the University of Oxford in October 2015, where she also completed an MSc in social anthropology in 2011. For her doctoral research, she studied how Catalans use food and cuisine to express their national identity. Previously she studied business management at the Royal Agricultural University (2007–2010), and following her doctorate she spent a year in fund management and marketing research. She is currently a post-doctoral research associate with the School of Anthropology and Museum Ethnography at the University of Oxford. She is publishing a book based on her doctoral research, due in 2019.

Annaclaudia Martini is a PhD researcher, Department of Cultural Geography, faculty of Spatial Sciences at the University of Groningen, the Netherlands. She has degrees of Master in cultural anthropology and Bachelor in Japanese language and culture. Before her PhD she worked as an information architect and journalist. Current research focuses on emotional and affective experiences of tourists in places of dark tourism, specifically how foreign tourists negotiate their emotions and affects in visits to the disaster area in the region of Tohoku, Japan, hit in 2011 by an earthquake, a tsunami and a nuclear meltdown in the Fukushima nuclear power plant.

Brent Mckenzie, MBA, PhD, is an associate professor, Department of Marketing and Consumer Studies, at the University of Guelph, Guelph, Canada. Dr. McKenzie is a specialist on the Baltic Republics of Estonia, Latvia, and Lithuania, and the former Soviet Union. He has engaged in extensive research fieldwork, and conducted a number of academic and industry workshops, presentations, and seminars in these countries. His research has been widely published in both academic and practitioner journals. Dr. McKenzie is an Associate Editor for the *Baltic Journal of Management*, and a Regional Editor – Eastern Europe, for the *International Journal of Business and Emerging Markets*.

David McLaughlin, PhD, completed his doctorate in the geography department at the University of Cambridge in 2018. His thesis looked at literary guidebooks and travel writing about the world of Sherlock Holmes, written by readers, for readers. Its aim was to understand how these 'Sherlockians' have collectively recreated the Sherlock Holmes stories in their own image. He holds an MA in Australian studies from King's College London. His dissertation explored how Australian guidebooks represented Great Britain as a tourist destination. His most recent article 'The Game's Afoot: Walking as Practice in Sherlockian Literary Geographies' was published in the journal *Literary Geographies*.

Claudio Milano, PhD, based at the Ostelea School of Tourism and Hospitality, University of Lleida, Spain). His research focuses on sociocultural impacts of tourism (rural and urban), heritage and tourism, tourism, resistance protests and social movements. Previously, visiting lecturer, Federal University of Piauí (Brazil), the Strathmore University of Nairobi (Kenya), and the University of Colombo (Sri Lanka). Recent publications include: 'Otherness Anthropologies: Toward Ibero-American Anthropologies of Tourism' *American Anthropologist*; 'El turismo en el mundo rural ¿Ruina o consolidación de las sociedades campesinas e indígenas?' *Pasos - Journal of Tourism and Cultural Heritage* with J. Gascón.

Catherine Palmer, PhD, is an anthropologist, University of Brighton, UK, and a Fellow of the Royal Anthropological Institute. Her research focuses on identity, heritage and materiality; post-conflict/memorial landscapes; embodiment; tourism; and the coast/seaside. She is the joint book series editor for 'Routledge Advances in Tourism Anthropology' (with Jo-Anne Lester), and the author of the 2018 Routledge monograph *Being and Dwelling through Tourism: An Anthropological Perspective*. She is the editor of *Tourism Research Methods: Integrating Theory and Practice* (with Pete Burns and Brent Ritchie) and *Tourism and Visual Culture: Volume 1 Theories and Concepts* (with Pete Burns and Jo-Anne Lester).

Felicity Picken, PhD, is a lecturer in the School of Social Sciences and Psychology at Western Sydney University in Australia. When she is focused on land, her work examines the relationships between architecture, heritage, tourism and urban design with a particular interest in the way these constitute a reinterpretation and re-evaluation of relations with the environment. At sea, her work extends this focus to the increasing intensity and diversity of relations with oceanic worlds. In this she sees the emergence of the blue planet as a significant social actor and shaper of contemporary life.

Krupa Rajangam is a Bangalore based conservation architect and Research Scholar (MA in Conservation Studies, University of York, UK) with over 14 years' field-based conservation experience. An INTACH Research Scholar, NIAS Fellow, Charles Wallace Scholar and Zibby Garnett Fellow, she is Founder-Director of the collaborative heritage practice, Saythu – linking people and heritage. Currently she is PhD researcher for the National Institute of Advanced Studies, Bangalore, conducting ethnographic fieldwork focusing on the different 'communities' relationship with the 'heritage idea' at Hampi World Heritage Site, India.

Hayley Saul, PhD, is a lecturer at Western Sydney University in Australia and Director of the Himalayan Exploration and Archaeological Research Team (H.E.A.R.T). Her heritage and archaeology research in the Himalayas, operates at the interface with development agendas. H.E.A.R.T is partnered with Himalayan communities and a range of NGOs to operationalise research results and bring about positive benefits to rural Nepalese communities. Hayley undertook an AHRC-funded post-doctorate with the Early Pottery in East Asia Project and was a Japan Society for the Promotion of Science post-doctoral fellow, to investigate cuisine in prehistoric hunter-gatherer groups in Denmark, northern Germany and Japan.

Tina Šegota, PhD, is a lecturer at the Department of Marketing, Events and Tourism at the University of Greenwich. She holds a PhD in marketing communications from the Faculty of Social Sciences, University of Ljubljana, and she is also a PhD candidate in tourism at the Faculty of Economics, University of Ljubljana. Her research interests are seasonality and sustainable tourism development, with a passionate focus on local residents. She is also interested in destination image, self-congruity and destination advertising. She has published in leading journals and has co-authored several book chapters.

William Ling Shi is a PhD candidate in the Faculty of Hospitality and Tourism Management at Macau University of Science and Technology, Macau, China. His current research addresses the field of the heritage hotel, sustainable tourism, and tourism planning.

Jonathan Skinner, PhD, MA (University of St. Andrews) is reader in anthropology at the University of Roehampton. He has undertaken fieldwork in the Eastern Caribbean on the island of Montserrat (tourism and trauma, colonial relations and disaster recovery) and in the US/UK (social dancing, arts health, contested heritage). He co-edits the book series 'Movement and Performance Studies' for Berghahn Publishers with Professor Helena Wulff (University of Stockholm). Key tourism-related publications are: Skinner, J. (ed.) (2012) *Writing the Dark Side of Travel* (Berghahn); Skinner, J. and D. Theodossopoulos (eds) (2011) *Great Expectations: Imagination, Anticipation, and Enchantment in Tourism* (Berghahn).

Humberto Thomé-Ortiz, doctor in rural sciences from the Autonomous University of Chapingo. He is a full-time faculty at the Institute for Agricultural and Rural Sciences (ICAR) of the Autonomous University of the State of Mexico and a member of the National Researchers System. His research interests are local agro-food systems, territorial development and agro-food tourism. He is the principal investigator of the project 'Evaluation of the recreational dimension of wild edible mushrooms, their socio-economic interest and their prospects for rural development' funded by the Mexican National Council of Science and Technology.

Jacqueline Tivers, PhD, is an honorary research associate in geography at Oxford Brookes University, UK and a previous Chair of the Geography of Leisure and Tourism Research Group of the Royal Geographical Society–Institute of British Geographers. She has published several books, contributions to edited collections, and journal articles during her long career as a lecturer and researcher in geography. She is joint editor (with Tijana Rakic) of *Narratives of Travel and Tourism*, a previously published book within the GLTRG series.

Emma Waterton, PhD, is an associate professor in the School of Social Sciences and Psychology at Western Sydney University, and an institute fellow in the Institute for Culture and Society. Her research explores the interface between heritage, identity, memory and affect. She is author of over 80 publications in the field of heritage, including the authored monograph *Politics, Policy and the Discourses of Heritage in Britain* (2010), and the co-authored volumes *Heritage, Communities and Archaeology* (with Laurajane Smith; 2009) and *The Semiotics of Heritage Tourism* (with Steve Watson; 2014). She co-edits the book series *Critical Studies in Heritage, Emotion and Affect* (Routledge).

Philip Feifan Xie, PhD, is Professor of Tourism, Leisure and Event Planning at Bowling Green State University, the US. His research interests include cultural and heritage tourism, event management and the morphology of tourism.

Guojie Zhang, is a PhD candidate at the University of Otago (New Zealand). His current research interests lie in the areas of environmental philosophy and tourism development at urban ecological attractions.

Acknowledgements

Every book has a point of inspiration and the one for this book belongs to a conference panel on *New Directions in Heritage Tourism*, co-convened by us in 2016 as part of the Annual International Conference of the Royal Geographical Society with the Institute of British Geographers (RGS-IBG). Our panel was sponsored by the Geographies of Leisure and Tourism Research Group (GLTRG), which provides an intellectual home for 'thinking geographically' in relation to tourism. We would like to extend our sincere gratitude to the RGS-IGB and to the GLTRG for hosting our sessions. A big thank you to all the contributors to our panel and to the various members of each audience all of whom made the conference such a stimulating experience. The presentations and the discussions that flowed from them were highly enjoyable and enabled us, as editors, to refine the focus for the call for abstracts that has resulted in this book. We are particularly grateful to all the authors who responded to our open call for chapter proposals, many of which we were unable to accept due to the restrictions of a single volume. The selection process was not an easy undertaking.

A huge thank you also goes to the editorial and production team at Routledge for supporting us throughout the process.

1 Heritage for tourism

Creating a link between the past and the present

Catherine Palmer and Jacqueline Tivers

The traditional understanding of heritage is that it refers to stories about the past drawn from the events, activities, places, objects, landscapes, people and ideas venerated and reproduced over time as an inheritance for future generations. To speak of heritage is, therefore, to speak of a relationship that brings the past into the present. However, this is a socially constructed relationship because it is based upon the concerns of those individuals and groups that choose how the past should be used in the present. As such, what is labelled heritage in the present tells us as much about the here and now as it does about what took place in the past. The association of heritage with the notion that something of value, an inheritance, is being handed down for safe keeping to a legatee in the present is a well established theme in the literature, so it is not our intention to go over existing arguments (see Lowenthal 1998, Ashworth and Tunbridge 2000, Samuel 2012). Our intention here is to explore the ways in which that which is labelled as heritage is created in the first place and what this created heritage communicates about the experience of the past in the present. By focusing upon heritage *creation* in the context of tourism we move beyond debates about the extent to which what is presented is or is not 'authentic heritage' to focus on how something *becomes* heritage for use in the present.

The sense of there being a legatee is important here because it means that the experience that is created is always personalised; there is always a me, us, our or we written into the uses that are made of the past. Personalising the past is one of the ways in which individuals and communities come to understand their place in the world and its relationship with the world of others. As Graburn (2001: 68) argues heritage 'as both "own" and "owned" makes necessary the consideration of inter-generational cultural continuity, as well as the conception of "others" and "alterity"'. This is not to say that everyone who encounters the past as heritage through tourism feels a personal connection with what is presented; what matters is that the potential to do so lies at the heart of every heritage experience. This is important because the link between the past and the present needs to be understood on the basis of a felt experience with a past that *matters* in order to encourage people to visit heritage sites. Indeed, Timothy and Boyd (2006) have argued that the ability of heritage sites to create affective social, psychological and historical links with individuals highlights the significance of heritage in the twenty-first century.

This personalised felt experience could be in terms of the synergy created between the heritage values manifest in a particular site and the personal values of a visiting tourist. These values might, for example, relate to conserving the heritage of a region's natural biodiversity; thus UNESCO World Heritage Status has been granted to national parks that include the Everglades in Florida, The Serengeti in Tanzania, The Wadden Sea in the Netherlands and the Nanda Devi and Valley of Flowers National Park in India. On the other hand, the values that attract visitors could relate to what have been described as felt kinship ties (Palmer 2005), for example those experienced by a family member visiting a former coalmine where a parent or grandparent once worked or those relating to a wider national or diasporic family (Basu 2007, Levi-Ari and Mittelberg 2008, Gouthro and Palmer 2011). Nadel-Klein provides an excellent example of the motivation behind the drive to create a personal connection between the fishing industry in Scotland, once a thriving employment sector and the local or national heritage tourist; the fishermen felt:

> compelled to concretize and embody their memories in texts, collections, performances and displays – many of these housed in museums and heritage centres – so that their own descendants, as well as outside visitors, will not forget them. . . . a way of bequeathing something of 'to a future that looks increasingly bleak'.

> (2003: 173)

Although such experiences of the past relate to a past that has been socially (re) created by the present this does not mean that they are any the less enjoyable for those people who engage with the attractions and activities that comprise the heritage tourism sector. Nevertheless a heritage experience is marketed on the basis that it means something to someone and by engaging with heritage tourism the individual is made aware of the fact that he or she is engaging with a valued past, valued because it is highlighted as being significant to the present.

While the past as represented through heritage tourism is frequently offered as a safe place to visit there are clearly numerous examples where what is experienced is neither enjoyable nor uncontested, and neither does it contribute to a sense of closure between the past and the present. Sites, monuments and museums that relate to war, state-sponsored violence or genocide are illustrative of how present-day experiences of a difficult past provide a very different understanding of the notion of inheritance (Macdonald 2010, Mowatt and Chancellor 2011, Kidron 2013, Giblin 2014). The legacy of such examples has been described by Simon (2006) as 'a terrible gift', a useful description because it suggests that what is inherited from the past by current and future generations is the importance of 'not forgetting'. The creation of heritage in this sense relates to the creation of a wider set of cultural values associated with acknowledging and resisting the role of violence in disrupting as well as controlling human relationships.

A heritage label thus communicates an understanding of value as defined in relation to the prevailing social, political and cultural circumstances of the present. Apaydin's (2018) research at the medieval heritage site of Ani in eastern

Turkey provides a good illustration of how use and values often go hand in hand. Despite being used as a political tool to promote nationalism 'the heritage site also forms an important place in daily life for local communities whose relationship with the heritage site goes beyond this political level: by bringing out the meaning, value and sense of place at Ani' (2018: 491). Value is an interesting word here because it not only refers to the beliefs and ideals frequently understood in the wider sense as being representative of a particular way of life, it also, and increasingly so today, refers to what can be gained economically from a past labelled as heritage (Choi et al. 2010, Dümcke and Gnedovsky 2013). This is because what is valued in the present is the fact that heritage sells and as a result the word 'heritage' is attached to an ever-increasing number of products, services and activities, within and beyond the tourism sector. In the UK for example, the Heritage Window Company sells aluminium windows for domestic housing, 'value' here being associated with a heritage that is defined in terms of British engineering and quality standards (www.theheritagewindowcompany.co.uk). Such an example illustrates that heritage is not only something to be visited, it can also be part of everyday life; it can be bought and installed in your own home.

The underlying narrative in the majority of examples discussed so far is that of nostalgia. Nostalgia has a long association with what Samuel (2012) refers to as *Retrochic*, the aesthetic use of the past to persuade people in the present to purchase or experience a range of commercial products and cultural experiences. Literary tourism is one such example, which can create a sense of nostalgia linked to a longing for the world associated with the writer (Herbert 2001, Robinson and Anderson 2002). Although not all tourists look for or experience a sense of nostalgia when engaging with the history of a particular experience (see Caton and Santos 2007) *Retrochic* is a powerful force in the marketing of not just heritage tourism but also products and services (Brown et al. 2003, Cattaneo and Guerini 2012, Orth and Gal 2012); for example, the *Along Came Betty* range of 1950s-inspired cosmetics, the retro radio, and the above-mentioned Heritage Window Company. Despite the fact that not all tourists experience a sense of nostalgia when engaging with heritage tourism – there are after all many different types of heritage on offer – this particular sentiment cannot be ignored when focusing on the creation of heritage for tourism purposes. This is largely because of its role in creating and communicating the significance of the past in the present, communicating that which should be valued and conserved for future generations. As Smith (2006: 121) notes in relation to historic houses an 'entire nation is characterised as being overly concerned with gazing over its collective shoulder into a past reconstructed as more gentle and elegant than the present – a sense of elegance apparently personified by the country house'.

Heritage as represented by the country houses, castles, monuments and attractions that comprise the mainstay of heritage tourism does not provide a sufficiently detailed picture of the range of phenomena now claimed as 'heritage' for tourism purposes. Primarily for economic, but also in some cases for socio-cultural reasons, tourism sectors such as culinary tourism, ecotourism, cultural tourism and religious tourism, as well as destinations such as post conflict sites and sea ports 'adopted' by cruise companies, have employed the heritage label to attract tourists. Thus, the commodification of history has been extended to include the proactive production and reproduction of a multitude of heritage products and experiences (Macleod 2010, Tzanelli 2013). The island of Jersey's tourism offering marketed as Jersey Heritage, for instance, includes not only the usual references to heritage walks and ancient heritage sites but also the island's geological record dating back to the Ice Age. References to this record illustrate contemporary preoccupations with climate change providing an excellent example of what a focus on the past can tell us about what matters in the present:

> The dramatic landscape of Jersey, its coastline and inland landscape of valleys and fields, has been shaped by long time processes of climate change. The island has an exceptional geological record for the Ice Age documenting over a quarter of a million years of successive changes.
>
> (Jersey Heritage, 'Ice Age Jersey' 2018)

In many ways this is heritage as loss rather than as something to be gained, an inheritance that has been wasted rather than wisely invested for the future, hence, for example the naming of the British heritage attraction in Cornwall, The Lost Gardens of Heligan. UNESCO has attached the same description to some aspects of its World Heritage sites, for example the temple city of Khajuraho in the Himalayas includes The Lost Gardens of Khajuraho. The geological environment is not the only aspect of the past to be labelled as heritage in order to further contemporary understandings of what has been saved and what should be worth saving. Wincott (2017) provides a fascinating example of the politics of food whereby a heritage label is attached to seeds, crops and vegetables as a way to legitimise and normalise those who are considered to be appropriate guardians for the foods we eat. These guardians then go on to establish the kinds of places in which such 'treasured' resources should be secured, places such as seed banks and walled heritage gardens that are then managed by experts and commercially minded organisations. 'The treasure metaphor matters because of its use in establishing and justifying the power of some interest groups over resources for food and agriculture' (Wincott 2017: 13). Interestingly, it is not only the heritage gardens of the type mentioned above that feature as tourist attractions. The seed banks and vaults Wincott refers to have, in recent years also become an established part of the tourism sector; for example Kew Gardens' Millennium Seed Bank at Wakehurst in south-east England. It seems that the words 'heritage' and 'treasured' more effectively communicate contemporary conservation agendas because they speak of value in relation to potential loss to future generations.

The above discussion is significant because it demonstrates that the creation of heritage extends beyond the more usual types of attractions and experiences most closely associated with heritage tourism. Attractions such as buildings, the location of specific events, the physical artefacts from the past, and the ideas and inventions of particular people all have heritage value because of their influence on the present. The drive to label an ever-expanding range of phenomena and experiences as heritage for tourism purposes never seems to wane, largely because, as noted above, the past as heritage 'works'; it works economically and it works because it resonates with people, whether people as individuals and communities or people in terms of the human race or humanity (as is the case with heritage seeds, vegetables and crops). Our focus on the creation of heritage not only includes heritage as it relates to the built or natural environment it also encompasses intangible heritage in the form of language, dance, drinks and food as well as heritage in the form of literary works of fiction. All such aspects are imprinted with the cultural particularities of the group, community, region and nation to which they belong. This illustrates their importance for tourism because references to the heritage of a people are the mainstay of many promotional campaigns designed to attract both domestic and international tourists, whether this is in relation to the UNESCO World Heritage Sites of a country, or because the history of a particular town or city has defined it as having a distinctive heritage identity, for example Rome in Italy, Tallinn in Estonia and Petra in Jordan. Heritage is also put to work in terms of rebranding post conflict and post disaster destinations, for example the Balkan nations of former Yugoslavia – Montenegro, Serbia, Croatia, Macedonia, Slovakia and Bosnia-Herzegovina – and post-Katrina New Orleans (Gotham 2007, Vitic and Ringer 2007).

Within the context of the themes outlined above our purpose here is to explore how heritage is socially constructed; how it is created in the present, how it is 'used', interpreted and experienced. While the notion of heritage as a social construct is well established what is less well known is *how* heritage is created and with what consequences across different geographic and cultural contexts, both western and non-western. The wide-ranging examples and understandings of heritage tourism included in the chapters that follow go beyond the more usual European and North American contexts to provide significant insights into the ways in which heritage is created, used and experienced.

Chapters and case studies

The research-based contributions outlined below are drawn from many parts of the world and address a variety of contexts and subjects; for example, Brazil, Argentina, Mexico, Japan, Turkey, and Estonia, the Welsh language, the tango, mushrooms, coffee, cruise tourism and the techniques employed to construct tourist accommodation.

Following on from this chapter, Kimberly Berg focuses on Creating a destination through language: Welsh linguistic heritage in Patagonia. Berg argues that Chubut Province, in the Patagonian region of Argentina, is the site of a robust Welsh diaspora community, established in 1865 but now serving as a popular tourism destination for Welsh tourists seeking to experience the Welsh language in its pure form, spoken in the streets of the historically Welsh towns. The Welsh language has become central to a heritage narrative that recalls an idealised (though never truly realised) past where Welsh was the dominant language. This narrative has been the foundation on which the reverse-diaspora tourism market in Chubut has been built. Berg's discussion highlights the intricacies of these linguistic and cultural revitalisation efforts, and outlines the perceived benefits for the Welsh diaspora and the Welsh homeland communities.

Chapter 3, entitled Performing national identity in heritage tourism: observations from Catalonia by Venetia Johannes, provides an ethnographic account of how 'heritage' has been used in the nationalist and pro-independence movement in Catalonia. Johannes argues that Catalan heritage has taken on new significance as a symbol of resistance and separate history in the strained relationship with Spain. Her focus on sites of historic national memory, and the foods associated with these places demonstrates how promoting foodstuffs under official categories, simultaneously allows local actors to assert political will, create heritage, and encourage tourism. Her discussion covers issues such as the role of 'insiders' and 'outsiders' in heritage creation and tourism, the heritage 'label' in Catalan cuisine, and heritage as national identity performance.

Heritage defined and maintained through conflict re-enactments: the Estonian Museum of Occupations and the Forest Brothers Bunker (Chapter 4) by Brent McKenzie argues that museums can invite, or entice, visitors to come and experience the heritage of a country or its people. The main focus of his chapter is to examine the Museum of Occupations, and more specifically the introduction of an offsite attraction, the Forest Brother Bunker, in the Republic of Estonia. McKenzie aims to better understand how this attraction has been used to serve both as an additional source of museum revenue and also to further entrench the brand image of the Occupation Museum as the leading authority on Estonian heritage that was shaped during the period of Soviet occupation from 1944–1991.

Krupa Rajangam's focus in Chapter 5 is on Constructing heritage, shaping tourism: Festivals and local heritage governance at Hampi World Heritage Site, Karnataka, India, a popular and well-known national and international tourism destination. Using ethnographic research at Jathre (the Hampi temple's chariot festival) and Utsav (a government-sponsored cultural festival) she seeks to understand both the 'authorised' narrative of the site, as a 'group of monuments at Hampi', and its ground realities, as a place with overlapping layers of archaeological park, cultural landscape, embodied space and living heritage. She reflects on the limited official understanding of the actual usage of the site and its meaning to visitors, noting that the construction of heritage by local government serves certain vested interests within electoral, identity and cultural politics.

In Chapter 6, Creating heritage for cruise tourists, by Jacqueline Tivers, a neglected area of study is addressed through research into cruise passengers' space/time opportunities on shore and heritage in relation to the huge, growing, and specific demands of the cruise industry. The research on which her chapter is based concerns the 'creation' of heritage sites and heritage tourism experiences in cruise ship destinations and the ways in which this 'creation' is reflected in the publicity materials of shipping lines and the onshore activities of cruise passengers. Tivers's research methodology is autoethnographic, employing participant observation and the keeping of personal diaries alongside informal interviews with passengers and formal interviews with senior staff. Her discussion draws on examples from nine different cruises between 2014 and 2017.

'It's tango!' Communicating intangible cultural heritage for the dance tourist, by Jonathan Skinner provides the focus for Chapter 7. Here, Skinner argues that, typically, tourism – a global heritage-producing enterprise – is examined with reference to physical tangible heritage. However, his chapter focuses on intangible heritage, how it is created, grown into and dwelt in, produced, and commoditised and ultimately disseminated and sold to tourists and the public. He examines Argentine tango, an ostensibly improvised dance art form – a physical competence regarded as an example of embodied heritage made transnational by tango dancers and teachers, migrants who bear their skillset wherever they go – to engage with the question of these teachers' bodily dispositions (habitus), the Romanticisation of this movement system, and the alleged authenticity that students buy into and travel to experience and acquire.

Following on from Skinner's chapter David McLaughlin focuses on literary tourism in a chapter entitled Holmes as heritage: readers, tourism and the making of Sherlock Holmes's England (Chapter 8). Between 1983 and 2001 an American lawyer named David Hammer, a self-confessed fan of Arthur Conan Doyle's Sherlock Holmes stories, wrote a series of 'Sherlockian' travel guides to England. Hammer's series provides a case study of the role that ordinary people, not authors or tourism promoters, have played in the creation of heritage as a tourist commodity in the late 20th and early 21st centuries. McLaughlin argues that David Hammer used his travel guides as a means of creating Sherlock Holmes's England as a material manifestation of this idea of Holmes as heritage, a heritage that could and should be visited by Sherlockian reader-tourists. He used pieces of England's Holmes-related past – places from Doyle's life, locations from the Sherlock Holmes stories, and even sites from his own past – to create a new story of the past for Sherlockians one that made tourism into a necessary part of the Sherlockian reader's experience.

In Chapter 9, Creating heritage for tourism: 'consuming history', 'prosthetic memories' and the popularisation of a folk hero's story, Michael Fagence's focus is directed primarily at 'teasing' out the tangible and visual evidence of a story about a particular episode of history. He considers the creation of 'prosthetic memories', of 'being there' without actually 'being there', and of 'consuming history' through the medium of heritage-based tourism. Fagence's study draws particularly on the investigative and interpretative skill sets of 'thinking geographically' and 'the gaze' component of semiotics to unravel how heritage is created in the present, and in the forms which have attraction for tourism. These matters are put to the test in a case study of the nineteenth-century Australian bushranger, outlaw and folk hero, Ned Kelly.

Creating (extra)ordinary heritage through film-induced tourism: the case of Dubrovnik and Game of Thrones, written by Tina Šegota (Chapter 10) focuses on the practices of (re)producing heritage through film imagery within the UNESCO World Heritage Site of Dubrovnik. More specifically, Šegota discusses the recurrent practices of tour guides in reshaping and recreating the heritage of the city of Dubrovnik through film imagery related to the popular TV series, *Game of Thrones*. Her analysis finds that Dubrovnik's heritage has become a melting pot of three or more narratives that require highly skilled professional guides who are able to provide necessary and accurate interpretation of the heritage. However, the real issue for Šegota is whether Dubrovnik can continue to sustain itself as a significant heritage destination, since it has been increasingly profiled and promoted through time-limited film imagery.

Chapter 11 by Duccio Gasparri and Annaclaudia Martini, *Amachan*: the creation of heritage tourism landscapes in Japan after the 2011 triple disaster, takes as its focus the television drama *Amachan*, which, in 2013 received record-breaking ratings among Japanese viewers, generating significant tourism growth in the area in which it was set. *Amachan* portrays a countryside village's need to rely more and more on domestic tourism for revenue. In order to do so, the main characters reinvent their everyday occupations as tourist attractions. Railway employees, sea urchin divers, and even high-school students, plot and discuss how to make their village more attractive. Martini and Gasparri argue that *Amachan* offers a deep view on the bottom-up management of tradition in rural Japan. Their chapter analyses how the drama deals with heritage creation both within the plot, and in its real-life effects. Focusing on *Amachan* provides a novel analytical frame to address forms of heritage creation.

The next chapter, written by Felicity Picken, Hayley Saul and Emma Waterton (Chapter 12), is entitled Bedrock, metropolis and Indigenous heritage: rendering 'The Rocks' invisible. Here they focus on 'The Rocks' at Sydney Harbour, one of Australia's most visited colonial heritage attractions arguing that in the repertoire of modern nations it represents the symbolic birthplace of the nation. As a place that was quarried from the sandstone edges of the natural harbour, even the contours of the geological bedrock have been transformed. Within this highly inscribed and engineered environment one Indigenous tour group tells of the deeper history of the place and is able to render Indigenous heritage visible with almost no physical resemblance to the pre-colonial landscape. Without the pre-colonial 'country' that underpins Indigenous heritage, The Rocks Dreaming Aboriginal Heritage Tour accomplishes a unique heritage presence anyway and challenges common assumptions about 'historical evidence', continuity and discontinuity within dominant heritage management discourse.

George S. Jaramillo and Alan Hooper, in Chapter 13, Between the cliffs and the sea: St Kilda and heritage from afar, explore alternatives to the binary position of visitor and resident, by promoting the notion of custodianship through an ongoing study of a remote access heritage centre for St Kilda, Scotland. They discuss how heritage bodies, local people and tourists can come together in the co-creation of heritage, based on the notion that the tourist is an embodied practitioner in heritage-making rather than just a viewer. They argue that the new centre, with its potential for co-creating heritage and involving the tourist, not as consumer or even performer of heritage, but rather as custodian of it in the same way as the host, can lead to new approaches to theorising heritage – approaches that will continue to push the boundaries of what it means to claim rights over a historical place, to rethink the ways that heritage is performed and created, and to consider how ideas of rural innovation can be employed at a global level.

Chapter 14, written by Penny Grennan, Made in China: creating heritage through tourist souvenirs representation considers the influence that tourist souvenirs have on cultural stereotyping and cultural seepage, and their role in creating, contesting, and defining heritage and cultural value. This created heritage is, she argues, then appropriated by tourism and becomes part of touristic practices. The difficulties of locating and understanding heritage and culture are typified by the shifting narrative of souvenirs – a narrative which determines their value as well as contributing to slippery notions of the past. Souvenirs have cultural currency as a result of their origins and associations; however, notions of authenticity and representation are contested. Grennan aims to illuminate this in relation to the experience and interpretation of place thereby questioning what heritage means to tourists in the twenty-first century.

The next chapter, written by Giovanna Bertella and Maurizio Droli, Creative practices of local entrepreneurs reinventing built heritage (Chapter 15) views creativity as a key element informing the role that built heritage can play in terms of being a unique tourist attraction and a meaningful part of the life of local residents. Adopting a practice-based understanding of entrepreneurship, their study investigates entrepreneurs who reinvent the built heritage of an Italian village. The findings suggest that the reinvention process is a combination of innovation and imitation. The most creative entrepreneurs are characterised by exceptional creativity, sense of attachment to the local heritage, quite extensive social capital and sensitivity to the wellbeing of the community. Bertella and Droli argue that while these entrepreneurs' resources are applied to obtain benefits for the businesses and for the local area they illustrate how heritage is created through creative practice.

Chapter 16, Co-creating a heritage hotel for a new identity, written by Philip Feifan Xie and William Ling Shi, attempts to broaden understandings of co-creation by examining stakeholders who authenticate the meaning of a heritage hotel. The authors propose that a heritage hotel is not only defined in terms of the provenance of material and non-material aspects of a culture, but also by subjective criteria as applied by various stakeholders. Using the case study of the Hotel Estoril, the first Western-style casino hotel built in the former Portuguese colony of Macau, they show that government, community organisations and residents endeavour to co-create a new identity for adaptive reuse. Under the circumstances, a heritage hotel is characterised by a polyvocality of interpretations, reflective of the array of stakeholders involved.

Ilkay Tas Gursoy takes as her focus for Chapter 17 Turkish coffee: from intangible cultural heritage to created tourist experience. Turkish coffee culture was listed as part of Intangible Cultural Heritage of Humanity in 2013 as a unique feature of heritage. Gursoy demonstrates how on its route to the UNESCO list, Turkish coffee culture has been shaped by the interplay of political, economic and social conditions. She focuses on how Turkish coffee heritage is reproduced for tourism by various actors through interrelated practices. These interrelated practices for creating tourist experience out of coffee heritage range from cultural diplomacy and hospitality to performativity, materiality and connectivity.

Chapter 18, The reinvention of crab fishing as a local heritage attraction in Northeast Brazil written by Claudio Milano, engages with the contemporary trend to create a heritage label to attract tourists in relation to the crab fishing activity of Northeast Brazil. As a part of local heritage the identity of the occupational group – crab fishermen in Northeast Brazil – is used to promote culinary tourism. Milano's research is based on ethnographic fieldwork undertaken over 13 months from 2011 to 2014. The uça (*Ucides cordatus cordatus*) crab fishing in the Parnaiba River Delta perfectly illustrates the overlap between the different dimensions of heritagisation in touristic markets. Ultimately, Milano illustrates how in Northeast Brazil the role of the crab fisherman has changed as a result of the expansion of tourism.

Chapter 19 by Humberto Thomé-Ortiz is entitled Creating biocultural heritage for tourism: the case of mycological tourism in central Mexico and focuses on the creation of heritage in relation to wild edible mushrooms. Thomé-Ortiz argues that natural heritage is a central element in the new tourist dynamics of the region. Due to their aesthetic and culinary attributes, wild edible mushrooms are local resources with a high economic and cultural value, arousing the interest of tourists in the processes of locating, identifying, collecting and preparing these resources. His chapter analyses the relationship between biocultural heritage and mycological tourism through a case study in central Mexico, where biocultural heritage is recreated, used and interpreted for the production of a tourist experience. Thomé-Ortiz concludes that the study of the relationship between traditional ecological knowledge about mushrooms on the one hand, and tourism on the other, opens up a new heritage perspective in terms of the creation of a biocultural heritage in response to the logic of the tourist market.

Chapter 20, the final chapter of the book, is written by Guojie Zhang, James Higham and Julia Nina Albrecht. Their focus on (Re)creating natural heritage in New Zealand: biodiversity conservation and tourism development addresses the (re)creation of natural heritage in relation to biodiversity conservation and fenced ecosanctuaries in New Zealand. Ecosanctuaries are unique conservation projects which, while contrasting in approach, are generally committed to the protection of native fauna. This often involves the intensive management of the recovery of critically endangered bird species as part of the restoration of New Zealand's pre-human biodiversity. Through critically considering which types of nature are labelled as 'natural heritage' and how they are (re)created through conservation practice in the context of New Zealand's fenced ecosanctuaries, the authors conclude that ecosanctuaries represent critical opportunities to (re)create natural heritage through financial aid and environmental education, with important implications for both conservation management and nature-based tourism development.

References

Apaydin, V. (2018) The entanglement of the heritage paradigm: values, meanings and uses. *International Journal of Heritage Studies*, 24(5): 491–507.

Ashworth, G. and Tunbridge, J. (2000) *The Tourist-Historic History: Retrospect and Prospect of Managing the Heritage City*, rev. ed. Oxford: Pergamon.

Basu, P. (2007) *Highland Homecoming: Genealogy and Heritage Tourism in the Scottish Diaspora*. Abingdon, Oxon: Routledge.

Brown, S., Kozinets, R. and Sherry, J, F. (2003) Teaching Old brands new tricks: retro branding and the revival of brand meaning. *Journal of Marketing*, 67: 19–33.

Caton, K. and Santos, A. (2007) Heritage tourism on Route 66: deconstructing nostalgia. *Journal of Travel Research*, 45(4): 371–386.

Cattaneo, E. and Guerini, C. (2012) Assessing the revival potential of brands from the past: how relevant is nostalgia in retro branding strategies? *Journal of Brand Management*, 19(8): 680–687.

Choi, A. S., Ritchie, B. W., Papandrea, F., and Bennett, J. (2010) Economic valuation of heritage sites: a choice modelling approach. *Tourism Management*, 31: 213–220.

Dümcke, C. and Gnedovsky, M. (2013) *The Social and Economic Value of Cultural Heritage: Literature Review*. European Expert Network on Culture (EENC). Available at: www.interarts.net/descargas/interarts2557.pdf [accessed 15 January 2018].

Giblin, J. (2014) Post-conflict heritage: symbolic healing and cultural renewal. *International Journal of Heritage Studies*, 20(5): 500–518.

Gotham, K. F. (2007) (Re)branding the big easy: tourism rebuilding in post-Katrina New Orleans. *Urban Affairs Review*, 42(6): 823–850.

Guthro, M. B. and Palmer, C. (2010) Pilgrimage in heritage tourism: finding meaning and identity in the industrial past, in M. Conlin, and L. Jolliffe (eds.) *Mining Heritage and Tourism: A Global Synthesis*. London: Routledge, pp. 33–43.

Graburn, N. H. (2001) Learning to Consume: what is heritage and when is it traditional? in N. Alsayyad (ed.) *Consuming Tradition, Manufacturing Heritage. Global Norms and Urban Forms in the Age of Tourism*, London: Routledge, pp. 68–89.

Herbert, D. C. (2001) Heritage pasts and heritage presents: temporality, meaning and the scope of heritage studies. *International Journal of Heritage Studies*, 7(4): 319–338.

Jersey Heritage, Ice Age Jersey, 2018. Available at: www.jerseyheritage.org/heritage-landscape/ice-age-jersey [accessed 15 January 2018].

Kidron, C. (2013) Being there together: dark family tourism and the emotive experience of co-presence in the holocaust past. *Annals of Tourism Research*, 41: 175–194.

Levi-Ari, D. and Mittelberg, D. (2008) Between authenticity and ethnicity: heritage tourism and re-ethnification among diaspora Jewish youth. *Journal of Heritage Tourism*, 3(2): 79–013.

Lowenthal, D. (1998) *The Heritage Crusade and the Spoils of History*. Cambridge: Cambridge University Press.

Macdonald, S. (2010) *Difficult Heritage: Negotiating the Nazi Past in Nuremberg and Beyond*. London: Routledge.

Macleod, D.V.L. (2010) Power, culture and the production of heritage, in D.V.L. Macleod and J.G. Carrier (eds). *Tourism, Power and Culture: Anthropological Insights*. Channel View: Bristol, pp. 64–89.

Mowatt, R. and Chancellor, C. (2011) Visiting Death and life: dark tourism and slave castles. *Annals of Tourism Research*, 38(4): 1410–1434.

Nadel-Klein, J. (2003) *Fishing for Heritage: Modernity and Loss along the Scottish Coast*. Oxford: Berg.

Orth, U. and Gal, S. (2012) Nostalgic brands as mood boosters. *Journal of Brand Management*, 19(8): 666–679.

Palmer, C. (2005) An ethnography of Englishness: tourism and national identity. *Annals of Tourism Research*, 32(1): 7–27

Robinson, M. and Andersen, H. C. (eds.) (2002) *Literature and Tourism: Essays in the Reading and Writing of Tourism*. Thomson: London.

Samuel, R. (2012) *Theatres of Memory: Past and Present in Contemporary Culture*, rev. ed. London: Verso.

Simon, R. (2006) The terrible gift: museums and the possibility of hope without consolation. *Museum Management and Curatorship*, 21: 187–204.

Smith, L. (2006) *Uses of Heritage*. London: Routledge.

Timothy, D. and Boyd, S. W. (2006) Heritage Tourism in the 21st century: valued traditions and new perspectives. *Journal of Heritage Tourism*, 1(1): 1–16.

Tzanelli, R. (2013) *Heritage in the Digital Era: Cinematic Tourism and the Activist Cause*. Abingdon, UK: Routledge.

Vitic, A. and Ringer, G. (2007) Branding post-conflict destinations: recreating Montenegro after the disintegration of Yugoslavia. *Journal of Travel & Tourism Marketing*, 23(2–3): 127–137.

Wincott, A. (2017) Treasure in the vault: the guardianship of 'heritage' seeds, fruit and vegetables. *International Journal of Cultural Studies*: 1–16.

2 Creating a *destination* through language

Welsh linguistic heritage in Patagonia

Kimberly Berg

Introduction

The heritage tourism industry is continually challenged to establish new and unique forms of heritage to be marketed and consumed by tourists. Heritage is taking increasingly dynamic forms in various global destinations. Language, notably in areas of the world where minority language revitalisation is on the rise, is quickly becoming a heritage tourism commodity. Such is the case with the Welsh language in Patagonian Argentina. While this region may seem an unlikely *Welsh* heritage destination, the seeds of the contemporary situation were sown over 150 years ago, beginning with an arduous journey across the Atlantic by a small group of Welsh settlers, who intended to establish a robust and thriving and, most importantly, Welsh-speaking, colony in the Patagonian region of Argentina. This migratory event, while additionally orchestrated on the grounds of achieving religious, social, and economic autonomy, had as its cornerstone the prerogative to speak the Welsh language. Today, the language remains a central aspect of Welsh–Patagonian identity, albeit with decades of newly layered ideologies and associations by community members in both Argentina and Wales. Welsh heritage- (and more specifically Welsh language) tourism has become a niche market offering in Chubut Province, Argentina. This chapter will investigate the intricacies of how and why the language has come to be a tourism commodity in Argentina, as well as highlighting the political and social ramifications of this for Welsh language revitalisation efforts in both the homeland and the diaspora. Before exploring the contemporary context of the Welsh language in Argentina, it is pertinent to briefly review the historical context of contemporary Welsh language ideologies in Argentina and Wales.

From history to heritage tourism

English political, social, and economic domination was ever-present throughout Wales in the eighteenth and nineteenth centuries, and life under the umbrella of British rule resulted in minimal economic or social opportunities for the Welsh (Jones 1992). British political and social control over Wales was most blatantly seen through attempts to *civilise* and *control* the Welsh population. This meant mandating English-medium schools, an English-only legal administration, and domination of the nonconformist religious sector that served as the hub of social organisation for many Welsh communities (Williams 2009). The Welsh were often pressured to assimilate, linguistically and culturally, especially in urban areas already experiencing high immigrant populations from other countries (Baur 1954). English attempts at order were successful in some ways, for example in creating a stigma against speaking Welsh in public. However, these pressures simultaneously resulted in a stronger Welsh nationalism in some regions and provided the incentive to revive and maintain a uniquely Welsh identity. One mechanism for the latter was significant out-migration, in pursuit of cultural, religious, linguistic, and economic freedom. The United States, Canada, and Australia were all considered viable locations for the creation of new Welsh settlements, due to the already established British presence in these newly formed nations. In many cases, religious leaders acted as figureheads for these movements, using charismatic revivalist rhetoric to persuade settlers to join their movements (Knowles 1995). Thus, in 1865, Michael D. Jones convinced 153 Welsh people to sail to, and settle in, Patagonia. Unlike the previous waves of migration to Anglo-settled countries, the colony in Argentina was envisioned as a last-ditch effort to create an entirely Welsh-speaking community in a land where there would be no English influence (Baur 1954).

Several subsequent waves of Welsh migrants arrived in Chubut during the next half century. Within two decades of arrival, the Welsh community in Argentina experienced heavy pressure to assimilate from the highly centralised Argentinian government. The language of administration was Spanish and, after state Spanish-medium schools were mandated in 1896, chapels became the only remaining Welsh linguistic centres (Owen 1977). As chapel attendance declined, however, the Welsh language also waned in status within the community (Williams 1991). For several generations, the youth were no longer being educated in the Welsh language and the regular usage of the language declined, which only accelerated the assimilation of the Welsh-dominant communities within a Spanish-medium Argentinidad (Owen 1977). At this point, the changing community values were in direct conflict with the emotional goals on which the community had been founded. This discrepancy caused similar tensions to those felt in English-Welsh conflicts in Britain. In the Welsh settlers' attempt to escape British hegemonic control, they entered into a new hegemonic arrangement whereby the Welsh were now expected to act as full members of Argentinian society, linguistically, socially, culturally, and politically.

While the dream of an unassimilated Welsh colony did not persist, the Welsh legacy nonetheless remains firmly rooted in Chubut provincial memory. Welsh language is central to identity, despite the language of daily exchange having changed over time to primarily Spanish. This change has influenced much of the contemporary ideology surrounding Welsh language usage in the province and, it can be argued, the contemporary incentive for Welsh revitalisation in Patagonia. The latter offers a lucrative community resource, through the development of Welsh-themed tourism throughout the Chubut Province, and has also helped to shape a narrative that substantiates the central role of the Welsh language in the lives of Welsh descendants in Patagonia.

Welsh heritage in Patagonia

Welsh heritage, by any measure, is the most visible, economically viable, and prominent heritage in Chubut Province. The story of settlement has lent itself to the creation of a romantic, survivalist narrative that is easily captured through heritage sites and communicated to tourists who may be unfamiliar with the intricacies of the Welsh story in Argentina. However, this specific niche of the heritage tourism industry is relatively new to Patagonia; it is only within the last couple of decades that *Welsh Patagonia* has become a destination for, by and large, Welsh nationals. There are also some groups of domestic, and non-Welsh international, tourists which visit the Welsh heritage sites in Chubut. Interestingly, the development of a specifically Welsh heritage tourism industry has simultaneously been taking place on the national level in Wales, notably since the early 1990s. Welsh heritage tourism has provided a new, unique tourism offering, apart from the British-English tourism market (Pritchard and Morgan 2001). In fact, parallel branding trends have been underway in Patagonia and Wales; the Welsh dragon, for example, is as much recognised in Chubut as it is in the homeland.

Welsh, and likewise Welsh–Patagonian, branding has been largely perpetuated by the institutions and programmes that support Welsh language revitalisation efforts. For Welsh Patagonia, one programme has been particularly influential – the Welsh Language Project, funded by the British Council and the Welsh Assembly. This began in 1997 and is the primary entity responsible for hosting and supporting Welsh language instruction in Argentina.[1] Each year, two or three teachers from Wales are selected to live and work in Argentina, teaching Welsh language courses in the (former) Welsh towns in the province. Frequently, courses are attended by members of the community, who either have Welsh ancestry and wish to learn the language, or who spoke Welsh as children and want to sustain their Welsh competency. However, some non-Welsh descendants attend these courses out of curiosity and the desire to speak another language. This attendance, by those from outside the community, reflects some of the most salient values that have been constructed around the Welsh language in Argentina. For some non-Welsh people in Patagonia, there is a perception that the Welsh language, and engagement with this cultural heritage, is an important factor in accruing significant social and cultural capital. Similar values operate for Welsh descendants, who have had the opportunity to either learn or maintain their ancestral language, or even better, have had the chance to travel to Wales. Collectively, then, the Patagonian community has, in many ways, rallied around *Welshness*.

Graham and Howard (2008) attest that heritage is not inherently valuable; rather, communities and institutions attribute value for various political, social, and economic reasons. Welshness in Patagonia provides a prime example of such valuing processes. The language ideologies, the creation of a specifically Welsh identity and the structure of the community heritage resources – in both the Welsh–Patagonian and Welsh national communities – have encouraged increased investment from Wales and the deepening of relationships between the homeland and its diaspora. This has resulted in the construction of a Welsh–Patagonian *destination*, specifically for Welsh tourists to see and experience the Welsh language being utilised in a profoundly different part of the globe. Bodies in Wales, such as the British Council, the National Assembly, the National Library of Wales, the National Museum Wales, the BBC Wales orchestra, the television channel S4C, among other more community-based organisations as well as individual celebrities, have all been complicit in building and sustaining the image of the Welsh–Patagonian community as the quintessential, successful Welsh settlement, where language usage and traditions remain robust. However, the reality of Welsh descendants' daily experiences is far from that of an idealised bastion of Welshness in the heart of Patagonia (Johnson 2009). While several members of the community have been able to carve out a living working in the handful of Welsh teahouses that serve as tourist attractions, or teaching Welsh at one of the three Welsh–Spanish primary schools, most community members do not have Welsh-themed livelihoods.

Hiraeth, a Welsh term defined simply as longing, but with layered associations to include the desire or sense of bond felt with a place that may or may not exist, operates on both sides of the heritage equation for the Welsh homeland and its diaspora (Kielar 2016). This sentiment has provided the motivation, not only for diaspora members to travel back to the homeland for a multitude of reasons (including intensive Welsh courses, visiting family, and invited collaborations with entities in Wales), but also for Welsh nationals to make semi-long-term or regular visits to the diaspora, to experience a different type of Welshness that is constructed as more *traditional*, given the geographic context of the community as supposedly free from English influence. The literature on diaspora communities within tourism studies discusses the idea of belonging as being particularly salient to roots tourists who travel to what they consider their ancestral homelands in search of a missing piece of themselves. These are typically members of globally recognisable diaspora groups that left their homelands due to large-scale push and pull factors (Coles and Timothy 2004). Interestingly, and somewhat in contrast to the model that Coles and Timothy have identified, members of the Welsh national community actively seek to make the journey to the diaspora in order to experience what is often described as a simpler, more wholesome and quaint Welshness. This mythologised nature of the Welsh–Patagonian settlement encourages members of the Welsh national community to travel to Argentina to reunite with those who have been constructed, through Welsh national institutions and literature, as long-lost Welsh brothers and sisters (Morgan and Pritchard 2004). As will be defined below, many Welsh tourists are motivated to experience life in the Welsh diaspora due to complex language ideologies from the homeland, which serve to influence, likewise, the Welsh national and Welsh diaspora communities.

Language ideology and heritage tourism in Welsh Patagonia

Welsh language ideology, and more broadly the ideology of Welsh nationalism, is not straightforward. The homeland, the nation of Wales, is highly complex with regard to people's perspectives on speaking Welsh, and the motivations of teachers and tourists for coming to teach in or tour Patagonia are also complex. Generally speaking, in the homeland, language ideologies are divided on class lines. The unintended consequences of language revitalisation efforts are inter-language hierarchies. In Wales, this has resulted in working-class speakers, who have had access to fewer language augmentation resources, tending to speak what is considered a less prestigious form of Welsh, if any at all. This form of Welsh does not carry the same linguistic capital as does the more formalised, academic Welsh that others with greater means have accessed through formal, Welsh-medium education. This more proper form of Welsh is very prestigious and deemed to be important in all contexts – most specifically, official and institu-tionalised venues, and notably those involved in revitalisation efforts. Those who speak the less prestigious version of Welsh deem English to be the only important language in official contexts. Welsh national tourists in Patagonia often consider the dialect of the Welsh language there to be an older, more traditional form of Welsh, and speak highly of this form of the Welsh language upon their return to the homeland. This has consequences for the homeland, as it not only substanti-ates a perception of the robustness of Welsh in Patagonia, it also unintentionally devalues forms of the Welsh language in Wales that might be considered *less proper*. Accordingly, the Welsh linguistic hierarchy in Wales is influenced by the values ascribed to the Welsh–Patagonian community.

A linguistic hierarchy also exists in the Welsh–Patagonian community, but in this case between Welsh and Spanish. Spanish is considered the necessary language, and is deemed valuable and necessary for most activities outside the Welsh-themed activities in Chubut, that is, for *official* business. Welsh, in Patagonia, carries prestige and social capital, but does not serve a practical utility function. Within the community there is an unspoken rule that you are not *truly* Welsh unless you speak the language. Similar to the situation in the Welsh homeland, foreigners, or non-Welsh descendant Argentinians, who speak Welsh are welcomed into the community more than those who do not (Madoc-Jones et al. 2013). In fact, there are several non-Welsh people who have learned Welsh in an effort to gain sta-tus in the community, and thus may appear *more Welsh* than Welsh Argentine descendants who do not speak Welsh. In this way Welsh language ideologies of the homeland have been adopted by and adapted to the Welsh–Patagonian community in Argentina. In consequence, when Welsh tourists visit, they often perceive Welsh usage to be much more frequent and regularised than is necessarily the case.

Few studies have thoroughly investigated the Welsh language and its usage in Patagonia, though there has been increased scholarly attention in recent years, as the profile of the community has been elevated through exchange efforts between the Welsh homeland and the diaspora. Ian Johnson (2009) found that members of the community who had a closer relationship to the Welsh language, whether through ancestry or engagement in the various Welsh-themed activities and events, were more optimistic regarding the future of the language in Argentina, while those who were more distant from the language were more pessimistic. In considering the cultural geography of the Welsh-settled towns in Chubut, Johnson identified a few which are now considered the Welsh *centres* for the community as a whole. These centres, somewhat unsurprisingly, align with the cities that are considered the tourism destination cities for Welshness in Chubut, namely, Trelew, Gaiman, and Trevelin. There are a few other towns with reputations of Welshness, including the cities of Puerto Madryn, Rawson, and Esquel, but while these are included in Welsh–Patagonian history and are a part of the Welsh story, they are not the must-see towns on the Welsh heritage tourism circuit. This situation is related to the nature of institutional support from Wales, and the role that connections between various Welsh national institutions and entities and the heritage organisations in Chubut have played in bringing only select towns to the forefront of Welshness in Patagonia.[2]

The data for this chapter were collected principally throughout a ten-month, ethnographic field season in 2015, during the 150th anniversary celebration of the establishment of the Welsh community in Argentina, but also from two shorter field trips to Argentina and during three field seasons in Wales. In addition, some context for this project has also come from ongoing engagement with the Welsh-North American community, within which Welsh–Patagonian heritage narratives also circulate. All data were collected through qualitative research methods, including participant observation and in-depth interviewing.

Tourist profiles and experience

It is important to capture the tourist experience in order to more fully grasp not only the role of language within the Patagonian tourism industry, but also the impact of language ideologies and sentiments surrounding the Welsh language in the homeland. The time spent by Welsh tourists in Chubut was one of the most influential factors impacting their reflections on their stay in the region and also what they chose to communicate about their experience on returning to Wales. Those on very short-term visits typically gave nothing but positive responses to their time in the community and looked forward to communicating their experiences to their family and friends back home. Those undertaking intermediate length stays (three to four weeks) had often very mixed, and sometimes even negative, thoughts on their tourist experience in Chubut. However, with longer-term stays (from two to six or eight months), the satisfaction with the visit increased. In all cases, engagement with and usage of the Welsh language heavily influenced individual impressions of touristic experience. Unpacking the nature of these trips further, it became clear how and why the range of tourist experiences might result in variability of feelings toward the narratives that surround, and the reality of, Welsh Patagonia.[3]

Typically, for those travelling to Welsh Patagonia for up to ten days, the experience in the community was favourable. These trips were frequently with tour groups, either Welsh specific from Welsh national tour providers such as Teithiau Tango,[4] or from other domestic tour companies. Occasionally, they were excursions from the many cruise ships that docked in Puerto Madryn during the summer months. Due to the short time within the Welsh towns, and the highly orchestrated nature of Welsh activities for these tours, the tourists would often gain the experience of bustling, Welsh-speaking hubs in the towns they visited, namely, Gaiman, Trelew, and Trevelin. They would see and experience Welshness and Welsh speakers, and often extrapolate from this experience to conclude that Welsh language and traditions were central to the daily lives of most individuals within the Welsh–Patagonian community.

It was those visitors who stayed for three to four weeks that often had the least favourable experiences. In some instances, Welsh visitors had been oversold the degree of Welsh language usage within the community and undersold the usage of Spanish. For example, the image many undergraduate students on short-term exchanges and scholarships had in their minds, prior to arriving in Chubut, was that Welsh was present in every aspect of daily life, and that there was really no need for Spanish.[5] What they came to realise, however, is that, while Welsh was spoken widely in very particular contexts, day-to-day conversations by and large took place in Spanish. One of the students mentioned how disappointed he was in seeing the heritage nature of the Welsh language in Patagonian, and that he could not help but feel slightly discouraged for the future of the Welsh language both at home and abroad.

Once visitors transitioned into the long-term visitor category (as defined in this paper), the feelings of favourability toward the community substantially increased. This makes good sense if we think about the nature of relationships that are formed as a consequence of long-term engagement and residence in a community. These longer-term visitors often became something akin to community members themselves, attending Welsh community events and non-Welsh activities as well. They were able to use their Welsh sufficiently often to see its utility, but experienced non-Welsh Chubut as well, and often gained positive feelings toward Argentina as a whole. It must also be said that those with the financial capital to participate in longer-term stays were often those from the more elitist, Welsh nationalist segment of society, who greatly valued the language usage, and would seek every opportunity for this in Patagonia. These visitors often spoke *proper* Welsh, which certainly shaped their experiences in Chubut. They were proud to observe the usage of Welsh in general, given their orientation toward pro-Welsh language revitalisation. Because these longer-term visitors valued the language so strongly, and were often the most visible and memorable visitors to the community, their language ideologies also left more permanent marks on the community, shaping community responses to the Welsh language. In addition to sheer visibility, these visitors contributed to the local, micro-economy by renting space from community members and purchasing food and other supplies from local shops and this helped shape their positive reception by the community.

Discussion

Lowenthal (1985) argues that heritage can be used to 'set the record straight' regarding historical or past misinterpretations. I suggest that this is the way in which Chubut heritage is constructed – as a means to interpret the Welsh story correctly, by emphasising the value of the Welsh language and the fact that

Welsh language and cultural traditions live on in Patagonia despite historical forced assimilative strategies similar to those experienced in Britain during the eighteenth and nineteenth centuries. For the Welsh in general, the loss of their language is a historical injustice with contemporary implications. Raising the status of the language in the diaspora, and better still, utilising its newfound prestige as a mechanism through which to attract tourism dollars, can be seen as one means to restore the place of the language in the historical record.

Graham et al. (2000: 19) note the need for communities to '"recreate" what could or should have been there but never actually was', through heritage. This idea corresponds precisely with the concept of *hiraeth* and is no more apparent than in Welsh Patagonia, where it is rooted in the rhetoric of the initial nationalistic migratory processes that led to the establishment of the Welsh community, a rhetoric premised on linguistic and cultural freedom and the unhindered preservation of Welsh values and traditions in a new location. Unsurprisingly, these aspirations rarely work out in idealised ways, evidenced by the fact that, contemporarily, the entire Welsh–Patagonian community speaks Spanish and identifies as Argentinian, but of Welsh descent. However, time and again, my respondents referred to Welsh values when asked to identify what people gain from maintaining Welsh heritage in the region. While economic and political benefits were mentioned by a few of my more critical participants, and then only briefly, the majority of people with whom I spoke referenced 'los valores de galeses'.

In the homeland, decades of Welsh language demoralisation and accompanying historical events resulted in the decline of Welsh language usage, and also associations of the language with stupidity and backwardness. The effect of these processes was deeply ideological and personal. Similar defacing of the language did not happen to the same degree in Argentina. There were some periods of negative sentiments toward Welshness by the wider Argentinian national community, but in general the Welsh community and language have been received with respect by the Patagonian community at large. Thus, the preservation of the language has held, and continues to hold, different significance in the homeland and the diaspora. Consequently, when the usage of the Welsh language in Argentina is referenced as a motivation or justification for all those in Wales to speak Welsh, this overlooks the more complex ideological battle in Wales surrounding Welsh language usage, training, and entitlement to language services and support

Borrowing from Lowenthal (1985, 1998), Welsh heritage may be situated within a broader discussion of the benefits of participating in heritage in general. He notes that heritage is required in the contemporary period to enable people to orient themselves relative to the past, within the present, and to look forward to their future selves or to an idealised future society. Such is undoubtedly the case with Welsh heritage, both in Wales and also in Patagonia. Given the tumultuous nature of Welsh-English relations throughout the last several centuries, it is not difficult to see how participation and revitalisation in Welsh heritage serves as a mechanism to validate a separate history and justify the need for its revival and maintenance. The founding of the Welsh–Patagonian community marked a critical moment in Welsh history, when one (now defined as highly nationalistic) group of settlers altered the trajectory of Welshness in both Wales and Argentina.

As I learned during my various trips to Wales, including attending Welsh classes and attempting to speak Welsh in the community, there are much stronger divides in Wales about significant government resources being invested in language maintenance. Many who do not speak Welsh, and who had no access to language instruction in their early years, would argue that monies spent on Welsh language revitalisation are a waste, especially since, outside of the country, the Welsh language is not used as a language of exchange. Some people hold additional animosity toward the Welsh Assembly for investing a portion of these language and heritage revitalisation funds in Argentina when, according to these respondents, there are many more worthwhile causes that would support the Welsh people in the homeland. They argue that such language maintenance does not have practical benefit for the people of Wales (yet they witness some of the outcomes of these investments in Chubut through various news specials, documentaries, and other programmes, broadcast in Wales to raise the profile of the Welsh–Patagonian community). In a sense, these people represent a very distinct form of Welsh nationalism which, rather than focusing on investment in heritage/language, argues that investments should be made in public services and infrastructure for the direct benefit of Welsh nationals. In contrast, the version of Welsh nationalism focused on language revitalisation heavily supports the international exchange of resources, in order to bolster the significance of that marker of identity deemed most salient to being Welsh, the ability to speak the language. Therefore, we can see that the battle over language is much more than simply a battle about desire or commitment to speaking the language; it is also about reclaiming an identity which, for some, no longer exists. Yet, fragments of this identity can still be seen in the diaspora and are subsequently reflected back to the homeland through the tourism industry, where they then become additionally distorted and used in contradictory and exclusivist ways. The primary mechanism for the exchange of these values is through the Welsh–Patagonian heritage tourism industry, and associated enterprises.

Conclusions

In conclusion, the unique and timely example of the language of Welsh as a heritage product in the diaspora, and the associated values that Welsh–Patagonian heritage tourism communicates back to the homeland, indicate that not only is heritage taking on new forms but that the form which heritage takes, and the tourist interactions with this, have a great impact on cultural and linguistic nationalism and revitalisation efforts both in the Welsh homeland and the diaspora. The language is one of the most definitive markers of Welsh identity and a form of heritage deemed invaluable and in need of preservation in Argentina. Reclaiming and bolstering the Welsh language in Patagonia serves to rewrite the Welsh legacy, and provides a case for claiming the resilience and strength of Welshness. Thus, the maintenance of the language ensures not only rightful heritage ownership over the province, but also justifies capitalising on such heritage for the preservation of Welshness (primarily through tourism), given the historical struggles of the Welsh national community, as well as those of the Welsh diaspora community in Chubut. In addition to these ideological stances, we must not forget the economic impetus for a focus on heritage. While the idealistic preservation of culture is a partial motivator for heritage development, the latter is also an important economic force, of which the Welsh descendant community in Patagonia is the rightful beneficiary. Ultimately, as Graham et al. (2000) suggest, heritage is not simply a bounded place or location, it is also an internal state of identity and informs the self-concept of a group. Multiple layers must be accounted for when attempting to understand a heritage destination and the new forms heritage is taking in the twenty-first century. Transforming the Welsh language into a heritage product ensures its restoration to its rightful place in Welsh society, helping to reorient the contemporary narrative and, more importantly, to rectify mistaken narratives of the past that sought to silence the Welsh language.

Notes

1 https://wales.britishcouncil.org/en/programmes/education/welsh-language-project.
2 Interestingly, the Welsh–Patagonian centres, as identified above, have all undertaken Welsh-Spanish, and in one case even indigenous, language signage. That is, in preparation for the 150th-anniversary celebrations in 2015, Trelew, Gaiman, and Trevelin all, either through the department of tourism or culture, implemented signs throughout their towns that demarcated points of interest in, minimally, Spanish and Welsh. This has served the important function of increasing visibility for the Welsh language in Chubut, which perpetuates the image of its regularised usage to tourists from Wales.
3 While several community members do speak Welsh, Welsh is infrequently used in the home, or between individuals as the language of exchange. Usage on these personal levels is often generational and, on occasion, reflective of kinship. That is, one may find a handful of older individuals who use Welsh to communicate with one another, but this is by no means common for the majority of the community. Similarly, the vast majority of families, even if they are Welsh descendant families, do not speak Welsh at home nor do they utilise Welsh as the first language for their children. Welsh is more accurately a heritage language, used within specific contexts and functions, the heritage tourism industry being one of the most notable (Kelleher 2010).
4 www.teithiautango.co.uk/en.
5 One common sentiment that I heard from both Welsh people that had visited Patagonia, and also those that had never been but had familiarity with the community, was: 'wow—they speak Welsh in Patagonia, so it is only right that we speak Welsh here.' On a basic level this sentiment makes complete sense, but ideas like this definitely overlook the reality of the situation. It is true that Welsh is spoken in Patagonia but the number of speakers is not high and the language is represented on generational lines, whereas In Wales, despite the internal differences of Welsh usage, the ability to speak Welsh is generally considered a group unifier. One student I met, studying Welsh–Patagonian heritage, was Welsh by birth and had grown up in Wales, but was from an English-speaking family. She did not speak Welsh, nor did she attend a Welsh medium school. She did speak Spanish, but this was not considered *good enough* by her, as she was from Wales. Generally, this individual had an overwhelmingly negative and isolating tourist experience, because she found herself subject to the complexities and ideologies that surround the Welsh language in Wales, but in the middle of Patagonia. So, while there is a general, positive reception toward Welsh tourists (since, after all, tourism is

an economic endeavour as well as a social one), tourists who spoke Welsh experience a different, more positive and engaging side of the community as opposed to non-Welsh speaking tourists.

References

Baur, J. (1954) The Welsh in Patagonia: an example of nationalistic migration. *The Hispanic American Historical Review*, 34 (4): 468–492.

Coles, T. and Timothy, D. (2004) 'My Field is the world': conceptualizing diasporas, travel and tourism, in T. Coles and D. Timothy (eds.) *Tourism, Diasporas and Space*. London: Routledge, pp. 1–30.

Graham, B. and Howard, P. (2008) Introduction: heritage and identity, in B. Graham and P. Howard (eds.) *The Routledge Research Companion to Heritage and Identity*. Farnham: Ashgate Publishing, Ltd., pp. 1–19.

Graham, B., Ashworth, G.J. and Tunbridge, J.E. (2000) *A Geography of Heritage: Power, Culture, and Economy*. London: Routledge.

Johnson, I. (2009) How green is their valley? Subjective vitality of Welsh language and culture in the Chubut Province, Argentina. *International Journal of the Sociology of Language*, 195: 141–171.

Jones, R M. (1992) Beyond identity? The reconstruction of the Welsh. *The Journal of British Studies*, 31(4): 330–357.

Kelleher, A. (2010) What is a heritage language? Heritage briefs, 2016. Available at: www.cal.org/heritage/pdfs/briefs/What-is-a-Heritage-Language.pdf [Accessed 28 July 2017].

Kielar, S. (2016) Hiraeth: word of the week, 2 April. Available at: https://sites.psu.edu/kielarpassionblog2/2016/04/02/hiraeth [Accessed 28 July 2017].

Knowles, A K. (1995) Immigrant trajectories through the rural-industrial transition in Wales and the United States, 1795–1850. *Annals of the Association of American Geographers*, 85(2): 246–266.

Lowenthal, D. (1985) *The Past is a Foreign Country*. Cambridge: Cambridge University Press.

Lowenthal, D. (1998) *The Heritage Crusade and the Spoils of History*. Cambridge: Cambridge University Press.

Madoc-Jones, I., Parry, O. and Jones, D. (2013) The 'chip shop Welsh': aspects of 'Welsh speaking' identity in contemporary Wales. *Studies in Ethnicity and Nationalism*, 13(3): 394–411.

Morgan, N. and Pritchard, A. (2004) Mae'n Bryd I ddod Adref—it's time to come home: exploring the contested emotional geographies of Wales, in T. Coles and D. Timothy (eds.) *Tourism, Diasporas, and Space*. London: Routledge, pp. 233–245.

Owen, G D. (1977) *Crisis in Chubut: A Chapter in the History of the Welsh Colony in Patagonia*. Swansea: Christopher Davies.

Pritchard, A. and Morgan, N. (2001) Culture, identity and tourism representation: marketing Cymru or Wales? *Tourism Management*, 22(2): 167–179.

Williams, C. (2009) Commentary: the primacy of renewal. *International Journal of the Sociology of Language*, 195: 201–218.

Williams, G. (1991) *The Welsh in Patagonia: The State and the Ethnic Community*. Cardiff: University of Wales Press.

3 Performing national identity in heritage tourism

Observations from Catalonia

Venetia Johannes

Introduction

In this chapter, I will provide an ethnographic account of the ways that 'heritage' has been used in the Catalan Autonomous Community (Catalonia), in northeast Spain. Catalonia has long been known for its sense of difference from Spain, a difference that was implicitly recognised in the 1978 Spanish constitution.[1] However, following disagreements about Catalonia's tax situation, and a sense of hostility from the Spanish central government, support for independence from Spain has soared, polarising the population into those for and those against. Most recently, the Catalan government held a referendum on October 1 2017, the final outcome of which remains uncertain (they previously held a similar referendum on 9 November 2014, but the ruling party rebranded it as a non-binding 'symbolic' referendum following pressure from Madrid). It is now therefore a politically sensitive time, when Catalan heritage has taken on new significance as a symbol of resistance and separate history in the strained relationship with Spain.

In Catalan, the word 'heritage' is generally translated as 'patrimoni', which has the same root as the English word 'patrimony', from the highly emotive Latin word 'patria', or 'fatherland'. As a result, discussions of heritage, or more accurately 'patrimony', are already implicitly bound up with deeper notions of belonging to a homeland, nation or family. This shared root demonstrates the strong link between concepts of heritage and nationalism. Both concepts are malleable and manipulable social constructs that can be marshalled to justify or persuade. Both can express power and agency, either as a top-down exertion of control from the upper echelons of a social hierarchy or as a grassroots movement to oppose this control.

As the editors of this volume have pointed out, heritage tourism has broadened from an emphasis on places to include culinary and cultural tourism. In this chapter, 'heritage' is taken to mean both sites of historic memory (real or imagined) with nationalist associations and also the culture, food and drink associated with these places. The potential interrelationship of heritage and food is not a new concept; it has been subject to extensive debate both outside and inside academic circles. A driver in this area has been the efforts of various official bodies to recognise food products and cuisines as 'heritage'; for instance, UNESCO's recognition of culinary cultures as intangible heritage and the European Union's system of Protected Designation of Origin (PDO/PDI). Tourism, and the role that recognised products and cuisines play within that industry, adds an extra dimension of complexity.

Catalans take great pride in performing their cultural and culinary heritage, using these to express their national identity both in individual and collective ways. However, the presence of a highly successful tourism industry catering to non-Catalans is impossible to ignore, especially in the capital city of Barcelona; in 2015 Catalonia received a quarter of Spain's total tourist visitors (Turespaña 2015). As in many places, this is a double-edged sword. Some local pro-independence activists see tourism as an opportunity to raise awareness of a separate identity while decrying the touristic homogenisation that is turning Catalonia into another region of Spain. More recently, Barcelona's mayor, Ada Colau, enacted legislation to curb tourist numbers (Plush 2017) and in August 2017 tempers flared with anti-tourist activities perpetrated by Arran, the youth wing of far left political party CUP (Burgen 2017). The region has experienced a terror attack in Barcelona in September 2017 and continuing political instability since October 2017, following an illegal independence referendum, widespread protests and the Spanish government's imposition of direct rule (at the time of writing, in December 2017, this situation remains unresolved). These events contributed to a 4.7 per cent drop in tourist numbers in Catalonia in October, in contrast to the rest of Spain (Tadeo and Goyeneche 2017), while tourist bookings for the first quarter of 2018 are down 10 per cent from the previous year (Michel 2017).

In line with this volume's goal of understanding how heritage is socially constructed, I will use Catalonia as a case study to understand the complex dynamic between heritage, tourism and food. I will first consider the issue of representing heritage through national identity performance, using the example of historical re-enactment during the 1714–2014 Tercentenary Celebrations of the Siege of Barcelona, celebrated on Catalonia's national day, the *Diada* (11 September). I will focus in particular on the way that food was used as part of this memorialisation. Next I will discuss some of the attempts to recognise Catalonia's culinary heritage through official designation, for instance by UNESCO. There was a recent, and now sadly failed, attempt to have Catalan cuisine recognised as UNESCO intangible heritage of humanity, following the first recognition of culinary cultures in 2010. This was led by an organisation called the Fundació-Institut de Cuina Catalana i Gastronomía, (Foundation-Institute of Catalan Cuisine and Gastronomy, or FICCG), which I will discuss further here. A successful UNESCO intangible heritage initiative, the recognition of the Mediterranean diet in 2013, was a partial inspiration for the campaign. Research by the University of Barcelona was crucial in allowing the bid to go through, as was its promotion by a cadre of academics (Medina 2009), a model the FICCG tried to follow.

The chapter proceeds by discussing how Catalans experience their national identity through internal tourism and the role that heritage plays in this experience. Before concluding, I will also give a brief exposition of a theme that will run through this chapter, that of the intended audiences of touristic heritage activities, whether they are Catalans experiencing their own culture, or non-Catalans. I am aware of the dangers of categorising different types of tourists (Waldren 1997) but, in my experience in Catalonia, it is possible to do this via language, as Catalan is so rarely spoken by outsiders.

Heritage and memory in the 1714–2014 tercentenary celebrations

2014 was an important year for Catalans, as it marked three hundred years since the disastrous Siege of Barcelona in 1714. The siege marked the end of the War of the Spanish Succession (1702–1715), a Europe-wide conflict to decide who would occupy the Spanish throne. The Catalans backed the losing, Habsburg faction, against the victorious Bourbon claimant, Philip V, who favoured centralisation of government in Madrid and an end to the Catalan Parliament (Generalitat). As the last remaining Habsburg stronghold, Barcelona capitulated on 11 September 1714 after a protracted and bloody siege. As punishment, the new monarch swept away Catalan governmental institutions, banned Catalan in legal documents, and instituted ruinous taxes. This day is memorialised today as Catalonia's national day, the *Diada*. Catalans recognise the irony that such an important day in the national calendar recalls a defeat and the dissolution of Catalan institutions and privileges. Yet their destruction created a sense of difference and a lingering resentment, which became a rallying cry for the later Catalanist movement.

The year 2014 saw a remembering of 1714 in all manner of popular acts. This included the creation of historic guided tours, product merchandising (especially food products) and the opening of a museum, the Born Cultural Centre, which showed houses destroyed in the siege and artefacts from the era. The *Diada* celebrations on this day were a focal point of the entire tercentenary, centred on Barcelona, the site of the original event. Historical re-enactment has always formed a part of these celebrations, but the performances in 2014 took on particular significance, for instance through re-formed groups of *Miquelets*, or Catalan infantry regiments, from the early eighteenth century.

The new museum, the Born Cultural Centre, is located in a tourist hub, a short distance from several popular attractions in central Barcelona. It is an impressive space, situated in a large, glass-roofed, former food market, with the main walkways overlooking the ruins. Open on four sides and including useful conveniences, it was clearly designed to cater to the influx of tourists in the area (Figure 3.1) and 670,000 visitors passed its doors in the first four months of opening (Catalan News 2014).

It is a place that demonstrates the sense of injustice at Catalonia's treatment during and after the war. Information boards (accessible without admission charge and written in Catalan, Spanish and English, the most common languages at Barcelona tourist sites), around the edges of the ruins, display emotive stories about the residents, the experiences of the siege, and its aftermath. Here, heritage has a dual purpose – as a site of traumatic collective memory for Catalans, and also to raise awareness of Catalan history for tourists, showing them that

Figure 3.1 The Born Cultural Centre in Barcelona. Note the information boards on the walkway to the right

Catalonia is different from Spain. This theme was also present in other popular museums, such as the Catalan National History Museum in Barcelona, which created an exhibition, entitled '300 years of 11th September'. The museum is a popular destination, welcoming 776,000 people in 2013 (ibid.), and situated in the port, a prime tourist hotspot. The museum's permanent display depicts national history and myths in great detail for tourists. Again, most of the exhibition was in Catalan, Spanish and English, to ensure that external visitors would understand the nature of the celebration and the events of 1714.

Of relevance to the issue of food and heritage, one wing of the Born Cultural Centre is occupied by a restaurant run by Moritz (Barcelona's brewer), called 'The 300 of the Born', a reference to the tercentenary. Moritz also designed a specific beer called 'Born 1714', imitating production techniques from the era. The space is marketed as an area where 'gastronomy converges with history thanks to an extensive menu based on historical cuisine', according to the Moritz website (Moritz 2016). The location of the Born Cultural Centre is itself note-worthy from a food perspective, as it is on the site of the original Born Market, active 1876–1971, and the site of Barcelona's wholesale fruit and vegetable market from 1921 (Ajuntament de Barcelona 2017). This was celebrated in an exhibition at the centre, entitled 'Born, Memories of a Market', taking place between March and November 2017. Recent research by Josep-Maria Garcia-Fuentes et al. (2014) has found that Barcelonan markets and food halls have been key to promoting and preserving economic and social spaces in the city, as well as Catalonia's gastronomic heritage. The location of the Born Cultural Centre therefore demonstrates a subtle underscoring of the relationship between food, heritage and national history.

The menu of Born 300 shows a thorough attempt to associate Catalan food of today with the siege of three hundred years ago, even down to humorously renaming the dishes on offer to evoke the era; for instance, *Xuixos*, sweet tubular pastries, are called 'Cannons . . . to remember the cannons that were the protagonists of the confrontation'. Other entries include '*Miquelet* sandwiches' – 'The mounted cavalry, eighteenth century *tapas*', '*Bombardejats*', for *bombes* (bombs), a stuffed croquette, 'so as not to forget that Barcelona has been bombed many times', 'Traditional and historic *platillos*', 'White bread of the French aristocracy' or 'Catalan black bread of the siege'. Dishes are also named by the restaurant after historical figures, places or events, such as *Bombes del Comte-duc d'Olivares*, or *Coca de recapte tradicional de Cardona*. On the back of the menu, one can find more detail on these figures, events, and the social context of the era, thus allowing food to perform an educational role.

The main focus of *Cuina*, Catalonia's foremost cooking magazine, in September 2014, was 1714. Its contents include a 'Menu from 1714: with recipes from three centuries ago', and an in-depth discussion of historical cuisine, food culture and cookbooks. An advertising feature markets the 'Born 1714' beer. The magazine also organised a series of talks (*Cicle Cuina 1714*) on food in Barcelona in the eighteenth century. The Catalonia-focused travel magazine *Descobrir* promoted the 1714 campaign with an entire issue dedicated to 'Catalunya 1714: We travel to the key scenes of the War of Succession.'

There was also a food route called 'Gastronomía 1714', designed by the FICCG and accompanied by a website and a promotional book, *La cuina del 1714* (Cuisine of 1714, Cases et al. 2014), subtitled as 'a gastronomic route through our history'. The first half of the book is a guidebook to the different locations on the route. The second half is a cookbook of recipes taken from FICCG's *Corpus* of Catalan recipes and some quotes of recipes from old cookbooks. The idea is to travel through Catalonia, visiting different locations that were significant in the war, to learn about their history and experience the places through the foods associated with them, by either consuming them in the location or cooking them at home. This book shows very well the connection between place, history and food – which is the crux of how heritage is being interpreted for tourism. It must be said that it is not certain all these foods actually *were* present in the early eighteenth century, and certainly not in the form we know them today. Yet this historical connectedness is key to the marketing of heritage in Catalonia today, via the celebration of particular landscapes, historic locations and a selection of foods that are seen as typically 'Catalan'. This is also true of Mortiz's 'the 300 of El Born', where the dishes on offer are normal Catalan foods, marketed under names associated with the past.

Culinary heritage was also central to the advertising for the *Ruta 1714* (1714 Route), led by the Generalitat de Catalunya.

Figure 3.2 Front cover of the magazine *Descobrir* for its 'Catalunya 1714' issue

The catchline for the campaign was 'Relive our history with five senses: monuments, landscapes, gastronomy' [my translation], and often included links to the 'Gastronomía 1714' campaign website (seen in this image in the bottom left, and with the exhortation 'Cuisine of 1714, taste it!').

Various food products were created (and sometimes redesigned or repackaged) to take advantage of the tercentenary celebrations. A Barcelona chocolatier, Enric Rovira, for example, designed a set of chocolates for the tercentenary, where he sought to imitate the taste of chocolate from that time; he created a pack of two chocolates, one an 'historic' chocolate called '1714' and another a 'modern' chocolate called '2014' to represent the present day.

Figure 3.3 Main poster for promoting the *Ruta 1714*, as part of the tercentenary celebrations. Used with permission of Consultes XTEC, Generalitat de Catalunya

Figure 3.4 Packaging for Enric Rovira's 1714–2014 chocolates, created for the tercentenary celebrations. Used with permission of Enric Rovira

However, as is noted in an accompanying text, solid chocolate was not actually available three hundred years ago:

> History says that on the eleventh of September 1714, the day the troops of Philip V entered Barcelona and abolished Catalan self-government of Catalonia, chocolate was only a drink based on water, cocoa, sugar and spices . . . Solid chocolate didn't appear until 1847 in England. Despite this historical reality we wanted to imagine how the solid chocolate of the era could have been considering the existing ingredients and culinary culture in Barcelona at that time.
>
> [My translation]

Rovira's patriotism is palpable from his description of the historic events in this text, but the wording also demonstrates how heritage was both an inspiration and a commercial strategy for making his chocolate relevant and appealing to his fellow compatriots. As to its use in marketing Catalonia to an external audience, the situation is less clear. The language used is Catalan, and while Rovira's products are a staple in most of Barcelona's tourist shops, I more often recall seeing the '1714–2014 chocolate' for sale in local, Catalan sweet shops and bakeries.

However, actual ethnographic experience suggested that some of these memorialisations might have been out of place. A tour guide told me that, in her rural town, no one had wanted to go on any of the 1714-inspired history routes or tours. Few of my close friends were aware of Enric Rovira's chocolates or the 1714 Gastronomic Route. I tried to attend a class in eighteenth-century cuisine, organised as part of the tercentenary celebrations; the class was cancelled due to lack of numbers. Despite this, there was a strong awareness of the tercentenary campaign generally, which the Generalitat began promoting a year before the event.

Official recognition of culinary heritage: ups and downs

The prime agent for many of these developments was often the Catalan regional government (Generalitat), either at regional level or further down the governmental hierarchy in individual municipalities. Heritage tourism may thus be viewed almost as a weapon in the complex power play between the Catalan Parliament and the central government in Madrid. The Generalitat has been particularly active in supporting the campaign for recognising Catalan cuisine as UNESCO intangible heritage and also the successful bid for Catalonia to be European Region of Gastronomy for 2016. The UNESCO bid has now been shelved; while the reasons are hazy, the most likely cause is the tense situation the UNESCO bid would involve, as any bid would need to go through the capital, Madrid. As the Generalitat has been so involved in promoting Catalan culture, it would be awkward to have to route this pro-Catalan project through a Madrid-based government that has historically been critical of the Gerneralitat, its initiatives, and Catalan identity in general. The referendum in October has compounded this impasse.

Catalonia has 20 products registered under the European Union's three-tier Protected Designation of Origin scheme: 11 Protected Designation of Origin products (PDO, meaning production is entirely in one area), nine Protected Geographical Indication products (PGI, with at least one stage of production in an area), and finally one Traditional Specialities Guaranteed product (TSG, a regional food product of specific character). A tradition of making a product in a certain area is central to achieving PDO, PGI or TSG status, so recognising a product under this system also recognises its role in culinary heritage. In 2003, the Catalan government also created a compilation of 240 *Productes de la Terra* (literally 'Products of the Land'), with a similar goal in mind, that of protecting Catalonia's ethno-alimentary heritage (Generalitat de Catalunya 2003).

Throughout Europe, the decision to protect certain products and take advantage of a certain *terroir* has become a means of self-promotion and national identity assertion (DeSoucey 2010), as well as an opportunity for touristic opportunity and income generation (Leynse 2006, Demoissier 2011). Looking specifically at the Catalan case, Robert Davidson (2007) has described how food is a medium through which the Catalan government engages in a new relationship with the rural by officially denominating areas and the products linked to them. Taste has now been officially recognised as a means by which a government-sponsored identity can be developed, or as Davidson puts it, a means of 'literally packaging a nation' (Davidson 2007: 40). Thus the government manages the image, acting as the protector of products, place and, by extension, cultural patrimony.

Despite the lack of success with UNESCO recognition, the Fundació-Institute de Cuina Catalana i Gastronomía (FICCG) continues to promote culinary heritage and identity through research for the recipe book created by the foundation, the *Corpus del Patrimoni Culinari Català* (Corpus of Catalan Culinary Patrimony), as well as through other publications. Preserving Catalan cuisine is the main goal of the organisation, and was part of the motivation for the UNESCO bid. With this in mind, the FICCG created the *Marca Cuina Catalana*, an official recognition given to restaurants that prepare Catalan dishes according to recipes in the *Corpus*. These measures generally receive a favourable reaction in Catalonia, just as there is almost always a positive attitude to the preservation and promotion of any aspect of Catalan culture. Moreover, this international recognition furthers and even celebrates awareness of Catalan identity outside its borders, ensuring touristic and, by extension, economic potential from the activities of the FICCG.

Yet, even within Catalonia, the UNESCO bid (and the FICCG) has its detractors. Some Catalans I knew found it hard to understand how Catalan cuisine could be controlled and managed by an organisation. As one chef remarked, while he is in favour of initiatives like the *Marca Cuina Catalana* and the UNESCO campaign, he did not want Catalan cuisine to become 'a work of art from grandma, which is hung up and does nothing'. Another of my informants, a food journalist, felt there was a risk of turning Catalan cuisine into 'the offerings of a museum. Because it doesn't move, it's immutable, codified'. This demonstrates well one of the main problems with marking any cultural performance (including cuisine) as heritage;

it codifies and freezes that performance in a specific time, and sometimes prevents further adaptations that would keep the performance relevant over time.

Debates about who really 'owns' heritage, and which foods represent 'culinary heritage', are prevalent throughout Catalonia. At the same time, the commodification of culinary heritage often leads to an increase in price. I recall the leader of a cultural organisation complaining about this very problem when he visited the county of Cerdanya in the Pyrenees. A typical activity in Catalonia is visiting particular regions to try local specialities (discussed further in the next section). The local speciality of Cerdanya is the *trinxat*, a dish of mashed cabbage, potatoes and bacon. My friend found it cost an exorbitant 12 euros; for comparison, the average three-course lunch menu is 10–15 euros. This made him feel he was being priced out of his own culture, a situation he blamed on promotion of the dish as the regional, heritage food of the Cerdanya.

Experiencing national (and culinary) heritage through tourism

One phrase I often heard in the field was 'The cuisine of a country is its landscape put into a pot'. What this means in a practical sense is that the physical aspects of that landscape give rise to the produce that is available there, and even affect the way that food is cooked. The phrase is attributed to Josep Pla, who was one of the most important Catalan writers of the twentieth century; he wrote a book about Catalan food, called *What We Have Eaten*, which is an elegy to a cuisine that he saw as disappearing (Pla 1972). Along with other Catalan writers under the Franco dictatorship, Pla used his writings to try to preserve a Catalan heritage that he envisaged as being lost.

Representative of a general trend present in Catalan nationalism since the nineteenth century is a movement called *excursionisme*. This is often translated as 'hiking', especially by the anthropologist Josep Llobera (2004). However, I would give it a broader definition, especially today in the context of heritage tourism: going on outings, visiting other parts of Catalonia, becoming familiar with the landscapes, towns and villages that make up the region. The Catalan government has long been aware of the strategic importance of this activity in promoting Catalan identification, as demonstrated in the tourist poster from 1930, shown in Figure 3.5 (see Congdon 2017).

One example of *excursionisme* is the visiting of other parts of Catalonia to try certain foods, such as a trip to the Ebre Delta in the far south to try rice dishes, to the north-east to experience *mar i muntanya* cuisine (literally, 'sea and mountain' dishes, such as chicken and prawns), or to the central, agrarian Plain of Vic for pork products. Ideally, Catalans will develop a love and affection for their native land through the experience of walking through it and by experiencing its different cultural and culinary heritages. The landscape becomes the symbol of the nation, which residents and visitors come to know intimately. This intimate knowledge is best encapsulated in one food-based, excursionist activity – *busca-bolets*, or mushroom finding – as participants need to know every part of the landscape of particular sites across Catalonia. In the last few years, there has been a noticeable

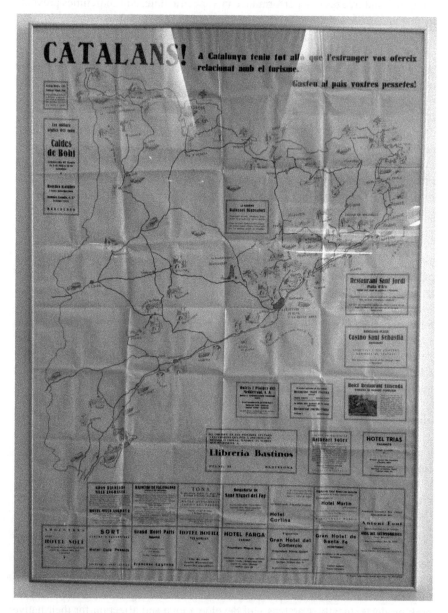

Figure 3.5 Catalan poster from 1930 encouraging Catalans to participate in local tourism

increase in the popularity of this activity and it has been promoted extensively in the popular press and media throughout the region. From a heritage and identificatory perspective, this serves two purposes. Firstly, Catalans believe that most other cuisines across Spain rarely use mushrooms (except in the Basque country).

Mushroom finding is therefore an expression of a distinct culinary identity. Secondly, mushroom finding is an historical activity that has been performed by rural Catalans for centuries. While the *busca-bolets* is now carried out for leisure rather than subsistence purposes, it allows Catalans to perform a piece of heritage that connects them to an activity they associate with their ancestors. This idealisation of the rural is typical of other examples of nationalism and part of what nationalism theorist, Ernest Gellner (1983: 57), describes as 'symbolism drawn from the healthy, pristine, vigorous life of the peasants'.

It is also important to note that heritage and *excursionisme* are also related in another way, in the preservation of built heritage. In the nineteenth century there were several instances of Catalanist excursionists coming across Romanesque and Medieval monasteries and churches, in so doing rediscovering 'lost' heritage from Catalonia's 'Golden Age' (the 11th to 14th centuries ad). These places now provide a connection with the past. A classic example is the Monastery of Sant Benet in Bages, one of Catalonia's most splendid monasteries from this period, which had been abandoned by the nineteenth century. It was rediscovered, bought and restored by Catalan intellectuals later in the nineteenth century and became the family home of a well-known artist of the Catalan Modernist period. By imitating the heritage of the medieval era, these intellectuals sought to create a new Catalan 'golden age'. Today, the museum celebrates both these eras with audio visual displays and tours around the building. Food heritage is also integral to this site, as it is the headquarters of the Alicia Foundation, a research and educational institute that promotes awareness of food, nutrition and culinary heritage throughout Catalonia.

Even today, the *excursionist* ideal is alive and well. The top three of Catalonia's most popular publications are keen to promote this ideal of travel in Catalonia, whether on walking trips, weekends away or day trips. These magazines – *Cuina* (literally 'Cooking'), *Descobrir* ('Discover', a travel magazine) and *Sapiens* ('History') – stress the need to experience Catalan places by travelling to them to experience the local cultures and especially their foods.

Insiders and outsiders, Catalans and non-Catalans

Tourists now play an important part in preserving culinary and monumental heritage. Tourism is one of Catalonia's most important industries, employing 11.6 per cent of the Catalan population in 2013, while in Barcelona alone it generated €20 million per day (Ajuntament de Barcelona 2013). The economic potential of tourism was recognised as early as 1930 with the development of internal tourism, as evidenced in the poster, shown in Figure 3.5, which contains the exhortation 'Spend your pesetas in the country!' Language is a pertinent point to consider here. Catalan and Spanish have equal weight in Catalonia, although Catalan is the preferred language in most areas outside of Barcelona. The use of these languages, plus English, is a useful indicator of the intended audience. Language demonstrates whether material is for in-group consumption amongst Catalans or for dissemination outside this group, either to Spanish speakers (tourists or local residents) or English-speaking visitors from outside Spain. When it comes to raising aware-ness, beyond Catalans, of Catalonia as a distinct unit with its own identity, it is the latter group of tourists that is most important. That is why, in large pro-independence protests, many of the banners have been written in English; they can then be understood in the global Anglophone media. The presence of tourists offers an ideal opportunity to continue this process. It is now almost impossible for non-Catalan tourists to be unaware of Catalanist events and the sentiments behind them. Thus some of the presentation of heritage to tourists has the secondary purpose of raising awareness of Catalan identity and struggles, an activity sometimes called *fer pais*, literally 'making country'. This is particularly prevalent in the arena of food, due to common misconceptions about Catalan food.

It is a common trope that the best food to eat in Barcelona is *tapas* with *sangría*, even though these items are not commonly consumed by Catalans. Indeed, many Catalans I knew found it offensive that their cuisine was seen only as 'tapas', which they often consider a separate cuisine, representing a different kind of heritage and a hangover of attempts in the Franco period (1939–1975) to destroy Catalan cul-ture and make Catalonia just another region of Spain. Opening the country to mass tourism in the 1960s aided that process, as Spanish authorities presented a simpli-fied vision of Spain as the land of sun, sea, *sangría*, bullfighting, flamenco, *paella* and tapas; of these, only *paella* has any connection with Catalan culture. Barcelona also received large numbers of immigrants from other parts of Spain in the Franco period, a move encouraged by the government to further dilute Catalan identity. Despite the efforts of the Catalan government to make amends, through many of the initiatives I have discussed here, there is a sense that Barcelona's Catalan iden-tity has been diluted, creating a negative heritage in a culinary and cultural sense. This is the reason why Catalan municipal governments are keen to encourage non-Catalan tourists to travel out of the city of Barcelona into other areas of Catalonia. Not only does this spread tourist income throughout the region, but the tourists get to see the 'real' Catalonia that is clearly different from the rest of Spain.

Conclusion

What does the Catalan nationalist movement today teach us about heritage from a touristic perspective? Much has been written about the power dynamics implicit in performing for tourists (Pi-Sunyer 1978, Boissevan 1996), but the examples outlined here have shown that many of the performances and manifestations of heritage in Catalonia are more for Catalans themselves than for non-Catalans. Richard Wilk (1999), a key theorist on national cuisine, believes that tourism has been essential to the creation of Belizean culture and cuisine, but in the Catalan case the situation is more complex. I have not focused so much on *Spanish* tourists as a separate category, nor on their reactions to the promotion of Catalan identity through heritage tourism, as I have insufficient data concerning their attitudes. However, what is certain is that tourism, and in particular heritage tourism, is a means of promoting awareness of Catalonia as different from the rest of Spain.

Of greater importance than external tourists are internal, Catalan tourists, who are key to developments, debates and reformulations of cultural performance and culinary heritage. Heritage tourism, in particular during the 1714–2014 tercentenary, was a means of identity expression, reformulation and in-group discussion for Catalans. The current of both historiography and identity passes through heritage-focused touristic developments. Catalans are using culinary heritage as a means of recreating what has become a significant moment in national history, and getting in touch with a national past that is central to present-day Catalanism. This reliving of a national past through the senses is a novel way of promoting and experiencing a perceived national heritage. Moreover, the Catalan case reveals how heritage, be it culinary, place-centred or cultural, gains new importance in a situation of contested national identity.

Note

1 The Constitution is based on the indissoluble unity of the Spanish Nation, the common and indivisible homeland of all Spaniards; it recognises and guarantees the right to self-government of the nationalities and regions of which it is composed and the solidarity among them all (Second Article of the Spanish Constitution, Congreso de los Diputados, 1978).

References

Ajuntament de Barcelona (2013) Tourism and Hospitality: Sector Report 2013. Available at: http://w27.bcn.cat/porta22/images/en/Barcelona_treball_Informe_sectorial_Tourism_and_hospitality_gen2013_en_tcm43–32845.pdf [Accessed 25 July 2017].

Ajuntament de Barcelona (2017) El Born Mercat. Available at: http://elbornculturaimemoria.barcelona.cat/en/el-born-market [Accessed 24 July 2017].

Boissevan J. (ed.) (1996) *Coping with Tourists: European Reactions to Mass Tourism.* Providence and Oxford: Berghahn Books.

Burgen, S. (2017) Barcelona anti-tourism activists vandalise bikes and bus. *The Guardian,* 1 August [Online]. Available at: www.theguardian.com/world/2017/aug/01/barcelona-anti-tourism-activists-vandalise-bikes-and-bus [Accessed 5 September 2017].

Cases A., Gassó M., de Meià S., Miras Llopart J. and Pérez Samper M.A. (2014) *La cuina del 1714.* Barcelona: Comanegra.

Catalan News (16 May 2014) Catalan museums received 21.5 million visitors in 2013 [Online]. Available at: www.catalannews.com/culture/item/catalan-museums-received-21-5-million-visitors-in-2013 [Accessed 24 July 2017].

Congdon, V. (2017) Regionalists and excurstionistes: Catalan 'regions' and national identity, in J. Riding and M. Jones (eds.) *Reanimating Regions: Culture, Politics and Performance.* Oxford and New York: Routledge, pp. 79–94.

Congreso de los Diputados (1978) Spanish Constitution (English). Available at: www.congreso.es/portal/page/portal/Congreso/Congreso/Hist_Normas/Norm/const_espa_texto_ingles_0.pdf [Accessed 27 July 2017].

Davidson, R. A. (2007) *Terroir* and Catalonia. *Journal of Catalan Studies,* 1(1): 39–53.

Demossier, M. (2011) Beyond terroir: territorial construction, hegemonic discourses, and French wine culture. *Journal of the Royal Anthropological Institute,* 17: 685–705.

Garcia-Fuentes, J.M., Guàrdia Bassols, M. and Oyón Bañales, J.L. (2014) Reinventing edible identities: Catalan cuisine and Barcelona's market halls, in R.L. Brulotte and M.A. Di Giovine (eds.) *Edible Identities: Food as Cultural Heritage.* Farnham: Ashgate, pp. 159–174.

Gellner, E. (1983) *Nations and Nationalism.* Oxford: Blackwell.

Generalitat de Catalunya (2003) *Productes de la terra.* Barcelona: Generalitat de Catalunya, Departament d'Agricultura, Alimentació i Acció Rural.

Institut Català de la Cuina (2011) *Corpus del Patrimoni Culinari Català.* Barcelona: RBA Libros.

Leynse W.L.H. (2006) Journeys through 'ingestible topography': socializing the 'situated eater' in France, in T.M. Wilson (ed.) *Food, Drink and Identity in Europe.* Amsterdam and New York: Rodopi, pp. 129–158.

Llobera, J.R. (2004) *Foundations of National Identity: From Catalonia to Europe.* New York and Oxford: Berghahn Books.

Medina F.X. (2009) Mediterranean diet, culture and heritage: challenges for a new conception. *Public Health Nutrition,* 12(9A): 1618–1620.

Michel, E. (2017) Explainer: how the independence drive has stalled the Catalan economy. *The Local.es,* 15 December [Online]. Available at: www.thelocal.es/20171215/ explainer-what-the-independence-drive-is-doing-to-the-catalan-economy [Accessed 28 December 2017].

Moritz (2016) El 300 Del Born. Available at: http://moritz.com/en/section/el-300-del-born [Accessed 28 July 2017].

Pi-Sunyer, O. (1978) Through native eyes: tourists and tourism in a Catalan maritime community, in V.L. Smith (ed.) *Hosts and Guests: The Anthropology of Tourism.* Oxford: Blackwell, pp. 149–155.

Pla, J. (1972) *El que hem menjat.* Barcelona: Edicions Destino.

Plush, H (2017) Barcelona unveils new law to keep tourists away. *The Telegraph,* 27 January [Online]. Available at: www.telegraph.co.uk/travel/destinations/europe/ spain/catalonia/barcelona/articles/barcelona-unveils-new-law-to-keep-tourists-away [Accessed 5 September 2017].

Tadeo, M. and Goyeneche, A. (2017) Tourists gave Barcelona a miss as Catalonia crisis raged. *Bloomberg,* 1 December [Online]. Available at: www.bloombergquint.com/ onweb/2017/11/30/tourists-gave-barcelona-a-miss-as-catalonia-crisis-raged [Accessed 28 December 2017].

Turespaña (September 2015) Turísticos en fronteras. Available at: http://estadisticas. tourspain.es/es-ES/estadisticas/frontur/mensuales/Nota%20de%20coyuntura%20 de%20Frontur.%20Septiembre%202015.pdf [Accessed 27 July 2017].

Wilk, R. R. (1999) 'Real Belizean food': building local identity in the transnational Caribbean. *American Anthropologist,* 101(2): 244–255.

Waldren, J. (1997) We are not tourists, we live here, in S. Abram, J. Waldren and D.V.L. Macleod (eds.) *Tourists and Tourism: Identifying with People and Places.* Oxford: Berg, pp. 51–70.

4 Heritage defined and maintained through conflict re-enactments

The Estonian Museum of Occupations and the Forest Brothers Bunker

Brent McKenzie

Introduction

There exists extensive research into the impacts of heritage-related museums, attractions, and tourism sites (see Kirshenblatt-Gimblett 1998, Corsane 2005, Alvarez et al. 2016). Babić (2016) examines how the growth of interest in heritage research aligns with the roles and aims of the operation of museums as well as the wider field of museum studies and museology. Amineddoleh (2014) explores the impact that museum artefacts have on the study of cultural heritage, while Schouten (1995) focuses on the consumer experience at heritage attractions. The historic roles played by heritage sites have been examined in terms of experience and culture by Smith (2006), while the integration of theory with the practice of heritage has been investigated in the case of tourism, by Bourdeau et al. (2017), and in that of sustainability, by Auclair and Fairclough (2015).

Museums comprise one of a number of different places where heritage is preserved by way of displaying collections of memories and artefacts. They invite, or entice, visitors to come and experience the heritage of the country or its people. But as is the case for many public, and private, educationally oriented institutions, while there is the requirement to maintain historic relevance, there is also the need to adapt and adjust to changing marketing realities, including the increasing importance of tourism. The overarching question is how this is to be achieved. The aim of this chapter is to address this question by way of an analysis of the Museum of Occupations (*Okupatsioonide Muuseum*) in Tallinn, Estonia. More specifically this research examines how the introduction of an offsite attraction, the 'Forest Brother Bunker' (*Retked metsavendluse radadel*) has been used both as an additional source of Museum revenue, and as a way to further entrench the brand image of the Occupation Museum as the leading authority on Estonian heritage, shaped during the Soviet period of 1944–1991.

Beginning with an outline of the historic roots of the Estonian Forest Brothers, the chapter will review the extant literature on the role that historic re-enactments have played in heritage development, maintenance, and advancement. Following this, background will be provided on the purpose, success, and controversies of the Museum of Occupations located in Tallinn, the capital of Estonia. The creation of the Forest Brothers Bunker as a re-creation exhibit for the Museum of Occupations will be discussed, with support from an interview by the author with the Director of the Museum of Occupations and the Curator/Creator of the Forest Brothers Bunker attraction. This section also provides insight into the role that such an exhibit has had on wider concepts of Estonian heritage, culture, and nationality. The chapter concludes with an integration of the literature and the specific case study and considers the contribution of the research to the fields of heritage study and tourism practice.

The Estonian 'Forest Brothers'

Estonia and the other two Baltic states of Latvia and Lithuania shared a troubling, and often horrific, second half of the twentieth century. Created as independent states following World War I, they were caught up in the infamous Molotov-Ribbentrop Pact between Adolph Hitler and Josef Stalin. The three nations were put 'under the sphere' of the Soviet Union and were subsequently occupied. This occupation lasted until 1941, with the commencement of Operation Barbarossa, Nazi Germany's reneging of the Molotov-Ribbentrop Pact and the subsequent replacement of the Soviet occupation by that of Nazi Germany. The Nazi occupation lasted until the Soviet Union retook the region in 1944, which resulted in the incorporation of the three countries as part of the USSR, until re-independence was achieved in 1991 (Kasekamp 2010).

In the case of Estonia, the original Soviet occupation resulted in mass arrests, executions and forced relocations to Siberia (Raun 1987). The Nazi occupation continued with arrests and executions, while the second Soviet occupation led to further arrests, executions, and deportations. During the Second World War, Estonians fought in three different ways. Some volunteered for, and some were forcibly conscripted into, fighting for Nazi Germany, while some volunteered for, or were forcibly conscripted into, fighting for the Soviet Red Army. But it is the third group on which this chapter is focused; the 'Forest Brothers' ('*Metsavennad*') were a group of Estonian partisans and members of the resistance movement who lived in the forests and conducted surprise attacks on the Soviet forces.

The 'Forest Brothers' are also known by a number of other names (Brothers of the Forest; Forest Brethren; Forest Brotherhood). Depending upon the source, these were partisans actively engaged in a guerrilla war against Soviet occupation (Vitkus 2012) or, alternately, a renegade group of domestic terrorists who had no choice about opposing Soviet rule as they had fought on the side of Nazi Germany against the Soviet army (and, by extension, against the Allied powers (Anušauskas 2006)). Interestingly, the Soviet Union itself created films and propaganda about the role that partisans could, and did, play in protecting Soviet Russia from the Nazi advancement into the Soviet Union in 1941 (Stites 1995). What is of lesser contention is that from approximately 1945 until the last known Forest Brother in Estonia was found (August Sabbe was discovered by KGB agents in 1978 and drowned himself in a river to avoid capture), the Forest Brothers were credited with having killed thousands of Soviet soldiers in Estonia (Lowe 2012). Arguably of greater significance, both objectively and mythically, has been the ongoing fight by the Forest Brothers for Estonia's return to independence (Laar 1992).

The legacy of this has been the continuation of a strong reverence for the Forest Brothers movement across the three Baltic States. The movement remains an active component in terms of Estonian history education, both inside and outside of Estonia (Raun 1987).

The Museum of Occupations

The Museum of Occupations is centrally located in the capital city of Estonia, Tallinn. As noted on its website:

> The Museum of Occupations provides a comprehensive overview of Estonian society during three periods of occupation: the first Soviet occupation 1940–1941, the German occupation 1941–1944, and the second Soviet occupation 1944–1991. Audio-visual displays and photos highlight the events of the era, repression and national resistance, as well as showing how people coped with the day-to-day realities of this difficult period.
> (www.okupatsioon.ee, accessed 1 February 2017)

The Museum of Occupations was founded in 2002–2003, using a large donation from a member of the Estonian diaspora, Dr. Olga Kistler-Ritson, who also created the Kistler-Ritso Estonian Foundation that continues to control the operations of the museum (Haven 2011). Although a privately run museum, it did receive official support from the Estonian government when it opened in June 2003 (Tamm 2013). In subsequent years the museum has continued to receive a degree of support, but has also provoked controversy. The Russian Federation press, for example, views the museum as a propaganda tool of the Estonian government, in terms of suppressing the controversial positions that some Estonians played in supporting Nazi activities during World War II (Burch and Zander 2008). The museum has also received the attention of a number of academic and industry publications. Mark (2008), for example, compares and contrasts the focus of the Museum of Occupations with that of the Museum of Genocide Victims in Vilnius, Lithuania, while Williams (2007) examines photographs within the museum in terms of their political impact on Estonian independence issues. Other studies that have used the Museum of Occupations as a basis for their research include that of McKenzie (2018) who examines the role that the retail and marketing of souvenirs has on museum success.

Beginning with its 4th edition (2006), a popular tourism guide, the *Lonely Planet guide to Estonia, Latvia and Lithuania*, listed the Museum of Occupations as the 'Museum of Occupation and Fight for Freedom', stating that the museum focused on Estonian struggles (Williams and Blond 2006, Bain 2009), while the subsequent 6th and 7th editions again mentioned the struggles, but also noted the excessively disproportionate focus on the Soviet period and the limited focus on Nazi crimes, particularly those related to the Holocaust (Presser et al. 2012, Dragicevich et al. 2016). The present study also reviewed the Bradt travel guides (Williamson 1997, Arnold 2014). Beginning with the 'Baltic Capitals', 2nd edition

(Taylor et al. 2003), the guides heralded the opening of the occupations museums within a discussion of other geographically close sites relating to the Nazi and Soviet occupations. The associated 'Baltic Cities' title (Taylor 2008), provided a more detailed review of the history of the museum, but interestingly included the comment that 'to the Estonians, the Russians and the Germans are equally guilty' (p. 52). This would appear to contradict the criticism noted above. The use of the terms, 'Russians' and 'Germans', rather than 'Soviets' and 'Nazis', should also be highlighted. This conflation of terms, particularly in the case of the Russian/Soviet identifiers, may be viewed as troubling, since Estonian Russians represent approximately one-quarter of the population of Estonia (Statistics Estonia 2017).

Public tourist reviews have mirrored these points. For example, the leading online travel website, TripAdvisor, contains approximate 500 forum postings about the Museum of Occupations (www.tripadvisor.ca/Attraction_Review-g274958–d281978–Reviews-Estonian_Museum_of_Occupations-Tallinn_Harju_County.html). The museum is in the top 10 per cent of 'things to do in Tallinn'. These types of postings have been shown to provide a degree of understanding and insight into traveller perceptions and experiences (Lee et al. 2011). As of July 2017, the average overall review was positive, with over three-quarters of the reviews awarding a score of 4 or 5 out of 5. A sample of headings tended to support the industry publication reviews: 'A bit lopsided but still very interesting'; 'Informative and harrowing'; 'Interesting details about the history of Estonia'. In terms of negative reviews, one posted in 2016 elucidates Lonely Planet's concerns about the limited focus on Nazi atrocities:

> Disturbing in a wrong way
> This museum disturbingly underplays the atrocities committed by the Nazis in 1941–44. This apparently is to point out the Soviets as the real enemy without too much distraction. Watch for example the video on the second screen of the tour, which is concerned with WWII but hardly mentions mass murders committed by the Germans, and features Nazi propaganda images without putting those in a critical context.
>
> (TripAdvisor review [www.tripadvisor.co.uk], accessed May 2018)

The relevance of these third-party reviews becomes of greater interest if there is a blurring or lack of understanding of the original purpose of such a museum. As a private enterprise facility, the Museum of Occupations may find that without government or public support there is no choice but to cater to a wider audience, regardless of the fact that the original focus was on communicating to and educating those within and outside Estonia concerning the acts and events that occurred during the Nazi and Soviet occupations. In 2016 it was announced that, as of 2018, the Museum of Occupations in Tallinn will be renamed 'Vabamu', which in Estonian means 'freedom'. Although the change in title is intended to reflect the expansion of the museum (Cavegn 2016), there has been an immediate backlash over the impact that such a change might have, specifically a belief that the new name would reduce the focus on the period of occupation by Nazi Germany, as well as marking a movement towards political correctness with respect to Estonia's history (Kolga 2016).

The Forest Brothers Bunker

As noted above, knowledge of the history of the Forest Brothers themselves, and the role that the Forest Brothers movement played in Estonia during the Soviet occupation, was very great. Although the scope of the movement in Estonia has been argued to be of less prominence than in Latvia and Lithuania (Anušauskas 2006), the education of Estonian youth (and the Estonian diaspora) about the Forest Brothers has remained significant. With the expectation that such interest and education would continue, the Museum of Occupations created an interactive exhibit, the Forest Brothers Bunker (FBB) in 2013.

The aim of the FBB was to provide both Estonian and international tourists with the opportunity of experiencing how Estonian culture evolved during the twentieth century. As culture and heritage were suppressed, often overtly so, through forced incorporation into the Soviet Union, the FBB would help to ensure a continued focus on a lengthy but infrequently studied heritage, while also assessing the impact that a conflict based tourist attraction might have on Estonian identity. The original exhibit, a reconstruction of an example of a FBB, was opened at the Museum of Occupations in February 2013. It was on display until November 2013, after which arose the question of whether and how to continue offering such an education about the Forest Brothers, which meant so much to visitors and historians alike. The decision was taken to recreate the Museum bunker within the woods of Estonia (McKenzie 2017). The original exhibit was taken down and moved about 60 km to Rapla County. The specific location was the site where the Soviet NKVD (the Soviet secret police, or security force, and the predecessor to the KGB) had attacked such a bunker at the end of 1947. A commemorative stone had already been placed there in September 2007 to honour the Forest Brothers that were killed during the attack. A more durable reconstruction of what a Forest Brothers Bunker site would have looked like, was designed and built by a member of the Museum of Occupations. The 'cabin' had weatherproofing and a proper roof; in essence it was a 'hiking' cabin since people could stay in it. There was no charge to visit. In general, the only official tours made to the FBB were organised by schoolteachers for their students, although there were some one-off tours, based upon request, conducted by the creator of the site (McKenzie 2017).

Interview findings

To gather additional insights into the position and future of the museum for the research project, the author met with the museum curator, who was also the creator of the Forest Brothers Bunker attraction. A qualitative approach was selected as the best way to examine the underlying concepts of culture and heritage (Nevid and Sta. Maria 1999) within the context of the Museum of Occupations.

Qualitative research techniques, such as interviews, have been previously used to investigate how images of tourist sites in former communist countries have developed (Hughes and Allen 2008) as well as to study the growth of tourism in Estonia following the end of the Soviet period (Jaakson 1996). The interview lasted approximately 90 minutes and the author created detailed notes from the meeting. The interview commenced with a review of the current state of the Museum of Occupations and key insights, challenges, and opportunities that the museum was experiencing. Although paraphrased for clarity, the interview responses are presented in detail, as this is the first known empirical investigation into the concepts of culture and heritage as they relate to this type of museum. The key questions of the interview are listed below, together with responses from the creator/curator:

(1) How would you view heritage as against culture?

I think it is a very interesting question, a political question. Philosophically, who says 'what is heritage'. For example a couple of years ago in Iceland, two buildings were burning. The people in the city never cared about these buildings until they were gone. Thus (one) starts to understand something is important just before it is gone, which is the same with artefacts we cover. Old Estonian artefacts are valued. Items such as Soviet cupboards, sofas, were never of value, but after certain distance something will become nostalgic. This is a form of reflexive nostalgia in Estonia. Estonian people are scared of the Soviet period as it could become nostalgic, but as the more you have distance from that time the more of a nostalgic feel, as represented in restaurants or cafes . . . a goal is not to tell the truth so that the truth can be used as a political tool. That may be the goals of politicians and political institutions, but the museum needs to be focused on ensuring the discussion can take place even if it is not always easy. The Museum has, and does show many contradictory exhibits – not everyone agrees as that is the basis of a democracy.

(2) How does the Museum of Occupation help to enhance or to educate visitors about Estonian Heritage and Culture, and how is this done?

When you look at museums, ten, twenty years ago, they were collections and scientific work . . . education is the most important. Forming what it means to be a museum is something we are struggling with how to deal with . . . if an artefact is old, for people born in 1920s and 1930s, they will understand the Soviet period and most of those types of items. But for those born in 2000 or after re-independence from the Soviet Union, what is the significance of a radio?

(3) What would be the opportunities or challenges that exist for a privately owned versus a publically funded museum in terms of focusing on the periods of occupation in Estonia?

I don't want to say that there would be any difference, as I hope Estonia is a democratic country, so the national museums can also make their own decisions as well as to what they show, and what they show is not dependent upon gaining funding. Our museum gets a little money from the Government as well. I would like to hope it is not; that the value in Estonia of democracy is bigger than the political interests . . . our Museum is a museum of discussion. There is also a psychological perspective. Estonians want to be liked by others, which perhaps is a legacy of the Soviet period, I don't know. During the Soviet period you had to get along, and not draw attention. If there is no conflict, it is easier to exist during that type of system. Maybe this fear that existed during the Soviet period continues as change can bring unwanted attention, it is easier to keep the same narrative.

(4) If the majority of the visitors to the Museum are foreign tourists, how do you know that Estonian culture and heritage is being understood?

Our most recent records indicate that of all our visitors, 81 per cent were tourists, and 12 per cent were from Estonia. This was up from the typical 5 per cent, which was not unusual as the museum is 13 years old, and the increase was because the museum was in the news. Estonians know the Museum exhibits and only those interested in politics and history would come again, as most of the Estonian population have moved on from the period. They have moved on with their life. If you have lived through the Soviet period or know of it, you don't want to come see it . . . during the Soviet period the message was that I want to be free in Estonia . . . the Soviet system could not take away meaning from people, they could change the items, songs, and so on, but they can't take away what these artefacts mean to the Estonian people.

(5) How would this compare to how Estonians interpret the museum with respect to Estonian Culture and Heritage?

For the Estonian visitors to the museum, I think there are unfortunately big gaps between the generations. For the older Estonians, they need to know that the stories about the suffering are being told. For the younger generations, leave the suffering and move on. Estonian stories should be about e-technology, Skype, how successful Estonians have become. For the Museum the feeling is that this focus on the suffering as part of the Museum's message is being maintained by the Estonian diaspora. Many who escaped Estonia and did not live through the Soviet period, felt that they were the ones that kept up the fight to maintain Estonian culture. When in fact Estonian culture continued to live and evolve even through the Soviet period . . . 1991 is a long time ago.

(6) How does the Forest Brothers Bunker align with Estonian culture and heritage and how does this type of attraction aid in this education?

We do tours there for school groups in the springtime. The hiking cabin is open for anyone. They can read about the Forest Brothers, and see the reconstruction of the bunker ruin from 1947. As it is an interactive site, the visitor can use their imagination about Forest Brothers experiences. The fact that you are in the nature, you see a hole in the ground. The visitor learns about how the Forest Brothers used the bunker. The visitor gets to look at the hole, and in the hole, which helps to tell the story. For those that criticise the bunker as it is not authentic, why do people not make similar criticisms of artefacts that you see behind the glass? When you think about the process of learning it is an active process, and the Forest Brother Bunker provides people with something to do by learning. It is the experience of learning what the artefact means and not the actual 'artefact'.

In summary, the findings from the interview helped to place the Museum of Occupations, and the Forest Brothers Bunker specifically, within the context of Estonian culture and heritage. The perspective of the museum is that it plays a key role in both communicating to and educating non-Estonians about how the Soviet period has shaped, and continues to shape, Estonia. Even though the vast majority of visitors are foreign tourists, the museum indirectly has an impact on how Estonians, both domestic and within the diaspora, interact with Estonian culture.

Discussion and conclusions

What then can be learned from the study of one museum, and arguably one exhibit with respect to the maintenance of culture? Although the partisan conflict in Estonia was smaller in scale than that in the other Baltic states of Latvia and Lithuania, the Forest Brothers Bunker allows for a coalescing of heritage stories and experiences that can be passed on from generation to generation. Since the conflict depicted in the interactive exhibit is set against dominant Estonian culture, the Soviet/Russian culture of the second largest group of residents in Estonia adds a level of complication that needs to be addressed or at least clarified in terms of the context of the exhibit, in order to prevent outrage from defenders of Russian heritage. The Museum of Occupations has attempted to mitigate this inherent roadblock in order to appeal to the larger potential visitor base that is generally unaware of the various players, as well as to the Russian ethnic tourism market. As demonstrated, the aim of the Forest Brothers Bunker exhibit is to inform, educate and immerse the museum visitor in a more dynamic and interactive experience than merely observing and reading about historic artefacts and items (Brændholt Lundgaard and Thorek Jensen 2013). It is expected that this type of attraction will continue to gain prominence over time (Kovaleva et al. 2017).

The question of how the Occupations Museum and the Forest Brothers Bunker aid in the maintenance of Estonian heritage, and by extension Estonian culture, is less clear. Due to the often conflicting views from the various players (museum owners/board, museum managers, city officials, visitors and so on), one can suggest that greater analysis and study will be needed to best understand the role that these sites can play. As the management and focus of a museum changes, there is an inherent risk that the interpretation of existing exhibits may alter over time in order to match the larger outside voices, or more importantly, as a private enterprise, the financial stakeholders' agenda.

In conclusion, as discussed by Crane (1997), museums provide the public with the opportunity to experience history, culture, nature, science and art. They can directly contribute to public perception of their area of focus, while also having the spill over effect of attracting tourists to their country or city (Altinbasak and Yalçin 2010). With respect to the addition of the Forest Brothers Bunker, visitors have the opportunity to experience Soviet period demonstrations as well as to participate personally in the historic activities of the Forest Brothers, but how does this align with a larger narrative of Estonian heritage? As this chapter has shown, a museum, and interactive exhibits, can and do have different impacts on different types of tourist. A stated need and desire to convey Estonian culture and heritage to visitors who come to the Museum of Occupations and the Forest Brothers Bunker is complicated by the effect that the exhibits and attractions may have on Estonians themselves.

Over the years the percentage of Estonian visitors to the museum has fallen. But this fact has not stemmed the growth of conflict between how the residents of Estonia, in comparison to those of the Estonian diaspora, view the way that the museum should be conveying Estonian culture and heritage. This debate about culture and heritage between locals and diaspora is not new. What this chapter has brought to light is how that debate adds an extra challenge for a business entity, in this case a museum, whose *raison d'être* is to focus on culture and heritage. In order to meet this challenge, it is suggested that museums must ensure they do not stray too far from their main focus, but should also have the flexibility to update the museum exhibits. In addition, the ability to add immersive type attractions, beyond the footprint of the museum, can lead to the ongoing and increased relevance of the museum. Finally, the study of organisations, such as the Museum of Occupation, helps to advance our understanding of the benefit of ethnically and culturally oriented museums and attractions, both within and outside the Baltic Sea region, that aim to champion local heritage through conflict tourism.

References

Altinbasak, I. and Yalçin, E. (2010) City image and museums: the case of Istanbul, *International Journal of Culture, Tourism and Hospitality Research*, 4(3): 241–251.

Alvarez, M.D., Go, F.M. and Yüksel, A. (eds.) (2016) *Heritage Tourism Destinations: Preservation, Communication and Development*. Oxfordshire: CABI.

Amineddoleh, L. (2014) Protecting cultural heritage by strictly scrutinizing museum acquisitions, *Fordham Intellectual Property, Media and Entertainment Law Journal*, 24(3): 729–781.

Anušauskas, A. (ed.) (2006) *The Anti-Soviet Resistance in the Baltic States*. Vilnius: Genocide and Resistance Research Centre of Lithuania.

Arnold, C. (2014) Review of Bradt travel guides to Tajikistan and Uzbekistan, *Asian Affairs*, 45 (1) 151–153.

Auclair, E. and Fairclough, G. (eds.) (2016) *Theory and Practice in Heritage and Sustainability: Between Past and Present*. London: Routledge.

Babić, D. (2016) Bridging the boundaries between museum and heritage studies, *Museum International*, 68(1–2): 15–28.

Bain, C. (2009) *Estonia, Latvia and Lithuania*, 5th Edition. Lonely Planet Publications Pty Ltd.

Bourdeau, L., Gravari-Barbas, M. and Robinson, M. (eds.) (2017) *World Heritage Sites and Tourism: Global and Local Relations*. New York. NY: Routledge.

Brændholt Lundgaard, I. and Thorek Jensen, J. (eds.) (2013) *Museums: Social Learning Spaces and Knowledge Producing Processes*. Copenhagen: Kulturstyrelsen.

Burch, S. and Zander, U. (2008) Preoccupied by the past: the case of Estonian's Museum of Occupations, *Scandia*, 74(2): 53–73.

48   *Brent McKenzie*

Cavegn, D. (2016) *Museum of Occupations to be Expanded and Renamed Vabamu.* Available at: http://news.err.ee/v/Culture/db2ca4ab-9136–4e42–be80df4f23d8aa5f/museum-of-occupations-to-be-expanded-and-renamed-vabamu [accessed 21 July 2017].

Corsane, G. (ed.) (2005) *Heritage, Museums and Galleries: An Introductory Reader.* London: Routledge.

Crane, S. (1997) Memory, distortion, and history in the museum. *History and Theory,* 3(4): 44–63.

Dragicevich, P., McNaughtan, H, and Ragozin, L. (2016) *Estonia, Latvia and Lithuania,* 7th Edition. Lonely Planet Publications Pty Ltd.

Haven, C. (2011) Stanford takes Estonia's 'Museum of Occupations' under its wing. Available at: http://news.stanford.edu/news/2011/september/library-estonia-museum-092111.html [accessed 19 July 2017].

Hughes, H.L. and Allen, D. (2008) Visitor and non-visitor images of Central and Eastern Europe: a qualitative analysis, *International Journal of Tourism Management,* (10): 27–40.

Jaakson, R. (1996) Tourism in transition in post-Soviet Estonia. *Annals of Tourism Research,* 23(3): 617–634.

Kasekamp, A. (2010) *A History of the Baltic States.* London, UK: Palgrave Macmillan.

Kirshenblatt-Gimblett, B. (1998) *Destination Culture: Tourism, Museums, and Heritage.* Berkley: University of California Press.

Kolga, M. (2016) Welcome to the e-Occupation Museum, Estonian Life. Available at: www.eestielu.com/en/life/lifestyle/165–estonianlife-eestielu/opinion-arvamus/comment-kommentaar/5132–marcus-kolga-welcome-to-the-e-occupation-museum [accessed 21 July 2017].

Kovaleva, A., Epstein, M. and Paril, I. (2017) National heritage branding: a case study of the Russian Museum of Ethnography. *Journal of Heritage Tourism,* online 1–15.

Laar, M. (1992) *War in the Woods: Estonia's Struggle for Survival, 1944–1956.* Washington: Compass Press.

Lee, H.A., Law, R. and Murphy, J. (2011) Helpful reviewers in TripAdvisor, an online travel community. *Journal of Travel and Tourism Marketing,* 28(7): 675–688.

Lowe, K. (2012) *Savage Continent: Europe in the Aftermath of World War II.* London: St. Martin's Press.

Mark, J. (2008) Containing fascism: history in post-communist Baltic occupation and genocide museums, in O. Sarkisova and P. Apor (eds.) *Past for the Eyes: East European Representations of Communism in Cinema and Museums after 1989.* Budapest: Central European University Press, pp. 335–369.

McKenzie, B. (2017) How heritage can be defined and maintained through historic re-enactments. Interview with M. Piipuu, and M. Andreller on 2 January. Tallinn, Estonia.

McKenzie, B. (2018) Death as a commodity: the retailing of dark tourism, in P. Stone, R. Hartmann, T. Seaton, R. Sharpley, and L. White (eds.) *The Palgrave Handbook of Dark Tourism Studies.* London, UK: Palgrave Macmillan.

Nevid, J.S. and Sta. Maria, N.L. (1999) Multicultural issues in qualitative research. *Psychology and Marketing,* 16(4): 305–325.

Presser, B., Baker, M., Dragicevich, P., Richmond, S. and Symington, A. (2012) *Estonia, Latvia and Lithuania,* 6th Edition. Lonely Planet Publications Pty Ltd.

Raun, T. (1987) *Estonia and the Estonians.* Stanford: Hoover Institution Press.

Schouten, F. (1995) Improving visitor care in heritage attractions. *Tourism Management,* 16(4): 259–261.

Smith, L. (2006) *Uses of Heritage*. New York: Routledge.

Stites, R. (ed.) (1995) *Culture and Entertainment in Wartime Russia*. Bloomington: Indiana University Press.

Tamm, M. (2013) In search of lost time: memory politics in Estonia, 1991–2011. *Nationalities Papers*, 41(4): 651–674.

Taylor, N. (2008) *Baltic Cities (Bradt Travel Guide)* Chalfont St Peter, UK: Random House.

Taylor, N., Patrick, C., Baister, S., and Jarvis, H. (2003) *Baltic Capitals, 2nd: Tallinn, Riga, Vilnius and Kaliningrad* Chalfont St Peter, UK: Random House.

TripAdvisor website, accessed May 2018.

Vitkus, G. (2012) 'Forest Brothers' and the consequence of the metropole-periphery distinction elimination in the 'correlates of war' typology. *Journal of Baltic Studies*, 43(4): 515–527.

Williams, N. and Blond, B. (2006) *Estonia, Latvia and Lithuania*, 4th Edition. Lonely Planet Publications Pty Ltd.

Williams, P. (2007) *Memorial Museums: The Global Rush to Commemorate Atrocities*. London, UK: Berg Publishers.

Williamson, J. (1997) The Bradt Guide to Venezuela, *Reference Reviews*, 11 (3) 46–47.

5 Constructing heritage, shaping tourism

Festivals and local heritage governance at Hampi World Heritage Site, Karnataka, India

Krupa Rajangam

Introduction

This chapter seeks to examine the complex and contradictory processes of local heritage creation and governance at the UNESCO Cultural World Heritage (WH) Site of Hampi in Karnataka, India, through the lens of tourism. The site itself is a well-known cultural heritage destination on both national and international tourism circuits. However, the nature of tourism at the site is complex; individuals and groups are difficult to fit into neat categories as, for example, religious, cultural, adventure or leisure tourists. This is because, although the site is officially promoted by local government (various authorities which manage the site) as 'ruins' and 'monuments', in reality it is much more than that. It is a combination of monuments (ASI[1] 2011), archaeological park, cultural landscape (UNESCO[2] 2008), living heritage (INTACH[3] 2004) and metaphysical (Lambha 2007) or embodied space (Low 2003), all intersecting at one location[4]. Accordingly, international and domestic tourists do not come here seeking only 'ruins to sketch' or 'landscapes to photograph' but for the mix of nature and culture that the site offers. There are also many regional visitors, mainly pilgrims or religious tourists, who can be seen at various locations on-site throughout the year participating in a regular cycle of events.

However, as far as local government is concerned, such regional visitors are not tourists; the 'ideal tourist', or 'tourist' per se, is one who comes, sees the ruins, photographs them and leaves 'without causing any mess'. Such a definition excludes the majority of the site's visitors and the reality of most parts of the site – an agricultural landscape that encompasses ruins, monuments, temples, fields, settlements, villages, people and their day-to-day life. Since 1982, when the International Council on Monuments and Sites (ICOMOS) expert team visited the site to review its WH inscription, there have been unsuccessful attempts to incorporate such daily activities into the site's official designation (by changing it from group of monuments to cultural landscape: see Thakur 2007a and b). I argue here that this lack of success stems from the particular construction of Hampi's heritage, which serves certain vested interests within electoral, identity and cultural politics. In this chapter I present narratives and observations of different actors around the *Jathre* and *Utsav*. The former is the chariot festival of Virupaksha temple, one of the principal 'living' temple complexes[5] on-site.

The event could be interpreted as an expression of the site's 'livingness' or 'intangibility', but local government bodies deem it, and its visitors (mainly regional pilgrims), a hindrance to the 'proper' management of the site. The *Utsav* is a government-sponsored mega cultural festival set 'amidst the magnificent ruins of Hampi', where the 'ideal tourist' is welcomed; in fact it is an orchestrated public performance 'govern[ing] by spectacle' (Harvey 2006), the portrayal of Hampi that most suits such a performance being ruins and grand monuments (see Guha-Thaukrta 2004, Singh 2004). The various observations and ethnographic vignettes presented here derive from fieldwork carried out between January 2016 and April 2017; each field period was planned around a cycle of major events at the site. My work seeks to understand the 'heritage idea' among different individuals/groups, especially resident communities living in a particular cultural and geographical context. I build on this understanding to examine possible intersections, including convergences and/or divergences among different notions of 'heritage' and how they impinge on both place and people.

Introducing the actors: site, events, local government and tourism

The site

Hampi, named after the temple (and village) at its heart, is a 236 km² UNESCO Cultural World Heritage site in Karnataka, India, that encompasses the capital region of the Vijayanagara Empire – a significant fourteenth- to nineteenth-century South Indian kingdom, which at its peak ruled peninsular India. The capital region (also called Vijayanagara, City of Victory) is considered '[an] outstanding archaeological site of Hindu Asia' and 'the most completely preserved medieval Hindu capital in India' (Fritz et al. 1986: 22, 25). Hampi was one of the first cultural sites in India proposed for WH inscription (in 1982; finally inscribed in 1986). The widespread physical remains (ruins, archaeological mounds, fortifications, palace complexes, temples and water systems) are scattered in a cultivated landscape that includes 30 villages along with their revenue boundaries, in a series of valleys interspersed by rocky hill ranges. The 'spectacular setting' is dominated by the Tungabhadra River (UNESCO n.d.). The WH core zone (see Figure 5.1), an area of about 42 km², encompasses four villages – Kamalapura (now a town), Kaddirampura, Hampi and Anegondi – all originally agriculture-based. Observations and archival study of site chronology, however, show that Hampi village, at the heart of the site near the Virupaksha temple complex, has evolved organically into a 'tourist service village' offering basic infrastructure and visitor facilities.

The events

The temple complex dates back to at least the seventh century AD when a *kshetra* or pilgrimage centre was located here – *Pampakshetra* or *Hampé* (Settar 1990, Sundara 1997). Today, as the most significant temple of the region, it attracts large numbers of visitors through the year, but the most important event is the week-long

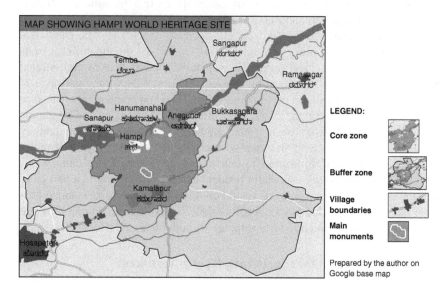

Figure 5.1 Hampi World Heritage site, showing core and buffer zones, villages and major monument complexes

Jathre (March/April), which celebrates the marriage of *Shiva* and *Parvati*. Its highlight is undoubtedly the *Rathothsava* or Chariot festival on the 7th day, which takes place in Hampi's Bazaar Street in front of the temple. Participants tend to be relatively local residents. The *Jathre*, like other religious events on-site, is largely run by pilgrim volunteers. It is presided over by descendants of the Vijayangara Dynasty in the presence of the head of the Vidyaranya *Matha,* the hereditary religious institution associated with the temple. One of the more widely believed foundation myths of the Empire is that the teacher-founder of this *Matha* helped establish the Dynasty and Empire. Historians consider the temple was probably a key factor in the founding of the Capital Region (Settar 1990, Kamath 2004).

Hampi or Vijaya *Utsav*, on the other hand, is an annual cultural festival at the site promoted by the state's Culture and Tourism Ministries since 1995. It is usually held over three days in winter (November/January). The site's ruins and monuments are presented as an ideal backdrop for cultural performances, given the history of patronage to 64 art forms by the Vijayanagara Kings. Before the involvement of a party leader and minister from the district, it was a fairly low-key sporadic celebration held in the Virupaksha temple at the culmination of *Dussehra* festivities (Ahiraj 2005). Once adopted by the state it began to be promoted as a tourism spectacle, much like South Karnataka's Mysore *Dussehra*.[6] Over the years it has metamorphosed into an event with a mega budget that brings in Bollywood singers and musicians to perform at various venues. The last *Utsav* I observed (November 2016) had nine stages with parallel performances over three days.

Local government bodies

The Archaeological Survey of India (ASI) protects 56 monument groups with their surrounding designated protected areas.[7] The State Department (DAMH – Department of Archaeology, Museums and Heritage) controls eight villages as a protected area under a 1988 notification and has at least 1200 structures in its list of protected monuments at the site. Cutting across these zones are other governmental boundaries like those of the Hindu Endowment Board (that deals with living temples), Police, Irrigation Department, Inland Waterways and of course Tourism Departments (state and central). Finally, in 2002, due to a number of reasons (see Rajangam 2017b) including the site being put on the WH in Danger List, the Hampi World Heritage Area Management Authority (HWHAMA), or *Pradikara* as it is known locally, was constituted by Karnataka State as the nodal agency to coordinate across various government departments working within the WH boundary. Simultaneously, the core and buffer zones of the site were redefined to include 30 villages along with their revenue boundaries, in keeping with UNESCO WH recommendations. The *Pradikara*'s mandate was to manage the WHS, including the coordination of site conservation, management, interpretation, and tourism activities.

Tourism and tourists

It is not an exaggeration to state that the site is Karnataka State's poster child for cultural heritage. The Stone Chariot of the Vithala complex (one of the major ruined complexes at the site) and the *Gopuram* or tower of Virupaksha temple (amidst rocky riverine landscape) feature prominently in state government publicity and tourism material, while the Golden Chariot, the state-run luxury train, makes a protracted stay at Hampi. Various government campaigns invite one to visit 'the site of the magnificent and glorious kingdom of Vijayanagara' (see Figure 5.2). Altogether, 'brand Hampi' is used to promote the state as a cultural destination par excellence. Hampi village, located at the heart of the site, gets most of the limelight and, as a result, has evolved organically into a 'tourist service village'.

Because the income of residents depends on tourism, they have become attuned to reading and interpreting visitor types and their varied needs; for example, they mentioned 'hippies' (earlier foreigner, now increasingly Indian) and their defined circuits (Goa, Hampi, Gokarna, Varkala) and noted that this group only wants a place to relax and feel at home, while 'commercial tourists' stay in the larger hotel chains in Hospet, the nearest city with a rail link, and arrive in their own or chauffeur-driven cars. Guides I spoke to felt this latter group is rather cut off from the site: 'they don't want the dust and heat; you won't see them at the *Jathre*, for example'. Resident communities consider pilgrim-visitors, who come throughout the year for rituals like *Jathre* associated with various temples, to be 'non-commercial tourists'. I spoke to a number of such groups at different religious events on-site (e.g. the all-night festival of Shivaratri) and found that

Figure 5.2 Hampi's ruins as promoted by the Tourism and Culture ministry: Karnataka state government advert in a leading English daily newspaper inviting delegates of the IT biz event to visit Hampi World Heritage site (the view foregrounds the rocky landscape around Virupaksha temple)

they also took the opportunity to visit Hampi's famous ruins or picnic on the river bank. While I was walking around the Bazaar, Guru, a pilgrim-visitor from Gangawathi questioned my presence at the *Jathre* – I was an obvious misfit in the scene. When I replied that I had come from Bangalore to observe the event, his response was *'bengaluru indha beri Jathre nodakke bandhra?'* (What! you came all the way from Bangalore just to see the *Jathre* . . . really?)' (interview April 2016).

Other visitors, who could be called 'tourists', rejected the label as derogatory. Their general advice to me was, 'don't waste your time talking to me/us. You should rather be talking to the typical tourist. You know the ones who come in groups, take pictures at various must-see spots and leave'. I never found such individuals. Everyone I interacted with was seeking something beyond the 'typical tourist experience' – undiscovered ruins to sketch, newer landscapes to photograph, and boulders to climb. The Hampi site offers ample opportunities for all these varied activities. As a visitor told me,

> at Hampi it is still possible to get lost, not really be lost, you know, more like feeling alone in a primal landscape. This is not possible at other destinations where you are always tripping over someone wanting to take photographs or pose for selfies.

A well-known artist and former 'hippie' said: 'when we came here in the late 60s it was almost like Hampi belonged to no one, each of us [different actors] could stake claims to parts of it and we did' (interview July 2016). In the view of Hampi residents *not* dependent on tourism, and some heritage authorities and experts, they (the Hampi village residents) are not really catering to tourists just some backpackers.

It became clear that the term 'tourist' does not reflect a homogenous category at Hampi. Visitors reject the label, while residents understand it in a nuanced manner and are able to adapt accordingly. So who is this 'tourist' that local government caters to and welcomes at Hampi? The complex answer became clearer as I observed the *Jathre* and *Utsav*.

Local governance and tourism at the festivals

In mid-April 2016 I arrived at Hampi village to observe *Jathre* preparations. I noticed that traders had begun to mark out their stalls along Bazaar Street and that banners were making an appearance in different villages announcing the upcoming *Jathre* with the images of Lord *Virupaksha* and *Vidyaranya Matha Swamiji* being displayed prominently. Three days before *Rathothsava* I saw carts loaded with provisions, cooking utensils and gas cylinders, pulled by gaily coloured bullocks, making their way to Bazaar Street. In the street families were roping off *mantapa* sections to mark their temporary possession of the space. The scene was one of continuous activity with a sense of anticipation in the air (see Figure 5.3).

Figure 5.3 Families taking over sections of Hampi Bazaar mantapas during the Jathre. The barricade erected in the foreground is to prevent people from entering the mantapa zone and is enforced strictly except during festivals

However, when I came back in November 2016 to observe the *Utsav*, any signs of preparation were absent until a week before inaugural day. When I remarked about this apparent lack of preparation, Raju, a former Hampi resident, quipped:

> See, they [the organisers] are the government. They do not need any time. The *Utsav* committee has the DC [District Commissioner, in this case of Bellary] on it, Culture Ministry is backing it, even a couple of days is more than enough time for them to mobilise all concerned departments.

I watched such mobilisation take place. The day before inaugural, the WH site was a hive of activity. Road barricades had materialised overnight, directing the movement of people and traffic, hoardings were being put up announcing the *Utsav* programme, information kiosks were being set up, water wagons and Portaloos were being transported to different locations on-site. All vehicular movement was diverted away from the core WH area to temporary parking bays during both events. However during *Utsav* regional public transport buses were co-opted to provide free services from various locations to the parking bays (people were left to make their own way to Bazaar Street during *Jathre*). About 500 additional police personnel were posted around the site for traffic control and safety. Straight after the three day *Utsav*, I revisited the various venues, curious to see if any clean-up was being undertaken (in contrast to the lack of concerted cleaning efforts post-*Jathre*) and found a small army of sanitation crew at work. They had been co-opted from the whole district and had been hard at work since the early hours, segregating and clearing trash, moving it away in dump trucks and trailers. By late morning when I reached the main stage, they were already half way through clearing it. Such large-scale mobilisation was not seen during *Jathre*.

In November, government adverts appeared in leading daily papers promoting the *Utsav* and inviting tourists to participate in the festivities, but there was no such promotional campaign before the *Jathre*. Walking through Hampi village in April 2016, I expected to see 'tourists' traversing the narrow streets, followed by locals proclaiming their wares or offering guide or transport services. In contrast, I saw children playing on the streets, women sitting in front of their homes exchanging gossip, while preparing for the day, and men idling on street corners. The near complete absence of the figure of the 'tourist' made the scene feel more 'real'. One obvious reason was that it was summer and 'off-season' so there was no need for residents to put on 'tourism personas' (Hochschild 1983, Bunten 2008). Any visitors I observed over the next few days were accidental visitors, in that they were unaware of the *Jathre* before coming to the site. As Raju's father told me:

> No tourists come for the *Jathre*, only pilgrims. Those days [his childhood] they would come in bullock carts from Hospet. There was no road, only rocks and boulders and people had to travel over them. Gradually private vans started to ply during festival times. *Jathre* time especially lakhs of people would come . . . you couldn't see the ground, only people's heads wherever you looked. They would stay in the mantapas of Hampi Bazaar for a week to 15 days. Tourists started coming very late. Only after 1986 when the site was declared a WH site. Even then numbers were less. Around 1992–93 with roads and government buses numbers gradually increased.
>
> (Interview March 2016)

On the other hand, in November, during *Utsav*, I did see some visitors who could be considered 'tourists' but generally near the main stages at Vithala or Bazaar Street. They were typically armed with VIP passes that gave them access to cushioned seats in cordoned off areas and permitted their cars to be parked near the stage, unlike 'general' audience, who had to walk about 1 km from the nearest public transport bay to the main stage. Notably, there was no public transport to the other main stage at Vithala, so those without private vehicles had to walk at least 2 km to this stage or take rickshaws (drivers charged a premium during such events). This made it very clear who was welcome at particular locations. However, much like the *Jathre*, the majority of the audience comprised residents of the region.

I also observed that, besides regional visitors, the occasional tourist and a few police personnel, local government was largely absent from the *Jathre*. However, during *Utsav*, government presence was quite marked, whether the Chief Minister flying in by helicopter or cars with flashing beacons rushing around the site. The rhetoric from various political leaders and bureaucrats over the three days made it clear that the event was not really a tourism spectacle but an orchestrated public performance put on by government to serve its interests. As a resident remarked, 'if the *Utsav* is in November we know it's a Congress *tamasha* (spectacle), if it's in January we know it's a BJP one' (both national political parties). The various speeches were easily summarised as, 'there can be no better location for the *Utsav* than the land of the great rulers of Vijayanagara. The magnificent ruins around us are an apt background for a celebration of our past glory. Let us all work together to bring this greatness back'. The Hampi backdrop thus served the interests of 'governing by spectacle' (Harvey 2006).

Besides electoral politics, the *Utsav* also served the interests of identity politics. The events tended to merge with celebrations of Karnataka State founding day (*Rajyostava*) and there were calls to bring back North Karnataka's greatness, just like during the glory days of Vijayanagara. Interestingly such narratives were not limited to regional politics (North Karnataka pitted against South), but ranged from local (particular community laying claim to part of the site as their heritage), sub-national (as a symbol of the unified linguistic state of Karnataka) to national (the last great Hindu Empire of India's historical period). Cultural sites are never 'politically neutral' (Massey 1996, 2005, Harvey 2014) and they can be ascribed multiple shifting meanings, which can affect the materiality of the site and consequently its management (Rajangam 2017a). Hence not just archaeology (Meskell 2002, Guha-Thakurta 2004) but also heritage practitioners need to be aware of the 'politics' around heritage sites.

Discussion: in the name of the tourist

The *Pradikara* has planned and continues to plan certain development projects at Hampi in the name of improving tourism facilities in general and particularly for events like the *Utsav*; for example, running battery operated vehicles (BoVs) at Vithala complex and installing chemical toilets. Normal vehicular movement is apparently forbidden because it could disturb underground archaeological remains and adversely affect the *mantapas*. However, all the resident communities (and some heritage experts) I interviewed cited these two projects as examples of Pradikara wanting to make money by selectively interpreting the integrated management plan. One respondent said:

the Pradikara picked whatever they could make some money out of. 15–20 chemical toilets costing lakhs each, set up at odd locations [I observed that they were set up in proximity to *Utsav* stages – most of these locations were otherwise not visited], 20–30 BoVs at 5–6 lakhs each. The toilets didn't remain usable for very long, most of the BoVs are rusting and piled up in an ugly shed near Vithala complex, only 4–5 vehicles run now. How come vehicular vibrations don't affect Krishna temple [another major attraction at the site]? Big buses go right through it! In fact once or twice buses have got stuck in the gateway and they have had to move beams to get them out. And the BoVs – 20Rs per ticket, who pockets the money? And they have 'local' women drivers so it looks good in front of tourists but you talk to the girls – they aren't happy. Recently when they put out a call for more women drivers no one responded'.

(Interview February 2016)

The examples above, of day-to-day management programmes, arbitrary or otherwise, could be labelled pro-tourism, but local government defended one of its larger interventions on-site – the demolition of homes, shops and lodges in Hampi Bazaar's mantapas and the removal of 328 families – by attributing it to undesirable tourism. Guru, the pilgrim-visitor mentioned earlier, said to me at the close of our conversation:

> This is all nothing, you should have come to Hampi *Jathre* earlier, it was really very nice then, there was life in the place. You would feel like staying back for a few days, now it has become lifeless, 'thiruga haal Hampi *maadbittidaarey*' (they have turned Hampi back into a place of ruins) . . . this was some years ago, they came with a JCB and all and demolished peoples' houses and asked everyone in Bazaar Street to leave, there's some rule that no one can stay within a few kilometres of the old structures, I'm not sure exactly . . . they [District Commissioner, local government] said bad things happened here, murders took place, foreigners brought weed and so on . . . I don't know how true all this is but this is what I heard . . .

The government's main defence is that, while they might have considered letting the 'illegal' structures remain had they just been houses, these structures were 'commercial'. Residents were running shops, restaurants and lodges in them, which were not only harming monuments (the *mantapas*) but also the sacredness of the 'living' site. They said, for example, that such establishments were often a cover for malicious activities – tourists would drink, use drugs, our youth was getting corrupted by the loose morals of the tourists, pilgrims were getting disturbed and the site's sacredness was getting affected.

The immediate reaction of heritage practitioners (for example, Fritz and Michell 2012) to the 2011 demolition was to attribute it to a limited understanding of the site's heritage-ness by the authorities. Residents and scholars, consider the ruins just one part of the site:

> The Hampi landscape has existed long before and after the Vijayanagara Empire, why focus only on that? These monuments are actually causing the destruction of 'living heritage'. Authorities are more concerned with conserving material remains instead of documenting local traditions, customs, cultures, lifestyles and communities . . . . which are rapidly vanishing.
>
> (Interview January 2016, Professor Tribal Studies)

> Local people should not be alienated from local heritage. That is something they have preserved and given to us. Between 1536 and now it is they who protected Hampi and now you want to uproot them and drive them away? Tomorrow you will say car festival [*Jathre*'s *Rathotsava*] is a nuisance and take it away. Where does it end? The Bazaar Street was unplanned which was not right but today it has become a desert. Pilgrimage doesn't mean only visiting the main shrine [Virupaksha], Bazaar is part of 'living' heritage.
>
> (Interview January 2017, Hampi scholar)

However, over time it has become apparent that the demolitions were the result of a number of vested interests intersecting at that point in time (Sattva Trust 2011). Campbell (2015a, 2015b) notes that they appeared to stem from a combination of limited understanding of the site, lack of participatory planning and UNESCO's concerns that, if left unchecked, the commercialisation of Hampi village might overpower the site. Bloch (2017) attributes the principal reason to a brand of religious (Hindu) nationalism that sees tourists as 'barbarians' spoiling the site's sanctity. Building on Herzfeld (2006), she considers the demolitions 'spatial cleansing' of the site. However, religious motives, monument protection and maintaining Outstanding Universal Value (as defined by UNESCO) do not appear to be the only reasons. According to residents there were other political-economic reasons as well: 'the local MLA (Member of Legislative Assembly) was heading Hospet Hotels Association at that time. Some of us saw them conducting hush-hush meetings before the demolitions, some hotels paid the JCB drivers – we spoke to them'. They further pointed out that in the years following demolition the number of hotels in Hospet had increased exponentially.

True or not, the rumours reflect people's anxieties as they struggle to make sense of governmental processes that appear contradictory. In the case of *Utsav*, for example, local government welcomes tourists, while at *Jathre* they consider them a hindrance. In day-to-day management, tourism becomes a source of bribes, but moral corruption is said to be the reason for the demolitions. Such actions look less contradictory if one considers that, as a far as local government is concerned, the term 'tourists' excludes 'hippies' and 'pilgrims', or indeed any group that causes a mess in the picturesque landscape. During an interview a local heritage official exclaimed: 'see, these people, they are all uneducated, they don't know anything. They will sleep and eat anywhere, even on top of monuments, leave their trash behind and we have to mount a cleaning operation afterwards. Have you seen the state of the site after *Jathre*?' (Interview February 2017).

The government's enforcement of its imagination of both the site and tourism has begun to interfere with peoples' daily lives. Hampi residents told me the following:

> Vijayanagara ruins survived because of us . . . we were looking after ruins in the middle of our fields . . . they moved us out of our fields and homes even. If we weren't living in Hampi Bazaar the mantapas would have disappeared long ago just like Vithala or Krishna Bazaar . . . heritage authorities came into existence only recently, maybe late 70s. Where was ASI before that? Or Pradikara? And today they call us illegal in the name of monument protection. If we didn't continue to worship at Virupaksha or conduct the *Jathre* year on year would the Bazaar have survived?

At the close of the *Jathre* I was sitting at a tea stall near Bazaar Street, a favoured observation post throughout the course of my field work. The owner asked me if I had enjoyed the *Jathre*. I said that I had and remarked that I had found it quite crowded. The response was, 'maybe to you but I have been here many years and the numbers are gradually reducing year on year'. Indeed, when I came back in April 2017, the number of stalls and participants seemed fewer than in 2016. One said: 'this year many people decided not to come as they were not sure if the *Jathre* would be permitted. They didn't want to be caught in any tangle with authorities'. It was rumoured that there might not be a *Jathre* the following year (2018) because ASI was planning to excavate Bazaar Street and the area would be cordoned off. Whether true or not, such rumours clearly reinforce the continued, and justifiable, sense of anxiety among residents of Hampi village about their future. In July 2017, the remaining residents of Hampi village were issued notices to stop all 'illegal' activities at the site, which term included all commercial activities, whether restaurants, lodges or selling any kinds of goods and services. Although the notices were subsequently postponed, their future remains in question.

Conclusion

The idea that cultural tourism will encourage (local) development can be partly attributed to UNESCO's once-favoured policy of advocating tourism at WH sites. That this vision is unfounded is well documented; Brockington et al.'s (2008) work on natural sites, for example, shows that, far from economically empowering local communities, tourism (and attempts to promote it) has largely alienated them, while Winter's work at Angkor Wat (2007) argues that tourism and heritage, combined to create a particular aesthetic imagination of the site for 'visual pleasure', does not take local people or culture into account. However, at Hampi the tourism industry was not the result of plans or policies; rather, it grew organically, possibly in an uncontrolled manner. Initially tourists and some residents did benefit (maybe unequally), until such time that local government, a rather late entrant to the scene, stepped in and decided that such tourism was unwelcome.

Although the pressure is not unidirectional, resident communities continue to lose out today. When I questioned a resident on why local authorities did not object to people setting up stalls or camping in the *mantapas* during various events (given that they were the ones who had evicted people from the *mantapas*), he retorted, 'of course, authorities don't mess with people during such festivals, they don't wag their tails when big numbers are involved. They only oppress us as individuals . . .' Local government has the power to undertake certain courses of action that interfere and sometimes oppress people in their daily lives. At Hampi WHS the *Jathre*, the definitive core of the site's 'livingness', has now reached a point where people are beginning to question its continued existence and the village at the heart of the WH site is being squeezed out of existence.

Acknowledgements

National Institute of Advanced Studies and my SAC committee, comprising my guide Sharada Srinivasan and members Carol Upadhya, Muthatha Ramanathan and Gill Chitty, for their constant support and guidance. INTACH for their grant which made the 15 months assigned to fieldwork a reality. Lynn Meskell for an extremely fruitful brainstorming session on my dissertation and emerging themes.

Notes

1 Archaeological Survey of India.
2 United Nations Educational, Scientific and Cultural Organization.
3 Indian National Trust for Art and Cultural Heritage.
4 Based on work in critical heritage studies and geography, I accept an all-encompassing 'heritage idea', whereby it is not possible to classify heritage as tangible, intangible, living, monumental. However, I use such distinctions in this chapter based on how various actors define the terms.
5 'Living' temple: a structure where divine worship continues. Some government bodies equate living temples with living heritage and exclude communities living in and around such sites from the latter definition. Others disagree and include communities but only if they are able to claim ancestral ties to the place.
6 Mysore *Dussehra*: a Royal procession in Mysore city at the culmination of the nine day annual *Dussehra* festivities. It was initiated by the Wodeyar dynasty but traces its origins to the *Maha Navami* procession initiated by Vijayanagara Kings at Hampi.
7 Each monument boundary is called a protected area and 100 m from this line is defined as a prohibited zone. A further 200 m from the second line is defined as a regulated zone. DAMH follows a similar nomenclature but in practice is not as strict about the implementation as ASI.

References

Ahiraj, M. (2005) As Dussehra ends focus shifts to Hampi Utsav, *The Hindu, Bellary* [Online], 14 October. Available at: www.thehindu.com/2005/10/14/stories/2005101404960400. htm [accessed 23 November 2016].
ASI (2011) AMASR Act. Available at: http://asi.nic.in/pdf_data/6.pdf [accessed 12 December 2014].
Bloch, N. (2017) Barbarians in India. Tourism as moral contamination. *Annals of Tourism Research*, 62: 64–77.
Brockington, D., Duffy, R. and Igoe, J. (2008) *Nature Unbound: Conservation, Capitalism and the Future of Protected Areas*. London: Earthscan.
Bunten, A. C. (2008) Sharing culture or selling out? Developing the commodified persona in the heritage industry. *American Ethnologist*, 35(3): 380–395.
Campbell, M. (2015a) Hampi Bazaar Demolition I. *Economic & Political Weekly*, L (25) June 25, 2015.
Campbell, M. (2015b) Hampi Bazaar Demolition II. *Economic & Political Weekly*, L (29) July 18, 2015.
Fritz, J.M. and Michell, G. (2012) Living heritage at risk. *Archaeology*, 65(6): 55–62.
Fritz, J.M., Michell, G. and Rao, M.S.N. (1986) Vijayanagara: the city of victory. *Archaeology*, 39(2): 22–29.
Guha-Thakurta, T. (2004) *Monuments, Objects, Histories: Institutions of Art in Colonial and Postcolonial India*. Delhi: Permanent Black.
Harvey, D. (2006) The political economy of public space, in S. Low and N. Smith (eds.) *The Politics of Public Space*. London: Routledge, pp. 17–34.
Harvey, D.C. (2014) Heritage and scale: settings, boundaries and relations. *International Journal of Heritage Studies*. http://dx.doi.org/10.1080/13527258.2014.955812.

Herzfeld, M. (2006) Spatial cleansing: monumental vacuity and the idea of the West. *Journal of Material Culture*, 11(1/2): 127–149.

Hochschild, A. R. (1983) *The Managed Heart: Commercialization of Human Feeling*. Berkeley: University of California Press.

ICOMOS (1982) ICOMOS Evaluation and Recommendation: Group of Monuments at Hampi.

INTACH (2004) INTACH India Charter. Available at: www.intach.org/about-charter.php [accessed 12 June 2015].

Kamath, S. (2004) *A Concise History of the Vijayanagara Empire*. Bangalore: Archana Prakashana.

Lambha, A.N. (2007) The Cosmic site of Vijayanagara, *Seminar*, 572. Available at: www. india-seminar.com/2007/572.htm [accessed 4 April 2016].

Low, S.M. (2003) Embodied space(s): anthropological theories of body, space, and culture. *Space & Culture*, 6(1): 6–18.

Massey, D. (1996) A global sense of place, in S. Daniels and R. Lee (eds.) *Exploring Human Geography: A Reader*. London: Arnold, pp. 237–245.

Massey, D. (2005) *For Space*. London: Sage.

Meskell, L. (2002) The intersections of identity and politics in archaeology. *Annual Review of Anthropology*, 31: 279–301.

Rajangam, K. (2017a) Shifting meanings, mutable materiality: material culture in nation building narratives at Hampi World Heritage Site. Paper presented at NIAS National Conference, January.

Rajangam, K. (2017b) Looking forward, looking back: narratives of hope and glory from the bridge at Hampi World Heritage Site, India. Paper presented at IIICH International Conference, Ironbridge, UK, July.

Sattva Trust (2011) Hampi Living Heritage, Blog. Available at: https://hampiheritage. wordpress.com [accessed 27 May 2017].

Settar, S. (1990) *Hampi: A Medieval Metropolis*. Bangalore: Kala Yatra.

Singh, U. (2004) *The Discovery of Ancient India: Early Archaeologists and the Beginnings of Archaeology*. New Delhi: Permanent Black.

Sundara, A. (1997) *Hampi: Ancient Kishkindha – Vanara's Capital*. Anegondi, Hospet: Sri Vidya Vijayanagara Hampi Heritage Trust.

Thakur, N. (2007a) Hampi World Heritage site: monuments, site or cultural landscape? *Journal of Landscape Architecture*, 16: 31–37.

Thakur, N. (2007b) Integrated Management Plan (IMP) for Hampi World Heritage Site, Final Plan – Draft, July 2007. New Delhi: Department of Architectural Conservation, School of Planning and Architecture.

UNESCO (n.d.) Group of monuments Hampi. Available at: http://whc.unesco.org/en/ list/241 [accessed 12 November 2011].

UNESCO (2008) Operational Guidelines for the implementation of the World Heritage Convention. Available at: http://whc.unesco.org/en/guidelines/ [accessed 18 November 2008].

Winter, T. (2007) *Post-Conflict Heritage, Postcolonial Tourism: Tourism, Politics and Development at Angkor*. London and NY: Routledge.

6 Creating heritage for cruise tourists

Jacqueline Tivers

Introduction

Academic research on cruise tourism has been limited in the past and patchy in coverage; for example, the topic is not listed as one of the 'key concepts in tourist studies' by Smith et al. (2010). It is now growing in volume (Morgan and Power 2011, Papathanassis and Beckman 2011, De Cantis et al. 2016), but this growth by no means parallels the explosive increase in the cruise-tourism sector itself. According to Cruise Lines International Association (CLIA) statistics, published in December 2016, more than 25 million passengers worldwide were expected to sail on cruise ships in 2017, compared to 15 million in 2006 (and 1.4 million in 1980, when the organisation published its first annual report). There is no sign of a decline in the near future; indeed it is 'the fastest growing segment in the travel industry . . . (increasing) at almost twice the rate of land based tourism' (Brida and Zapata 2010: 206). It is planned that 97 new ships will be built in the period 2016–2026. Approximately half of all cruise tourists originate from North America, with one-fifth coming from Europe and smaller, but increasing, percentages from China and Australia.

The most significant contributions to the cruise-tourism research field are the edited volumes by Dowling (2006) and Dowling and Weeden (2017). Interest by researchers, perhaps not surprisingly, has been focused primarily on economic and management issues (Hall and Page 2006), one of the most important of which is the provision of appropriate and sufficient resources within port destinations to support the increasing number of tourists who arrive on a daily or weekly basis. Nevertheless, there have been only brief mentions by researchers (e.g. Timothy and Boyd 2008) about *heritage* in relation to the huge, growing, and specific demands of the cruise industry, despite an increased emphasis on heritage tourism *in general* as a way 'to expand the number of attractions and destinations to accommodate . . . huge numbers of tourists' (Richter 1999:110). There has also been an almost complete lack of research on cruise passengers' space/time behaviour on shore (De Cantis et al. 2016; but see Jaakson 2004, Teye and Paris 2011).

The research that forms the basis of this chapter concerns the creation of heritage sites and heritage tourism experiences by tourism authorities in cruise ship destinations and the way in which this 'creation' is reflected in the publicity materials of shipping lines and the on-shore activities of cruise passengers.

The methodology of the study was autoethnographic (Moss 2001), employing the techniques of participant observation, informal interviews with passengers and senior staff and the keeping of my own personal diaries. In addition, printed literature relating to the destinations visited was scrutinised; this included travel magazines, holiday information books and 'port guides' to each destination (distributed on the ships to all passengers) as well as tourism brochures handed out on shore. The research investigated nine different cruises between 2014 and 2017, varying in length from 11 to 44 days (251 days in total), altogether visiting 71 port destinations throughout the world, several for two consecutive days or on more than one occasion. The majority of examples cited here, however, come from the Caribbean region, the most important world region for both current cruises and expected growth.

Cruise passengers' experience of place

Weaver (2005: 346) asserts that the ships themselves, rather than their ports of call, are promoted as the 'main holiday destinations for tourists' (see also Sheller 2004, Hall 2005, Momsen 2005, Dowling 2006, 2017, Duval, 2007). According to Wood (2006), cruise tourism is an example of 'globalisation at sea', involving a 'deterritorialisation' of the world and of capital. He proposes (Wood 2004: 134) that 'people go on a "cruise" more than they go to a place', and hence that cruise ships are in competition with 'real places'; indeed, that 'the mass-market cruise ship experience is deliberately detached from the region in which it cruises'; for example, that 'food and drink on board do not reflect the cruise region' (ibid.: 140). This detachment from the world's geography has certainly not been the case in my experience; rather, the ships I have travelled on have *emphasised* their specific geographical locations through, for example, relevant lectures, the prominent display of navigation charts, the inclusion of local foods on the menus and the welcoming of local people on board to entertain guests with indigenous cultural offerings of music and dance. These elements have all been clearly related to (perceived) demand by passengers for access to exotic cultures and traditions.

The extent to which this demand carries over into pressure on land-based resources is, however, open to question. Many researchers (e.g. Jaakson 2004, Momsen, 2005) have indicated that the majority of cruise passengers do not leave their ship at all during port stays, but instead stay on board to enjoy activities there. Writing about Caribbean cruise tourism, Momsen (2005: 218) asserts that 'the ship provides the view, and the islands of the Caribbean are the background, the focal points of the seascape'. Wilkinson (2006) suggests that only 10–15 per cent of Caribbean cruise tourists actually go ashore, due to misperceptions about safety and poverty, to some extent generated by cruise companies whose best interest is served by keeping tourist 'spend' on board. Douglas and Douglas (2004) assert that, on Pacific Island cruises, most passengers choose not to go ashore if there is a need to use a tender vessel. Brida and Zapata (2010: 215), while not claiming quite such high figures, state that 'it is well known that a substantial minority of cruise ship passengers do not even disembark in the different port destinations that are visited'. However, studying the behaviour of passengers in the port of Palermo in the Mediterranean, De Cantis et al. (2016) found that 80 per cent left their ships to go on visits, while Teye and Paris (2011: 26) recorded even higher percentages in their study of Caribbean cruise ports, noting that 'the opportunity to explore multiple destinations, cultures, and to sample destinations are strong motivating factors for those who go on cruises'.

My own experience of cruises, worldwide, has accorded with this latter view. As an example, the ship on which I travelled to the Caribbean in 2016 carried about 3,000 passengers. According to the ship's Excursions Officer, in each destination visited, about 1,000 guests took prearranged tours and a further 1,000 left the ship and 'did their own thing', which included taxi tours, locally organised minibus trips, public transport journeys and walking tours (mainly in parallel with the tours and activities organised by the Excursions Office), as well as shopping and strolling in the immediate vicinity of the ship. My informant said that nearly 1,000 passengers (fewer than one-third of the total) stayed on board during port days, primarily due to advanced age and/or disability and the subsequent difficulties involved in leaving the ship and getting around on shore. Personally, every passenger I interviewed, or met casually, had left the ship at at least one destination during the cruise and this has been true on all the cruises I have taken. On a voyage to New Zealand in 2017 (with 562 passengers on board), the Destinations Concierge confirmed that virtually everyone (including two women aged over 90) left the ship at ports, with about one-third going on excursions organised jointly by the shipping company and land-based tour operators; the Tours Manager said that the percentage taking organised tours varied between 15 and 98 per cent, 'depending on the place'. One woman, who was forced by illness to remain on the ship when it docked at Callao, Peru, commented afterwards that the experience was 'like the *Marie Celeste*, with everyone off the ship'. It was also clear that Pacific Island stops, requiring the use of tender vessels, were no less popular, even among the elderly and mobility impaired, thanks to the active assistance of crew. The same situation, of almost everyone leaving the ship at ports was also apparent on the ship on which I travelled from Australia to the UK, later in 2017.

It is useful to consider whether the age structure of the body of cruise tourists is a predictor of the sort of destination-place experience that passengers are seeking (Hall and Page 2006). On one of my cruises, in 2015, the average age of passengers (calculated by a senior officer) was 72 years and there were many passengers in their 80s and 90s. Other cruises, including a 2016 Caribbean cruise and the 2017 cruise to New Zealand, had a larger number of middle-aged people but, despite Dowling and Weeden's (2017: xviii) assertion that 'a much younger generation has discovered cruising', the vast majority of passengers on *all* my cruises have been retired people. During interview, the Excursions Officer for the 2016 cruise commented that many people on cruises, and especially older people, were now looking for more interesting things to do when they arrived at destinations than simply going to the beach; they wanted to visit places, to understand local cultures, and to learn about the history of places.

Studying the printed information available to guests on the different cruises, I noted that the main emphasis, both in magazines distributed to cabins before the cruises started and in individual 'port guides' was placed on 'exploring' and that the chief focus of attention was on places of interest, the people and their traditional costume, local food and drink, simple language expressions, flora and fauna, and *history* (with, outside Europe, an emphasis on *colonial* history – British, French, Spanish or Portuguese – and remaining colonial buildings). There was, wherever relevant, reference to beaches and the part they played in defining the character of islands and coastal regions, and certainly beach stops and transfers were always offered in the excursions programmes, but the main emphasis was on 'sightseeing'. The Excursions Officer for the 2016 Caribbean cruise and the Hotel Manager for the 2017 cruise to New Zealand both pointed out that many passengers take several cruises each year – three, four, or even more. Many are revisiting the same places, often again and again, so shipping line officials and their contacts on shore constantly need to create new trips and experiences to attract their customers. This accords with the comments of Weeden et al. (2011: 26) on the 'demanding expectations of experienced cruisers' and goes rather against the assumptions of McCalla and Charlier (2006), among others, that long-haul cruise passengers are relatively indifferent to the specific destinations visited, by comparison with other aspects of their cruise.

Cruise destination developments

Many cruises operate in less developed parts of the world, stopping at ports that often have poor infrastructure and a lack of tourist resources, located on small islands with low population densities, frequently lying at great distances from each other and from mainland areas (e.g. Pearce 1999). In these destinations cruise passengers may comprise over 50 per cent of all visitors (Brida and Zapata 2010). Papathanassis and Beckman (2011: 156) note that 'the increasing size of ships, not mentioning the volume of concurrent visitors ('overcrowding'), are posing significant demands on the infrastructure of ports and surrounding resorts. Such demands are associated with significant economic, social and environmental implications' (see also, Weaver, 2007, Klein 2011, Boniface et al. 2012, Kerswill and Mair 2015). In order to boost their economies, the countries concerned seek to attract cruise operators by building huge port extensions (e.g. Philipsburg, the capital of St Maarten in the eastern Caribbean, constructed a terminal for eight large cruise ships). As a by-product of dredging the deep channels necessary for ships to enter port, large areas of reclaimed land have been created (for example, at Road Town, Tortola); these are subsequently occupied by 'ocean villages' (see below) in order to generate income for the countries concerned, in part to offset the costs of constructing the port facilities to attract the shipping lines in the first place (see also, Duval 2007).

Cruise passengers are normally restricted to a few hours only at destinations and thus tourist resources must be concentrated relatively close to port areas (Hall 2005). The main focus for many 'tropical island' tourists (in the Caribbean, or the

Pacific or Indian Oceans) is the many beaches of golden sand and waving palm trees that fringe the islands, especially those close to docking points so that local taxis/buses/walking can be used to access them. However, while bringing some economic benefits, the increasing scale of cruise tourism is in many cases stretching the resources of the ports and proximate beaches to breaking point. As noted above, port authorities have responded by creating shopping and eating/drinking opportunities within designated, restricted access areas ('ocean villages') adjacent to shipping berths (for example, Port Zante in St. Kitts), as well as in relevant town centres. Such developments mainly comprise duty-free shops, selling high-end jewellery, perfume, and fashion clothing, together with many smaller stores and stalls retailing beachwear and the inevitable T-shirts, made in China or India but stamped with the logo of whichever country the development is located in. Thus, passengers glimpse only a stereotyped impression of a place and its culture (Boniface et al. 2012). The port authorities are desperate to create uniqueness (see also, Scheyvens 2002, Teye and Paris 2011) but finish up with largely similar products to offer tourists. However, 'there is strong evidence that cruise ship passengers . . . are not particularly interested in authenticity in handicrafts' (Douglas and Douglas 2004: 258) and stalls selling such goods do, at least, provide one way for local people to benefit from the arrival of cruise ships. Richter (1999: 119) notes that 'some groups are adept at seizing the tourism initiative by creating an affordable, tourist-friendly heritage' in the form of local pottery or jewellery, newly developed but described as 'traditional'.

Port-based shopping opportunities may be generally desirable, but cruise destination authorities are aware that many cruise visitors are seeking indicators of local identity, including historic buildings and places, cultural performances, indigenous industries, and exotic natural environments. There is some attempt to provide a 'local feel' through 'cultural acts, displays and exhibitions' within port complexes (St Kitts port leaflet), but also a committed drive to establish new places of interest to tourists away from the immediate port vicinities. The terms 'history' and 'heritage' are widely employed to cover this broad variety of offerings; as Hannam and Knox (2010: 141) say, 'everything has to have heritage stories attached to it – if it is to be considered worthy of the tourist gaze'. In an extreme example of this phenomenon, Antigua constructed a (so-called) 'Heritage Pier' adjacent to its shipping berths, while Tortola labelled its newly built port extension 'Heritage Quay'; in both cases buildings were constructed in a generalised 'heritage' style, reminiscent of many dockside developments in the UK.

According to a local information leaflet, Pusser's Landing on Tortola, the chief sailing centre of that island, displayed 'a vibrant waterside area full of character and history'; on the contrary, I noted in my diary that it was 'a modern sailing marina development, built to look like 'heritage' buildings – very expensive and non-Caribbean in style'. Another example was seen on the island of St Maarten where, according to the publicity leaflet, the port development 'offers cruise passengers a new venue to visit and sample the products and services available in eight ginger-bread houses that reflect the national heritage', but where, at the same time, developers had destroyed real 'history' in order to create 'heritage';

Figure 6.1 Heritage Pier, Antigua

in fact, an historic cannon had been dropped into the sea, just off shore, together with a helicopter and a mini-submarine, for snorkellers to look at under water! An equally bizarre 'heritage-creation' trend noted was the presence of private islands, purchased by shipping companies in order to bypass crowded and expensive ports, and the marketing of 'these entirely simulated environments as providing an "authentic" Caribbean experience no longer possible in the real place' (Wood 2004: 140). Of course, some islands and coastal areas do have more 'genuine' features to offer and cruise ships also offer well-promoted visits to many World Heritage Sites, both Cultural and Natural, in different parts of the world.

Landscapes, more broadly, were considered as 'heritage' in on board talks and publications. Sheller (2004: 17) says that 'the Caribbean is constantly reassembled as a primeval, untouched site of luxuriant profusion' and this is also true of other 'tropical' areas of the world. Cruise port guides and other information books and leaflets commonly used terms such as 'picturesque', 'scenic', 'paradise', 'exotic' and 'idyllic' to promote coach and minibus 'panoramic' tours, and off-road 'jeep adventures', as well as inviting participation in more active tourist attractions like guided hikes, aerial tramways and zip lining through rain forest, river tubing, biking, kayaking and so on – activity tourism, but with a 'natural heritage' basis. The natural environment is clearly very important as a tourist draw; in my diary entry for Tortola, for example, I noted that 'it was a small island with a very small population, so there really wasn't a lot to see apart from the forested mountains'. Similarly, the coral reefs and clear waters that lie off shore of many islands, both in the Caribbean and in the Pacific and Indian Oceans, were treated as 'island heritage' and 'a natural wonder' (port guide to Bora Bora, French Polynesia) in brochures advertising whale, dolphin, sea lion and turtle spotting trips and sailing, swimming and snorkelling activities.

So far as significant buildings are concerned, visitors were encouraged (through cruise ship excursions as well as published literature) to view churches, monuments, fortresses and plantation houses. The forts, like Brimstone Hill Fortress in St Kitts and Fort George in Grenada (eastern Caribbean), remind tourists of the region's colonial history, as do the preserved plantation houses, such as Sunbury Plantation House in Barbados (an island described in on-board literature as having an 'inescapable colonial "feel"' with its 'superior collection of antiques') and St Nicholas Abbey, where not only could the original house and furnishings be seen but also the sugar cane fields and (working) refinery. On other islands, visits were recommended to Stony Hill Great House in St Lucia, and to Fairview House in St Kitts, the latter described as a 'restored 300–year old colonial style property' with 'authentically decorated rooms'. Elsewhere, plantation houses have been destroyed leaving a few ruins and associated signage, as at Romney Manor in St Kitts where a new building housed Batik clothes production and sales, acting as one of the chief attractions for day trip tourists on this island; according to the port guide, 'you can watch local crafts women produce colourful batiks, based on scenes of Caribbean life, West Indian motifs and Carib Petroglyphs'. In Martinique, the grounds of a former plantation house have been reinvented as an ecotourism and cultural heritage centre, offering a museum of local history and guided walks in the rain forest.

If the island scenery was described as 'picturesque' and 'idyllic' in cruise information, and the prominent public buildings labelled 'historic' and 'colonial', domestic buildings tended to be portrayed as 'quaint' and 'rustic'; in Antigua, for example, we noted a 'rustic beach shack' (newly built!) serving lunch and visited an *historic* Georgian shipyard 'refurbished as a pretty colonial style village' (access controlled by entrance guards), while in Barbados 'brightly painted rum shops and chattel houses' were pointed out on a coach tour. In 'historic' Bridgetown, a walking tour claimed to bring 'the past to life. You'll get a feel for local life and have the opportunity to view some of the buildings that have played a part in Bridgetown's heritage'. A tour of Martinique emphasised the town history of St Pierre, a settlement destroyed by a volcano in 1902, and also 'the point where Columbus landed in 1502'. At the rum distillery in St Lucia, the information book noted that 'a village street, spice market and 'carnival' had been recreated to give an insight into the lifestyle and spirit of St Lucians'. In St Kitts, a journey on the old railway was recommended in order to experience 'a colourful narrative history of the island', while a further 'heritage' attraction, included in several day trip itineraries, was the so-called 'Amazing Grace Experience', set in a house once owned by the former slave trader, John Newton, who penned the famous hymn there in 1779. According to port guides, a 'Caribbean style buffet lunch' with 'delicious local dishes' was a prominent part of many tours of the islands; these would be accompanied by steel pan music, 'dancers in flamboyant carnival costume' and considerable and unlimited quantities of 'traditional' rum punch. 'French Caribbean' cookery demonstrations were on offer in St Martin, while a 'local life' trip to an estate farm and a pineapple plantation was available in Antigua.

Beyond the Caribbean, I have encountered similar 'heritage'-style developments. In Lima, Peru, a crowded city with a colonial heart and 2,000–year-old pyramids (which has World Heritage Site recognition), we were instead taken to visit a (1920s) private house containing 'a bizarre collection of nativity scenes. I asked the guide who was taken to this site and she said, only cruise ship tourists!' (personal diary). In American Samoa (South Pacific Ocean), on a cruise in 2014, we visited a village where we watched a 'cultural performance' and ate local food, alongside several other coachloads of cruise tourists, and a similar excursion was offered in Rarotonga (in 2017), where passengers were invited by the 'Destinations' brochure to 'explore the culture, traditions, people and history of the Cook Islands' and 'to personally relive Polynesian yesterdays'. In Mauritius (Indian Ocean) one popular cruise tour took us to three remaining plantation houses connected to tea production.

Local industries are also exploited as 'heritage', a notable example of this being in Grenada (eastern Caribbean), the nation promoted as the 'spice island', the home of nutmeg. The 'heritage' of spice was represented by a nutmeg processing station at Gouyave (visited in 2016, along with several hundred other people from the ship) and a newly created, but temporarily closed, attraction called 'The Spice Basket', advertised as 'the home of our culture' and a museum of the spice industry. Both of these were located several miles from the port, but offered much needed alternative capacity to the limited resources in the capital city and port area and supplemented the beach provision that absorbed the majority of day visitors to the island; both places were well represented on trips organised by shipping lines. In my diary I noted that the nutmeg processing site was in fact 'just a working factory. It was Sunday, of course, so everyone had come in just for us – our guide had walked 4 miles to get there'. Rum distilleries were also promoted as part of the history of the islands; at Mount Gay in Barbados, for example, the visitor was invited to taste and see the production of 'the rum that invented rum', while in St Martin (the French half of that island) the 'century old tradition of 'how to create' flavoured rum' could be investigated by tourists.

Another very good example of heritage tourism development was seen in La Reunion (South Indian Ocean) in March 2017; here we visited a vanilla plantation (and plantation house) from which products have been exported for 200 years but which, according to the tour guide, now relies totally upon cruise tourists for sales of vanilla (40 ships having already patronised the site since the beginning of that year). However, perhaps the best example I have encountered anywhere in the world was in Manta, Ecuador. I quote from my diary (January 2017):

Who would ever visit this part of Ecuador apart from cruise tourists? Manta is a useful port from which to take trips to the Galápagos Islands and also to the Amazon Forest. But not everyone, by any means, goes to these major attractions, so the local tour company has to find *something* for the majority to do! So they take them to various 'artisan' workshops displaying the 'material heritage' of Ecuador – nut carving, weaving, and hat making, which are located in poor, industrial areas.

It would seem that, in the absence of sufficient attractions to cope with the flood of cruise tourists, *anything* can be labelled as 'traditional', 'historic' or 'heritage' to form the basis of a visitor attraction and a stop on a coach or minibus trip. As Gill and Welk (2007) assert, heritage tourism depends on tourists' motivations and perceptions rather than on the attributes of specific sites. Hannam and Knox (2010: 157) comment that 'heritage tourism is not so much about presenting people with the "truth", but about confronting them with something that they will believe to be either the truth itself or a pretty good simulation of such'. Such 'proactive production of heritage' (Macleod 2010: 64) may, at the least, be problematic, since it emphasises 'the parties who are able to actively manipulate their environment in pursuit of creating something that represents their notion of their heritage' (ibid.). As Hollinshead remarked some 20 years ago, 'the presentations of history and heritage are presentations of choice and bias' (Hollinshead 1997: 171).

Figure 6.2 Hat making, Ecuador

One example of this that I encountered concerned cricket in Antigua. A cruise tour on this island offered the chance to meet a living 'cricket legend', a worthy aim in a country for which cricket is such an important part of tradition. However, the actual site of historic cricket matches was not promoted and has been almost entirely unvisited since the opening of a new stadium; in my diary I noted that 'we followed directions to the old cricket ground. We asked to visit the club room. Here we saw the honours boards for past Test Matches – Lara's 400 was there . . . it was all rather run-down'. This seemed to me a wasted opportunity to attract heritage tourists, compared to the predictable encouragement from port literature to visit 'historic' Redcliffe Quay, where 'a selection of colourful, renovated buildings create an atmospheric warren of interest, and the old trade buildings are now shops, boutiques, and art galleries'.

It was telling that a notable exception to the heritage-creation trend observed in many places was any emphasis on the histories of indigenous people. There was, for example, one museum in Martinique based on Amerindian heritage, but this was not represented on any cruise tour. I visited it myself to try to understand why this was the case and found that the information in the museum was entirely in French. Since, according to Boniface et al. (2012), more than 90 per cent of cruise tourists in the Caribbean derive from North America (and many of the remainder are British), this seemed rather a lost opportunity to showcase 'real heritage'. The short 'histories' of the islands, included in port guides for the 2016 Caribbean cruise, were extremely dismissive of indigenous people and their culture, while the massacres and extermination of Caribs by Europeans were mentioned very casually; instead, *history* implied the colonial era and the conflicts between French and English military forces for control of the islands, together with blood-curdling stories of pirates. A similar emphasis on 'colonial', rather than indigenous, history and heritage was also noted in other parts of the world.

Nevertheless, the primary historical lack in the eastern Caribbean was any emphasis on the African 'heritage' of the islands (see also, Wilkinson 2006). Richter (1999: 119) says that 'heritage tourism today in many societies is much more willing to confront the shameful legacies of the past'. However, according to Best and Phulgence (2013), Caribbean governments seek actively to downplay the role of slavery in the history of their islands, seeking to put past traumas behind them, despite the increasing demand for 'heritage' experiences by tourists. A good example I noted was Speightstown in Barbados, described in on-shore literature as ''Little Bristol' from its considerable trade with that English port' without any mention of the slavery that formed the most important aspect of the trading. Indeed, apart from one or two monuments commemorating abolition, and despite its huge importance in the history of the region, I encountered virtually no mention of slavery anywhere in the eastern Caribbean. The only exceptions were in St Kitts, where a surviving Bell Tower at Romney Manor was pointed out as echoing the story of a kind master who was active in the anti-slavery movement, while there was a small display in one side room at Brimstone Hill Fort which, as a World Heritage Site, was presumably required to present the hard truths about slave heritage rather than avoid them. Elsewhere in the world I have not encountered such a determined resistance to historical truth about slavery; indeed, the heritage of slave or indentured labour was well displayed in Bonaire (south Caribbean, 2017 cruise), Mauritius (Indian Ocean, 2017) and Louisiana in the southern United States (2015 cruise), in each case forming a significant 'heritage' attraction.

Conclusion

Based on extensive cruise experience and research, this chapter has attempted to show that, with the increasing importance of cruise tourism and the unceasing demand for new tourist experiences in cruise destinations, it appears inevitable that various types of created 'heritage' will figure largely in the offerings of excursions offices and their local counterparts on shore. These may include some or all of the following: buildings, work places, 'historic sites', landscapes, flora and fauna, food and drink, and cultural performances. However, what counts as 'history' and 'heritage' will inevitably be biased towards the aspects expected to draw tourists (and their money) from the 'bubbles' of their ships, as well as to provide viable alternatives to the mass attraction of beaches and port-side shops.

References

Best, M.N. and Phulgence, W. (2013) The contested heritage of sugar and slavery at tourism attractions in Barbados and St Lucia, in L. Jolliffe (ed.) *Sugar Heritage and Tourism in Transition*. Bristol: Channel View.

Boniface, B., Cooper, C. and Cooper, R. (2012) *Worldwide Destinations: The Geography of Travel and Tourism*, 6th Edition. London: Routledge.

Brida, J.G. and Zapata, S. (2010) Cruise tourism: economic, socio-cultural and environmental impacts. *Journal of Leisure and Tourism Marketing*, 1(3): 205–226.

Cruise Lines International Association (CLIA) (2016) *2017 State of the Cruise Industry Outlook*.

De Cantis, S., Ferranto, M., Kahani, A. and Shoval, N. (2016) Cruise passengers' behavior at the destination: investigation using GPS technology. *Tourism Management*, 52: 137–150.

Douglas, N. and Douglas, N. (2004) Cruise ship passenger spending patterns in Pacific Island ports. *International Journal of Tourism Research*, 6(4): 251–261.

Dowling, R.K. (ed.) (2006) *Cruise Ship Tourism*. CAB International.

Dowling, R.K. and Weeden, C. (2017) *Cruise Ship Tourism*, 2nd Edition. CAB International.

Duval, D.T. (2007) *Tourism and Transport: Modes, Networks and Flows*. Clevedon: Channel View.

Gill, A. and Welk, E. (2007) Natural heritage as place identity: Tofino, Canada, a coastal resort on the periphery, in S. Agarural and G. Shaw (eds.) *Managing Coastal Tourism Resorts: A Global Perspective*. Clevedon: Channel View, pp. 169–183.

Hall, C.M. (2005) *Tourism: Rethinking the Social Science of Mobility*. Harlow, Essex: Pearson Education.

Hall, C.M. and Page, S.J. (2006) *The Geography of Tourism and Recreation*. London: Routledge.

Hannam, K. and Knox, D. (2010) *Understanding Tourism: A Critical Introduction*. London: Sage.

Hollinshead, K. (1997) Heritage tourism under post-modernity: truth and the past, in C. Ryan (ed.) *The Tourist Experience: A New Introduction*. London: Cassell, pp. 170–193.

Jaakson, R. (2004) Beyond the tourist bubble? Cruiseship passengers in port. *Annals of Tourism Research*, 31: 44–60.

Kerswill, M. and Mair, H. (2015) Big ships, small towns: understanding cruise port development in Falmouth, Jamaica. *Tourism in Marine Environments*, 10(3–4): 189–199.

Klein, R.A. (2011) Responsible cruise tourism: issues of cruise tourism and sustainability. *Journal of Hospitality and Tourism Management*, 18(1): 107–116.

Macleod, D.V.L. (2010) Power, culture and the production of heritage, in D.V.L. Macleod and J.G. Carrier (eds.) *Tourism, Power and Culture: Anthropological Insights*. Bristol: Channel View, pp. 64–89.

McCalla, R.J. and Charlier, J.J. (2006) Round the world cruising: a geography created by geography?, in R.K. Dowling (ed.) *Cruise Ship Tourism*. CAB International, pp. 206–222.

Momsen, J.H. (2005) Uncertain images: tourist development and seascapes of the Caribbean, in C. Cartier and A.A. Lew (eds.) *Seductions of Place: Geographical Perspectives on Globalization and Touristed Landscapes*. London: Routledge, pp. 209–221.

Morgan, P. and Power, L. (2011) Cruise tourism, in M. Robinson et al. (eds.) *Research Themes for Tourism*. CAB International, pp. 276–288.

Moss, P. (2001) *Placing Autobiography in Geography*. New York: Syracuse University Press.

Papathanassis, A. and Beckman, I. (2011) Assessing the 'poverty of cruise theory' hypothesis. *Annals of Tourism Research*, 38: 153–174.

Pearce, D.G. (1999) Tourism development and national organizations in small developing countries: the case of Samoa, in D.G. Pearce and R.W. Butler (eds.) *Contemporary Issues in Tourism Development*. London: Routledge, pp. 143–157.

Richter, L.K. (1999) The politics of heritage tourism development, in D.G. Pearce and R.W. Butler (eds.) *Contemporary Issues in Tourism Development*. London: Routledge, pp. 108–126.

Scheyvens, R. (2002) *Tourism for Development: Empowering Communities*. Harlow, Essex: Pearson Education.

Sheller, M. (2004) Demobilizing and remobilizing Caribbean paradise, in M. Sheller and J. Urry (eds.) *Tourism Mobilities: Places to Play, Places in Play*. London: Routledge, pp. 13–21.

Smith, M., Macleod, N. and Hart Robertson, M. (2010) *Key Concepts in Tourist Studies*. London: Sage.

Teye, V. and Paris, C.M. (2011) Cruise line industry and Caribbean Tourism: guests' motivations, activities, and destination preference. *Tourism Review International*, 14(1): 17–28.

Timothy, D.J. and Boyd, S.W. (2008) Heritage tourism in the 21st century. *Journal of Heritage Tourism*, 1(1): 1–16.

Weaver, A. (2005) The McDonaldization thesis and cruise tourism. *Annals of Tourism Research*, 32(2): 346–366.

Weaver, D.B. (2007) Resort structure and 'plantation' dynamics in Antigua and Coastal South Carolina, in S. Agarural and G. Shaw (eds.) *Managing Coastal Tourism Resorts: A Global Perspective*. Clevedon: Channel View, pp. 204–215.

Weeden, C., Lester, J.-A. and Thyne, M. (2011) Cruise tourism: emerging issues and implications for a maturing industry. *Journal of Hospitality and Tourism Management*, 18(1): 26–29.

Wilkinson, P.F. (2006) The changing geography of cruise tourism in the Caribbean, in R.K. Dowling (ed.) *Cruise Ship Tourism*. CAB International, pp. 170–183.

Wood, R.E. (2004) Cruise ships: deterritorialized destinations, in L.M. Lumsdon and S.J. Page (eds.) *Tourism and Transport: Issues and Agenda for the New Millennium*. London: Routledge, pp. 133–145.

Wood, R.E. (2006) Cruise tourism: a paradigmatic case of globalization? in R.K. Dowling (ed.) *Cruise Ship Tourism*. CAB International, pp. 397–406.

7 'It's tango!'

Communicating intangible cultural heritage for the dance tourist

Jonathan Skinner

Introduction

Tuesday afternoon and we are sitting exhausted in a café in Wimbledon, West London. 'Liam' tells 'Betsy' and me:

> This is the worst of your problems. When qualified, no matter how good you are as a dancer, you won't be THE Argentinian dancer. You won't have 'it' – what the punters want, no matter how good you are as a dancer or teacher!

Betsy, Liam's teaching partner and fellow student, expands on his advice: 'It's not authentic. You're not the real dancer, no matter how good you are. It's always happening. They want someone from Buenos Aires'.

Betsy, Liam and I are teacher-training students at the London Argentine Tango School (LATS), one of the longest established UK tango schools, run by Leonardo and Tracey. Liam is an accomplished ballroom dancer and instructor who gives tango classes in Brighton, where Tracey started her dancing. He is assisting Leo and Tracey during our monthly tango-teacher training session. Betsy and I are working towards our level one examination: an oral and a demonstration of a dance lesson. Today, Leo has been drilling us with warm-up moves and the lead and follow underpinning his *lapiz* and *enrosques* (a leader's leg extension that becomes a spiral action into the standing leg as the follower rotates around the leader). The conversation about the struggle to teach tango in the UK as a non-Argentinian matches the struggle, not only to imprint the moves into our muscle memory, but also to be able to dance both 'lead' and 'follow' and explain and teach the move to each other.

This chapter is about the 'it' that Leo has. It is more than the ability to execute a move with poise, precision, timing and typical élan. Leo lives the move. He embodies it and demonstrates this every day and every night in his classes and his improvised dances. We buy into 'it', whether during the classes, the weekend Milonga party, or the dance holidays held in Sardinia and Buenos Aires each year – liminal times in the year for transformation and self-improvement (Skinner 2015). Leo's 'it' is an indigenous knowledge that he grew into, 'a second-skin' (Skinner 2007) that he is able to wear and utilise, like the cosmopolitan salsa teacher who relocates for work and relies on their physical prowess (and Latin looks). The question for this chapter is whether or not 'it', as indigenous heritage, is a form of *habitus*; a memory embodied. Does Leo's skillset, which he commoditises as intangible cultural heritage, dwell in his body and is it something that can be acquired by the student and tango tourist?

Describing the seemingly natural movements of the salsa dancer from Cuba, Puerto Rico or Central and Southern America, the common refrain is that 'it's in his hips'. This extends to the environment where the dancer resides, whether this is where they grew up or where they migrated to. Shelagh Pietrobruno studied salsa dancers in Montreal, and refers to their movements as 'movement heritage', a 'corporeal vernacular' of the body that she theorises through sociologist Pierre Bourdieu (1990: 68) and his habitus concept where the body is conceived of as a 'living memory pad', some form of blotting paper that soaks up movements by practical mimesis. Interview research into salsa dancing in Sacramento (California) and Belfast (Northern Ireland) attests to this self-ascription among dancers or its projection upon the Latin dancer, no matter their generation (Skinner 2007). It is seen as a genetic propensity to move with a Cuban action, with hips swaying from side to side. Similarly, Heike Wieschiolek (2003) notes that the dance is associated with a Latin identity in Hamburg clubs; it is taught to local Germans but is seen as inherent in Latin migrants, who therefore do not need the classes. Dance anthropologist Juliet McMains (2015) draws upon the anthropology of tourism literature to make the point that Latino dance teachers actively play with their personas. She takes Alexis Bunten's (2008) point about tour guides' 'self-commodification' of their identity to engage the tourist. Latina salsa teachers, especially, have self-exoticised their body language to market lessons in how to move hands, ribs and hips with femininity. They capitalise on ethnic and gender stereotypes, manipulating the dancing desires of their pupils. In her study of salsa in New Jersey, Katherine Borland (2009: 485) similarly describes the women practising moves so that they become a part of their muscle memory – a repertoire that they can draw from in their improvisations: 'As each dancer inhabits the move, she makes it her own, and basic competence gives way to playful improvisation'. The key word here is 'inhabit', meaning to dwell within the body. Borland (2009: 485) goes on to characterise these learned movements that correspond to sexualised notions of femininity as 'carefully learned artifice'. Dancers use their bodily movements to 'self-fashion' their identities, often enjoying the dance floor as a place of escapism and self-expression. 'Salsa dance taps into a natural sensuality that exists prior to culturally imposed inhibitions on women's self-expression' Borland claims (Bock and Borland 2011: 17). In its cultural transmission it is both constructed as Otherness and courted as an essentialist ability.

To return to McMains (2006), Latin dances such as the salsa, but also very much the tango (particularly the ballroom codified version of the dance as opposed to the Argentine tango), rely on Western stereotyping of Latin emotion and aesthetic for their appeal. This cultural imperialism is pithily summarised by Marta Savigliano (1995) as a 'political economy of passion'. McMains (2006: 112–113) qualifies this appropriation and revision in her account of tango's spread to European and American ballrooms:

The sudden popularity among the cultural elite of Paris of what had been a lower-class dance form associated with violence and prostitution in Argentina created an atmosphere of scandal that further heightened its appeal . . . In fact, the idea of tango – its mythologised origins in the brothels, its boiling passion, its image of domination and rebellion – proved to be more profitable and marketable than the dance itself. Tango students in Europe were either unprepared to learn the complexities of the dance, ill-informed about the technique, or uninterested in the movement style practised in Argentina. Instead, a proliferation of new dances circulating under the same name emerged as dance teachers codified and redefined the dance for Western consumption.

Where McMains focuses on the codification of ballroom dance, Savigliano (1995: 119) discusses the grotesque caricaturisation of the social dancing of the past in Argentina in show-tango performances that are choreographed contrasts between 'airy elegance and tumultuous earthiness'. Latin America scholar Mike Gonzalez and Venezuelan journalist Marianella Yanes (2013: 77) credit tango's arrival in Paris at the turn of the twentieth century, and the ensuing cosmopolitan frenzy for the dance among the 'gilded youth on their own version of the Grand Tour', for lending the dance an air of acceptability and respectability. It gained 'the European seal of approval' (Gonzalez and Yanes 2013: 77) and allowed it to find its voice and come out of the shadows back in Buenos Aires. As a dance, it still represents that history as a lived heritage, rehabilitating the traditional rural gaucho into a cosmopolitan national figure (Bockelman 2011: 580). For Gonzalez and Yanes (2013: 184), 'the tango's past is always present'. It represents the sadness of sexual relations, and a nostalgia for a glorious past in the Golden Age of 'big band' tango (1935–1952), but it also resonates with 'the demi-monde of prostitutes, pimps and red-light districts' of tango's origins in the barrios of Buenos Aires (ibid.: 187). This exotic, physical, transgressive association attracts its up-market students with alter-egos to indulge at home and abroad.

Tango tourists in search of 'it'

In 2003 UNESCO adopted the definition of intangible cultural heritage as 'the practices, representations, expressions, knowledge, skills – as well as the instruments, objects, artefacts and cultural spaces associated therewith – that communities, groups and, in some cases, individuals recognise as part of their cultural heritage' (UNESCO 2003). The international recognition of intangible heritage (such as song, music, cuisine, craft skills, dance, drama and festival) as a non-material expression of culture redresses a previously Eurocentric approach to heritage dominated by European monumental and material examples. It now attends to the level of community identity and to how tacit knowledge is transmitted and renewed (Cominelli and Greffe 2012) and thus includes body-movement systems. In 2009 the UNESCO Intergovernmental Committee on Intangible Cultural Heritage held in Abu Dhabi inscribed the tango tradition, defined as a 'musical genre' (UNESCO 2009), referring in their public justification to dance, music, songs and dance hall practices:

The Argentinian and Uruguayan tradition of the Tango, now familiar around the world, was developed by the urban lower classes in Buenos Aires and Montevideo in the Rio de la Plata basin. Among this mix of European immigrants to the region, descendants of African slaves and the natives of the region known as criollos, a wide range of customs, beliefs and rituals were merged and transformed into a distinctive cultural identity. As one of the most recognisable embodiments of that identity, the music, dance and poetry of tango both embodies and encourages diversity and cultural dialogue. It is practised in the traditional dance halls of Buenos Aires and Montevideo, spreading the spirit of its community across the globe even as it adapts to new environments and changing times. That community today includes musicians, professional and amateur dancers, choreographers, composers, songwriters, teachers of the art and the national living treasures who embody the culture of tango. Tango is also incorporated into celebrations of national heritage in Argentina and Uruguay, reflecting the widespread embrace of this popular urban music.

(UNESCO 2009)

Both countries agreed to safeguard this intangible cultural heritage through the creation of specialised training and documentation centres, the establishment of an orchestra, and construction of museums and preservation trusts dedicated to tango (see also UNESCO 2008).

Those who dance the tango illustrate their 'distinctive cultural identity'. They practice and disseminate the art of tango by using their bodies, externalising and projecting the group identity they are embodying. These proponents of Argentina and Uruguay's national heritage are 'national living treasures' to be respected and revered. The tango dance teacher is one of those 'treasures', a living embodiment of intangible cultural heritage, whether in South America or 'across the globe' adapting to their new circumstances. Liam implies that *Leo* embodies tango intangible cultural heritage but *we* do not and will never be seen to do so. As the lessons continued, Leo slipped in anecdotes about growing up dancing tango, learning from his father, listening and singing along with the tango singers that visited. He practised his tango walk alone for years (from the age of seven) before he was allowed to walk and dance with a partner. He then danced for years around Buenos Aires before he came to the UK as a tango teacher. When he arrived he spent much of his time deconstructing the work of other tango teachers, working intensively with his partner Tracey, who came from a ballroom background where moves and routines are learned and choreographed together. For Leo, the tango is about interpreting the music with your partner, improvising dynamic moves through an intense connection with each other:

To dance the proper tango we must first catch the music. You must feel the musicality. It is about playing. If you are going to improvise you need to know how to play. Listen to the body.

In Argentine tango we dance in reality. Not for stage and to develop choreography. It is the most pure form of art. The connection with Tracey makes this thing a reality, not a fiction. We don't teach a sequence. Lose the magic and adventure if you know the sequence. It's an adventure to discover how she moves. The adventure gives me the idea to know you. I want to know you.

Learning 'it' from Leo – picking up, appropriating, paying for his intangible cultural heritage – took place over the many months of the tango teachers' course, specifically year one, level one (posture, embrace, musicality, improvisation, tango history, teaching technique). We watched, copied, danced to, and danced with, Leo, learning how to move as Leo moved. He and Tracey had spent years stripping back the tango to the core elements that they wanted to share with others in their teaching, their teacher-training and their self-published tango guidebook (Acosta and Tyack-King 2015). Their advertising stresses 'the authentic, social art form of Argentine Tango' (ibid.: back cover), 'long may it be danced and loved' (ibid.: 3). This is also stressed in their public lessons, workshops, milongas, tango dinners at the Waldorf (where the tango was first danced in London in 1910), at their annual Tango Festival and during their tango holidays (typically monthly weekends away on the coast, a fortnight in Buenos Aires early in the year and a summer holiday, such as to Sardinia for their annual Tango Festival). Recently, Leo celebrated fifty years of dancing tango and spoke about its importance as an improvised art form, distinctive and unique throughout the world for being present in the moment, live and alive for dancers and audience. For him, 'it's something very nice in the world and is something very important to support.' For Tracey, Leo's tango upbringing lends his dancing, if not his teaching, a standard that can be admired and imitated but never reached; 'he really is the real thing', she says admiringly.

Students are attracted to Leo and Tracey through the Romantic image of tango – an intimate and passionate dance that, for many, is more sophisticated and elegant, more classy and challenging than other social dances such as jive or salsa. They want to learn from the real person, to get as close to the origins of the dance as it is represented – one foot removed, so to speak. This allows Leo and Tracey, among other dance teachers, to make a profession out of their skills, showing them the dance in its context, especially when visiting Buenos Aires. Virginia Gift (2008: 24) rightly refers to Buenos Aires as 'the Mecca' for tango tourists, estimating that some 25,000 'hardcore tango enthusiasts' (ibid.: 117) travel to Buenos Aires each year, attracted to the 100+ milongas each week, the street shows and dinners with performances. They go to dance, learn, experience the atmosphere and buy tango shoes. The attraction for Gift (ibid.: 47) is the intensity of the vacation: '[t]he heady atmosphere of "total immersion" at tango events especially favours swift, intense friendships and camaraderie reminiscent of the magic of children's summer camps'. This is a unique form of tourism for its participation and immersion, for possessing the tourist gaze but also being gazed upon as Anthony Shay asserts (2016: 144). With a group of tango tourists on their retreat from Bristol to Toulouse, I found that tango and tourism were intertwined – a leisure practice in a leisure location (Skinner 2015). Dancers could come back from this liminal time renewed and re-enskilled, as well as refreshed. Such tango enhancement through tourism was a more prominent feature than on jive holidays that were more about enjoyment (Skinner 2011), as though there were more cultural capital attached to dance learning as opposed to just dance doing.

'Frances' went on holiday with Leo and Tracey to Sardinia. For her, the seaside reminded her of her childhood summers: 'The tango enriches the holiday. It makes it feel more special. The freedom of movement and the music makes you feel good!' In other words, tango tourism combines a holiday with an activity. It creates bonds between dancers who share a common interest. This 'holiday +' or 'common-interest holiday' theme was apparent in a number of interviews with dancers around London, where I dance, teach and research tango.

'Noel' is in his eighties, a widowed financier who dances regularly in London, keeping him active, mentally and physically. The tango dancing relaxes him and gives him something to look forward to in the day. For him, there is more room to dance on London dance floors; in Buenos Aires the dance floors are packed and a tight embrace and small compact moves are necessary. For him, the Argentine tango teachers are better dancers because they have been born into the tradition. It belongs to them authentically: 'the Buenos Aires teachers are better because they're born with it. They've just got it in their soul. No teacher born in London is as good. They're not authentic, you know. Leo feels it. John is a good local teacher but it's mechanical'. Berlin – Amsterdam – Budapest – Paris – Miami – and through Italy and Spain: Noel tangoed with his wife. They became not just tango tourists but 'tango globetrotters' after retirement: 'we had many tango travels; my wife decided where to tango on holiday. We had all day sightseeing and all night dancing!'

'Tango is an endless source of interest' for 'Amanda', a divorced architect living in Balham who has danced tango for eight years. She loves the music and the ability to express herself through it. The tango is a quiet reflective time for her when she is able to relax and meditate and pray whilst she glides across the dance floor. In tango she can both connect with another and find communion with herself and her God. She is aware that the best dancers are not always the best teachers, able to break down a move or correct moves in pupils. Amanda has been on a range of tango holidays – to Italy, India and the USA, and also on a Mediterranean tango cruise – preferring to travel with familiar dance groups and teachers. These holidays have their social scene 'ready-made'. They make her 'anew in the craziness of [her] world'. Amanda's experience of visiting Buenos Aires on a tango holiday was to travel with a group and have tango lessons with that group. She found the teachers there too mercenary and believes that she can get the same quality of lessons from Argentinians in London, like Leo, without feeling that the teachers are profiteering from 'their natural heritage'.

'Freddie' is a retired journalist who dances ballroom and Argentine tango with his wife. They attend tango lessons and milongas locally but have travelled extensively on tango holidays. After long weekends in Bournemouth with several dance teachers, they have ventured to Italy several times, to Sardinia with Leo and Tracey, and to Buenos Aires on a self-planned visit with a group of tango dancers of different levels of ability. The holidays are the most authentic experiences for Freddie and his wife. They learn new moves that they can execute back home on the local dance floor. They also get advice on posture, frame, musicality and dance. But it is also very much a holiday with dancing in it for Freddie: 'It's really good: interesting places – see the place and have entertainment and a few lessons thrown in. I suppose we're tango tourists as we're taken to local milongas. A different way of seeing the place.' The highpoint of Freddie's tango tourism was the trip he organised to Buenos Aires for dance friends who came by cruise ship and flew in from visiting Brazil or direct from the UK. They stayed in a tango hotel and booked lessons and dance nights with a show and social dancing:

> Six of us went to Parakultural. It was fantastic! . . . [W]e were the only tourists there and still mingled in. It was all very friendly. The place to go! I'd like to go back but my wife feels that we have done BA and all the sights. We're very lucky in London with Argentinians here that teach it. You need that. John is a very good teacher but you need a little bit of that reassurance. Buenos Aires' tango is the gold seal. Dancing and doing it in the environment it comes from should be the best competence. You can't teach 'Leoism'!

'Mary' went with two tango girlfriends to Buenos Aires and danced, shopped and toured some of the sites. Her photograph album was passed round the tango group and suggestions and recommendations were made for other dancers' visits. 'Jeremy' is retired and currently on a five-week visit to Buenos Aires 'to crack [his] tango on its head!' He will take lessons, join practicas and attend milongas and come back a more competent tango dancer. This will make him more popular in the London tango scene. 'Macy', on the other hand, a Mexican attendee of Leo and Tracey's classes and milongas, is going/returning to Buenos Aires with her husband, a non-tango dancer. She is slanting her private lessons in London towards the milonguero style found on the crowded dance floors. She will pay for a tango escort to accompany her to the dance nights. She is not interested in lessons – she can get quality lessons in London – but to return to Buenos Aires and to tango this time will be a dream come true.

Each of these dancers is an avid follower of tango, a number seeking 'Leoisms' from his native country. This extends to such an extent that they spend time and money going away to improve their dancing, to develop skills through their regular teachers, and to experience Buenos Aires – where 'it' all comes from. They return with added tango cachet. Amanda and Freddie and his wife have attended a number of tango tours, including Leo and Tracey's holidays in Sardinia. They have all travelled the 7,000 miles from London to Buenos Aires as tango tourists, except Frances who will visit later in 2018. Each dancer has also used the tango to travel – to Europe's leading cities, across the Mediterranean, and as far as India. The students admire and want to emulate their teachers; they want the 'it' that the teachers bring with them to their dance classes.

From a Romantic perspective, the dancers want to tap into the intangible heritage they see before them and are paying for. Folklorist Regina Bendix (1997: 47) associates debates on authenticity and expressive culture with Romanticism's nationalistic underpinnings. She distinguishes between individual genius and the anonymous community of an idealised past, the folk community. Here, in tango tourism, we have both. We have the creative teacher inspiring their students to visit Buenos Aires, to travel, learn and develop more as dancers, to gain confidence and credibility in their tango, to acquire tango heritage from specific barrios but also to be able to use tango to improvise and express themselves through the music. But as one UK tango teacher noted, 'this is an invention and clever marketing of the tango'. Sociologist Maria Törnqvist (2013: 61) studied tango tourism in Buenos Aires and describes it as 'an intimate dance economy' where teachers and dancers promote and provide the authentic 'feel' of the dance for hungry tourists. These tourists crave the authentic *abrazo* (embrace) from an Argentinian tango dancer/teacher in Buenos Aires. It cannot get any more real than that for them. And once sampled, either the desire continues or it is assuaged and the tourist, such as Mary, continues with her 'bucket list' of activities to do before she dies (the Northern Lights are next on her list).

The habits of heritage

UNESCO Chair in Cultural Tourism, Maria Gravari-Barbas (2012, 2018), recently elaborated on her thesis that tourism is a heritage-producing machine by suggesting that the two co-produce each other. Tourism both prescribes and produces heritage (Gravari-Barbas 2018: 7). Her examples focus on physical monuments, but this thesis could equally extend to intangible cultural heritage such as tango where the tourist dancer trades in the dance moves and experiences, and the tango dancer trades off their embodied knowledge. The two come together in a delicate interplay on the dance floor. The knowledge traded is a 'bodywork', to return to Törnqvist (2013: 110, 113, 218): the teachers trade *accessibility* in tango technique and as dance hosts; they also trade in *temporality*, offering a shortcut to the dance skills that might have taken decades to master. This is more than their habitus, referred to by Bourdieu as a bodily disposition, a culturally learned way of moving, being, interacting – 'a system of durable and transposable dispositions' (Bourdieu 1972: 261). Bourdieu's student Loïc Wacquant defends this attempt to build a science of practice, to mediate between the subjective and the objective – perhaps even between the tangible and intangible, to return to heritage – and to show how the socio-symbolic becomes sedimented in people's actions. Wacquant (2016: 65) includes 'trained capacities and patterned propensities' in this habitus, an inclusive and ambitious gambit that opens up the nascent background of the tango teacher but also the prescient learnings of the tango tourist. History and society hypothetically embodied in dance returns us also to Bendix and her examination of the influence of Romanticism. Leo's habitus, Leo's 'Leoism', Leo's 'it' comes from his father, his family, his barrio, and is formative and transferrable – though presumably not so malleable and permeable as to include his UK experiences.

According to Swartz (2002: 63S), this habitus is 'an active residue of (one's) past'. Unconscious, pre-reflective, and generally unobservable, it has been constructed with the weight of inertia about it as much as the weight of history. To apply Bourdieu to tango and tango tourism would be to give in to an historical determinism (we are bound and enmeshed in the world around us). We dwell in it and it dwells in us. And yet the tango can be taught and it can be learned. Further, tango changes in its conventions, codifications, styles and meanings. Gustavo Fares (2015: 180) suggests that, as such, tango is a free signifier associated with modernity and easily adaptable by those with increasing access to leisure time. It is, though, just a commodity. Nevertheless, Wacquant (2016: 68) would have us distinguish between primary and secondary habitus (or second nature even) – the one, family socialisation by osmosis, the other, a more learned, grafted disposition; his amateur boxing and my social tango effectively belong to the latter. Certainly walking, whether down the street or across the dance floor, constitutes an expression of this habitus. It is found in the body hexis dispositions, 'a durable way of standing, speaking, walking' that Bourdieu (1990: 70) controversially extends with the clause 'and thereby of feeling and thinking'. And yet with tango, our walking changes significantly in style, posture, momentum, pacing: Leo's lessons with Liam, Betsy, myself, Freddie, Frances and Macy in London and Sardinia are about adding cadence to the walk to match the music; using the heel, passing the ankle, brushing the floor, engaging the metatarsals, turning out for stability, keeping the weight forward, projecting and using intentionality until we no longer have to think about 'it'. The Romantic interpretation of this teaching and learning is that we are renegotiating our habitus.

Writing about a cleft 'habitus' from jarring confrontations in working class education environments, Ingram and Abrahams (2016) suggest that habitus is not static but can be confronted, changed, destabilised, reconciled, abandoned. The tourist's way of walking is challenged in tango tourism: one minute viewing a site and walking Buenos Aires, the next practising their walk with their tango maestro, and then performing it on the dance floor. In the lessons with Leo we hear stories of knife fights with gauchos warily circling each other. This is the body movement we seek to adopt. Tracey throws in a comment that she saw one of Leo's father's jackets with a long inside pocket to carry just such a knife. The students appreciate this story and increase their regard for Leo and his authenticity. It confirms the biographical Welcome on their website:

> The London Argentine Tango School run by Leonardo and Tracey teaches the authentic, social art form of Argentine Tango. Leonardo Acosta, from Buenos Aires, has danced Tango for over 48 years. Based on his years of teaching and dancing, they have defined his style and now have a comprehensive teaching methodology to help others dance this beautiful dance. It is named in honour of Leo's father, who was also a Tango Teacher.
>
> (LATS 2017)

Practitioners of intangible cultural heritage are not passive purveyors of a skill. They are more than a living archive of a nation's adopted representations of itself. They are agents in the cultural production and development of the improvised movement system that is a lifestyle, an art, and a means to a living. Kirshenblatt-Gimblett (2004) makes this point about the application of understandings of intangible cultural heritage that, for me, approximates the critique of Bourdieu for his static application of habitus. For her, there is a tension and an irony about heritage coming to represent modernity and carriers of heritage being preserved when cultural practice is processual and motile. She writes: 'The asynchrony of historical, heritage, and habitus clocks and differential temporalities of things, persons, and events produce a tension between the contemporary and the contemporaneous [. . .] a confusion of evanescence with disappearance' (ibid.: 59). To move from the Romantic approach to this authentic and laden way of walking to the cynical, one teacher let down his guard when explaining to his advanced class in the UK that the designer walk with cadence from particular barrios in Buenos Aires was a marketing invention, a form of auto-exoticisation to attract interest. Tango in the barrio is part of what Morgan Luker (2016) refers to as the 'tango machine': a brand and service for consumption, an example of modern day expediency. To illustrate this, Luker (2016: 6) interrogated the Argentine social anthropologist Mönica Lacarrieu as Director of the Commission for the Preservation of Historic and Cultural Patrimony:

'So what about tango as intangible heritage?' I asked her.

'Ah, tango,' she replied. 'It sometimes seems like we are the only office in the whole city government that doesn't deal with tango. You see, we deal with real intangible heritage, not stuff for some tourist show.'

Conclusion

Luker was writing about the tango machine, a commercial enterprise found across the streets of Buenos Aires. This is akin to the glamour machine found by McMains in the world of Dancesport that advertises a fantasy of youth, sexual desirability, romance, social acceptability, success, classiness and passion. All of these feature in tango as taught and as travelled. Where these illusions persist only within the walls of the dance studio for the competitive ballroom dancer, in tango they exist on the streets of Buenos Aires and in the public milongas for the Argentine tango social dancer. In both dance environments the students become addicted to the fantasy (although it is interesting that tango lessons generally take place without the walls of mirrors found in dance studios – these were only needed when Liam, Betsy and I worked with Leo as he transferred his intangible cultural skills into an intangible cultural asset). For McMains (2006: 55), this can be explained almost as a masquerade of social inadequacy: '[t]he Glamour Machine obscures the failure of society to provide, for example, adequate physical and emotional intimacy in an increasingly isolationist culture'.

This is a jaded view of both the dance environment and the social world where more Romantic interpretations carry sway. Freddie would love to return to Buenos Aires and to sample the tango at its heart again; in the meantime he can only mention his jealousy of Jeremy with his extended stay in the city and prepare for more local and European tango holidays himself. Before specialising in tango with Leo, both Liam and Betsy made their own pilgrimages to Buenos Aires and found it added 'credibility' to their classes, validating their teaching and ways of dancing. 'We're not a community of dancers like in Buenos Aires,' Liam laments. 'We are Saturday nights, here, dancers of tango. The closest we have to their tango community is our tea dance. But we'll never get it.' That is, until Leo turns up with 'it'.

References

Acosta, L. and Tyack-King, T. (2015) *The ABC of Argentine Tango*. Self-published volume, hardcopy and iBook.

Bendix, R. (1997) *In Search of Authenticity: The Formation of Folklore Studies*. Madison: The University of Wisconsin Press.

Bock, S. and Borland, K. (2011) Exotic Identities: Dance, Difference, and Self-fashioning. *Journal of Folklore Research*, 48(1): 1–36.

Bockelman, B. (2011) Between the gaucho and the tango: popular songs and the shifting landscape of modern Argentine identity, 1895–1915. *The American Historical Review*, 116(3): 577–601.

Borland, K. (2009) Embracing difference: salsa fever in New Jersey. *Journal of American Folklore*, 122(486): 466–492.

Bourdieu, P. (1990) *The Logic of Practice*. Cambridge: Polity Press.

Bunten, A. (2008) Sharing culture or selling out? Developing the commodified persona in the heritage industry. *American Ethnologist*, 35(5): 380–395.

Cominelli, F. and Greffe, X. (2012) Intangible cultural heritage: safeguarding for creativity. *City, Culture and Society*, 3(4): 245–250.

Fares, G. (2015) Tango's elsewhere: Japan. *The Journal of the Midwest Modern Language Association*, 48(1): 171–192.

Gift, V. (2008) *Tango: A History of Obsession*. London: Amazon Publishing.

Gonzalez, M. and Yanes, M. (2013) *Tango: Sex and Rhythm of the City*. London: Reaktion Books Ltd.

Gravari-Barbas, M. (2012). Tourisme et patrimoine, le temps des synergies? in C. Khaznadar (ed.) *Le patrimoine, mais quel patrimoine?* Internationale de l'imaginaire, No.27, Paris: Maison des Cultures du Monde, pp. 375–399.

Gravari-Barbas, M. (2018) Tourism as a heritage producing machine. *Tourism Management Perspectives*, 26, April: 5–8, https://doi.org/10.1016/j.tmp.2017.12.002.

Ingram, N. and Abrahams, J. (2016) Stepping outside of oneself: how a cleft-habitus can lead to greater reflexivity through occupying 'the third space', in J. Thatcher, N. Ingram, C. Burker and J. Abrahams (eds.) *Bourdieu: The Next Generation: The Development of Bourdieu's Intellectual Heritage in Contemporary UK Sociology*. London: Routledge, pp. 140–156.

Kirshenblatt-Gimblett, K. (2004) Intangible heritage as metacultural production. *Museum International*, 56(1–2): 52–65.

LATS (2017) Argentine Tango: Welcome! www.lat-s.co.uk, accessed 23 December 2017.

Luker, M. (2016) *The Tango Machine: Musical Culture in the Age of Expediency*. Chicago: University of Chicago Press.

McMains, J. (2006) *Glamour Addiction: Inside the American Ballroom Dance Industry*. Middletown: Weslyan University Press.

McMains, J. (2015) *Spinning Mambo into Salsa: Caribbean Dance in Global Commerce*. Oxford: Oxford University Press.

Pietrobruno, S. (2006) *Salsa and its Transnational Moves*. Oxford: Lexington Books.

Savigliano, M. (1995) *Tango and the Political Economy of Passion*. Boulder, CO: Westview Press.

Shay, A. (2016) *Ethno Identity Dance for Sex, Fun and Profit: Staging Popular Dances Around the World*. London: Palgrave Macmillan.

Skinner, J. (2007) The salsa class: a complexity of globalization, cosmopolitans and emotions. *Identities* (Special Edition on Emotions and Globalization), 14(4): 485–506.

Skinner, J. (2011) Displeasure on 'Pleasure Island': tourist expectation and desire on and off the Cuban dance floor, in J. Skinner and D. Theodossopoulos (eds.) *Great Expectations: Imagination, Anticipation, and Enchantment in Tourism*. Oxford: Berghahn Books, pp. 116–136.

Skinner, J. (2015) Tango Heart and soul: solace, suspension, and the imagination in the dance tourist, in M. Harris and N. Rapport (eds.) *The Imagination: A Universal Process of Knowledge*. Oxford: Berghahn, pp. 61–76.

Swartz, D. (2002) The sociology of habit: the perspective of Pierre Bourdieu. *The Occupational Therapy Journal of Research*, 22: 61S-69S.

Törnqvist, M. (2013) *Tourism and the Globalization of Emotions: The Intimate Economy of Tango*. London: Routledge.

UNESCO (2003) Text of the Convention for the Safeguarding of the Intangible Cultural Heritage. UNESCO, https://ich.unesco.org/en/convention (Accessed 13 December 2017).

UNESCO (2008) El Tango. Parte de Cafe de los Maestros (DVD), www.unesco.org/archives/multimedia/?pg=33&s=films_details&id=319 (Accessed 13 December 2017).

UNESCO (2009) Decision of the Intergovernmental Committee: 4.COM 13.01. https://ich.unesco.org/en/decisions/4.COM/13.01 (accessed 13 December 2017).

Wacquant, L. (2016) A concise genealogy and anatomy of habitus. *The Sociological Review*, 64(1): 64–72.

Wieschiolek, H. (2003) 'Ladies, just follow his lead!': salsa, gender and identity, in E. Archetti and N. Dyck (eds.) *Sport, Dance and Embodied Identities*. Oxford: Berg.

8 Holmes as heritage

Readers, tourism and the making of Sherlock Holmes's England

David McLaughlin

Introduction

When considering places associated with the England of Sherlock Holmes, we might think of Undershaw, Arthur Conan Doyle's home in the Surrey countryside. We might, perhaps more naturally, think of 221B Baker Street in London, a place that readers and fans of the Sherlock Holmes stories have been visiting for more than a century (Reijnders 2013). Yet, we should also think of Cairo, in Egypt, as an important site in the making of Sherlock Holmes's England. It was in Cairo, in the late 1970s, that self-professed devotee of Doyle's Sherlock Holmes stories (or 'Sherlockian') David Hammer had the idea for a Sherlock-themed tour of England; although, since no such tour existed, it fell to him to create it. Therefore, between 1983 and 2001, he wrote a series of travel guides to England, as the Great Detective would have known it. There were four books in all: *The Game is Afoot* (1983), *For the Sake of the Game* (1986), *The Worth of the Game* (1993), and *A Deep Game* (2001).

Hammer's travel writing can be understood as one manifestation of a larger proliferation of Holmes-inspired literary tourism, which developed in the latter years of the twentieth century – laying the foundations of a reader-led industry of sorts which continues to this day (McLaughlin 2016, 2017; examples include Alexander 1984, 1999, Sundin 1985, and Christopher 2012). This explosion in Sherlockian literary tourism was broadly characterised by readers who used their travels to and through places associated with the Sherlock Holmes stories in order to practise what I have termed expansionary literary geography: 'It is a deliberate endeavour to turn personal and embodied experiences of actual-world places into extensions of Holmes's fictional world – and to influence fellow Sherlockians' imaginative encounters with that world – that are the hallmarks of this practice' (McLaughlin 2017: 32).

Many examples of Sherlockian literary tourism share a ludic belief that Sherlock Holmes was a historical figure and not simply a fictional character. It was the strength of this professed belief among early Sherlockians that famously led G.K. Chesterton (in Saler 2012: 106) to exclaim that, if these readers continued like this, there would come a time when many people genuinely believed 'that Sherlock Holmes really existed and that Conan Doyle never existed'.

Yet, if we look again at his memoirs and the ways in which Hammer talks about his own work, we can get a sense of a somewhat different purpose to Hammer's literary tourism. Writing about the genesis of his Sherlockian literary tourism, Hammer admitted that:

> I never really believed that Holmes had lived. I still don't, but I do believe that he was real; so real, in fact, that if he has not become a figure of history, he has of heritage, which surely constitutes a significant form of reality.
>
> (Hammer 2001: 10)

In this chapter I will argue that David Hammer used his travel guides as a means of creating Sherlock Holmes's England as a material manifestation of this idea of Holmes as heritage, one that could, and should, be visited by Sherlockian reader-tourists. I will show how he used pieces of England's Holmes-related past – places from Doyle's life, locations from the Sherlock Holmes stories, and even sites from his own past – to create a new story of the past for Sherlockians, one which made tourism into a necessary part of the Sherlockian reader's experience.

Literary tourism and heritage

Literary tourism has long been associated with what Robert Hewison has called the 'heritage industry' (in Harrison 2010: 16; see also Plate 2006, Hendrix 2008, Reijnders 2009, 2011, 2013, Westover 2012, James 2013, Van Es and Reijnders 2016). Robinson and Andersen argue that this is because literature possesses, 'some sort of public legacy expressed in emotional as well as spatial terms' (Robinson and Andersen 2002: 26). In this way, literary works can be seen as 'cultural reference points that sit with conceptions of social and cultural identity, ideas and ideals of nationality and nationhood, and popular discourses of historical development' (Robinson and Andersen 2002: 26). Harald Hendrix classifies writers' houses as 'destinations of literary pilgrimages *and other manifestations of heritage tourism*' (Hendrix 2008: 1, emphasis added).

Further, scholars have suggested that there is at present a general 'conflation of literary tourism with that of heritage tourism, conceiving of this practice to be the "corollary of the present-day obsession with heritage and cultural memory"' (Van Es and Reijnders 2016: 5). The causes of this association between literary tourism and cultural heritage is not hard to discover. Nicola Watson argues that it was a short leap from literary tourism's necessary act of 'imaginative (re)possession and (re)discovery' (Watson 2006: 4), to a place where the 'emerging national literary canon [could be] seized upon in order to effect a sort of interiorised national mapping', abetted by the fact that literary pilgrimages in Britain effectively 'allowed travellers [from Britain and abroad] to make themselves imaginatively at home across the nation through the medium of literature' (Watson 2006: 14; see also Bulson 2007: 4). Into the twenty-first century, literature and tourism remain associated with the idea of re-living an imagined or half-remembered, past. Thus,

Robinson and Anderson write that, 'nostalgia is important here and it seems like literary tourism increasingly plays to an audience that wishes to travel in time as well as space' (Robinson and Anderson 2002: 26).

The artificiality of this association between literary places and cultural identity is such that 'heritage has been fundamentally understood as a possession, the "spoils" claimed by nations and ethnicities for both moral and immoral ends . . . the placed literary past was regarded as a possession over which collectivities could be defined' (Zemuglys 2008: 40). Thus the purpose of literary tourism, with its focus on places to be possessed as a means of defining one's social group is, in part, the creation of literary heritage. It is important, here, to remember David Lowenthal's comments that, first, 'the relics of time help us both to know the past and to bend it to our own uses' and, more forcefully, that heritage 'clarifies pasts so as to infuse them with present purposes' (Lowenthal 1998: xv); in other words, 'It is a past entirely fitted to the present' (Zemgulys 2008: 1).

This recognition that literary heritage is a dynamic and imaginative act of possession and creation, combining places, literatures and present purposes, can help us to understand the role that Hammer's travel books play in making Holmes's England a site that Sherlockian tourists would want to visit, explore and possess. Importantly, despite his claim that Sherlockians, 'are essentially time-travellers, committed to another time, and perhaps worse, to places where we never lived, and for some, have never seen' (Hammer 1997: 2), Hammer's travel books represent less a nostalgic attempt to capture an imagined or half-remembered past. Rather, as I will argue, Hammer used his travels and resulting guides in order to *create* a heritage for Sherlockians, as a particular sociocultural group. His literary tourism practices, through which, as I will demonstrate, he both creates and venerates literary heritage sites connected to Sherlock Holmes, work to justify the dynamic and creative reading practices of Sherlockiana and to concretise those practices in the world.

Literary heritage contains within it a tension, between the individuality of fictional encounters and the collective, controlling impulse of heritage (as a form of authorised and collective remembrance). Literary tourism, as an act of commemoration, involves a 'return to the original places of creation', where 'that return doubles as return to the *original scene of reading*' (Zemgulys 2008: 45, emphasis added). For Sherlockians this tension is further complicated by the explicit existence of a community of readers encountering these stories together (McLaughlin 2016). In this chapter I shall attempt to show how these elements of literary heritage – the places of creation, the scenes of reading and the awareness of other readers – inform Hammer's act of creating Sherlock Holmes's England as a place of Sherlockian heritage.

The acid test: places of creation

The first element in the creation of England as a place of Sherlockian heritage is a focus on the places of literary creation. Hammer's Sherlockian tourism began with a desire to know and to encounter the places of Holmes's England.

He said as much to the SAS tour agent with whom he first discussed the idea of a Holmes-inspired tour of England: 'if I knew the sites, I wouldn't need the tour' (Hammer 2001: 9). As a self-described 'site-maven' (Hammer 1997: 3), he put this in rather colourful language in the preface to his first travel guide, *The Game is Afoot!* (1983). He explained that his aim was 'to put the Canon to the acid test – to return to the original source' (Hammer 1983: 7). Hammer's original source was England itself:

> I was convinced from the number of sites near his Norwood home that Doyle had seen places on his constant walks and related his already developed story ideas to them. I believe also that the sites themselves sometimes created the stories, and certainly they always influenced them.
>
> (Hammer 2001: 10)

Later, in *The Worth of the Game*, he justified including Doyle's childhood neighbourhood around Picardy Place in Edinburgh in his guide by reasoning that, 'Whether one chooses to regard Dr. Doyle as the father of Mr. Holmes or his literary *accoucheur*, he was necessarily author or agent, and in either capacity his antecedents and environment are well worth the enquiry' (Hammer 1993: 6).

On the surface, Hammer's justifications for including Doyle's homes and haunts in his work were aimed at his fellow Sherlockians, who leaned more toward the idea 'that Sherlock Holmes really existed and that Conan Doyle never existed' (Saler 2012: 106) – or at least that one did not need to recognise Doyle as his creator to write about Holmes as a living man. Yet, Hammer's insistence on including Doyle also suggests that he is practising what Andrea Zemgulys has called 'association'. As she explains it, in relation to nineteenth-century literary tourism:

> factual and fictional worlds coincided loosely, through expansive speculation rather than precise labeling. Associations made almost any landscape relevant to the memory of a writer; they encompassed . . . sites just reminiscent of fictional settings, sites simply curious and interesting to those who wished to know more.
>
> (Zemgulys 2008: 23)

Yet, it is important to note that although Hammer apparently began his quest with an image of places associated with Doyle – those country lanes along which the author would walk and think – his end point is rather different. In his published travel guide, Hammer uses association to gather together sites from Doyle's life and from his stories under the heading of 'the English haunts of *Mr. Holmes*' (Hammer 1993: xi, emphasis added). In doing so, Hammer blurs the line distinguishing places of authorial inspiration from places of narrative importance. In *A Deep Game*, his London-specific travel book, Hammer includes the former offices of *The Strand Magazine* among his list of Holmesian sites around Trafalgar Square. It was here, he tells his readers, that 'two neat holographic manuscripts . . . were submitted by an unknown writer, a Dr. A.C. Doyle of

2 Upper Wimpole Street' (Hammer 2002: 15). The overlap between his discussions of Doyle's writing career with his mapping of places central to *Holmes's* life means that Hammer's Holmesian and Doylean geographies are collected together; the places of Doyle's life become as important a part of Holmes's England as are the locations of the story.

Hammer's travels are not simply devoted to marking literary sites on a pre-existing map: they indicate that tourism is the agent by which Sherlock Holmes's England is itself created. This act of creation depends on possession as well as discovery. For instance, In *The Worth of the Game* (1993) Hammer visits Doyle's school at Stonyhurst. Hammer reserves perhaps his greatest excitement, and some of his most descriptive language, for this visit. He confesses that 'I had long wished to see Stonyhurst because so much of Doyle remained there' (Hammer 1993: 27). His visit to the place where 'the boy Doyle became the man Doyle' (ibid.: 25) brings out the Romantic in Hammer. 'We followed for a time the course of the River Ribble', he writes, 'on its eager way to the Irish Sea, and were intrigued by the road signs for the Trough of Bowland, just to the north. The area around Stonyhurst was summer-verdant in the river valley, with the forest foliage lush and luxuriant' (ibid.: 28).

We can understand Hammer's visit to Stonyhurst as an act of possession in the name of creating literary heritage in two ways. First, following Lennard Davis, Hammer's Romantic descriptions of his journey to Stonyhurst can be understood as more than the result of artistic rapture. Davis argues that the representation of places through linguistic description has long been a tool for asserting possession of those places. In an artful piece of metaphor, he likens the role of linguistic description of represented spaces to Robinson Crusoe's practice of 'describing' his living space by drawing a line around it; by 'describing' his space, Crusoe claims it for his own. In much the same way, says Davis, 'the refashioning of the terrain through language and extended description is a development in political [or, in this case, sociocultural] control' (Davis 1987: 73).

Secondly, it reflects many literary tourists' curiously possessive attitude towards authors' homes and haunts, which scholars of literary tourism and literary heritage have identified. (Trubek (2010) calls it an 'irrational allure'.) Hammer's desire to see the place where 'the man Doyle' – the author of Hammer's beloved stories – was made is an act of what Zemuglys calls 'finding the person in the place' which, she argues, 'made creation legible and understandable, and made authority approachable and life-sized' (Zemuglys 2008: 47). It was Hammer's cultural forebears, curious readers who, in late nineteenth-century America, during the 'interim between the occupation of this first [American] generation of literary houses by their authors and their establishment as museums' began to engage in 'surveying all their spaces and contents, and probing the details of the private lives once contained therein' (Hazard 2006: 27). Hammer's visit to Stonyhurst repeats these early acts of probing and surveying, transforming the school from a living educational establishment into an artefact of the past, a 'relic of time' (Lowenthal 1998: xv), ripe for being bent to Hammer's purpose of creating Sherlock Holmes's England as a *Sherlockian* tourist destination.

At The Chequers: scenes of reading

The second element in Hammer's heterarchical collection of time-relics that contribute to his creation of Holmes's England is his own memories of what Zemgulys calls 'scene[s] of reading' (Zemgulys 2008: 45). These scenes of reading are important to Hammer's creation of England as a site of *Sherlockian* heritage because they locate the meanings of literary places in readers' acts of literary creativity as much as in authors' lives; that is to say, these places belong in the England of Sherlock Holmes because they are a part of David Hammer's life as a Sherlockian reader.

The practice of locating literature in place, is 'the enactment of the return to the "original" scene not just of creation but of *reading*' (Zemgulys 2008: 19, emphasis in original). For Zemuglys, as for Watson before her (Watson 2006), this foundational act of literary heritage involves an attempt to gain a greater connection or sense of intimacy with the author (see also Wells 2012). Notably, these attempts at gaining emotional connections with authors depend on recognising readerly agency:

> literary geography fantasizes a personal relation to the author by catering to a sense of readerly gratification, of knowing and closeness. It also fantasizes such a relation by creating a sense of readerly definition, by representing the reader as a self, as a person grounded in his or her own experiential past.
>
> (Zemuglys 2008: 57)

If 'the visit to writer's places [was] a recollective act performed by the reader *of* the reading' (Zemuglys 2008: 57, emphasis in original), then Hammer's inclusion of his visit to The Chequers public house in *The Worth of the Game* (1993) recognises the role of Sherlockian readers' encounters with fiction in the making of this literary heritage.

His visit to this pub in Oxford – at which, supposedly, Holmes and Watson stayed in 'The Adventure of the Creeping Man' (2009) – owes as much to his own memories of drinking there as a student as it does to his reading of the Sherlock Holmes stories. He notes that this story was set in 'Camford', an amalgam of Cambridge and Oxford, and that the usual Sherlockian basis for deciding which town is really Camford 'falls along lines of loyalty – alumni loyalty' (Hammer 1993: 50). Thus, by drawing on his reading of 'The Adventure of the Creeping Man', and equally on his university experience, Hammer creates an association, of the kind Zemuglys discusses, between a place from his own life and Sherlock Holmes's England. With this association, Hammer implies the equal importance of readers and authors as sources of this particular literary heritage.

Whereas Hammer's representation of The Chequers as a scene of reading arguably establishes a personal relationship between himself and Holmes, it also represents an image of Hammer as a reader who is 'grounded in his or her experiential past' (Zemuglys 2008: 57). This is because his discussion of The Chequers is led not by the similarities between the textual description of the Camford pub and the establishment Hammer finds himself in (as he does elsewhere, see Hammer 1997); rather, it is led by his own recollections of the pub over time, beginning by admitting that 'when in Oxford in the late 1960s, I learned of The Chequers, erroneously believing that it was the Oxford inn where Shakespeare regularly stayed enroute [sic] to Stratford on Avon' (Hammer 1993: 50). Hammer devotes another page and a half to this story, telling of his enquiries with the local council and the pub's owner, and his eventual discovery that the pub was first recorded in 1681 – too late for Shakespeare to have drunk there. In the middle of this story about his personal connection to the pub over the years, Hammer inserts a fleeting reference to Sherlock Holmes – at the end of a sentence about the Shakespeare mystery: 'there the matter [of the Shakespeare connection] stood until 1979 when I made the connection with Sherlock Holmes' (ibid.: 51).

Hammer's writing further presents himself grounded in his experience as an active participant in making, rather than simply recognising, Holmes's England. He devotes the majority of the chapter to his own visits to the pub, past and present, and, like his visit to Stonyhurst, Hammer's return visit to The Chequers is made in a spirit of possessing the space once occupied by, in this case, 'a figure of heritage' (Hammer 2001: 10). On page 52, Hammer lists five lines from 'The Adventure of the Creeping Man' which mention The Chequers; two of these refer to eating or drinking in the pub. It is no coincidence, then, that Hammer's chief means of experiencing the pub is to eat and drink there:

> Audrey and I dined well on pub-plus food, a bit above the ordinary pub fare, and we learned that the establishment no longer proffered rooms to travellers. May today's travellers dare hope that the decision did not result from an earlier transient's pock-marking a rented wall with a patriotic VR? No, strike that, it was 1903 so would have had to have been a patriotic ER.
>
> (Hammer 1993: 56)

With these closing remarks – relocating a ballistic act from 'The Adventure of the Musgrave Ritual' (2009) into a setting from 'The Adventure of the Creeping Man' – Hammer affirms the central place of his own creative engagement with the Sherlock Holmes stories in the making of Holmes's England.

By drawing this textual image of himself and his wife dining in The Chequers, Hammer seeks at once to gain a greater sense of intimacy with Sherlock Holmes and to put himself on an equal creative footing with Doyle. If, as Zemgulys argues, the inn, tavern or drinking house was a popular site of literary tourism and ripe for possession as literary heritage, because 'it had been favoured by the (conversing, observing) writer and offered a glimpse of the working writer at rest' (Zemgulys 2008: 21; see also Watson 2009), then in this scene there is a type of ghostly reflection at work. Hammer raises the spectre of Holmes 'at rest', firing bullets into the wall from his sofa, while depicting himself, as the author of this account of Holmes's England, at rest in that quintessentially authorial haunt, the pub.

Their own special visions: other readers

The third and final part of this heterarchical collection of elements which inform Hammer's literary tourism – and the part which best identifies Hammer's project as the creation of literary *heritage* ripe for touristic exploration– is the presence of other readers in Hammer's writings. In his memoir, Hammer wrote that the decision to bring other Sherlockian readers along for the journey had been a deliberate one. He explained that his first publisher, Jack Tracy:

> convinced me that the manuscript [of *The Game is Afoot!*] needed to show how the sites were located, adding personal details of the search to make it more interesting. What I had regarded as hubris he saw as engaging detail, making the reader a fellow passenger on the search.
>
> (Hammer 2001: 13)

Later, in *The Worth of the Game* (1993) Hammer indicated that what had begun as an act to engage his readers more fully had come to define his approach to the making of Holmes's England as a place of Sherlockian heritage. 'Just as the poets their special visions possess', he wrote, 'so do we Sherlockians each hold in secret possession our own private view of the immediate world of the doctor and the detective' (Hammer 1993: xiii). Knowledge that each Sherlockian possesses their own idea of Sherlock Holmes's world precluded Hammer from offering his own travels as a definitive guide to the places therein. Instead, he wrote that: while Sherlockians 'each invoke our own visions, the little book which follows is intended to buttress your particular dream' (ibid.: xiv).

The idea that Sherlock Holmes's England is made from the 'own particular dreams' of every American Sherlockian (or, rather, every reader of Hammer's books) might at first seem at odds with the idea of heritage as an authorised or controlling narrative of the past. After all, as Hammer's excursion to The Chequers suggests, many of these particular dreams of Holmes's England are plausibly based in readers' own recollections of reading – of their encounters with the Sherlock Holmes stories in particular places and times. And memory and heritage are arguably poles apart. 'Memory is defined by scholars', writes Zemgulys, 'as . . . pointedly distinct from representations of the past such as heritage' (Zemgulys 2008: 69). She defines heritage as 'regulating, institutional, totalizing, closed' and memory as '"unruly", subjective, open and fragmentary', arguing that they 'would not seem to belong on the same page' (ibid.).

Yet, I would suggest that there are two ways to think about Hammer's inclusion of other readers as the key to understanding his creation of the England of Sherlock Holmes as a project to create a literary heritage. The first is to accept literary heritage as a form of 'collective memory':

> Literary heritage, with its memorials and museums, patently represents a project of memory: it constructs the past as accessible in the present, one moreover continuous and grounding. Its tourists, further, bring the past into

active relation with the present . . . The celebration of national writers and transnational readers further allow us to understand literary heritage as a project of 'collective memory'.

(Zemgulys 2008: 69)

Notwithstanding their attempts to immortalise a *fictional* character, Hammer's travel guides, with their emphasis on discovering the specific locations for events in Holmes's life (including the locations of his creation), arguably represent a form of memorialisation; moreover, one produced for a specific group of people, the Sherlockians who form Hammer's core audience. Furthermore, Hammer's responses to Holmes-associated locations such as The Chequers, imagining the spectral figure of Holmes performing well-known actions in some other room, reflect the thoughts of many literary tourists in the museum-homes of famous authors: it is the feeling that 'the writer might at any point re-enter' the room (Robinson and Andersen 2002: 19).

Hammer's promise that his travel guides are 'intended to *buttress* your particular dream' (Hammer 1993: xiv, emphasis added) indicates his awareness that collective memory needs a focal point around which to coalesce. Indeed, Zemgulys argues that 'Understanding literary heritage as collective memory explains how its appeal to private and individual recollection is both energizing and destabilizing of community' (Zemgulys 2008: 69). Hammer's travel guides may be seen as textual equivalents of statues or museum-houses: sites which provide a starting point over which individuals can lay their own recollections and places where memory becomes heritage through the power of community.

The second means of understanding the presence of other readers as a vital element in turning literary tourism into the creation of literary heritage becomes apparent with a reconsideration of David Lowenthal's argument that heritage 'clarifies pasts so as to infuse them with present purposes' (Lowenthal 1998: xv). For David Hammer, as a Sherlockian, the present purpose with which the (newly created) past of Sherlock Holmes's England is infused is the expansionary literary geography (the practice of creatively expanding on the literary spaces of Holmes's world through adding their own stories and adventures, often made through tourism) that characterises much of Sherlockiana. By making his readers 'fellow passengers' in his search for the locations of Sherlock Holmes's England, Hammer refrains from presenting each site as a given and, rather, focuses on the embodied, mobile *process* of locating these Holmesian places. The following passage, relating to the quest for the eponymous Wisteria Lodge, is typical:

If Watson's description of the Esher-to-Wisteria Lodge walk that raw March evening is substantially accurate, the Lodge is not too far distant from the Heath Road. The villa has historically been placed in the region between Esher Common and Oxshott Heath . . . Despite a careful scrutiny and a retracing of the route more than once, we found no dwellings along the road which had either the antiquity or the style of the original Wisteria Lodge.

(Hammer 1983: 111)

By focusing on the process of finding the sites such as the Wisteria Lodge, Hammer creates a new image of a set of past events – the creation of the literary spaces of Holmes's world by Arthur Conan Doyle in his texts. This new image is permeated with a present purpose: to represent the literary spaces of Sherlock Holmes as ever-under-construction, always being shaped by the activities and imaginations of Sherlockian readers. Hammer's guides simulate his experience for readers and encourage others to do what he did, to use tourism as a means of creating and possessing the England of Sherlock Holmes as a heritage site and to regard that heritage site as an invitation to future tourism.

Conclusion

In *The Heritage Crusade and the Spoils of History* (1998), David Lowenthal reminds us that:

> Fiction is thus not the opposite of fact but its complement, giving our lives a more lasting shape . . . That myths are batty and irrational does not spoil their worth. Camelot and the Grail lack historical credibility but convey psychological authority . . . these rooted mythologies lend cosmic meaning to our own lifetime quests.
>
> (Lowenthal 1998: 146)

With this idea in mind, and a recognition of the power of '"true" lies' (Lowenthal 1998: 146), Hammer's description of Sherlock Holmes as not so much a figure of history as one of heritage – 'which surely constitutes a significant form of reality' (Hammer 2001: 10) – comes into greater focus.

In this chapter I have read Hammer's tourist guides, written just before the dawn of the twenty-first century, as seriously shaped by his belief that Sherlock Holmes has become a figure of heritage for Sherlockians. I have demonstrated how Hammer's embodied travels help give these 'true lies' about Holmes and Watson and their half-real lives a material place in the world. By following the practices of literary heritage creation, as identified by Zemgulys, his guides created Sherlock Holmes's England as a place of Sherlockian literary heritage; they emphasise the creative agency of Arthur Conan Doyle, but also importantly of readers, in shaping the 'true lie' of an England of, or belonging to, Sherlock Holmes the fictional character.

Further, in their appeal to other readers' special visions and private views of this place, they reveal the sociocultural *purpose* of Hammer's use of the relics of the past in this way. They are enticements to, and guides for, readers to do those practices which will put their own pasts and experiences on the same register as those of Doyle and of Holmes himself; to justify the Sherlockian group practices of expanding on Holmes's world, of creating new stories and new places in which the Great Detective can live on forever.

By writing *tourist guides*, rather than a descriptive monograph or a series of articles, Hammer further emphasises the importance of Sherlockian tourists' visits to these sites of their literary heritage – as an act of commemoration but also, vitally, as an act of creation, one which will make anew Sherlock Holmes's England as a destination for literary tourists for as long as there are tourists willing to make it so.

References

Alexander, A. (1984) *On the Scent: A Visitor's Guide to Sherlock Holmes's London*. Seal Beach, CA: The Bullpup Press.

Alexander, A. (1999) *Hot on the Scent: A Visitor's Guide to Sherlock Holmes's London*. Ashcroft, BC: Calabash Press.

Bulson, E. (2007) *Novels, Maps, Modernity: The Spatial Imagination, 1850–2000*. London: Routledge.

Christopher, J. (2012) *The London of Sherlock Holmes*. Stroud: Amberley Publishing.

Davis, L. (1987) *Resisting Novels: Ideology and Fiction*. London: Methuen.

Doyle, A.C. (2009) *The Penguin Complete Sherlock Holmes*. London: Penguin.

Hammer, D. (1983) *The Game is Afoot: A Travel Guide to the England of Sherlock Holmes*. Bloomington, IN: Gaslight Publications.

Hammer, D. (1986) *For the Sake of the Game: Being a Further Travel Guide to the England of Sherlock Holmes*. Indianapolis, IN: Wessex Press.

Hammer, D. (1993) *The Worth of the Game: Being a Final Travel Guide to the England of Sherlock Holmes*. Bloomington, IN: Gaslight Publications.

Hammer, D. (1997) *A Dangerous Game: Being a Travel Guide to the Europe of Sherlock Holmes*. Dubuque, IN: Gasogene Press.

Hammer, D. (2001) *The Game is Underfoot!: The Memoir of a Sherlockian Publisher*. Shelbure, ON: The Battered Silicon Despatch Box.

Hammer, D. (2002) *A Deep Game: The Traveler's Companion to the London of Sherlock Holmes*. Indianapolis, IN: Gasogene Books.

Harrison, R. (2010) What is Heritage? in Harrison, R. (ed.) *Understanding the Politics of Heritage*. Manchester: Manchester University Press, pp. 5–42.

Hazard, E. (2006) 'A realized day-dream': excursions to nineteenth-century authors' homes. *Nineteenth Century Studies*, 20(1): 13–33.

Hendrix, H. (2008) *Writers' Houses and the Making of Memory*. London: Routledge.

James, K.J. (2013) Literary tourism, the Trossachs and Walter Scott. *Journal of Tourism History*, 5(1): 93–96.

Lowenthal, D. (1998) *The Heritage Crusade and the Spoils of History*. Cambridge: Cambridge University Press.

McLaughlin, D. (2016) The game's afoot: walking as practice in Sherlockian literary geographies. *Literary Geographies*, 2(2): 144–163.

McLaughlin, D. (2017) Mobile Holmes: Sherlockiana, travel writing and the co-production of the Sherlock Holmes stories. Unpublished PhD thesis, University of Cambridge.

Plate, L. (2006) Walking in Virginia Woolf's footsteps. *European Journal of Cultural Studies*, 9(1): 101–120.

Reijnders, S. (2009). Watching the detectives: inside the guilty landscapes of Inspector Morse, Baantjer and Wallander. *European Journal of Communication*, 24(2): 165–181.

Reijnders, S. (2011) Stalking the Count: Dracula, fandom and tourism. *Annals of Tourism Research*, 38(1): 231–248.

Reijnders, S. (2013) *Places of the Imagination: Media, Tourism, Culture*. London: Ashgate.

Robinson, M. and Andersen, H. (eds.) (2002) *Literature and Tourism: Reading and Writing Tourism Texts*. London: Continuum.

Saler, M. (2012) *As If: Modern Enchantment and the Literary Prehistory of Virtual Reality*. Oxford: Oxford University Press.

Sudin, G. (1985) *Sherlock's London Today: A Walking Tour of the London of Sherlock Holmes*. Des Plaines, IL: Sherlock's Bookshop.

Trubek, A. (2010) The Irrational Allure of Writers' Houses. *The Chronicle of Higher Education*, Available at: http://search.proquest.com/docview/816274065/abstract/614B461B7D604B06PQ/1 [accessed August 2 2016].

Van Es, N. and Reijnders, S. (2016) Making sense of capital crime cities: Getting underneath the urban façade on crime-detective fiction tours. *European Journal of Cultural Studies* (online): 1–19.

Watson, N. (2006) *The Literary Tourist: Readers and Places in Romantic and Victorian Britain*. Basingstoke: Palgrave Macmillan.

Watson, N. (2009) *Literary Tourism and Nineteenth-Century Culture*. London: Palgrave Macmillan.

Wells, J. (2012) *Everybody's Jane: Austen in the Popular Imagination*. London: A&C Black.

Westover, P. (2012) Inventing the London of literary tourists: walking the romantic city in Leigh Hunt's 'Wishing-Cap' essays. *European Romantic Review*, 23(1): 1–19.

Zemgulys, A. (2008) *Modernism and the Locations of Literary Heritage*. Cambridge: Cambridge University Press.

9 Creating heritage for tourism

'Consuming history,' 'prosthetic memories' and the popularisation of a folk hero's story

Michael Fagence

Introduction

> We need landmarks, icons and local stories to identify the places we live in and visit. We want to retain collective memories of the past because they tell the story of a place and the habitat of many previous generations and construct our identities.
>
> (Jansen-Verbeke 2016: 279)

Myriam Jansen-Verbeke's comment sets the scene for what is considered in this chapter. Her comment identifies a need, and then offers reasons for meeting that need. This chapter follows a similar form. Formally, and unquestioningly, it accepts the need to 'create heritage for tourism' and especially in the forms listed by Jansen-Verbeke: landmarks, icons, and local stories. It then proceeds to negotiate a pathway to reveal what the 'story of a place' may be, and what the 'collective memories of the past' at that place may be. This sets history-linked and heritage-based tourism into a role in popularising history, and in a position to make a serious contribution to 'consuming history' (De Groot 2009, 2015). In doing this it is faced with the challenge of creating 'prosthetic memories'; this is because the lapse of time between the historic event and the present is likely to frustrate any attempt through tourism to achieve anything other than an imagined past. As with most other forms of historic and heritage re-construction and substitution, tourism has to engage with challenges about accuracy and authenticity, and although that is a serious matter, it is not addressed here. There are carefully crafted and accessible published sources which have done that so well (see, for example, Smith 2006).

The principal and general focus of this chapter is to consider the content and process of creating heritage for tourism. As a second focal point, attention is directed to the potential contribution which may be made by heritage-based tourism to 'consuming history' as the stories from history become mediated and commoditised (Gyimothy et al. 2015). A third important focal point takes aim at exploring evidence of 'prosthetic memory-making'. These points are then used to underpin the focus of a selected case study, as it is probed speculatively to expose both the nature and the content of the task of creating heritage for tourism.

Tourism's capacity to meet many of the challenges faced in communicating matters concerned with past periods rests on its ability to tell stories and to provide experiences by drawing into its net of communication both tangible and intangible items, and then moulding them into products that can be delivered to groups of consumers who may not even share the same level of interest in the subject matter. The scales of these challenges are enormous. Lowenthal (1996: xi), for example, has claimed that 'all at once heritage is everywhere . . . the chief focus of patriotism and a prime lure for tourism. One can barely move without bumping into a heritage site'. Prentice (2003) supports this with his references to the heterogeneity of heritage-tourism attractions, while Jordanova (2006: 132) has explained that the huge appetite for the past 'is met by displays of 'history' and by ways of approaching the past that are not narrowly academic, but more akin to tourism'. Even before these observations, Sobchack (1996) and Rosenstone (1995) had already canvassed the breadth and depth of public interest in the presentation of stories from history, expressing views that popular audiences considered themselves to be not only spectators of history, but also participants in and adjudicators of it.

Tourism would seem to be ideally placed to meet the challenges of communicating the experiences of history, and to contributing to the making of 'prosthetic memories' (Landsberg 2004). Ideas for constructing an operational comfort zone for such memories would flow easily from, for example, Jansen-Verbeke's (1998) pioneering study on the 'tourismification' of historic districts, Cartier's (2005) functional interpretations of 'touristed landscapes', Garden's (2009) tool for 'heritagescape' assessments, Gunn's (1997) diversity of spatial models, and many of the commentaries about tourism micro-clusters (Jackson and Murphy 2002). There is a definite pathway here that links these various considerations of creating heritage for tourism with the earlier and pioneering efforts of Meinig (1979) and others at 'seeing, reading, interpreting and making sense of cultural landscapes'.

To help unravel the intricacies and nuances being faced, the story of the nineteenth-century Australian bushranger Edward (Ned) Kelly is used here as a case study. The intentions are to 'tease out' a pool of evidence which can be fitted to 'creating heritage for tourism', to marshal that evidence to meet the purposes of 'consuming history' and creating 'prosthetic memories', and to speculate how that evidence can be spatially configured as an 'emblematic landscape'.

Creating heritage for tourism

There is a rich vein of literature which considers the confluence of heritage with tourism, and some of it has attention-seeking subtitles referring to, for example, 'usable pasts', 'engaging the past', 'encounters with popular pasts', and 'history which is being used'. Many of the published papers and chapters have been written from privileged disciplinary positions in archaeology, architecture, geography, history, sociology, and increasingly from nuanced positions in the study of landscape, and from cultural and film studies, caught up in the cultural 'turn' which has influenced studies in the humanities and social sciences, and where the focus has been on signs, symbols and sites in emblematic landscapes. One conspicuous element of this has been a process that has included, for example, recovery, re-construction, re-animation, re-contextualisation, re-configuration, and re-presentation; this has been referred to in some sources as 'heritagisation'. From the pool of speculation about these matters two issues are given brief consideration here.

One of these issues has been manifested as a readily identifiable product: a popular history boom. In this boom, 'new' audiences are encountering matters and 'things' of history through a diversity of expressions of popular culture, including tourism (De Groot 2009). What is encountered by the public (whether through films, novels, plays, folktales or even in the open air through staged re-enactments) is 'created history'; and it becomes a heritage product as it is taken from a bank of evidence (resources), and then mediated, commoditised and transmitted to match the search for particular experiences by the various categories of popular audience (Pearce 1998; Sobchack 1996). One commentator has even speculated that tourism has become a creative arena itself by placing its own stamp on how stories from history can be told (Richards 2011). The circumstances underpinning much of the selection process – which stories to tell and how to tell them – resonate well with Urry's (1992) insistence that if resources are to attract the attention of tourism they must be 'distinctive', with specific identity, significance, and symbolism, and with an emblematic and particular landscape and setting.

The second issue is the spatial and networking implications of the growth of history-linked and heritage-based tourism. Although conventional linear, nodal and district configurations seem to suit the spatial needs of industry and commerce, Jackson and Murphy (2002) favour the adoption of a cluster form to meet the types of linkages commonly experienced with tourism-related activity. It was their judgement that a nuanced cluster form would be most suited to exploiting the distinctiveness of local heritage and sense of place, functioning in a similar way to the use of that form with the development of creative and cluster industries. This is shown in the loosely-formed nodal-cum-cluster structure for the study area depicted in Figure 9.3. That Figure has been constructed by applying to the 'natural' distribution of places in the Kelly corridor the principles of Pearce's (2014) tripartite cluster formation, and by responding to the primacy of distinctiveness championed by Urry (1992).

Study methods

The approach to this study has followed the conventional pathway of heuristic research. Using this loose and adaptive approach, the constant intention has been to better understand 'heritage' and 'heritage-tourism', and to do that by responding to the challenge posed by Jamal and Kim (2005: 56) to develop 'a well-theorised integrated framework showing the complexity, dynamism, scale and scope of doing a research study related to heritage and tourism', and by working with a framework which has the capacity 'to better tease out . . . the ways in which tourist sites are artfully constructed' (Knudsen et al. 2008: 1).

The case study in this chapter has drawn on a bank of evidence which started with a baseline study in 2007. The pool of information has been regularly

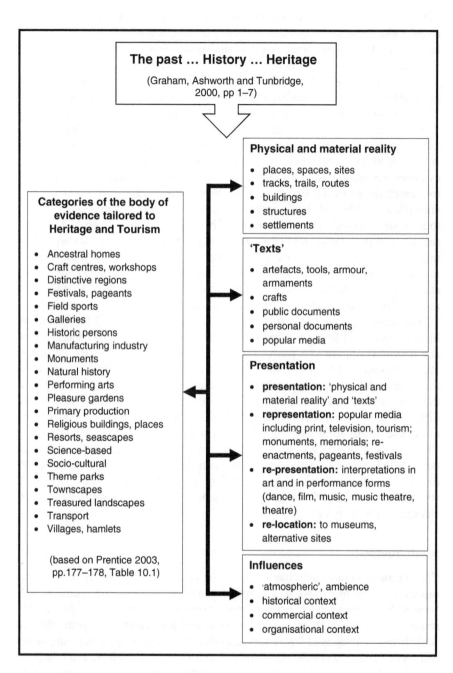

Figure 9.1 Principal categories of evidence

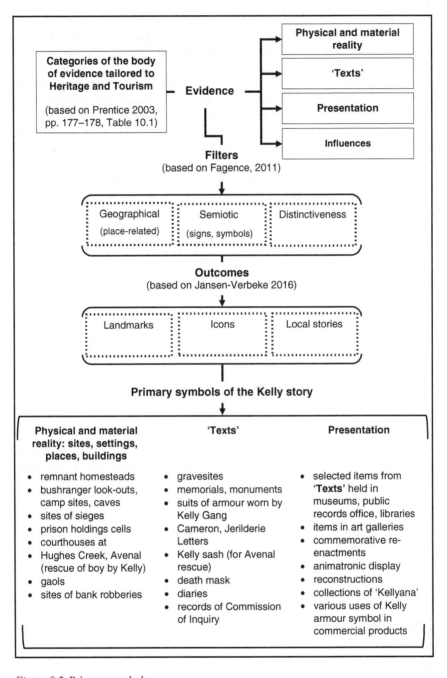

Figure 9.2 Primary symbols

augmented, revised, updated, improved, reclassified and re-interpreted, while staying within a previously set and narrowly defined corridor of disciplinary comfort (Fagence 2011). Elements of this bank of evidence are assembled to meet the special challenges of each project, and a specially focused selection has been made from the bank of evidence to suit the peculiarities of this study. For the current study, the information to be used was marshalled into four groups: physical and material reality, 'texts', presentation, and influences (see Figure 9.1). To increase the usefulness of the evidence for the purpose of this study, selected portions of it were 'passed through' a number of discipline-linked filters (as described below). The next step in the process was to align the accumulated and interpreted evidence with Jansen-Verbeke's (2016) categories of landmarks, icons and local stories, and then to reconfigure that preliminary sorting into a tentative list of the primary symbols of the Kelly story (Figure 9.2).

A combination of three investigative and interpretive approaches (or filters) has been used here. Of these, one has come from the disciplinary approach of 'thinking geographically' (Hubbard et al. 2002, Shurmer-Smith 2002) and a second from the 'the gaze' component of Peircean semiotics (Pearson and Warburton 2005, Waterton and Watson 2014). To this framework of epistemological pluralism was added the advocacy of Urry (1992) that 'distinctiveness' is a desirable characteristic. His claims are that 'it is the distinctiveness of the visual that gives to all sorts of activities a special or unique character' (ibid.: 172), and that 'there has to be something distinctive to be gazed upon . . . the signs collected by tourists have to be visually extraordinary' (ibid.: 173). There can be a reasonable claim that what has been done in this study follows on from the intellectual legacy of the pioneering studies on creating cultural landscapes (see Meinig 1979).

The heritage 'touristed' landscape of the Ned Kelly story

As Pearce et al. (2003) have commented, it is rare for studies of folk heroes and others who fit awkwardly into that description (Seal 1996) to attract much attention in the process of tourism attraction building. Ned Kelly is almost an exceptional case, although, with his chequered history of confrontation and his involvement in criminal activity, there is a degree of dissonance that engulfs his story and this has tended to impede its full potential being realised. Despite the difficulties which are faced with the communication of the Kelly story through various expressions of popular culture, and especially tourism, public interest in the story has been instrumental in successfully sustaining some elements of the story as centrepieces of popular culture presentations. Many opportunities have been taken to seize the maxim that once 'the hero' is dead the stories are malleable and can be fitted to any form of presentation.

The Ned Kelly story

There are really two Ned Kelly stories and they were acted out in parallel through the 25 years of his life (1855–1880). One of the stories is a good fit with the common accounts of an Australian family's responses to the cultural, economic, environmental, political and social challenges which were faced in rural Victoria during the final years of the nineteenth century. Such were those challenges that it was certainly not a 'good' time to be rural, to have Irish and convict ancestry or sympathies, to be land-less, to have few skills, to be poor, to have a tense relationship with government officials (especially the police and the judiciary), or to be linked with family or district-based 'clans' or gangs. These were all characteristics of the Ned Kelly family, and they were not distinctive to that family.

A second, and parallel, story formed around a set of drama-filled events that spanned the short period 1878 to 1880. Those events were set in a period already economically, politically and socially inflamed by the Eureka rebellion of 1854, which took place on the goldfields in another part of Victoria. Some commentaries claim that the stories of the Eureka and Kelly-related events only have a high profile because Australian history generally lacks the rebellions and popular heroes of the histories of some other countries. Even if this is so, it is the drama-filled final years of Ned Kelly's life, sometimes referred to as 'the Kelly Outbreak' (McQuilton 1979), which contribute to the high profile of the Kelly story and which are the foundation stones of the story's potential for tourism.

In a period marked by constant bushranging and outlaw-like activities, and high levels of tension between Kelly family members and the powerful forces of the police, local government and the judiciary, there was a simmering high probability of drama-fuelled events. A brief inventory of these events includes the legal declaration of the Kelly Gang as outlaws, two bank robberies, a siege and gunfight at a rural campsite at which three policemen were killed, a second siege (at the township of Glenrowan, conventionally now referred to as the Kelly Gang's 'last stand'), the murder of a suspected police informer, an attempt to derail a train, the preparation of two quasi-political manifestos outlining rural grievances, the formation of a 'shadowy' group of sympathisers, and finally the capture, arrest, trial, imprisonment, and execution of Ned Kelly. It is this period that makes the Kelly story distinctive and, in summarising the situation, Seal (1996: 145) suggests that the Ned Kelly story is 'a compelling example of the potency of the outlaw hero tradition . . . [and that Kelly is now] the closest thing Australia has to a national hero'. It was this phase (1878–1880) which underpins the distinctiveness of the Kelly story, and it is from this short period (with few exceptions) that the symbols may be drawn to match with Jansen-Verbeke's (2016) formula of landmarks, icons and local stories. The outcome of this exercise is depicted in Figures 9.1 and 9.2.

Symbols of the Kelly story: the tangible evidence

A significant advantage to the investigation and interpretation of the Ned Kelly story is its substantial factual basis. Much of the evidence of the events has been captured by photographs, by concurrent news reports, by proceedings of Commissions of Inquiry, by court transcripts, and by diary notations, and these materials have been supported by the discovery of distinctive artefacts. The story worked its way into history from happenings in a readily identifiable rural area of north-east Victoria, approximating to a corridor measuring 300 km in length by 100 km in width, hemmed in by a periphery of hill ranges, with the internal plain punctuated by a number of river systems, and traversed by the major Sydney to Melbourne road corridor (Figure 9.3). It has always been a distinctively rural area with a short history of mining activity accompanied by population immigration during the period of the gold rush (1850s–1860s). That temporary gold rush urban network survives mainly with remnant forms (as in Woolshed Valley). The stories of the Kelly corridor have been based on some of the previously-mentioned listed accurate sources, and on embellishments and augmentations through folk-tales, doggerels, legends and myths. It is the mixture of these sources that has been captured in Figures 9.1 and 9.2, firstly in the categories of physical and material evidence, and 'texts', secondly in the presentations, re-presentations, re-presentations and re-locations of materials and records, and thirdly in what can be referred to as the influences on and 'atmospherics' of the story, the places, the events and the people. The Kelly story has a rich repertoire of evidence, which fits well into what has been described elsewhere as an 'emblematic landscape'.

An extensive interpretive commentary on the evidence of symbols of the Kelly story is impossible here due to lack of space. Instead, brief commentaries (of up to three dot points of evidence for each nodal point – place, site, township – which experienced some impact from the Kelly story) is recorded in Figure 9.3. Thirteen nodal points or clusters have been identified. Of these, two – Beechworth with Woolshed Valley, and Melbourne – are used here for particularly-focused commentaries.

One of the 'thickest' concentrations of physical and material evidence in the Kelly corridor is to be found in the two 'nodes' which form a loose cluster composed of the township of Beechworth with the adjacent area of Woolshed Valley. Beechworth has a definable heritage precinct, which includes buildings associated with the peak activity of gold mining in the districts around Beechworth; these include the telegraph station, the former gold warden's office, and the Chinese Protector's office. However, its particular distinctiveness is drawn from the buildings and spaces with close links to the Kelly story. Among the most prominent of these are the courthouse used for the committal trial of Kelly, the stone lock-up cells, the police paddocks and stables, and the former sub-treasury building (now used as a museum – the Ned Kelly Vault). Adjacent to this precinct are public and commercial buildings (Post Office, Bank of New South Wales, Bank of Victoria, Oriental Bank), the former Shire Hall, and a number of hostelries, many of which have changed little since the Kelly period. The recently decommissioned gaol is one of the gateway markers to the precinct. Close to the precinct, but not contiguous with it, are the former premises of the photographer responsible for recording many of the Kelly incidents and court appearances, the house of the magistrate who issued the remands for the arrest of Kelly sympathisers, and the offices of the law firm which provided the defence counsel for the Kelly family. From the stock of the built environment, it is the courthouse where the committal trial of Ned Kelly was held before his transfer to Melbourne that forms the focal point of

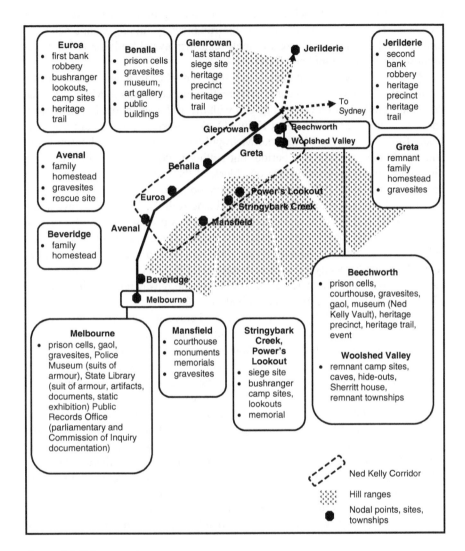

Figure 9.3 Primary nodes

tourism attraction. Although now decommissioned as a district court, the interior has been preserved and is used as the centrepiece for the trial re-enactment which is held during the annual Ned Kelly weekend (usually in August).

In the adjoining Woolshed Valley, a number of temporary gold rush townships were created in the decades of the 1850s and 1860s (Eldorado, Napoleon Flat, Sebastopol Flat, Woolshed), but most of the remaining evidence is only remnant. The principal evidence in this district includes remnants of the homes of Kelly Gang member Joe Byrne (in Sebastopol) and of the police informer Aaron Sherritt (in Woolshed), the rough camp sites and caves used by the police and Kelly Gang members (for watching each other), and the meeting places of the Kelly Gang members. There are remnant sites of the rudimentary mining camps scattered throughout the valley, and there are small-scale displays of Kelly-period artefacts in museums in Sebastopol and Eldorado.

Melbourne's contribution to the Kelly story is marked by a much looser spatial configuration of physical, material and 'text' evidence. It was in Melbourne that the drama-fuelled action came to its end with the trial, conviction, imprisonment, and finally the execution of Ned Kelly (11 November 1880). The old Supreme Court Building and the Melbourne Metropolitan Prison (Old Melbourne Gaol) still stand as markers of that period, but neither building remains in use for its nineteenth-century purpose. Only one block of the original gaol remains and it has been used since 1972 as a tourism attraction and museum. In one wing of the original building one cell is marked as being Kelly's, another displays a facsimile model of his death mask, and yet another is used to display the official diary record of prisoners, their convictions and their date of execution. The original scaffolding used for the executions, once removed to another gaol, has been reinstalled. Just as Kelly's life was dogged with mystery and myth, despite its largely factual basis, the whereabouts of Kelly's body was forensically finalised and determined only in 2012. Kelly's body was formally and finally buried with other members of the Kelly family in unmarked gravesites (in Greta), but mystery still attends the whereabouts of Kelly's skull. Apart from the significance of the judicial and custodial buildings, Melbourne has almost certainly the largest collections of public history Kelly 'texts'. The collections include the Commission of Inquiry Reports, parliamentary transcripts, photographic and media evidence, the Jerilderie and Cameron letters (the so-called quasi-political manifestos of Kelly), other Kelly-authored correspondence, three of the four suits of armour worn by gang members at the Glenrowan siege, and a collection of artefacts from the excavations at Glenrowan. These items are curated variously in the State Library, the Public Records Office, and the Police Museum. Although there is no commemorative monument to mark the life and times of Ned Kelly, there are, in Melbourne General Cemetery, memorials to, and the gravesites of, the trial judge (Sir Redmund Barry), the doctor at the execution, three jurors at Kelly's trial, Kelly's legal counsel, and both the police superintendent and the commissioner in charge of the search for the Kelly Gang.

Symbols of the Kelly story: beyond the tangible evidence

The Kelly story is encircled by three strands of what may be described as intangible cultural evidence. One of these is the authentic historical context in which the story is embedded. A second is the context of controversy and dissonance that engulfs not only the story, but also the attitudes about how (or whether) the story should be told, and the responses of government and special interests to sustaining the evidence of the story. There is also a third strand, which may be described as an 'atmospheric' element, in that it draws a link between some aspects of the Kelly story and some of the ambience which has become almost a hallmark of

Australian-ness: anti-authoritarianism, egalitarianism, independence, resource-fulness, larrikinism and mateship.

Accompanying the factual evidence of the Kelly story are embellishments related to the fantasies, myths, legends and folktales which have been created around the lifestyles of the rural families, the bushrangers and the larrikins of nineteenth-century Australia, and the incendiary conflicts those sections of the community had with the agencies and agents of government, the banks, some landowners and businesses. Most commentaries report that the Kellys were expe-rienced participants in these various frictions, and it is this which contributes so much to the 'atmospherics' of the Kelly story and to the romantic linkage of the story to the rich history about outlaws, bandits, highwaymen, and popular rebel-lions. It is both the 'atmospherics' of the story, and the clear record of criminal activity, which generate the popular polarisation of attitudes towards members of the Kelly family. Some commentaries consider the Kelly Outbreak to be one of the most controversial and embellished chapters of Australian history, but it might well be this very fact that has attracted the attention of popular culture. The Kelly story, quite apart from dominating entries in bibliographies, biographies, and novels about bushranging and bushrangers, has been exposed for example:

- in eleven feature films, seven theatre dramas, a television mini-series and two stage musicals;
- in a series of signature paintings from the Australian artist Sidney Nolan (the 1946–1947 series of 27 paintings);
- as the principal or complementary focus of static and touring exhibitions across Australia;
- and adapted as symbolism in the opening ceremony of the Olympic Games in Sydney (2000), in commemorative stamps issued in Australia (1980 and 2003) and in Ireland (2001), and for roadside direction signs and road maps of what may be referred to loosely as Kelly Country.

Telling the story of Ned Kelly has a reach beyond the factual evidence of the events, and it seems to be the 'atmospherics' that give the story its special identity and that contribute significantly to binding together the various nodes and clusters of action across a dispersed rural region.

Conclusions

At the beginning of this narrative, the aim was to explore the implications of Myriam Jansen-Verbeke's assertion that 'we need landmarks, icons and local sto-ries to identify the places we live in and visit', and to do that by teasing out from a pool of evidence those items from a selected story that could contribute positively to the act of 'consuming history', to the creation of 'prosthetic memories' and to spatial ordering into an 'emblematic landscape'. Overall, the intention was to seek evidence of all of this within the scope of popular culture, and especially through history-linked and heritage-based tourism; the loose target was to speculate about 'creating heritage for tourism'. That there is an exceptionally large volume of published commentary about the history of the Australian bushranger Ned Kelly, and that there is already extensive exposure of the selected story about him in various expressions of popular culture, and that the tourism industry has already 'found' the story and is presenting it, provided a foundation of reasonable confidence that the Ned Kelly story held potential for speculations about 'creating heritage for tourism'. Negotiating the preliminary questions using the 'teasing out' process proved to be a not too difficult task. For many stories from history there are pools of evidence about events and happenings, about places and spaces, and about people as individuals and in groups. This means that film, drama, music, literature and art, as expressions of popular culture, have an almost limitless portfolio from which to draw. The case of tourism is less fortunate, not because of a restricted portfolio, but because it is faced almost simultaneously with the challenge of multiples of dimensions (including agency, familiarity, memory, space, time) and multiples of senses (sight, smell, sound, smell, taste, touch). While absorption into the scope of 'consuming history' can be achieved with ease, and the presentation as a substitute experience through 'prosthetic memory'-making may be not too troublesome, there can be a real challenge in those cases where the presentation (whether on-site or on another site, and whether as an original or substitute or copied item) has to face a simultaneous and multi-faceted combination of challenges that other expressions of popular culture are able to avoid. Additionally, of course, tourism has to face the challenge of dispersed resources. In the Ned Kelly case, the story unfolds across a rural region and a capital city, with spatial clusters of evidence which, if they are to be engaged in the process of learning about the story, present to the would-be tourist demands of cost, energy, interest, stamina, and time that are not usually included in the personal budget for encounters with other forms of popular culture.

Stories about the history of interesting characters may be told through tourism and may fit into the prospectus of 'consuming history' and popular culture with ease. However, the conversion or transposition of them is unlikely to be a routine tourism-attraction-making exercise. Even if the evidence is readily available (which would be rare), it is the marshalling of it to 'tell the story' which is the challenge. Similarly, the creation of 'prosthetic memories' is problematic if the challenge is expansive and inclusive of evidence across the spectrum of multiple dimensions and senses; for example, the 'prosthetic memory' demands of some of the 'popular audiences' listed by Sobchack (1996) would set severe challenges, especially in those stories where dissonance was rife. If the case were to be presented through drama, film or literature, the different viewpoints could be managed in private, but in tourism, the case is 'in the open', to be accepted, rejected or challenged from any viewpoint. Perhaps the most difficult of the challenges faced by tourism is in the telling of stories which are not tightly located in one place. The story becomes almost a pilgrimage, tour or expedition. Tourism development along trails with serial stopping points is one solution (Timothy and Boyd 2015), and Gunn (1997) has drafted a number of alternative regional spatial forms which may be suitable. Recent explorations with cluster forms offer other options for presenting stories that extend across regions. That the Ned Kelly story already has a presence in popular culture, and that it can attract a place in 'consuming history' by contributing 'prosthetic memories', is a measure of its historic and contemporary significance. It is also evidence which supports the contention of Pearce et al. (2003) that the stories of iconic individuals such as folk heroes have a distinctive role to play in developing and marketing tourism attractions, and in 'creating heritage for tourism'.

References

Cartier, C. (2005) San Francisco and the left coast, in C. Cartier and A. Lew (eds.) *Seductions of Place: Geographical Perspectives on Globalisation and Touristed Landscapes*. London: Routledge, pp. 148–168.

De Groot, J. (2009) *Consuming History: Historians and Heritage in Contemporary Popular Culture*. London: Routledge.

De Groot, J. (2015) *Remaking History*. Abingdon, Oxon: Routledge.

Fagence, M. (2011) 'Dead Men Do Tell Tales': 'teasing out' the contribution of the folk hero to heritage-based tourism. PhD thesis, La Trobe University, Melbourne (Australia).

Garden, M.-C. (2009) The heritagescape: looking at heritage sites, in M. Sorensen and J. Carman (eds.) *Heritage Studies, Methods and Approaches*. London: Routledge, pp. 270–291.

Gunn, C. (1997) *Vacationscape*, 2nd Edition. New York: Van Nostrand Reinhold Company.

Gyimothy, S., Lundberg, C., Lindstrom, K., Lexhagen, M. and Larson, M. (2015) Popculture tourism: a research manifest, in D. Chambers and T. Rakic (eds.) *Tourism Research Frontiers: Beyond the Boundaries of Knowledge*. Bingley, UK: Emerald Publishing Group, pp. 13–27.

Hubbard, P., Kitchen, R., Bartley, B. and Fuller, D. (2002) *Thinking Geographically*. London: Continuum.

Jackson, J. and Murphy, P. (2002) Tourism destinations as clusters: analytical experiences from the New World. *Tourism and Hospitality Research*, 4(1): 36–52.

Jamal, T. and Kim, H. (2005) Bridging the interdisciplinary divide. *Tourist Studies*, 5(1): 55–83.

Jansen-Verbeke, M. (1998) Tourismification of historical cities. *Annals of Tourism Research*, 25(4): 739–742.

Jansen-Verbeke, M. (2016) Tourismification of cultural landscapes, *Proceedings of TCL2016 Conference*, Budapest: INFOTA, pp. 276–281.

Jordanova, L. (2006) *History in Practice*, 2nd Edition. London: Hodder Arnold.

Knudsen, D., Metro-Roland, M., Sloper, A. and Greer, C. (2008) *Landscape, Tourism, and Meaning*. Aldershot: Ashgate.

Landsberg, A. (2004) *Prosthetic Memory: The Transformation of American Remembrance in the Age of Mass Culture*. New York: Columbia University Press.

Lowenthal, D. (1996) *The Heritage Crusade and the Spoils of History*. London: Viking.

McQuilton, J. (1979) *The Kelly Outbreak: The Geographical Dimensions of Social Banditry*. Carlton, Victoria: Melbourne University Press.

Meinig, D. (ed.) (1979) *The Interpretation of Ordinary Landscapes*. New York: Oxford University Press.

Pearce, D. (2014) Toward an integrative conceptual framework of destinations. *Journal of Travel Research*, 53(2): 141–153.

Pearce, P., Morrison, A. and Moscardo, G (2003) Individuals as tourist icons: a developmental and marketing analysis. *Journal of Hospitality and Leisure Marketing*, 10(1–2): 63–85.

Pearce, S. (1998) The construction and analysis of cultural heritage: some thoughts. *International Journal of Heritage Studies*, 4(1): 1–9.

Pearson, M. and Warburton, T. (2005) Semiotic approaches to image-based research: key concepts, in B. Somekh and C. Lewin (eds.), *Research Methods in the Social Sciences*. London: Sage, pp. 164–167.

Prentice, R. (2003) Revisiting 'heritage': a key sector of the (then) 'New' tourism, in C. Cooper (ed.) *Classic Reviews in Tourism*. Clevedon: Channel View Publications, pp. 161–191.

Richards, G. (2011) Creativity and tourism: the state of the art. *Annals of Tourism Research*, 38(4): 1225–1253.

Richards, G. and Marques, L. (2012) Exploring creative tourism: editors introduction. *Journal of Tourism Consumption and Practice*, 4(2): 1–11.

Rosenstone, R. (1995) *Visions of the Past: The Challenge of Film to Our Idea of History*. Cambridge, MA: Harvard University Press.

Seal, G. (1996) *The Outlaw Legend*. Cambridge: Cambridge University Press.

Shurmer-Smith, P (2002) *Doing Cultural Geography*. London: Sage.

Smith, L. (2006) *Uses of Heritage*. London: Routledge.

Sobchack, V. (1996) *The Persistence of History*. New York: Routledge.

Timothy, D. and Boyd, S (2015) *Tourism and Trails: Cultural, Ecological and Management Issues*. Clevedon: Channel View Publications.

Urry, J. (1992). The tourist gaze 'revisited'. *American Behavioural Scientist*, 36(2): 172–186.

Waterton, E. and Watson, S. (2014) *The Semiotics of Heritage Tourism*. Bristol: Channel View Publications.

10 Creating (extra)ordinary heritage through film-induced tourism

The case of Dubrovnik and *Game of Thrones*

Tina Šegota

Introduction

Central to tourist consumption is the tourist gaze: the fact that 'we look at, or gaze upon, particular objects, such as piers, towers, old buildings, artistic objects, food, countryside and so on' (Urry 1995: 131). These objects boast certain material and imagination-stimulating qualities that evoke a nostalgic sense of history and tradition and are, thus, able to attract tourists (Bærenholdt et al. 2004). Heritage sites create an anticipation of pleasurable experience that is very often constructed and sustained through non-tourism practices, such as popular culture in general and film-induced tourism in particular (Urry 1995, Beeton 2005, Urry and Larsen 2011). Film-induced tourism is considered a unique form of tourism that motivates visitors to experience on- and off-location sites used in films and/or TV series (Beeton 2005, Hudson and Ritchie 2006). Due to being featured in a film or TV series, a place or object otherwise considered an 'ordinary' object of tourist consumption very often gains the status of an icon (Riley et al. 1998). The use of film imagery to emphasise the extraordinariness of a place is the subject of a long-lasting debate among academics and business people (Riley and Van Doren 1992, Riley et al. 1998, Beeton 2005, Beeton 2010, Connell 2012). It is certainly a practice widely employed by tourism professionals.

Enriching heritage with fantasies and daydreams from films and TV series may not directly 'harm' the unique attractiveness of a place. By intertwining the heritage of the place with film imagery, tourists are attracted to certain places, gazing at particular objects 'in the level of what is *ordinary* and hence what people view as *extraordinary*' (Urry and Larsen 2011: 115, emphasis in original). Tour guides have the ability to transform and facilitate the identity of the place as interpreters and educators of its heritage (Imon et al. 2007), acting as a direct link between the identity of the heritage site and the visitor experience. On the one hand, they provide necessary and accurate interpretations of the site, while on the other they have the ability to enhance the quality of the visitor experience by complementing the 'ordinary' heritage sightseeing tours with unique stories and sites relating to the film or TV series. Hence, heritage becomes the subject of transformation and reformation influenced by popular culture; its identity is 'a *discursive formation* which consists of what the destination is and represents at the time and the historical and present practices involved in transforming it' (Saarinen 2001, 51, emphasis in original).

Limited attention has so far been paid to the practices of (re)producing heritage through film imagery in sites of (so-called) outstanding value to humanity. This chapter addresses this research gap by discussing the recurrent practices of tour guides in reshaping and recreating the heritage of the city of Dubrovnik, a UNESCO World Heritage Site since 1979, through film imagery related to the popular TV series, *Game of Thrones*. The chapter will start with a review of relevant literature concerning the influences of film imagery and tour guides on the tourist gaze. It will then describe the city of Dubrovnik and its heritage and present an analysis of the role of tour guides in transforming the heritage of that city in connection with the popular series, *Game of Thrones*. The chapter will conclude by discussing the implications of film-induced tourism for the heritage management of a destination.

On the creation and delivery of the mediated gaze

Tourism sets the stage for a very profound consumption of places because destinations represent 'a unique environment and stimulation apart from those ordinary shopping settings' (Oh et al. 2004: 309). The physical space itself becomes not only the location of tourist consumption, but the object of consumption per se (Jančič 1999, Urry 2002, Bærenholdt et al. 2004, Oh et al. 2004, Urry and Larsen 2011). Tourists visit places and gaze upon the objects, landscapes and traditions (as part of the physical spaces), in search of authentic and memorable experiences. What is 'sold' to the tourist is highly context-dependent, inseparable from the social and physical setting within which it occurs (Urry 1995). Ramkissoon and Uysal (2014: 114) suggest that an authentic experience, at least in part, arises from 'the nature of the interaction within the setting in which tourist experience is produced and consumed'. However, there have to be certain mechanisms in place to ignite a tourist's desire for authentic experiences, while the latter have to be carefully delivered at the visit site in order to be memorable.

Creating the tourist gaze for places of 'outstanding value'

Mechanisms that inspire a desire to travel are highly diverse, with destination branding as a common factor. Destination branding involves the selection of a consistent mix of brand elements, in order to identify and differentiate a tourism destination through positive image building (Cai 2002, Novčić Korać and Šegota 2017). The brand elements are embodied in pictures and videos in order to link *in situ* experiences and emotions with a destination (Šegota 2018). As such, they have the ultimate power to present the evidence of a destination's unique characteristics to target audiences (through destination marketing) or from one person to another (by word of mouth). Urry and Larson (2011: 115) recognise that the availability of visual media results in the propensity of people to 'keep demanding new out-of-the-ordinary experiences'.

Two much-debated mechanisms of positive destination image building are, firstly, inscription on the UNESCO World Heritage Sites list (for outstanding heritage) and, secondly, the presence of on-location filming sites. Very often, these two do not go hand in hand, but both are seen as key factors affecting the tourist gaze and communicating a destination's uniqueness to tourists. Being named a UNESCO World Heritage Site brings special attention to the natural or cultural endowments of a place (Cuccia et al. 2017), emphasising its outstanding value and stressing the pure and original heritage that needs to be preserved for humanity (Frey and Steiner 2013). Such inscription builds expectations of a certain unique experience and influences the interpretation of authenticity. The sites play a significant role in creating the atmosphere of tourist experience because of their effective charge; tourists often report that their lives have been enriched by the opportunity to visit these special places, due to the characteristics they possess (Urry and Larsen 2011, Lisle 2016). According to Lowenthal (1985), localities with old buildings display solidity, continuity, authority, and craft; they have survived developers, town planners, wars, erosion and earthquakes, for years and years; they link past generations to the present; they demonstrate that tradition and age are worthy of preservation; they were built without the help of modern technologies. This claim to authenticity is what distinguishes World Heritage Sites from other heritage sites. Frey and Steiner (2013) recognise that many tourism destinations which have the designation of 'World Heritage' become major attractions and icons of national identity and as such gain general popularity. The contemporary fascination with gazing upon such heritage contributes to economic growth (Arezki et al. 2009) and increases the attractiveness of wider regional areas (Mazanec et al. 2007, Frey and Steiner 2013, Patuelli et al. 2016). Destination management organisations (hereinafter, DMO) also use the World Heritage label for differentiating their specific tourism destinations from those of their competitors, presenting their own sites as must-see tourism products (Marcotte and Bourdeau 2012, de Fauconberg et al. 2017).

Other important tourism products are those localities featured in popular culture. When such sites are visited, people gaze on the scene to relive the elements or certain aspects of the events conveyed through popular culture media. In recent years, there has been specific interest in understanding the benefits of literature and film tourism to destination marketing and management (Beeton 2010, Larson et al. 2013, Šegota 2018). Bolan and Williams (2008) argue that film tourism benefits destination marketing in numerous ways, most importantly in reaching an audience (via film imagery) that would normally be unreachable through traditional marketing activities. In the first place, a destination's exposure through film generates awareness of a destination among viewers who may not be addressed by other tourism marketing tools. If a film is commercially successful, the market reach is even greater. Secondly, popular culture is considered an autonomous destination image formation agent, providing substantial information about a destination within a very limited time. Since popular culture is very often considered to be independent of the direct influence of DMOs, the information provided through film is likely to be evaluated as more objective and unbiased. Lastly, film imagery, which includes on-screen virtual characters, an appealing storyline, memorable music, and remarkable landscapes, generates out-of-the-ordinary experiences which are then materialised at the moment a tourist visits the destination and recreates similar experiences as those viewed in on-screen performances (Bolan and Williams 2008). Šegota (2018) asserts that the influence of film in emphasising the extraordinariness of 'ordinary' must-see tourism products (that is, landscapes, places, and sites) is undeniable.

Unquestionably, labelling an attraction as an important heritage site or a must-see filming location aids in destination marketing. Labels help DMOs to invent new destinations or to embellish ordinary destinations with imaginative geographies or novel stories and myths (Urry and Larsen 2011). In the case of film tourism, on-site filming destinations record a rapid increase in the number of visits and overnight stays due to the active tourism promotional work of DMOs. Prominent examples include the destination marketing practices of New Zealand in connection with the trilogies, *The Lord of the Rings* and *The Hobbit* (Croy 2010, Benton 2015, Li et al. 2016), of Forks, USA and the Italian towns of Volterra and Montepulciano in connection with *The Twilight Saga* (Larson et al. 2013), and of Croatia in connection with *Game of Thrones* (Šegota 2018). These destinations display the pull factors for film site visits (Riley and Van Doren 1992) and have become (so-called) fantasylands for tourists who consider themselves true fans of the films. They magnify pilgrimage to the point that the consumption of *un*mediated reality is impossible (Urry and Larsen 2011).

The role of tour guides in delivering the mediated gaze

People inspired to pursue the tourist gaze may do so individually or in groups, guided by tour guides, travel guides and tips, modern technology apps, or in random strolls around the destination. Eventually, those pursuing the tourist gaze come into contact with local residents, other tourists, and workers in the tourism and hospitality sectors. Urry and Larsen (2011: 77) recognise that those in tourism and hospitality, with face-to-face contact with tourists, 'literally work under the tourist gaze'. Moreover, for Del Casino and Hanna (2000), they are so much a part of the performance that they themselves become part of the gaze; these authors are referring particularly to tour guides, who are perceived as 'of crucial importance in cultural tourism, as theirs is the task of selecting, glossing, and interpreting sights' (Dahles 2002: 784). Many writers see tour guides as essential to enhancing visitors' satisfaction and experience and their understanding of a destination and its culture (Holloway 1981, Moscardo 1998, Ap and Wong 2001). For Wang et al. (2002), it is tour guides' communication and presentation skills that 'make or break' a tour, while Ap and Wong (2001) see these skills as crucial in transforming tourists' visits into experiences. Similarly, McIntosh and Prentice (1999) and Reisinger and Steiner (2006) say that tour guides play more roles than just providing information to tourists; they convey a sense of the place by interpreting attractions and sites, by explaining where to look, when to look, why to look, and how to behave. Cohen (1985) ascribes to guides the role of mentors, who select the experience and the narrative (which places to visit and which ones to omit), provide education through offering correct and precise information, and mediate the meaning between a tourist site and its visitors by fabricating or guarding the authenticity of the place. However, how the guides' roles are executed depends on historical and mediated narratives of the place. Here, historical and mediated narratives are seen as the content of tourism products that are commoditised to suit the perceived tourists' tastes and travel agendas (Urry 1995, Wong 2013). Some researchers suggest that tour guides do not manage to perform their roles in full, because postmodern tourists are not really seeking authenticity and in-depth understanding of heritage. Instead, guides have been placed in a difficult situation, where staging the narrative becomes superior to historical accounts of the site because the preference of tourists is for a visual experience and experiential enjoyment of the place (Nuryanti 1996, Desmond 1999, Blom 2000).

The above situation arises in the case of guided tours within film tourism. In order to attract visitors, tourism organisations and businesses promote guides, routes and maps with the content specifically highlighting filming location sites. Since the release of *The Lord of the Rings*, for example, the official New Zealand DMO has branded the country the 'Home of Middle-earth' (New Zealand Tourism 2017), one important focus of tours being the original Hobbiton Movie Set. Tourists may decide to visit this fictional and virtual environment on their own, or they can be guided through the mediated gaze (Urry and Larsen 2011, Benton 2015). In the case of the latter, the authenticity of the place is being fabricated (Larson et al. 2013) in order to meet expectations of the virtual experiences anticipated by fans of this popular culture phenomenon. However, tour guides in historic towns and heritage sites used as on-location filming sites are placed in an even more unenviable position in delivering the tourist gaze; one example concerns the TV series, *Game of Thrones*, a media phenomenon that has swept Europe since 2011. Tour guides have found that their encoding of a preferred narrative is contested by expectations over the mediated gaze. They have to decide how they will position themselves with respect to the particular accounts offered by heritage and fictional narratives: 'they may subscribe strongly to conveying a particular account, or may be less engaged, or perhaps even ironic' (Macdonald 2006). The research outlined in this chapter addresses the positioning of tour guides (with respect to heritage and fictional narratives) in the Croatian city of Dubrovnik. The study uses a qualitative interpretative research style, based on interviews with representatives of tourist agencies offering walking tours in Dubrovnik.

Case study of Dubrovnik and *Game of Thrones*

The city of Dubrovnik and its surrounding area cover the southernmost region of Croatia, stretching along the narrow Adriatic coastal belt under the Dinaric mountain peaks. The Old Town of Dubrovnik was formally established at the end of the twelfth century, when two Slavic settlements were fortified and strengthened within the City Walls (Visit Dubrovnik n.d.). From the thirteenth century onwards,

Dubrovnik became an important Mediterranean Sea power, as evidenced by its many and diverse buildings, such as Gothic, Renaissance and Baroque churches, monasteries, palaces, and fountains (UNESCO n.d.). In 1667 the city was severely damaged by an earthquake; however, the majority of the Old Town has been preserved to the present day. In the twentieth century the city became a well-known tourist destination and in 1979 it joined the UNESCO list of World Heritage Sites. In the 1990s, the city was yet again damaged during armed conflict; however, its restoration was coordinated by UNESCO in order to preserve the unique architecture of the Old Town. Nowadays, the city is one of the most famous tourist destinations in Croatia and in south-eastern Europe. The mountainous landscape, the crystal clear blue sea and the unique architecture have made Dubrovnik worthy of the nickname 'Pearl of the Adriatic'. What attracts tourists the most is the view of its preserved white stone defensive walls, endowed with numerous forts and towers, surrounding the medieval red-roof-top-houses and palaces (see Figure 10.1). Hence, the most famous tourist attractions are the Old Town, the City Walls and numerous fortresses, including Lovrijenac, Minčeta, and Bokar.

Since the early 2000s, and especially since 2011, the city of Dubrovnik has boasted an increasing number of tourist visits. In 2015, for example, there were almost one and half million tourist arrivals, while almost one million admission tickets were sold for the City Walls. Tkalec et al. (2017) attribute these record tourist numbers to HBO's 'megahit' TV series, *Game of Thrones*, suggesting that *Game of Thrones* film-induced tourism resulted in a 37.9 per cent increase in tourist arrivals, a 28.5 per cent increase in overnight stays and a 37.5 per cent increase

Figure 10.1 Entrance to the city of Dubrovnik
Source: Zoran Marinović and Dubrovnik Tourist Board

in City Walls admission tickets, compared to a mere 7 per cent increase in tourist arrivals, a 8.2 per cent increase in overnight stays, and a 2.1 per cent increase in City Walls admission tickets in the pre-*Game of Thrones* period. The TV series became highly successful immediately after its first screening on April 17, 2011. The original series was based on George R.R. Martin's bestselling series of fantasy novels, *A Song of Ice and Fire*, which portray chronicles of violent dynastic struggle among noble families for the Iron Throne while more threats emerge from the north of the continent and from distant eastern lands (Šegota 2018). With a production budget of up to US$100 million per season and a total of 38 Emmy awards, this record-setting TV series commands an average of 20 million viewers per episode, making it the most successful TV series in history (HBO, 2016). In 2011, during season one of the series, HBO producers moved some of the filming locations from Malta to Croatia, including those relating to the King's Landing, the most crucial place in the series, known for its Iron Throne. The majority of the filming took place in the Old Town of Dubrovnik and at nearby tourist attractions. Croatian DMO instantly recognised the economic benefits of a form of tourism driven by desire for an authentic experience of on-screen location sites in Dubrovnik and its surroundings. In both online and offline destination marketing activities, they strongly emphasised the city of Dubrovnik as a synonym for King's Landing. As a result, Dubrovnik became the pilgrimage destination for fans of *Game of Thrones* (Šegota 2018).

Touring the heritage: of Dubrovnik or King's Landing?

One tourism product that has gained popularity among visitors to Dubrovnik is dedicated walking tours of the city and its famous City Walls. These tours were initiated in the mid-1970s after the reconstruction of inaccessible walls. During the armed conflict in the 1990s the city and its walls reportedly suffered the most devastating destruction since the thirteenth century, but after the restoration the tours commenced again. Today, small tourism businesses provide most of the tours in the city, mainly focusing on local history and the popular TV series, *Game of Thrones*. Hence, the tours are largely organised according to scripts that meet tourist preferences for walking through the site and experiencing various gazes. The most important local heritage sites are sold under the meme, 'discovery tour', the history of politics and the challenges relating to the city's fortification are sold as the 'war tour', while the film-induced experience tours bear direct reference to the *Game of Thrones*. In the case of the last two, walks are being sold with an expectation that visitors are less attracted to the historical depth of the physical site than to its staged narrative.

In response to the discovery that some tourists are indecisive in their preferences over the mediated or historical gaze of the city of Dubrovnik, there are also tours which address both; the so-called 'two-in-one tours' combine experiences across heritage, history of wars and popular culture. These packages require well-trained professional guides with the ability to interpret, translate, and differentiate fact and fiction clearly. Representatives of Dubrovnik Walks™ and Dubrovnik

Walking tours™ stated that guides for such tours are equipped with high-level professional knowledge about the history of the place, but also share the utmost enthusiasm for *Game of Thrones*. In order to draw a clear line between factual tours and fiction tours, the *Game of Thrones* themed tours are delivered by guides that are real fans of the series themselves, while some guides for 'discovery' and 'war' tours voluntarily exclude themselves from any relationship with the popular culture phenomenon. 'Discovery' guides tend to position themselves as strongly committed to the historical narrative of the place, thus contributing to high levels of consistency between tours. Other guides may be less engaged with the cultural heritage and, instead, embark on a path of recreating the city's heritage through war or *Game of Thrones* storytelling. In this case, the tours management personnel encourage guides to deliver a one-of-a-kind tourist gaze by telling of their personal involvement with the TV series or giving first-hand accounts of living in a besieged town. These personal guides' stories represent a social setting that is highly context-dependent and inseparable from the physical setting within which it occurred. This kind of engagement increases the extraordinariness of place, with tourists having unique opportunities to meet those who contributed to the fictional or real heritage of the city.

Encouraging three different narratives of a place to exist, or even increasing the complexity by offering a mix of two (seemingly exclusive) narratives, entails complex visualisation work. Guides that deliver the 'discovery' tours build visualisation through their impeccable communication skills; they have to convey different layers of history through memorable stories and detailed descriptions of the sites. Other guides have to be skilled narrators as well; however, they show tourists the pictures and point to indicate where, for example, Daenerys Targaryen visited the House of Undying (Minčeta Tower) in Season Two searching for her stolen dragons, or, for example, which part of Stradun Street was bombed to rubble. In these cases, the work of linking the narrative of the war tour, or the *Game of Thrones* tour, to their original contexts has already been accomplished, in that tourists are familiar with images of the warfare or the TV series before they visit. The pictures used by the guides serve as visual triggers of the knowledge and the (un)pleasant memories they already possess, in order for them to grasp *in situ* the experiences that could not be delivered elsewhere.

Conclusion

> For the Game of Thrones fans out there, it all comes live in Dubrovnik. You will walk the same paths, touch the same walls and soak up the views you see on the show.
>
> Ed A. Jones (in Figueroa 2015)

The words of tour manager, Ed Jones, summarise the gaze that tourists anticipate when visiting King's Landing (the city of Dubrovnik, the 'Pearl of the Adriatic' and a UNESCO World Heritage Site). With the increasing popularity of the TV series, *Game of Thrones*, the city of Dubrovnik has gained the worldwide recognition for which it has longed for decades. However, this recognition has become tightly connected to the fictional heritage of film imagery. This has been greatly encouraged by the work of Croatian DMO in promoting the city as King's Landing on social media, which Šegota (2018) describes as unintentional practices gone 'great'. As a result, Dubrovnik's heritage has become a melting pot of three or more narratives: one about Gothic, Renaissance and Baroque architectural history and events; one about the political challenges, warfare, and fortification of the place; and one about the fictional chronicles of violent dynastic struggles of noble families for the throne. For small tourism businesses, intertwining the heritage of the place with film imagery has brought recognition and financial success. They instantly capitalised on the increasing tourist numbers by offering one-of-a-kind walking tours to *Game of Thrones* filming locations, enriched by personal stories of those contributing to its production. Moreover, tour management personnel recognised that tourists are indecisive in their perceptions of the place, so they now offer walking tours with mixed narratives. These require highly skilled professional guides who are able to provide necessary and accurate interpretation of the heritage as well as increasing visitor satisfaction, compared to 'ordinary' heritage sightseeing tours, by including unique stories and sites related to the TV series. Those delivering this mediated gaze are fans of the gaze themselves, because only 'true fans' know what people view as extraordinary.

Undeniably, Dubrovnik's heritage has become the subject of transformation influenced by popular culture. The label of UNESCO World Heritage Site from 1979 made its heritage outstanding; however, it was the popular culture label from 2011 onwards that made it extraordinary. Some tour guides remain strongly committed to a historical narrative of the city, while others increasingly succumb to postmodern tourists' preferences for instant authentic experiences and a superficial understanding of heritage. However, the fruits of this (what Saarinen (2001) calls) 'discursive formation' will shortly be evident, since the TV series will be concluding soon and filming has already finished in Croatia. There are strong fears that Dubrovnik and its tour guides will have a difficult task in transforming the heritage back to its initial pre-*Game of Thrones* stage. This will involve downgrading the film narrative, making it only equal to, or less important than, the war and historical narratives. The real issue is whether Dubrovnik can continue to sustain itself as a significant heritage destination. Since 'new Dubrovnik' has been increasingly profiled and promoted as King's Landing, the city is now at risk of acquiring the image of a destination for film enthusiasts that only lasts a decade.

References

Ap, J. and Wong, K.K.F. (2001) Case study on tour guiding: professionalism, issues and problems. *Tourism Management*, 22(5): 551–563.

Arezki, R., Cherif, R. and Piotrowski, J. (2009) *Tourism Specialization and Economic Development: Evidence from the UNESCO World Heritage List*. Washington, DC: UNESCO.

Bærenholdt, J.O., Haldrup, M., Larsen, J. and Urry J. (2004) *Performing Tourist Places*. Aldershot, Hants: Ashgate.

Benton, N. (2015) Magic of New Zealand's Middle-earth. *Australasian Leisure Management*, 111(Jul/Aug): 38–41.

Beeton, S. (2005) *Film-Induced Tourism*. Clevedon, UK: Channel View Publications.

Beeton, S. (2010) The advance of film tourism. *Tourism and Hospitality Planning and Development*, 7(1): 1–6.

Blom, T. (2000) Morbid tourism: a postmodern market niche with an example from Althorp. *Norwegian Journal of Geography*, 54(1): 29–36.

Bolan, P. and Williams, L. (2008) The role of image in service promotion: focusing on the influence of film on consumer choice within tourism. *International Journal of Consumer Studies*, 32(4): 382–390.

Cai, L.A. (2002) Cooperative branding for rural destinations. *Annals of Tourism Research*, 29(3): 720–742.

Del Casino, V.J. and Hanna, S.P. (2000) Representations and identities in tourism map spaces. *Progress in Human Geography*, 24(1): 23–46.

Cohen, E. (1985) The tourist guide: the origins, structure and dynamics of a role. *Annals of Tourism Research*, 12(1): 5–29.

Connell, J. (2012) Film tourism - evolution, progress and prospects. *Tourism Management*, 33(5): 1007–1029.

Croy, W.G. (2010) Planning for film tourism: active destination image management. *Tourism and Hospitality Planning and Development*, 7(1): 21–30.

Cuccia, T., Guccio, C. and Rizzo, I. (2017) UNESCO sites and performance trend of Italian regional tourism destinations. *Tourism Economics*, 23(2): 316–342.

Dahles, H. (2002) The politics of tour guiding: image management in Indonesia. *Annals of Tourism Research*, 29(3): 783–800.

de Fauconberg, A., Berthon, P. and Berthon, J.P. (2017) Rethinking the marketing of World Heritage Sites: giving the past a sustainable future. *Journal of Public Affairs* (online), March: 1–7.

Desmond, J.C. (1999) *Staging Tourism: Bodies on Display from Waikiki to Sea World*. Chicago: University of Chicago Press.

Figueroa, A. (2015) Croatia's tourism grows thanks to festivals and 'Game of Thrones.' *Travel Agency Central*. Available at: www.travelagentcentral.com/croatia/croatias-tourism-grows-thanks-festivals-and-game-thrones-52369 [accessed January 25, 2016].

Frey, B.S. and Steiner, L. (2013) World Heritage List. In I. Rizzo and A. Mignosa (eds.) *Handbook on the Economics of Cultural Heritage*. Cheltenham, UK: Edward Elgar Publishing Ltd, pp. 171–186.

HBO (2016) Available at: www.makinggameofthrones.com/production-diary//game-of-thrones-triumphs-2016-emmys [accessed September 20, 2016].

Holloway, J.C. (1981) The guided tour: a sociological approach. *Annals of Tourism Research*, 8(3): 377–402.

Hudson, S. and Ritchie, J.R.B. (2006) Promoting destinations via film tourism: an empirical identification of supporting marketing initiatives. *Journal of Travel Research*, 44(4): 387–396.

Imon, S.S., Dioko, L.A.N., Ong, C.E. and Kane, M. (2007) *Tourism at Cultural Heritage Sites in Asia: Cultural Heritage Specialist Guide Training and Certification Programme for UNESCO World Heritage Sites*, 4th Edition. Macao SAR: UNESCO and Institute for Tourism Studies (IFT).

Jančič, Z. (1999) *Celostni Marketing (Integrated Marketing)*. Ljubljana, Slovenia: Faculty of Social Sciences UL.

Larson, M., Lundberg, C. and Lexhagen, M. (2013) Thirsting for vampire tourism: developing pop culture destinations. *Journal of Destination Marketing and Management*, 2(2): 74–84.

Li, S., Li, H., Song, H., Lundberg, C. and Shen, S. (2016) The economic impact of film tourism: the case of *The Lord of the Rings* and *The Hobbit*. In *Tourism Travel and Research Association: Advancing Tourism Research Globally*. 7.

Lisle, D. (2016) *Holidays in the Danger Zone: Entanglements of War and Tourism*. Minneapolis: University of Minnesota Press.

Lowenthal, D. (1985) *The Past is a Foreign Country*. Cambridge, UK: Cambridge University Press.

Macdonald, S. (2006) Mediating heritage: tour guides at the former Nazi Party Rally Grounds, Nuremberg. *Tourist Studies*, 6(2): 119–138.

Marcotte, P. and Bourdeau, L. (2012) Is the World Heritage label used as a promotional argument for sustainable tourism? *Journal of Cultural Heritage Management and Sustainable Development*, 2(1): 80–91.

Mazanec, J.A., Wöber, K. and Zins, A.H. (2007) Tourism destination competitiveness: from definition to explanation? *Journal of Travel Research*, 46(1): 86–95.

McIntosh, A.J. and Prentice, R.C. (1999) Affirming authenticity: consuming cultural heritage. *Annals of Tourism Research*, 26(3): 589–612.

Moscardo, G. (1998) Interpretation and sustainable tourism: functions, examples and principles. *Journal of Tourism Studies*, 9(1): 2–13.

New Zealand Tourism (2017) Home of Middle-earth. Available at: www.newzealand.com/int/home-of-middle-earth [accessed July 12, 2017].

Novčić Korać, B. and Šegota, T. (2017) Branding of a (desti)nation with a deteriorated image: the case of Serbia. *Sociology and Space*, 55(1): 77–99.

Nuryanti, W. (1996) Heritage and postmodern tourism. *Annals of Tourism Research*, 23(2): 249–260.

Oh, J.Y.-J., Cheng, C.-K., Lehto, X.Y. and O'Leary, J.T. (2004) Predictors of tourists' shopping behaviour: examination of socio-demographic characteristics and trip typologies. *Journal of Vacation Marketing*, 10(4), pp. 308–319.

Patuelli, R., Mussoni, M. and Candela, G. (2016) The effects of World Heritage sites on domestic tourism: a spatial interaction model for Italy. In R. Patuelli and G. Arbia (eds.) *Spatial Econometric Interaction Modelling*. Cham: Springer International Publishing, pp. 281–315.

Ramkissoon, H. and Uysal, M. (2014) Authenticity as a value co-creator of tourist experiences. In N. K. Prebensen, J. S. Chen, and M. Uysal (eds.) *Creating Experience Value in Tourism*. Oxfordshire, UK: CAB International, pp. 113–124.

Reisinger, Y. and Steiner, C. (2006) Reconceptualising interpretation: the role of tour guides in authentic tourism. *Current Issues in Tourism*, 9(6): 481–498.

Riley, R.W., Baker, D. and Van Doren, C.S. (1998) Movie induced tourism. *Annals of Tourism Research*, 25(4): 919–935.

Riley, R.W. and Van Doren, C.S. (1992) Movies as tourism promotion. *Tourism Management*, 13(3): 267–274.

Saarinen, J. (2001) *Transformation of a Tourist Destination. Theory and Case Studies on the Production of Local Geographies in Tourism in Finnish Lapland*, Nordia Geographical Publications, Geographical Society of Northern Finland and Department of Geography, University of Oulu.

Šegota, T. (2018) (G)A(i)ming at the throne: social media and the use of visitor-generated content in destination branding. In C. Lundberg and V. Ziakas (eds.) *The Routledge Handbook on Popular Culture and Tourism*. Oxfordshire, UK: Routledge, In Press.

Tkalec, M., Zilic, I. and Recher, V. (2017) The effect of film industry on tourism: *Game of Thrones* and Dubrovnik. *International Journal of Tourism Research* (online) July: 1–10.

UNESCO (n.d.) Old City of Dubrovnik. Available at: http://whc.unesco.org/en/list/95/ [accessed July 12, 2017].

Urry, J. (1995) *Consuming Places*. London: Routledge.

Urry, J. (2002) *The Tourist Gaze*. London: Thousand Oaks.

Urry, J. and Larscn, J. (2011) *The Tourist Gaze*, 3rd Edition. London: Sage.

Visit Dubrovnik (n.d.) About Dubrovnik. Available at: http://visitdubrovnik.hr/index.php/en/26-uncategorised/cities-towns/570-about-dubrovnik-eng [accessed July 12, 2017].

Wang, K.-C., Hsieh, A.-T. and Chen, W.-Y. (2002) Is the tour leader an effective endorser for group package tour brochures? *Tourism Management*, 23(5): 489–498.

Wong, C.U.I. (2013) The sanitization of colonial history: authenticity, heritage interpretation and the case of Macau's tour guides. *Journal of Sustainable Tourism*, 21(6): 915–931.

11 *Amachan*

The creation of heritage tourism landscapes in Japan after the 2011 triple disaster

Duccio Gasparri and Annaclaudia Martini

Introduction

The popularity of the Japanese TV show *Amachan* is so widespread that in the months following its airtime, experts projected an increase of economic revenue in the area where it is set of around 3.3 billion yen[1] (over 30 million dollars), in addition to making everyone in Japan incessantly repeat the show's catchphrase 'jejeje'. *Amachan* is set in northern Sanriku, a rural area that sadly became famous for having been subjected to the brunt of the March 11, 2011 Great Eastern Japan Disaster, which took the lives of thousands of people and left many more homeless. Shot in 2013, the morning show did not engage directly with the disaster for most of its run, but had a significant impact on the recovering towns and their traditional activity, 'ama diving'. While, in Korea, ama diving has been added to the UNESCO intangible heritage list,[2] the few remaining Japanese examples have yet to be included. Nonetheless, through the show *Amachan*, the figure of the ama has become popular throughout Japan, boosting tourism and revitalising a declining tradition.

The story starts in 2009 and portrays the most important issues of a small fishing village – poverty, depopulation and the increasing need to rely on domestic tourism for revenue. These issues lead the main characters to reinvent their everyday occupations as tourist attractions during the summer season. Although intentionally humorous, *Amachan* illustrates how the Japanese media industry reimagines the landscape in order to pursue a specific narrative, within which rural traditional heritage is re-invented, reproduced and adapted in order to cater to tourists from all over Japan.

This chapter addresses the *Amachan* phenomenon in the light of its impact on tourism in the northern Sanriku area of Kuji city. We provide an overview of the drama, the context in which it is set and the literature on rural tourism and heritage building. We then discuss the types of heritage established (tangible, intangible and digital) when the drama impacted domestic tourism and how they work together. The popularity of *Amachan* in Kuji favoured not only the creation of new attractions and performances, but merged old traditions with new, hybrid features that enhance and make consumable for twenty-first-century tourists the history and memory of Japan's rural areas.

Context

The town of Kuji is located on the coast of Sanriku, which lies on the north-eastern side of Honshu Island, stretching from the southern Aomori Prefecture to the northern Miyagi Prefecture. Kuji is served by the Sanriku Tetsudō railway (commonly referred to as 'Santetsu'), connecting the town to the main railway and highway routes of northern Japan, all the way from Tokyo in the South to Aomori in the North. Sanriku is one of the most remote rural areas in Japan (Thompson and Traphagan 2006). In the Meiji era (1868–1912), the main economic revenue came from agriculture and fishery. With the beginning of the twentieth century and the development of deep-sea fishing, the prolonged absence of the fisher-men urged women to start gathering seaweed, abalone, and sea urchin for money (Martinez 2004). These women were called ama[3] (sea woman). Around the same period, the dawn of Japanese industrialisation led to a considerable drift of man-power from rural areas towards urban centres (Thompson and Traphagan 2006). This caused depopulation and socio-economic decline in peripheral municipali-ties including Kuji and its surroundings. During the 1970s and 1980s, both the central government and local authorities addressed countryside depopulation and economic shrinkage by promoting domestic tourism in rural areas as an alterna-tive source of revenue. In Kuji, this phenomenon focused on ama divers. Since the 1970s, a stream of tourists from urban areas has visited the town to observe the tradition of the ama, who dive, collect, and sell *uni* (sea urchins).

Domestic countryside tourism in Japan relies on feelings of nostalgia for the past, a return to nature, and to long-forgotten communal values; all this is con-densed into the term *furusato*, or 'native place' (Robertson 1991). As McMorran

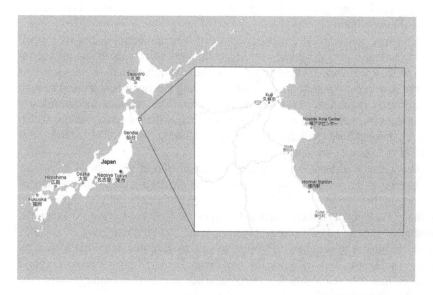

Figure 11.1 Map of the Kuji area in Japan

notes, 'while *furusato* can refer to one's actual birthplace or hometown, it generally refers to an idealised rural village that is spiritual home to all Japanese people' (McMorran 2008: 339). A dramatic change to the *furusato* tourism model in Kuji came on 11 March 2011, as an offshore earthquake of magnitude 9.0 generated a tsunami that hit the Sanriku coast and washed away entire towns, causing massive destruction to buildings and infrastructure and radically altering the seabed environment. This caused the halting of ama diving and, subsequently, the cessation of tourism. In an attempt to carry on with the tradition, in the summer of 2011 ama dived in the waters of nearby Kosode Bay to look for sea urchins, but came up empty-handed and covered in filth from the murky waters.

In 2012, amid the ongoing reconstruction of buildings and roads, and the removal of the debris from the seabed, Kuji was chosen as the main setting for the morning television programme, *Amachan*, to support recovery efforts. Japan's national broadcasting company (NHK) has a long history of actively promoting revitalisation and boosting the popularity of rural regions by using them as sets for its shows (called *asadorama*, morning dramas). The director, Kankurō Kudō, a native of the neighbouring prefecture of Miyagi, revealed that he 'hoped that the *dorama* would contribute to promoting a comeback of Japan's more depressed local areas, especially after the Great East Japan Earthquake' (Maynard 2016: 245). The 156 episodes of the witty and humorous story aired in 2013 and proved immensely successful, exposing Kuji and the ama divers to unprecedented national attention.

Amachan tells the story of Aki Amano, daughter of Haruko and niece of Natsu, an ama in the village of Sodegahama, near the town of Kitasanriku, both fictional places modelled on the actual Horinai village and Kuji city. In the 1980s Haruko, dreaming of becoming a singer, flees to Tokyo, intending never to return to her hometown. In the summer of 2009, worried about her mother's health, she comes back, bringing Aki with her. Aki is a gloomy and lonely young girl who has a troubled relationship with her assertive and bad-tempered mother, but as she enters the village she brightens up, quickly learns the local dialect and becomes an outgoing and talkative child. She befriends Yui, a spoiled but popular girl whose dream is to move to Tokyo and become a teenage singer/actress (an idol; see the 'Intangible heritage' section below). Aki joins the local ama, a group of elderly women led by her grandmother, who warmly welcome her, as they see the possibility of luring more tourists to Sodegahama if they have a young girl in their midst. Naïve and pretty, Aki becomes popular, turning into the main local attraction as a young ama and a precious resource for the town's touristic revenues. She forms an idol duo with her friend Yui and eventually receives an invitation from a Tokyo producer to become a professional performer. Aspiring to promote her adoptive hometown by becoming a starlet in the capital, Aki leaves Sodegahama. Yui, who could not join her, breaks up their friendship out of jealousy and bitterness. However, when the disaster strikes, Aki returns immediately to Sodegahama to reunite with Yui and support her friends and family, eventually going back to her local celebrity role in order to attract volunteers, fans, and funding opportunities for the reconstruction of their beloved hamlet.

The drama weaves together intergenerational conflict, the complex dynamic between Japanese urban centres and the peripheries, the transmission of tradition, rural revitalisation and the consequences of disaster in rural areas. *Amachan* superimposes its narrative on Kuji's geography, generating physical landmarks (such as the Sodegahama train station, several local buildings, and the ama's Kosode Bay), intangible features (the ama's activities, the local dialect), and places and activities created to cater to the drama's fans (museums, monuments, guided tours). All these elements contribute to creating a new, integrated form of heritage centred on the figure of the ama for the attraction of domestic tourists. The emotional narrative of *Amachan* gives meaning to a rural area with a traditional activity, elevating it from a local and declining attraction to a national phenomenon.

Methods

The research for this chapter was carried out between 2016 and 2017 and was based on semi-structured interviews with local residents, government officials, business owners, and ama divers. Informants were sourced through snowball sampling and convenience sampling. The interviews focused on domestic tourism in north-eastern Japan, the changes experienced by ama divers, everyday life in rural Sanriku, the impact of the 2011 disaster on socio-economic structures and the impact of *Amachan* on Kuji and the surrounding area. In addition, we carried out participant observation in northern Sanriku, and in the town of Kuji, concentrating on the most significant landmarks relevant to the drama: the Ama Center in Kosode, the Sodegahama train station, the tunnel and the *Amachan* museum. We also analysed the drama itself, as well as newspaper and online articles and reviews, academic articles on *Amachan* and archival material. All interviews, audio-visual media, written media, and field notes were analysed using critical discourse analysis.

Literature review

The anthropologist Marilyn Ivy (1995) addresses the shift in meaning that the Japanese countryside underwent during the twentieth century. During the Meiji era the government heavily pushed for industrialisation and Westernisation of the country, but excluded the peripheries, the home of Japanese historical modes of production, from the national discourse (Vlastos 1998), deeming Japan's rural origins a hindrance to becoming a modern nation. This negative conception of the *inaka* (countryside) shifted during the 1970s as Japanese policymakers began to focus on the conditions of underdevelopment and depopulation of the peripheries. One of the solutions proposed was the encouragement of domestic tourism in rural villages, now conceived as a repository of symbolic heritage amid a 'vacuum' of symbols of urban national identity (Befu 2001). Nostalgia for the countryside took shape in the idea of *furusato*, or native place (see Robertson 1991, Ivy 1995, Creighton 1997, Guichard-Aguis and Moon 2009). While *furusato* can refer to one's actual birthplace or hometown, it generally refers to an idealised rural village that is spiritual home to all Japanese people (MacMorran 2008); a place of a simpler, more intimate lifestyle and a reassuring past (Lowenthal 1995). *Furusato* usually conjures up emotional images or memories of childhood; in popular imagination it always refers to a rural landscape (Creighton 1997). As McMorran highlights, '*furusato* heritage can be said to consist of three key aspects, all of which are considered absent from city life, yet crucial to Japanese national identity: (1) a proximity to nature; (2) an architectural cohesiveness and familiarity; and (3) a sense of cooperation and community' (McMorran 2008: 339). Domestic tourism to rural areas is still popular today, as a way to reunite with Japanese identity and to overcome the sense of 'homelessness' felt by many urban Japanese (Creighton 1997) in the face of cultural transitions[4] that have left masses of people with feelings of loneliness and estrangement from others (Davis 1979). However, the Great Eastern Japan Disaster of 2011 interrupted the flow of rural tourism in that region.

Disasters have been explored as contexts for the development of political and social agendas, as well as grounds for activism, solidarity and new power relations (Oliver-Smith 1996). They have a social dimension, as they harness collective action and sentiment (Kleinman and Kleinman 1997) and manipulate narratives of tragedy to promote or hide interpretations of events (Forgash 2011). Such interpretations foster a complex dialogue between memory and history, in which memory 'poses questions to history in that it points to problems that are still alive or invested with emotions and value' (LaCapra 1998: 8). Memory, materialised through heritage, is important to history because of the centrality of trauma and the importance of traumatic events in the construction of identity (Athanasiou et al. 2012). Heritage production is, thus, a continuous process of presentation and interpretation (McCabe 1998), a projection in the present of certain elements of the past, shaped to cater to nostalgic longings and celebrate aspects that still hold value in present social and political discourses (Ashworth and Larkham 1994). Landscape, events, buildings, categories of people, or jobs, can all receive a new meaning and value, to reflect society's collective memory (McMorran 2008). Collective memories, in turn, shape national and local identity and can be crucial in including or excluding minorities from identifying with that heritage (Rose 1995).

Heritage can be formally classified as either tangible or intangible. Tangible heritage refers to 'buildings and historic places, monuments, artefacts, etc., which are considered worthy of preservation for the future' (UNESCO 2003a). These include objects significant to the archaeology, architecture, science or technology of a specific culture (ibid.). Intangible heritage includes 'practices, representations, expressions, knowledge, skills – as well as the instruments, objects, artefacts and cultural spaces associated therewith – that communities, groups and, in some cases, individuals recognise as part of their Cultural Heritage' (UNESCO 2003b). The development of new technologies has prompted the emergence of a new type of digital heritage, made up of computer-based materials of enduring value that should be kept for future generations (UNESCO 2003c).

Discussion

Heritage can manifest itself in unexpected ways. In every town in Japan a system of loudspeakers is used to air musical tunes at 8 a.m., 12 noon and 5 p.m. This is part of the cultural soundscape of Japan. In Kuji, since 2013, the morning chime has been Yoshihide Ōtomo's *Amachan* opening theme, creating the beginning of a new episode every morning in the north-eastern town. The programme has made a major contribution to tourism-related revenues in northern Sanriku, but after four years the initial momentum is dwindling. This has made necessary the institution of a more structured tourism circuit to attract both domestic and overseas tourists. In this section we discuss the processes of heritage building in Kuji since 2013 and how locals and visitors experience and negotiate the impact of *Amachan* on the coast. The discussion will be divided into three sections: the creation of tangible heritage such as landmarks, the creation of intangible heritage such as a hybrid dialect and the transformation of the figure of the ama, and the drama itself as a form of digital heritage. All these types of heritage are combined in a synthesis of peripheral traditions and contemporary trends aimed at closing the gap between pre- and post-disaster Sanriku, between past and present and, ultimately, between rural and urban Japan.

Tangible heritage

According to an informant from Kuji, 'Everything revolves around Aki. [Tourists] want to see what Aki saw, they want to stay where Aki lived. That's why people come here'. However, Aki's village, Sodegahama, and the nearby town of Kitasanriku are both fictional settings based on the real settlements of Horinai and Kuji. The municipality and inhabitants of Kuji see tourism as one of the main sources of revenue for the town. They have therefore created a tourism circuit, performances and attractions that would keep people coming to visit, even after a potential decline in the popularity of *Amachan*. Three categories of places have been defined, to provide a tangible, consumable experience for *Amachan* fans:

1   Locations significant to pre-*Amachan* local tourism, enhanced by how they were portrayed in the drama (Kosode Bay, the Kuji Ekimae building, the Sanriku railway).
2   Locations already existing, but not as tourist sites, which gained significance as recognisable features of Sodegahama and Kitasanriku (Horinai station and train tunnel).
3   Attractions specifically created for fans of *Amachan* (the *Amachan* Museum in Kuji, *Amachan*- related gadgets, events, memorial plates, etc.).

When visitors heading to Kuji climb on the Santetsu train, they have already started their tour. Indeed, the train car itself looks familiar to someone who has watched *Amachan*: cream-coloured interiors, bright red seats, and the comfortable simplicity of countryside trains. Gently creaking and rocking, the two cars ride beside the coast – now a fast succession of concrete seawalls, constructions sites and temporary housing, a common view after the Great Eastern Japan Disaster. Before reaching Kuji, visitors pass by the Horinai station and are greeted by the sign of the fictional Sodegahama stop and a blue bench where Aki and Yui often used to sit in the drama. Horinai and Sodegahama overlap in tourists' imagination and the addition of the sign and the bench, which belong to a fictional world, enhance this superimposition. Next to the station is a tunnel, portrayed many times in the drama, which has become the goal of a specific intangible practice (see below).

Once in Kuji, the reminders about the drama are omnipresent. Posters and fliers are everywhere, together with framed pictures of the *dorama* stationmaster, Daikichi, with his comical sidekick, Yoshida. In a corner, mannequins wear ama's *kasuri*, the official kimonos of the diving women (dark blue with a red and white geometrical pattern) and Aki's idol costume. There is also an acoustic guitar signed by Ōtomo Yoshihide, the composer of the drama's soundtrack. In front of the station stands the Ekimae building, where Daikichi and Sugawara, the head of the Kitasanriku tourism bureau, often plotted to revitalise their beloved neighbourhood. An *Amachan* museum was opened in 2014 and souvenirs are available everywhere in town: key-chains, pins and stickers, most of which have the dialectal expression 'je' or 'jejeje' on them. The 'Jejeje', a local dialectal exclamation of surprise, has become so popular that a dedicated plaque has been placed at Kosode Bay, where ama work and perform for tourists, to mark the place where

Figure 11.2 Tunnel at Horinai station

Aki first learned this expression, eating sea urchins and laughing with the divers in the first episode of the *dorama*.

All these diverse forms of tangible heritage contribute to the illusion of visiting the fictional places where *Amachan* is set, while on the other hand, they also create tangible attractions that ground the tourist experience in the intangible traditional practices and performances of Kuji and Horinai.

Intangible heritage

One of the most effective narrative devices of *Amachan* is to juxtapose the ama with one of the most popular contemporary female figures in Japan: the idol. In one of the first episodes of the show, Aki meets her soon-to-be best friend Yui, whose dream is to leave Kitasanriku and become a star in Tokyo (just as Aki's mother did years before). The scene climaxes with Yui stepping into the Sodegahama station tunnel and screaming at the top of her voice '*Aidoru ni naritai!*' ('I want to become an idol'). A Kuji town employee pointed out to us how many young girls come all the way from Sendai, Tokyo, or even Taiwan, just to make a brief stop at Horinai station, re-enact that liberating yell and go back home.

Japanese idols are described as a media oddity, having neither singing and acting talents, nor remarkable beauty (Sakai 2016), and yet being incredibly popular as media personalities because of their cheerful and inspiring cuteness. Since the 1980s, idols have become the main role models for teenagers, epitomising the possibility of conquering show business through sheer motivation.

Idolhood is a recurring theme in *Amachan* as both Aki and Yui end up pursuing a career as idols, but with opposite outcomes. Yui's excessive egoism leads her to bitter failure, while Aki's experience as an ama apprentice in rural Sanriku imbues her with a set of specific virtues: 'pure-hearted ambition and eagerness to please – the definition of idolhood' (Sakai 2016). The overlap between the characteristics of idolhood and those of the ama, represented by Aki, becomes crucial for heritage creation in Kuji, where women divers have always been the main tourist attraction. The ama of *Amachan* are introduced, not in a romanticised way (as the classic diver figure is presented all over Japan), but as the sunburned elderly matrons who welcome Aki into their midst and initiate her to the divers' ways. Viewers experience their everyday life directly and, through Aki's journey into idolhood and learn to associate the ama's spontaneity and determination with the virtues of the Japanese postmodern heroine par excellence – the idol. The hybrid figure of Aki, who embodies both the idol and the ama, is the driving force behind the revitalisation of Sanriku's ama practices. It has managed to re-popularise the ama, introducing teenagers to the ama tradition and at the same time providing much needed tourism revenues in post-disaster Kuji. The novelty of ama heritage after *Amachan* lies in the new way of presenting and interpreting traditions and practices by associating the ama with the idol, creating a hybrid figure that embodies values of both urban and rural Japan, packaged with the expectations and interest of young Japanese urbanites.

Another central feature of post-*Amachan* intangible heritage in Kuji is the dialect depicted in the drama. Aki absorbs almost immediately the fictitious

Kitasanriku dialect, which is a stand-in for everything that rural Sanriku and the ama represent. Together with the audience, Tokyo-born Aki learns the local dialect, establishing an emotional connection with the rural town of Sodegahama and the ama. Throughout the rest of the *dorama*, she is often identified by secondary characters as 'that girl with the Sanriku accent'. Significantly, Yui, who was born in the countryside, speaks only standard Japanese in order to assert her separation from the periphery and her aspiration to move to the capital. The dialect spoken in fictional Sodegahama approximates that of the actual region (Maynard 2016), enhancing easily recognisable and reproducible expressions, such as 'jejeje'. 'Je' is an exclamation of surprise (as previously mentioned), omnipresent in the episodes of *Amachan*. This expression was not common in Kuji prior to the show, only being kept alive by the elderly of Kosode in a slightly different form, 'je jee' (Tsuchiya 2013). Now, the exclamation 'jejeje' is popular throughout Japan, having become 'Buzzword of the Year' in 2013. 'Jejeje', initially an expression of provincialism, with which locals were embarrassed to be associated, has become the symbol of a heritage to be proud of, to the point of being adopted all over the country.

Digital heritage

National television dramas featuring young and cheerful heroines in rural settings are not a novelty in the Japanese media industry. These productions are explicitly aimed at:

> promoting a comeback of Japan's more depressed local areas. [. . .] This coincides with NHK's policies, which actively promote the broadcast of programs featuring rural communities. Such programming is expected to support tourism and the economic revitalisation of regions where, due to the absence of young residents, the population decline is severe.
>
> (Maynard 2016)

Amachan is the 88th morning drama (*asadora*) of this type. Although it may not be considered to create a 'proper' type of heritage, it does narrate many vital aspects of the everyday life and practices of the Kuji municipality. Tangible and intangible aspects of pre-*Amachan* heritage, especially ama traditions and practices, as well as some dialectal forms, are depicted in detail, presenting a durable, digitalised testimony. As in all heritage creation, the narratives are strongly oriented and interpreted; they aim at romanticising ama divers and bucolic life in rural towns. This is no different from what has been done in hundreds of other villages all over Japan and follows the patterns used to create *furusato* and *mura okoshi* (village revival). The show offers Kuji and Horinai an unprecedented visibility and has been used to enhance tourism in a post-disaster area. Because of the drama, fans and interested tourists are not only already informed about ama activities and practices and the regional language, and emotionally involved, but they can also take part in an ideal continuation of Aki's adventure in Kitasanriku by visiting and supporting Kuji. In this sense, they *do* visit a narrative space, as Tzanelli (2004) notes, but also the actual place that informs the narration. If *Amachan* as asadora is configured to appear more real than real, as Tzanelli (2014) illustrates in relation to *The Lord of the Rings*, the fictional reality bends back to actual locality in a deliberate attempt to interact with it.

Amachan as asadora consists of a deep generative layer of discursive and emotional contents as it ties together the geographical dimension of Kuji with its narrative counterpart, Kitasanriku and its surroundings. The central feature of this third heritage configuration is its recursive re-generation of places and practices. On the one hand, it represents people, activities, words and ideas from northern Sanriku; on the other hand, people, activities, words and ideas from the same area have been shifting over the last four years in order to meet Kudō, the director's vision. Coming originally from the region, he had knowledge of ama practices and was aware of the enormous potential in portraying national peripheries from the early stages of *Amachan* writing. A local ama explained:

> In 2012 we were introduced to Mr. Kurobe, the producer, and Mr. Nabe, the assistant director. When we first heard the idea [of *Amachan*] we were very worried that the screenplay would make fun of us, of people living in this area. After all, dramas come and go, but we still have to live here . . . So we put it as a condition, to collaborate with [Kurobe]. We didn't want anyone to be hurt by the contents of the drama, so we said 'Can we make it work without hurting anyone's feelings?' We put a lot of thought on this.
>
> (Kosode, personal conversation, May 2017)

Kudō manages to navigate these troubled waters by presenting a set of lovable characters: Daikichi the stationmaster, the tourism office representative, the members of the fishermen cooperative and many others struggling to keep up with modernity. More often than not, these seek the help of younger generations, in order to adapt Kitasanriku to current times. Aki and Yui act as mediators between their hometown and the wider world made up of idols, tourists, websites and promotional videos. This mediation is the core of *Amachan*'s narrative strength, and the most important aspect of the asadorama as heritage, as it mutates the geography of Kuji in a place of narrative informed by its locality (see Tzanelli 2014 on cinematic narrative). *Amachan*, then, provides a narrative undertext to ama practices and traditions, as well as commodifying the Sanriku railway and Kuji.

Conclusions

Amachan and its effects and impacts on the tourism industry in Kuji and nearby Horinai represent a unique configuration of heritage creation and representation. Previous studies (Tzanelli 2004, Watson and Waterton 2010) have examined how modalities of representation tend to alienate the social milieu from the construction of touristic heritage, and to model a dimension that is separated from the heritage construction discourse and the 'secret life' (Watson and Waterton 2010: 83), or actuality, of the places, practices and objects that constitute the space of tourism consumption (Watson and Waterton 2010). We propose that it is possible, in the case of *Amachan*, to add a layer of significance to such studies. In a world where news, shows and images are instantly reproduced, we have demonstrated through this paper that *Amachan* is informed by places, performances, and traditional heritage in Kuji to as great an extent as features used for tourism in post-*Amachan* Kuji and Horinai have been reshaped and modelled to represent the fictional towns of Kitasanriku and Sodegahama. We thus argue that *Amachan* in Kuji operates, on a more subtle level, as a phenomenon of heritage creation by presenting for entertainment and tourism purposes precisely those aspects of the Japanese countryside perceived as negative (backwardness and depopulation), as well as the tragic effects of the 2011 Great Eastern Japan Disaster.

In the fictional universe of *Amachan*, as the disaster hits Sanriku on 11 March 2011, Aki is in Tokyo, rehearsing for her debut show as an idol. Immediately, she goes back to Sodegahama and, after finding her grandma alive and well, she decides to stay, reunites with Yui in their old singing duo and performs in order to gather reconstruction funds. The show ends with the two women cheerily singing on the Santetsu train car, surrounded by fans, friends and family, as three couples are married (Aki's producer Aramaki and his fiancee, Aki's mother and her former husband, and the stationmaster Daikichi and the ama Sayuri) and Kitasanriku town rejoices at the reconstruction efforts. At the same time Aki, in the real Kuji, extends her own agency outside the narrative dimension and becomes the motor through which ama divers, local dialects and tangible features of the landscape become a commodity for tourists.

To summarise, Kuji's local heritage before *Amachan* and the disaster, together with neutral elements belonging to local culture, were integrated by *Amachan* in a cohesive discourse. This discourse has produced new forms of heritage that are enhanced, revitalised and popularised by national recognition. The process of heritage creation has also had an impact on the residents, and the way they perceive Kuji and themselves. An unpublished study by Tohoku University researcher, Miwako Kitamura (2016), shows how locals received the drama and its direct outcomes (mainly the increased numbers of tourists) very positively. Kitamura reports a significant improvement in satisfaction with local image, local traditions and even disaster prevention measures, after the airing of *Amachan*. Many of Kitamura's interviewees stated that they not only found new pride in living in Kuji after the television drama had made it famous nationwide, but that it had also strengthened their resolve to rebuild the town and villages damaged by the 2011 disaster.

Notes

1 www.huffingtonpost.jp/2013/08/10/'Amachan'_n_3737069.html.
2 http://english.yonhapnews.co.kr/culturesports/2016/12/01/0701000000AEN20161201
006200315.html.
3 Throughout the whole text, we will use the term 'ama' for both singular and plural.
4 Prime Minister Kakuei Tanaka, who expressed in his 1973 bestseller *Nihon rettō kaisō ron* ('Proposal for remodelling the Japanese archipelago') his worries about the current state of depopulation and decline of the countryside. His plan for the rebirth of rural Japan consisted in the 'remodelling of the physical landscape' (Robertson 1991: 28) through relocation of industries and the construction of transport infrastructures in the countryside.

References

Ashworth, G. J. and Larkham, P. J. (1994) *Building a New Heritage: Tourism, Culture, and Identity in the New Europe*. London: Routledge.

Athanasiou, A., Hantzaroula, P.and Yannakopoulos, K. (2008) Towards a new epistemology: the 'affective turn'. *Historein*: 8–11.

Befu, H. (2001) *Hegemony of Homogeneity: An Anthropological Analysis of Nihonjinron*. Melbourne: Trans Pacific Press.

Creighton, M. (1997) Consuming rural Japan: the marketing of tradition and nostalgia in the Japanese travel industry. *Ethnology*, 36(3): 239–254.

Davis, F. (1979) *Yearning for Yesterday: A Sociology of Nostalgia*. New York.

Forgash, R. (2011) Touring Tohoku, serving the nation: volunteer tourism in post-disaster Japan. *The Applied Anthropologist*, 31(1): 30–36.

Guichard-Anguis, S. and Moon, O. (2009) (eds.) *Japanese Tourism and Travel Culture*. London: Routledge.

Ivy, M. (1995) *Discourses of the Vanishing: Modernity, Phantasm, Japan*. Chicago: University of Chicago Press.

Kitamura, M. (2016) *Sanriku railway disaster and the local community: The influence of Amachan on the disaster at Iwate*. Unpublished research presented at a seminar of the International Research Institute of Disaster Science, Sendai, Japan.

Kleinman, A. and Kleinman, J. (1997) The appeal of experience, the dismay of images: cultural appropriations of suffering in our times, in A. Kleinman, V. Das and M. Lock (eds.) *Social Suffering*. Berkeley, California: University of California Press, pp. 1–23.

LaCapra, D. (1998) *History and Memory after Auschwitz*. Ithaca and London: Cornell University Press.

Lowenthal, D. (1985) *The Past is a Foreign Country*. Cambridge: Cambridge University Press.

Martinez, D.P. (2004) *Identity and Ritual in a Japanese Village*. University of Hawaii Press.

Maynard, S.K. (2016) *Fluid Orality in the Discourse of Japanese Popular Culture*. Amsterdam: John Benjamins Publishing Company.

McCabe, S. (1998) Contesting home: tourism, memory, and identity in Sackville, New Brunswick, *The Canadian Geographer*, 42(3): 231–245.

McMorran, C. (2008) Understanding the 'heritage' in heritage tourism: ideological tool or economic tool for a Japanese hot springs resort? *Tourism Geographies*, 10(3): 334–354.

Oliver-Smith, A. (1996) Anthropological research on hazards and disasters. *Annual Review of Anthropology*, 25: 303–328.

Robertson, J. (1991) *Native and Newcomer: Making and Remaking a Japanese City*. Berkeley, CA: University of California Press.

Rose, G. (1995) Place and identity: a sense of place, in D. Massey and P. Jess (eds.) *A Place in the World? Places, Cultures and Globalisation*. Oxford: Oxford University Press, pp. 87–132.

Sakai, M. (2016) *When Idols Shone Brightly. Development of Japan, the Idol Nation, and the Trajectory of Idols*. Available at: www.japanpolicyforum.jp/archives/society/pt20160407013017.html [accessed 27 July 2017].

Traphagan, J.W. and Thompson, C.S. (2006) The practice of tradition and modernity in contemporary Japan, in C.S. Thompson and J.W. Traphagan (eds.) *Wearing Cultural Styles in Japan: Concepts of Tradition and Modernity in Practice*. New York: SUNY Press, pp. 2–24.

Tsuchiya, Kei (2013) Ama-chan: Je je je no shinsoo. *Mainichi Shinbun*, May 18. Available at: http://mainichi/jp/select/news/20130518k0000e040173000c.html [accessed 29 July 2017].

Tzanelli, R. (2004) Constructing the 'cinematic tourist': the sign industry of *The Lord of the Rings, Tourist Studies*, 4(1): 21–42.

UNESCO (2003a). Available at: www.unesco.org/new/en/cairo/culture/tangible-cultural-heritage [accessed 20 July 2017].

UNESCO (2003b). Available at: www.unesco.org/new/en/cairo/culture/intangible-cultural-heritage [accessed 20 July 2017].

UNESCO (2003c). Available at: http://unesdoc.unesco.org/images/0013/001300/130071e.pdf [accessed 20 July 2017].

Vlastos, S. (ed.) (1998) *Mirror of Modernity: Invented Traditions of Modern Japan.* Berkeley, MA: University of California Press.

Watson S. and Waterton M. (2010) Reading the visual: representation and narrative in the construction of heritage. *Material Culture Review*, 71: 84–97.

12 Bedrock, metropolis and Indigenous heritage

Rendering 'The Rocks' invisible

*Felicity Picken, Hayley Saul and
Emma Waterton*

Introduction: stories of disconnection

In Australia, 'authentic' Aboriginal heritage is almost exclusively recognised as 'pre-colonial' and non-metropolitan, with traces of such heritage seldom show-cased in Australian cities (Hinkson 2003, Byrne 2003). This confinement of 'authentic' Aboriginal heritage to pre-contact, rural Australia was commenced by anthropologists in the early twentieth century, but lingers today in the assemblage of State and Federal legislation developed to define and manage heritage. There, heritage is structured into three distinct 'domains' or categories: historic, natural and Indigenous. Such structuring, as Byrne and Nugent (2004: 5) observe, sub-mits that 'Aboriginal heritage has no place in the historic (post-contact) period. It implies, in other words, that Aboriginal heritage properly belongs to the time before 1788, as if Aboriginal culture and history after that date are no longer authentic or "real"'. While the implications of this division are well-explored within the fields of history, archaeology and heritage management, particularly in terms of Aboriginal visibility and representation, less frequently examined are those it has for Australia's tourism sector, where Aboriginal post-contact heritage in urban contexts seems almost to have 'permanently departed the scene' (Byrne and Nugent 2004: 5).

Our purpose in this chapter is to argue that the tourism precinct of 'The Rocks', located on the western side of Sydney's iconic harbour, perfectly exemplifies this circumstance. It is earmarked as one of Australia's most visited colonial heritage tourist attractions and, in the repertoire of modern nations, is understood to repre-sent both British settlement and, crucially, the birthplace of the Australian nation. Urban morphology clearly puts The Rocks at the heart of the global city of Sydney, where it is marketed as *the* example of the city's continuity and authenticity, com-plete with subsurface archaeological features, fragile relics and well-preserved, British-styled original buildings. Settlement, as the most prominent narrative of heritage associated with The Rocks, seems to fill most of the cultural space available for '*knowing* and *feeling*' its past (after Watson and Waterton 2017: 49, original emphasis).

At the same time, it is also emblematic of the way particular places can lose what was once significant and meaningful about them. As a site of historic heritage, most narratives surrounding The Rocks overlook the wholescale re-engineering of its pre-colonial materialities, and the far-reaching consequences this has had for the objects, places and cultural practices of the area post-contact. Indeed, as a place that was quarried right out of the sandstone edges of the natural harbour to make way for the wharves and aprons that became Circular Quay, not even the contours of the geological bedrock remain as they were at the time of contact. Stories of Sydney's settlement, then, as told in and represented by The Rocks, have for far too long masked an equally compelling tale of dispossession. At the same time, the term 'dispossession', as antonym of 'possession', is problematic in its conformity with the categorical errors made by settler societies and the violations of these on Indigenous ontologies (Carter 2010, Hinkson 2003, Byrne 1996). Therefore, this is also a tale of resilience and adaptation expressed through an Indigenous reformation of The Rocks.

Within this historically dynamic, highly engineered environment, prompted by a desire to attend to a sense of loss and change, one Indigenous tour group tells of the deeper history of The Rocks, using the barest of material evidence. This chapter examines how The Rocks Dreaming Aboriginal Heritage Tour, provided by Dreamtime Southern X, achieves a heritage presence in a place that bears almost no physical resemblance to the 'country' that existed before colonisation. It was in this promise of a Dreaming Aboriginal Heritage Tour that we imagined a different way of interpreting place.

Australian Indigenous heritage and tourism

Disconnection with the past 'is typical of societies that have undergone transformations that have moved people and communities, in significant numbers, from one place to another or changed the way they work and live' (Watson and Waterton 2017: 48). Colonialism through European expansionism is a clear and potent example of this, as it has permanently and decisively transformed many of the relationships between people, pasts and places. Like many other nations with a colonial past, Australia has made a concerted effort to reassemble what it presents as heritage in order to better reflect contemporary views of multiple histories, alternative archaeologies, complex identities, and coexisting, sometime irreconcilable, viewpoints that are all embedded in relations of power (Casella and Fredericksen 2004, Connell 2007, Hollinshead and Suleman 2017). What is now widely described as the 'post-colonial turn' is bringing into being very real changes to heritage sites and heritage tourism, prompted by new intellectual and practical negotiations and frontiers that face up to, and engage with, the 'aftermath of colonialism' (Taiwo 1993). This has seen heritage and heritage tourism take a greater role in reconciliatory efforts that attempt to honour multiple voices and historical experiences, and remain cognisant of the continued imprint of these in our everyday, contemporary lives (Bhabha 2012, Lydon and Rizvi 2016). In Australia, this involves a far greater inclusion of Indigenous heritage and Indigenous peoples' interpretations of place or 'country'. Before this, Indigenous cultural and heritage tourism experiences were almost exclusively limited to the remote, central and northern parts of the country, and to a narrow view of pre-contact Indigenous culture (Simons 2000, Hinkson 2002, Davis 2007). In the places 'most colonised', in the cities and urban coastal fringes, the 'cult of disremembering' is a retrospective term for explaining how Indigenous heritage appeared to vanish (Stanner 1969, cited in Hinkson 2003: 297) or retreat to the northern half of the country (Altman 1989, Byrne 1996, Waitt 1999, Povinelli 1999).

The idea that 'real' or 'authentic' Indigenous culture exists in the north, and, by contrast, that 'dead' or 'fragmentary' cultural remnants exist elsewhere (Hinkson 2003: 300), has remained particularly stubborn. This is rehearsed in the promotion of 'traditional Aboriginal culture' in the Australian outback, which is predominant throughout the tourism industry, particularly in marketing, where there is a continued emphasis on those traditional-as-authentic aspects of Indigenous culture (Pomering and White 2011). Despite evidence that shows this discourse is beginning to change, the range of 'indirect Indigenous experiences' (Hinkson 2003), including museums, galleries, discovery centres and Indigenous rock art sights, as well as direct experiences through music, performance and Indigenous tours, shows the continuing 'currency of essentialism' (Murray 1992, cited in Byrne 1996: 101). This reflects a wider politics of 'hastily reading' cultural differences to reproduce 'pre-given [. . .] cultural traits set in the fixed tablet of tradition' (Bhabha 2012: 2) that, according to Craik (2001: 110), is not solely a problem of Australia's colonial history, but its 'inability to deliver on a positively formed post-colonial Indigenous Australian identity'. The corollary is the suppression of contemporary Indigenous culture from breaking free of the shackles of 'declining authenticity' (Byrne 1996).

The political will to support Indigenous Australian participation in the tourism industry began with the ideal of niche tourism experiences that could produce cultural and economic empowerment and autonomy for Indigenous people (Schmiechen and Boyle 2007: 59). The policies of Commonwealth and State governments under the framing of Australian and Torres Strait Islander (ATSI) tourism were focused most upon improvements in economic autonomy and employment in remote Indigenous communities (Whitford et al. 2001). Indeed, in the case of many of these communities, tourism was considered the only option for Indigenous people to achieve these goals (Altman 1989). The Sydney 2000 Olympic Games served to amplify an already increasing interest in 'Aboriginal Australia' (Hinkson 2002), and to highlight, based upon global tourist trends, an area of unmet tourist demand (Whitford and Ruhanon 2010). To better meet that demand, particularly in gateway and urban destinations like Sydney, the Federal and State governments launched various initiatives such as the Indigenous Tourism Group and Indigenous Tourism Champions Program, which work towards increasing the volume of 'export ready' Indigenous tourism experiences (Austrade 2017). Programme 'champions', for example, are selected according to criteria that include Indigenous ownership, employment opportunities for Indigenous people, and training, mentoring and exposure in the tourism industry. Today, the promise of encounters with *the world's oldest surviving culture* is a claim that spearheads Australia's distinctive cultural and heritage assets, with the Australian Government's official message to tourists being:

When visiting Australia, whether you are in a city, travelling the outback or enjoying a coastal holiday, there are Aboriginal tourism experiences that can connect you with the world's oldest living culture.

(Discover Australia 2017)

An introduction to The Rocks

On the face of it, The Rocks conforms to the idea that Indigenous heritage is 'difficult to locate' and 'largely invisible' in urban Australia (Hinkson 2002: 62). Such places are typically representative of what Hinkson calls 'post-contact' Australia, which are distinct from those remote and less 'contacted' places that have long been described in more purist terms as 'authentic' Aboriginal Australia (Byrne 1996). By this definition, The Rocks is not only Australia's first mega engineering project to dramatically reorder the landscape, it is also one of the oldest, continuing post-contact sites on the continent. Since the 1960s its significance has been shaped by its comparative colonial intactness, and correspondent heritage value, against the vastly expanding metropolis (Waitt 2000). Following historical trends of a stark separation between Indigenous, historic and natural categories of heritage, The Rocks could be supposed to exclude an Indigenous presence. Two factors somewhat mitigate this trend: first, as the birthplace of the colony, The Rocks is always *implicitly* a site of Indigenous heritage, and second, and much more recently, as a place where many international tourists first disembark to 'discover Australia', The Rocks has become an explicit promoter of Indigenous tourism.

A well-known tourist precinct at the northern end of the city of Sydney, nestled between Circular Quay and the Sydney Harbour Bridge, The Rocks, as a bastion of colonial Australia, is marketed for its sandstone buildings and cobbled streets, both of which were fashioned from the very 'rock' that lends the place its name. Originally occupied by the Eora People, it was one of the first sites of white settlement in the late 1770s, largely due to its proximity to the natural harbour and fresh water sources, and to the sheltering safety offered by the sandstone cliffs to the west. Those shorelines quickly began to shift in support of urban expansion and coastal reclamation, as early settlement transformed the area into a vibrant colony and adjacent port. Such developments precipitated uneasy relations between European settlers and Indigenous populations, particularly as those initially transient populations began to drop roots, spawning brothels, boarding houses, a hospital complex, convict tents, a parade ground, stores, commercial buildings, a blacksmiths and various establishments of law and order (Lydon 1993). From those earliest colonial beginnings, The Rocks has been primarily occupied by sailors, wharfies, gangs, prostitutes and pub landlords, most of whom lived in squalid dwellings adjacent to the harbour and engaged in nefarious activities (Hayllar and Griffin 2005).

Circumstances in The Rocks remained much the same until the 1960s, when demand for dockside labour began to dwindle (Morgan 1991). As Hayllar and

Figure 12.1 Cadman's Cottage

Griffin (2005: 520) argue, the 1960s were a 'key turning point' in The Rocks' history, which saw a transformation of the area 'from a poor, crime-ridden and physically blighted part of Sydney into one of its most appealing tourism precincts'. In large part, that is because the area at the time became suddenly conspicuous to developers who, taking a keen note of its harbour-side location, saw it as a promisingly lucrative site for developing high-quality housing and contemporary, high-rise office blocks. Such plans were halted, however, by appeals to cultural, historic and social values (Lydon 1993) and tourism as an alternative form of economic development. The Rocks, which had previously been thought of as an 'enclave of working-class housing' became, as Morgan (1991: 78) has noted, 'a site of national heritage', containing Australia's oldest surviving extant building, Cadman's Cottage (see Figure 12.1). Today, the area is an acknowledged heritage area, and is marked out as such by numerous attractions, monuments and heritage-styled signage (see Figure 12.2).

In 2016, the precinct received 2.83 million tourists, over half of which were international (Destination New South Wales 2017), and is one of three 'must see' places in Sydney, along with the Opera House and Darling Harbour. The Dreaming Tour complements the trade in traditional and contemporary Indigenous art and souvenirs in the Argyle and Spirit Galleries, Indigenous heritage displays in The Rocks Discovery Museum and in the Bangarra Dance Theatre (see Figure 12.3).

Figure 12.2 Signs of heritage tourism in 'The Rocks'

Figure 12.3 Souvenir shops in 'The Rocks'

The Rocks Dreaming Aboriginal Heritage Tour

The Rocks Dreaming Aboriginal Heritage Tour (henceforth the Dreaming Tour) is one of three tours conducted by Indigenous enterprise Dreamtime Southern X. The tour company was developed by Indigenous woman, Aunty Margret Campbell, who continues to operate the tours in conjunction with a small group of Indigenous guides.

The organisation's website describes the experience in the following way:

> This leisurely walkabout around The Rocks uncovers the authentic history of the Aboriginal people's saltwater heritage within Sydney Harbour, their land and water use and their spiritual connection to the adjoining waterways and foreshores.
>
> Aboriginal guides will demonstrate how this place we now know as Sydney continues to weave the Dreamtime Southern X text into it's [sic] modern, built up environment. Discover how to experience contemporary Aboriginal society right in the heart of cosmopolitan Sydney today.
>
> Drawing upon knowledge populated from the oldest ecologists, conservationists, wildlife carers, botanists, astronomers, climatologists and marine biologists on the Earth today, the guides will explain how this ancient wisdom continues to reveal itself within the English settlement of The Rocks.
>
> (Dreamtime Southern X 2018)

Dreamtime Southern X is one of 50 Indigenous tourism operators selected for the *Indigenous Tourism Champions Program* and one of two 'champions' that operate in The Rocks. The tour has no 'home' at The Rocks in the sense that it has no fixed presence in the form of a ticket office or operations 'window' on site. Instead, the tour is most visible through its online presence, where information is provided and disseminated and tours are booked. The tour begins in the forecourt of Cadman's Cottage, the oldest remaining example of the colonial built heritage, and is navigated loosely around seven stops or sites positioned along the harbour foreshore. Most of the tour is conducted as a gentle, conversational stroll between each 'stop', and is loosely scripted around the telling of cultural, and sometimes personal, stories. The conversational structure adds an element of spontaneity to each tour. In this way, and in the daily flow of an international tourist place, the guides remain receptive to the 'first contact' and intercultural exchanging that the tour often performs. Traditional objects, as well as some drawings, maps and pictures, are used to enhance the story-telling.

Our efforts to engage with the Dreaming Tour were undertaken individually, with each of us taking the tour separately, guided by 'Aunty', in the winter months of 2017. Adopting an autoethnographic approach, we each took notes and photographs, and attuned ourselves to the messages on offer, to the stories and sounds, to the sights/sites and visuals, and to our feelings, including how we orientated ourselves in the spaces of the tour. Importantly, the following reflections are based upon our *own* experiences of the tour. We are mindful of the fact that 'Aunty' received permission from community elders to deliver cultural content during the tour, as such, we have respectfully limited the discussions that follow to our auto-ethnographies of the excursion.

Rendering The Rocks invisible

As we embark from Cadman's Cottage, Aunty seemed to skirt the centre of The Rocks and its legacy of confinement. It was here that the 757 convicts of the First Fleet were encamped. As we walk north along the reclaimed foreshore that now serves as the dock for cruise ships, we leave behind the archaeological echo of the old gaol from the 1800s, submerged in sediment beside the Tank Stream. Aunty doesn't say why we take this route. It's unclear whether it's because this place has marginalised her to the waterfront fringes, or whether she follows a line of her saltwater heritage. She describes The Rocks as one big cemetery, and seems barely able to look at the buildings as we dart passed them. It's not just the stone that she says makes her uncomfortable, it's the cement. Looking closer, tiny carcasses of sea creatures are suddenly made visible – spires and whorls crushed and compressed between sandstone geometry. These were middens, now rendered static. What's left is a strange sense that these tiny, dead creatures are straining to move, to chime together again as a wave tumbles them around.

Glancing up from this inspection of the miniature, the scale of the slaughter becomes more apparent: a twenty-hectare burial ground where confinement is built into the very urban fabric. Such simple shifts in our focus trigger a momentary realisation of a more hidden landscape, recalling Val Plumwood's (2008: 1) recognition of a 'shadow place'. These are the sites that lurk in the in-between, places that scaffold the comforts of our ecological and economic lives, but that we choose not to see. In the case of The Rocks, Aunty prompts us to attend to a hidden landscape that supports our *cultural* comforts. And yet, it is a 'shadow place' in plain view. In a literal sense, the middens compose the colonial built fabric, appropriated into the now dubious project of 'civilising' the foreshore. Aunty's tour not only invites another way of seeing into the 'shadowy' foundations upon which the fabric of The Rocks is established, it also launches us into a consideration of how Indigenous heritage might inhabit the urban fabric in other, perhaps obscured, ways. *How* did such heritage become concealed in the shadows; present but systematically disregarded as the precinct transformed historically? And in the following, we also consider how aspects of Indigenous heritage are perhaps revealed in a more complex consideration of not just Indigenous-settler binary factions but a 'messier' late-eighteenth to early-nineteenth century landscape, where forms of confinement, restriction and (in)justice were meted out to diverse portions of the new urban settlement.

As we stroll along the foreshore, past the buried remains of Wharf House built in 1802, the home of Robert Campbell, one of Sydney's success stories in the common narrative of 'prosperity against adversity at the frontier', Aunty quietly muses at the sorrow she feels for Sydney's convict communities. Compared to the tenement houses that were more common lodgings for ex-convict families, Wharf House was built on the spoils of wood and coal exports, and later whaling and sealing, boasting an oasis of ornamental gardens replete with peacocks (Magee 2005). Aunty's identification with the convicts' feelings of displacement and confinement arouses a sense that those on board the First Fleet who were *not* willing colonists were also contained within this rapidly transforming urban landscape, sharing the pursuit of emancipation with the Aboriginal Eora. It was to The Rocks that Captain Arthur Phillip directed the convicts from the First Fleet immediately upon landing in 1788 (Magee 2005). Archaeological evidence of the tenements that grew up narrates living conditions which were far more modest than those of Robert Campbell. The impermeable geology had repelled intentions to design The Rocks with wide, airy streetscapes (Magee 2005), and the sandstone resisted the cutting of effective drainage to carry away the effluence of its densely packed inhabitants. By 1810, most of some 50 licensed taverns crammed the streets of the precinct (Magee 2005), catering rum, cheap food and temporary lodgings to sailors and wayfarers. Excavations of numerous grog bottles at the Sydney Sailors Home, dating to the 1860s (Lydon 1993), underscore the reputation that The Rocks earned as an abode for the underprivileged, ex-convicts and sailors seeking oblivion and to marinade their disempowered spirits in rum.

Where settlement at The Rocks could not penetrate the hard geology, it spilled outwards to occupy most of the Peninsula by 1845. Historical survey maps between 1833 and 1845 (Historical Atlas of Sydney website) describe rapid urban expansion, especially in the swelling maritime trade centre of The Rocks, with its storehouses, taverns, brothels and gaming houses. Of the rare archaeological evidence for the Aboriginal Eora around the precinct, a midden at Lilyvale was quick to be subsumed under new construction, probably before the 1833 survey plans that record established lots of land. Here, along with another Aboriginal site at Jobbins Building in The Rocks, glass had been reused and reworked into knapped tools (Lydon 1993) – a rare glimpse of the Indigenous-settler communities that were now sharing the peninsula and navigating the injustices of its rapidly transforming confines. Such urban narratives of Aboriginal Eora remain only glimpses in the archaeological record, but Aunty's sympathetic consideration of the shared convict-Eora cityscape casts a more substantial glance towards a heritage with at least some overlaps in the experience of poverty, lost liberty and displacement. In a sense, then, in a cityscape designed to socially incarcerate convict-settlers to the harsh, rocky peninsula is a place also imbued and inhabited by Indigenous narratives of similar (though not equivalent) injustices.

Replacing earlier ideas of inevitable cultural erosion to the forces of modernising Europe, a more optimistic view of cultural resilience understands the post-contact landscape as 'overlaying' and 'overlapping' Indigenous cultural landscapes rather than replacing them (Byrne 1996: 85). The materiality of The Rocks' urban fabric takes on the guise of a palimpsest – though the 'erasure' of certain material remains occurs, the precinct is immersed in ongoing processes of inscribing new meaning (Bailey 2006), remembering certain pasts, accumulating attachments and forgetting others. Though erasure of Eora heritage is perhaps most apparent in a physical sense in The Rocks, in a palimpsest landscape these processes are always in interplay with novel or resilient inscriptions of meaning upon the transforming urban streetscape too. The Dreaming Tour and its ability to render the Dreaming visible and connect visitors to Indigenous culture is intimately conscripted into this.

The Special Place of the Dreaming

The Dreaming exists on the metaphysical plane and is therefore evocative more than descriptive. The term evokes Indigenous Australian 'beliefs and actions, the transmission of 'themes through Aboriginal folklore' over generations, societal rules governing the creative process, the sacred qualities of some Aboriginal folklore, and the complexities of ownership in Aboriginal societies' (Davis 2007: 287). It is 'a form or mode of experiencing the world in which symbols of collectivity are constantly recharged with intimations of the self'' (Munn 1970 cited in Byrne 1996: 86). Once considered to have been irreversibly denigrated through the disconnection to country that was wrought by colonisation, the Dreaming has proven resilient and continues to shape identity and ways of being, embodying the spirit lifeworld of Indigenous Australian cultures.

In the Dreaming Tour, the Dreaming is living cultural heritage. It is the gradual unfolding of the Dreaming that forms the architecture of the tour and serves to reconcile, by connecting and continuing, the spiritual culture of pre-contact Indigenous societies and contemporary Indigenous lives. It is also a means through which the place becomes enrolled in the telling of both specific and general, pan-Indigenous Australian heritage, sweeping between specific sites at The Rocks and Indigenous relations with 'country' more generally. The Dreaming is both what is communicated and a communication device that acquaints times and places, pasts and presents, visibilities and invisibilities, ideas and bodies, landscape and cosmos. As we clung to the open water of the harbour, we were all struck by Aunty's mellow, almost hypnotic, delivery. As she speaks, her cadence slow and deliberate, her breathing seems patterned with the sea breeze. She pauses often, inhales deeply, appreciates. Sometimes she breaks off to speak to the ancestors. Frequently, she closes her eyes or looks into the distance for her memories. It is part confession, part didactic poetry, carrying the vividness of self-revelation while also imparting subtle instructions for living better. Aunty Margret describes this effect as one in which 'the stories and richness of the Dreamtime landscape interweave with modern living in downtown Sydney, one of the world's most cosmopolitan cities' (Dreamtime Southern X 2017). It is this 'Dreaming' that is spoken, walked, presented, demonstrated, shared and celebrated along the tour and infuses it with a dimension that is extra-territorial, by which is meant it is not wholly dependent upon evidence of the past because the materiality of *now* is also a manifestation of the Dreaming. Interpreting Indigenous Australian culture and lifestyle has itself been regarded as a tool to promote both a sense and care of place among tourists (Walker and Moscardo 2016).

Conclusion: stories of reconnection

We commenced this research through our own professional interest in heritage and tourism at The Rocks and our intrigue upon discovering The Rocks Dreaming Aboriginal Heritage Tour. We were struck with the question of how an Indigenous heritage tour was able to enliven the heritage of a place that appeared to be completely dispossessed of any evidence of it. It seemed that in order to perform such a feat at The Rocks, *The Rocks* must first be rendered invisible. The enormity of such a task could not be underestimated since The Rocks so well attests to a seemingly complete transformation of place and stands as an exemplar of Australian colonial heritage. As an urban landscape and a colonial heritage icon, The Rocks met the implicit criteria of *exclusion* of Indigenous Australian heritage (Hinkson 2007). Within this place, there appeared very little space for any other story to be told.

The idea of rendering The Rocks invisible was a far more problematic proposition than was first appreciated, but not a wholly unviable one. There are ways in which the Dreaming Tour does render The Rocks invisible but this is not uniform nor always necessary, and neither is it particularly desirable in the making of Indigenous heritage. To *only* render The Rocks invisible is to accede to the privileging of pre-contact Indigenous culture, to locate Indigenous heritage there and to perpetuate its location 'outside time' (Hinkson 2003: 297). Such a reading of The Rocks would continue to ignore the 'heritage of contact' that is hidden in plain sight, like the shell middens made static and the un-signified ochre pods. Likewise, it would continue to misrecognise post-colonial Indigenous Australian culture. At other times during the tour The Rocks as a colonial place is rendered very visible, when contemplating, for example, the experience of colonisation from the perspective of the people of the Eora nation who witnessed its 'birth' and the strange new orders that emerged there.

Then there is the Dreaming itself, an historical continuity, that also evokes the disruptive potentialities that Indigenous cultures possess and that have been celebrated by anthropologists like Hollinshead (1998) and Hinkson (2017). We witnessed such disruptions as we strolled with Aunty among the taken-for-granted legibility and aesthetic styling of The Rocks, notable for the familiarity of urban form in lanes and streets. Though our heritage tourist gazes were receptive (Urry 2001), in the first instance, to a built environment that embodies in its architecture and engineering a period of time that is already widely recognised as *colonial* heritage, with Aunty's guidance we found ourselves resituated, if not wholly in the Indigenous landscape of The Rocks, at least in the complicated and 'messy' palimpsest in which Indigenous and Colonial cannot be drawn as so materially and temporally separate.

Aunty's poetry does this by drawing upon the kinship and knowledge yielded by native trees and plants in the area, a material relation that is not particularly important to the telling of colonial histories of The Rocks. Likewise, journeying to the higher, pre-colonial contour of the land at what fragments remain of the beach restores the sight lines across the harbour and the stories that relate The Rocks with the vitality of the saltwater community who live(d) there. In these ways, the Dreaming can be interpreted by giving emphasis to the *continuities* in the contemporary landscape. Like all heritage tours, the Dreaming Tour engages the senses. What is different is what is selected from the sensorium to be made visible, edible, tangible, scented, audible and knowable. In this selection, the tour enacts a process of rendering invisibilities visible, casting light upon the 'shadow place' (Plumwood 2008) which is the Indigenous landscape entangled among the colonial fabric. All of the components enlisted to do this are hiding in plain sight, within the interstices of 'sites' as the modern eye is trained to see them. They are in sight lines, vegetation, mortar, earth and stone and the ever present 'Dreaming' that binds them together. Byrne (1996) depicts this as a process of entanglement that describes an authentic meeting of cultures, an important quality that is found in the Dreaming Tour. Perhaps *as* important for that palimpsest to sway between erasure and inscription though is that Aunty's poetic rendering of the Dreaming urges *realisation* without relying on exclusive delivery of knowledge *content* with the effect that now, as when Europeans first sought to understand Indigenous cultural life, aspects remain somewhat 'imponderable' (Davis 2007: 287).

References

Altman, J. (1989) Tourism dilemmas for aboriginal Australians. *Annals of Tourism Research*, 16(4): 456–476.

Austrade (2017) Policy and Strategy. Indigenous Tourism Group. Available at: www.austrade.gov.au/Australian/Tourism/PolicyandStrategy/Tourism2020/Working-Groups/indigenous-tourism [accessed 30 October 2017].

Bailey, G. (2006) Time perspectives, palimpsests and the archaeology of time. *Journal of Anthropological Archaeology*, 26(2): 198–223.

Bhabha, H. (2012) *The Location of Culture*. London: Routledge.

Byrne, D. (1996) Deep nation: Australia's acquisition of an indigenous past. *Aboriginal History*, 20: 82–107.

Byrne, D. (2008) Heritage as social action, in G. J. Fairclough, R. Harrison, J. H. Jameson, and J. Schofield (eds.) *The Heritage Reader*. London: Routledge, pp. 149–173.

Byrne, D. and Nugent, M. (2004) *Mapping Attachment: A Spatial Approach to Aboriginal Post-Contact Heritage*. Hurtsville: NSW Department of Environment and Conservation.

Carter, J. (2010) Displacing Indigenous cultural landscapes: the naturalistic gaze at Fraser Island World Heritage area. *Geographical Research*, 48(4): 398–410.

Casella, E. C. and Fredericksen, C. (2004) Legacy of the 'fatal shore': the heritage and archaeology of confinement in post-colonial Australia. *Journal of Social Archaeology*, 4(1): 99–125.

Connell, R. (2007) *Southern Theory: The Global Dynamics of Knowledge in Social Science*. Sydney: Allen & Unwin.

Craik, J. (2001) Tourism, culture and national identity: policies, publics and programs, in T. Bennett and D. Carter (eds.) *Culture in Australia*. Cambridge: Cambridge University Press, pp. 89–113.

Davis, M. (2007) *Writing Heritage: The Depiction of Indigenous Heritage in European-Australian Writings*. Kew, Victoria: Australian Scholarly Publishing.

Discover Australia (2017) Discover Australia's Aboriginal Experiences. Available at: www.australia.com/en-ie/news/2015/july/discover-australias-aboriginal-tourism-experiences.html [accessed 31 October 2017].

Dreamtime Southern X (2018) The Rocks Aboriginal Dreaming Tour. Available at: www.dreamtimesouthernx.com.au/ [accessed 27th February, 2018].

Hayllar, B. and Griffin, T. (2005) The precinct experience: a phenomenological approach. *Tourism Management*, 26: 517–528.

Hinkson, M. (2002) Exploring 'Aboriginal' sites in Sydney: a shifting politics of place? *Aboriginal History*, 26: 62–77.

Hinkson, M. (2003) Encounters with Aboriginal sites in metropolitan Sydney: a broadening horizon for cultural tourism? *Journal of Sustainable Tourism*, 11(4): 295–306.

Hinkson, M. (2017) Beyond assimilation and refusal: a Warlpiri perspective on the politics of recognition. *Postcolonial Studies*, 20(1): 86–100.

Hollinshead, K. (1998) Tourism, hybridity, and ambiguity: the relevance of Bhabha's 'third space' cultures. *Journal of Leisure Research*, 30(1): 121–156.

Hollinshead, K. and Suleman, R. (2017) Time for fluid acumen: a call for improved tourism studies dialogue with the decolonizing world. *Tourism, Culture and Communication*, 17: 61–74.

Lydon, J. (1993) Archaeology in The Rocks, Sydney, 1979–1993: from Old Sydney Gaol to Mrs Lewis' boarding-house. *Australian Historical Archaeology*, 11: 33–42.

Lydon, J. and Rizvi, U. (eds.) (2016) *Handbook of Postcolonial Archaeology*. London: Routledge.

Magee, O. (2005) *How The Rocks Was Won: Plan vs Politics*. Riverwood, NSW: EA Books.

Plumwood, V. (2008) Shadow places and the politics of dwelling. *Australian Humanities Review*, 44: 1–9.

Povinelli, E. (1999) Settler modernity and the quest for an indigenous tradition. *Public Culture*, 11(1): 19–48.

Simons, M. S. (2000) Aboriginal heritage art and moral rights. *Annals of Tourism Research*, 27(2): 412–431.

Schmiechen, J. and Boyle, A. (2007) Aboriginal tourism research in Australia, in R. Butler and T. Hinch (eds.) *Tourism and Indigenous Peoples: Issues and Implications*, New York: Butterworth-Heinemann, pp. 58–72.

Taiwo, O. (1993) Colonialism and its aftermath: the crisis of knowledge production. *Callaloo*, 16(4): 891–908.

Taylor, N. (2009) Legibility and aesthetics in urban design. *Journal of Urban Design*, 14(2): 189–202.

Urry, J. (2001) *The Tourist Gaze*, 2nd Edition. London: Sage.

Waitt, G. (1999) Naturalizing the 'primitive': a critique of marketing Australia's indigenous peoples as 'hunter-gatherers'. *Tourism Geographies*, 1(2): 142–163.

Waitt, G. (2000) Consuming heritage: perceived historical authenticity. *Annals of Tourism Research*, 27(4): 835–862.

Walker, K. and Moscardo, G. (2016) Moving beyond sense of place to care of place: the role of Indigenous values and interpretation in promoting transformative change in tourists' place images and personal values. *Journal of Sustainable Tourism*, 24(8–9): 1243–1261.

Whitford, M., Bell, B. and Watkins, M. (2001) Indigenous tourism policy in Australia: 25 years of rhetoric and economic rationalism. *Current Issues in Tourism*, 4(2–4): 151–181.

Whitford, M. M. and Ruhanen, L. M. (2010) Australian indigenous tourism policy: practical and sustainable policies? *Journal of Sustainable Tourism*, 18(4): 475–496.

13 Between the cliffs and the sea

St Kilda and heritage from afar

George S. Jaramillo and Alan Hooper

Introduction

The story of St Kilda may be considered a narrative of the disastrous nature of human abandonment and environmental entanglements. The custodians of the island over many centuries eventually disappeared with the evacuation of the last inhabitant of St Kilda in 1930. However, now that ownership has been transferred to the state, the question has arisen as to who are the custodians of St Kilda. It could be said that the current owners, the National Trust, are the island's custodians or that, since inscription on UNESCO's World Heritage List, arguably everyone is a custodian due to its outstanding universal value. This fuzziness of custodial rights and responsibilities might be regarded as an opportunity for locals (hosts) and visitors (guests) to enter into an open and transparent dialogue in the co-creation of the cultural experience activated by the site.

This chapter describes how the small island community group of *Ionad Hiort* is experimenting creatively in the development of an island heritage centre that 'moves beyond the museum' and towards a new form of cultural experience. We explore how this ongoing project approaches both the concepts of tourism culture and of custodianship, in relation to St Kilda, through strategic design thinking and integration into the growing tourism of the proximate islands of Lewis and Harris. We look at how the needs of the community may be met through a remote access centre that can share St Kilda's story 'from afar', whilst promoting engagement with change and innovation within both 'host' and 'guest' communities. The planned St Kilda Centre in the township of Uig provides a case study for the resourceful and innovative development of Scotland's remote heritage assets. The concepts of custodianship and tourism culture align to establish a model for the co-creation by locals and visitors of a cultural experience that acknowledges not only past, but also present and future, artefacts and traditions; a situation where change is embraced and innovation encouraged. After all, human ingenuity and innovation are central to the establishment and narratives of remote communities, such as St Kilda, located in extreme and challenging environments, to which we remain drawn in the twenty-first century.

The paper stems from an ongoing seven-year project to develop this idea, in the community of Uig on the west coast of the Isle of Lewis, Scotland. It focuses on the period of 2014–2016, during which a variety of stakeholders including The Glasgow School of Art (GSA), the World Heritage Organization (WHO), and multiple design consultants have provided valuable insight and direction for the community group. The case study uses data from semi-structured interviews, desk research, and participant observation that reflect on the ongoing story of the project, focusing on key moments across its development. In this chapter, we first look at the history of St Kilda, followed by an exploration of heritage and its relation to tourism/economic development programmes. We explore this critically through the concept of the tourist gaze (Urry and Larsen 2011), followed by a theorisation of the term 'custodianship' (Canavan 2016). We then use the case study of the St Kilda Centre to investigate these themes, analysing its development through the lens of custodianship. We conclude with the next steps for the project.

St Kilda: beyond the fall from grace

St Kilda is an archipelago of small islands about 80 km off the coast of the Outer Hebrides in the North Atlantic Ocean (Figure 13.1). More than 2000 years of human habitation illustrate an entanglement between people and the elements of nature, including harsh weather, limited resources and the tenacity to develop a way of life on a small area of land surrounded by sea. Although not a unique example (Easter Island and Lord Howe Island in the Pacific are others), St Kilda has over the last two millennia maintained a tenuous relationship between the sea, the cliffs and the people who have lived within its territory (Figure 13.2). Its history

Figure 13.1 A map of the site including the location of St Kilda and the future building site on Lewis

Figure 13.2 A view from Hiort towards the sea stacks and Soay

has been broadly covered (Geddes and Gannon 2015) and will be explored only briefly here, beginning in the 1700s.

It was not until smallpox and cholera impacted the main island of Hiort in the eighteenth century that an outside influence began to play a major role, leading to the loss of a large portion of its small (180) population (Stride 2010). During this period, increased visitation and interest from the British mainland brought about new visitor/host relationships; the St Kildans would 'perform' their cliff climbing skills for the various visitors arriving ashore (Geddes and Gannon 2016). The population continued decreasing, to just under 100 in 1920 and eventually to 34 by 1930, when the British government decided to evacuate the final members of the village in what has been described by some as a forced eviction. Yet, the story of St Kilda does not end there.

Since the evacuation, the island has maintained an important military presence – as a listening station during the Second World War and in modern times as a radar station for the Royal Artillery (Hebrides) Missile Range. Today, the islands are managed by the National Trust for Scotland, with sections leased to the Ministry of Defence and conserved in collaboration with Historic Environment Scotland. In the last 30 years, the islands have been recognised by the World Heritage Organisation for their outstanding universal value across a variety of cultural and natural criteria. Scientists and researchers study the wildlife, marine life, and geological, archaeological and historical aspects of the islands. The number of visitors grows each year and there is a desire to increase access to St Kilda for cruise ships, yachts, and visitors from the Isles of Lewis, Harris, and North Uist.

However, the remoteness and unique biological and archaeological aspects of St Kilda are threatened by this increase in visitation and use; many consider that it is being 'loved to death'.

'Heritagisation' and heritage tourism

The term 'heritage' is defined by multiple agencies; in particular, ICOMOS (2015) defines cultural heritage as 'an expression of the ways of living developed by a community and passed on from generation to generation, including customs, practices, places, objects, artistic expressions and values'. The idea that heritage is something passed down is taken up by many national and local agencies, who attend not only to cultural heritage but also to the historic environment, which is 'the physical evidence for human activity that connects people with place, linked with the associations we can see, feel and understand' (Scottish Government 2013). In this sense, the idea that heritage is artefactual, but also linked with identity and significance of place and feeling, is of key importance in understanding how heritage or the historic environment is viewed in this region.

In Scotland, national organisations such as Historic Environment Scotland, the National Trust for Scotland and various other agencies carry out the conservation and preservation of structures, sites, and landscapes. These agencies are entrusted to protect the heritage of the nation, providing the AHD (authorised heritage discourse) (Smith 2006). This discourse proclaims the official story of a region and integrates it into the maintenance and development of a national narrative. For many researchers, heritage relates not to the past, but to the present; it is constructed by the people of the present and is informed by current perceptions of history, rather than the material entities of the past (Lowenthal 1985). In this view, conservation is the management of the past from the perspective of present needs, telling certain stories and omitting others. This storytelling construction, to Hall (1999: 3), is 'a complex of organisations, institutions and practises devoted to the preservation and presentation of culture and the arts . . . to keeping what already exists'. In line with this idea of institutional knowledge, heritage is the promotion of a 'consensus of history by state-sanctioned cultural institutions and elites to regulate cultural and social tensions in the present' (Smith 2006: 3). This form of heritage is influenced by Romantic ideals and serves to perpetuate a pastoral, agrarian lifestyle, void of labour and hardship (Riley and Harvey 2007).

Today, the 'post-productivist' society has led to a greater appreciation of St Kilda, not only as a place for recreation, but as a place to learn about the unique island culture; a place where heritage becomes the attraction. Edensor has cautioned about the commodification of heritage in fixing places in time (Edensor 2008: 330), whereas Urry and Larsen (2011: 154) see it not just as commodifying history but as 'reproduced through performances made possible through networked relationships between organisations, machines, and especially buildings'. The tendency of heritage tourism to lead to the 'heritagisation' of the heritage asset, where the indigenous community are cast as actors in a staged history for the consumption of visitors, is well documented (Smith 2006, Ronström 2008).

Whilst providing a financial model in the short term, heritage tourism, often described as providing 'the only road to survival' (Ronström 2008:1), may not necessarily be in the interests of the local community at large in the long term. Its idealist perspective drives many of the people's lives, being hailed as a force for the regeneration of a region (Riley and Harvey 2007, Urry and Larsen 2011). For example, throughout Britain, groups such as the Arkwright Society or New Lanark Trust carry out conservation and preservation of structures, sites, and industrial landscapes, not only in the interest of protecting a particular site, but in providing improvement to a region in economic decline. Heritage as economic regenerator has had a long history in the United Kingdom, with examples from as early as the 1960s and 1970s. For example, the regeneration of Wirksworth in the Peak District during the late 1970s, with the assistance of the Civic Trust, had significant economic results in terms of population growth, inward investment in communities and a growing creative sector. The achievements of the Winkworth Project were recognised through the presentation of a 'Europa Nostra' award in 1983 (Gordon and Percival 1984). In Scotland, the promotion to World Heritage status of New Lanark and its eventual protection and rehabilitation have trans-formed the former mill into a tourist attraction for the region, but possibly at the cost of the region's overall identity (Bramley 2001, Landorf 2009) and the estrangement of lower income townspeople, who have been forced to move away due to higher property values and lack of work.

The commodification of heritage may engender a situation where the artefacts and cultural history of a place are 'owned' by local interests that regard their role as the packaging and delivery of the visitor experience. The past, or more precisely a sanctioned version of the past, is then valorised and foregrounded, diminishing the space for change and more importantly for local innovation. The situation is particu-larly evident in those rural settlements geographically remote from urban centres and even more so in island settings, where the economic opportunities alternative to tourism are limited and the space to challenge tourism conventions is restricted. The notion of performing for the visitor is not new, as shown by Ronström (2008); his vision of a dystopian future of local actors and visiting consumers essentially disenfranchises local people from pursuing alternative futures to those founded on the re-packaging of the past. Similar to the cliff-top performances of St Kildans for tourists referred to previously, Ronström's vision highlights the tendency for herit-age tourism to promote remoteness, both geographically in relation to urban centres and temporally in relation to contemporary life, which in turn denotes such places as peripheral and marginal to the present world. One might distil Ronström's argu-ment into the following: present needs being met through promotion of a particular version of the past at the expense of the future, where the lens of nostalgia fails to register 'precisely that which made islands central to previous times' (Ronström 2008: 1), namely innovation and the exploitation of settlement networks.

The tourist gaze and Scottish 'wilderness'

The development of tourism in the West stems from the Ancient Roman aristo-crats attending to their empire, to the pilgrimage routes of Santiago de Compostela in the Middle Ages, and to the mass tourism of British seaside resorts in the nineteenth century. A tourist is thus someone who engages in something extraordinary, outside their ordinary everyday life (Urry and Larsen 2011). Although this binary can be challenged, it shows how tourism may be a useful tool in understanding how people identify with other cultures and their circumstances. The tourist is out to *see* – a perspective of view and gaze (Boyer 1996) where the landscape (or building, site, etc.) is something to be viewed like a painting or photograph, based upon the eye and what is present 'out there'. This 'tourist gaze' (Urry and Larsen 2011) is not, however, just about engaging with the eyes, but also with the body; the concept moves beyond simply looking and involves, rather, the relationships and social constructions of how visitors engage and perform with the place they are visiting. These embodied practices include walking and engaging in discourse with residents (or the indigenous culture). A collective performance is developed through these embodied practices within the tourist space. In the case of heritage and tourism the tourist and resident engage in a variety of performances and views that showcase the politics of the space where control and power, identity and the 'ownership' of the past is present.

Views of the Scottish Highland and Island landscape recall lonely figures gazing upon infinite spaces or castles in the distance, like Robert Gibb's painting of Borthwick Castle from 1831. In Scotland, this view and 'gaze' is translated into the countless Romantic views or 'romantic gazes' inspired by nineteenth-century paintings, twentieth-century travel posters and literature that harks back to a 'Golden Age' of the Highlands and Islands of Scotland. Urry and Larsen (2011) have described a romantic gaze as the individual's view within the landscape, taking in the entirety of what they see. A romantic gaze is exemplified by the way that personal views of lonely travellers, desolate beaches and uninhabited spaces bring the viewer into intimate connections with the landscape. This gaze is reinforced in tourism campaigns, advertisements and social media sites and thus is engrained in the mind of the visitor, engendering expectations of lonely places and a Scottish 'wilderness'. In the case of St Kilda, visitors to the islands from the twentieth century had similar visitor/host expectations, as the inhabitants would showcase their talents for cliff climbing to the mainlanders (Geddes and Gannon 2016). This embodiment of the romantic gaze, however, limits the way that the visitor engages with not only the landscape but also the heritage of the site. It also limits the way that the resident (or host) sees themselves and the tourist within the gaze, often resenting the tourist for commodifying their past or abusing them for having the 'right' to view their heritage. As has been suggested in the last two sections of the chapter, the AHD and other forms of heritage-making regard heritage as something 'claimed', as an extraction, and as an amalgamation of all stories into a single narrative. There is a need in the twenty-first century to move beyond these notions of commodity, asset, and gaze towards a fluid notion of co-creation and co-ownership.

Custodianship

Recent academic research defines heritage as an emergent material and immaterial process (Smith 2006, Harvey 2015). There is a presence and embodied practice inherently bound to heritage in which DeSilvey (2006: 415) sees a way of 'working with the grain' of materials, such that a repressed past comes to life and with it, a creation of aural, temporal and visual senses, with an emphasis on the physical (Tilley 1994). Heritage may thus be considered a process of makings, within a relational encounter with the material and immaterial components. This understanding resonates with Canavan's idea of tourism culture.

Canavan (2016: 229), in his exploration of the concept of tourism culture, describes a space where 'tourism culture can be seen as the product of the melange of host and guest cultures that occur in a destination'. In contrast to Ronström's model of heritagisation where locals are typecast, in turn typecasting visitors and engendering staged behaviours in both, Canavan highlights the opportunities for co-creation of cultural experiences where the hosts (locals) and the visitors (guests) play complementary roles in a creative alliance. In the heritagisation model, the past is often regarded as under threat from the present, the local role is defined as that of proprietor rather than facilitator, a conservative mentality is reinforced and innovation is stifled. The tourism culture model, on the other hand, through the blend of external influences and local traditions, anticipates and exploits change through innovation as the basis for sustainable tourism. Accordingly, neither locals nor visitors are trapped in a version of themselves; rather, they are encouraged to participate in a developing situation where the challenges and opportunities of their interactions are acknowledged and built upon. As Canavan (2016: 238) notes, the nuanced and flexible host/guest interactions recognise 'on the one hand the persistence of originating cultures, whilst on the other appreciating the evolution and change in these as a result of the wider influences including tourism.'

The concept of custodianship establishes an explicit relationship between the heritage asset and the inherent obligations of the present incumbents to those of the future and as such can be regarded as empathetic to the tourism culture model and antithetic to Ronström's heritagisation model. Whilst inheritance is central to the concept of custodianship, heritage seen through a custodial lens transforms the inheritor's role from that of proprietor to that of facilitator. The custodial acknowledgement of temporal possession potentially opens the space for a more open and diverse dialogue between local and external parties, in turn offering the opportunity for co-creation of the cultural experience and a more agile management and sustainable development of the heritage asset.

Ionad Hiort: towards co-creation of heritage

On the west coast of the Isle of Lewis is the small township of Uig. Its scattered villages hug the bay, protected from the brunt of North Atlantic storms. Known as the place where the famed Lewis Chessmen were discovered, the Uig area, though beautifully rugged, shares many of the island's problems. For the last 30 years, a steady decrease of families, young folk and jobs has limited the growth of the region (Hall Aitken 2007). The consolidation of schools, the loss of military installations and concerns of limited support from the council have exacerbated these problems and the local communities have had to develop new ways to keep their communities intact.

The community group of *Ionad Hiort* ('St Kilda Centre' in Scottish Gaelic) has been working towards a notion of custodianship in its development of a new type of heritage-making. Since 2010, *Ionad Hiort* has worked with a variety of stakeholders, including Historic Environment Scotland, The Glasgow School of Art, the local Council and the Highlands and Islands Enterprises, to develop a space that moves 'beyond the museum' and towards a new definition of heritage and identity through the development of an island centre. The project initially came about through the creation of the St Kilda Opera, a £1.5 million, five-country project, developed by Scotland's Gaelic Arts agency, *Proiseact nan Ealan*, in 2007. This opera, inspired by the cliffs, people and history of St Kilda used creative techniques to unite five countries in a live performance in Gaelic from the cliffs, presenting an hour-long story of the island narrative (McKenzie 2007). In 2010, the *Ionad Hiort* group was created to oversee the then nascent idea of creating a remote centre. Running parallel to these developments, the World Heritage Organisation selected St Kilda as a case study for remote access heritage conservation and interpretation (UNESCO 2012), in part due to the production of a 3D laser scan of the islands through the 2009 collaboration between Historic Scotland and the GSA's Digital Design Studio (since renamed School of Simulation and Visualisation), titled the CDDV.[1] The scans formed part of a larger project idea of remote access and its use as a telematic approach to heritage. After a three-year period of contentious competition across the Western Isles, *Ionad Hiort* won the final commission to work on a feasibility study for the development of the centre (Maclean 2010). In *Ionad Hiort*'s proposal it was recommended that a new centre using remote access technologies should be built overlooking the cliffs of Mangerstadh (Figure 13.3). The site was chosen for its similarity to the topography of St Kilda as well as for its visual connection back to the archipelago, making it a unique surrogate for the actual site (Ionad Hiort 2017). The heritage centre's visualisation technologies would not just provide virtual access to the islands during inaccessible times of the year, but would create a whole new type of experience that otherwise could not be achieved, even by physically visiting the islands. The aim of the project was to develop a twenty-first-century research and visitors' centre, through the combination of visitors, technologies, narratives and residents.

Much of this work has been done through local community investigations, revolving around workshops and one-to-one talks where narratives and ideas are held in 'creative tension' or 'negative capability' (McAra-McWilliam 2007), to seek not a single solution but many alternatives that would be able to work for the community. It was during this period of development from report and commission towards mission statement that The Glasgow School of Art's Institute of Design Innovation (GSA) was introduced to *Ionad Hiort* by Highlands and Islands Enterprises in 2013, with the intention that the GSA could be both a sounding board and critical friend or 'tourist'. Particularly, work over the course of six months in 2014 involved a series of visits where community members of *Ionad Hiort* met with staff of the GSA and reflected upon what a new type of island centre would be like (Jaramillo 2017). GSA staff in their adopted role as 'tourists' enabled alternative ideas to come forward and promoted an open attitude. In the end, *Ionad Hiort* created artefacts from drawings, charts, and stories

Figure 13.3 A view of the Mangerstadh cliffs at the Geodh' an Fhithich site of the
St Kilda Centre

to interpret what the community and group wanted from the centre (Figure 13.4). This co-creation of strategy provided the group with a much-needed boost to their confidence, pushing them towards a new co-created plan and prospectus.

From 2015 to 2016 *Ionad Hiort* moved towards the realisation of their strategy by commissioning three consultants to aid in developing the new heritage centre through the creation of a fund-raising prospectus. This had three briefs: content (Metaphor, London), design (Dualchas Architects and Reiulf Ramstad Arkitekter) and business (Steve Westbrook, economist). The consultants provided a unique opportunity for *Ionad Hiort*'s voice to be manifest and promoted. They worked with the group to understand its requirements through site visits, workshops, and in-depth interviews with local residents and also used the findings of the GSA and other previous work, including the Rebanks (2015) Report that established a sound economic basis for having a centre in Uig. Seasonal increases in visits by cruise ships to the Isle of Lewis has provided a new impetus for the establishment of a much-needed facility, with coaches from the main island settlement of Stornoway travelling to the west coast of the island where the proposed facility is to be located. Finally, in August 2017, there was a major step forward with the publication of the final prospectus and the presentation of the master plan at a

Figure 13.4 The proposed design for the heritage centre

St Kilda Symposium in Stornoway. Here, in front of major stakeholders, including the Heritage Lottery Fund, Historic Environment Scotland and the National Trust, *Ionad Hiort* presented a wholly new concept that was at its core the group's idea. The group now needs to move ahead with the establishment of funding cycles as the project has a relatively high capital cost.

The idea of the centre has been positively received by Peter Debrine of UNESCO and government ministers, including Lord Dunlop (Stornoway Gazette 2016). There is also support from the broader heritage sector, as the centre is seen as a way to generate local jobs and improve economic activity within the region. The specific plans, however, have not been without their critics; many believe that there could be other approaches to developing the centre than by constructing a £9 million structure. One possibility might be to build small structures in a phased development that would allow for the ebb and flow, and the fickle nature, of tourism. The accepted scheme could also be criticised for the fact that it used paid consultants, who provided their own agenda and had preconceived notions about the themes of the centre. Yet, the overall co-creation of this centre from art piece to community group, from art school to consultants, shows how custodianship and co-creation can be a way of developing a new type of heritage centre. A recent review of the work shows continued support for construction from government ministers. It is possible that, in the development stages of the project, further visitor input and the ongoing growth in visits from Stornoway will provide new ideas to enhance its design.

Conclusions

Communities in the Western Isles thrive, grow and work within the constraints presented by these islands. Currently many projects, located on the island fringes, are seeking innovative ways to attract, maintain and sustain healthy levels of community. The work of *Ionad Hiort* and its co-creation of heritage through the proposed St Kilda Centre is representative of such rural innovation. As has been discussed, there is some contention between the preservation of heritage and the commodification of that heritage for the consumption of tourists. This chapter has discussed how heritage bodies, local people and tourists may come together in the co-creation of heritage, based on the notion that the tourist is an embodied practitioner in heritage-making rather than just a viewer. The new centre, with its great potential for co-creating heritage and involving the tourist, not as consumer or even performer of heritage, but rather as custodian of it in the same way as the host, would lead to new approaches to theorising heritage. It is to be hoped that this project will continue to push the boundaries of what it means to claim rights over a historical place, to rethink the ways that heritage is performed and created, and to consider how ideas of rural innovation can be employed at a global level.

Acknowledgements

The authors would like to thank the members of *Ionad Hiort*, particularly Malcolm Maclean, Joni Buchanan, and Iain Buchanan, for working with them in exploring these concepts and for promoting a new direction in heritage tourism and development. They would also like to thank the communities of Uig and Stornoway for their hospitality and assistance in the various stages of this investigation.

Note

1 CDDV is Centre for Digital Documentation and Visualisation. Since 2015, Historic Scotland has been renamed Historic Environment Scotland.

References

Bramley, R. (2001) So you want to build a 'hall of fame'? in *CAUTHE 2001: Capitalising on Research; Proceedings of the 11th Australian Tourism and Hospitality Research Conference*. Canberra: University of Canberra Press, pp. 17–27.

Canavan, B. (2016) Tourism culture: nexus, characteristics, context and sustainability. *Tourism Management*, 53: 229–243.

DeSilvey, C. (2006) Observed decay: telling stories with mutable things. *Journal of Material Culture*, 11(3): 318–338.

Edensor, T. (2008) Walking through Ruins, in T. Ingold and J.L. Vergunst (eds.) *Ways of Walking: Ethnography and Practice on Foot*. Aldershot: Ashgate Publishing, pp. 123–142.

Geddes, G. and Gannon, A. (2015) *St Kilda: The Last and Outmost Isle*. Edinburgh: Royal Commission on the Ancient & Historical Monuments of Scotland.

Geddes, G. and Gannon, A. (2016) When tourism came to St Kilda. *The Herald (Scotland)* [Online] Available at: www.heraldscotland.com/news/14324289.When_tourism_came_to_St_Kilda [accessed 6 April 2016].

Gordon, M. and Percival, A. (1984) *The Wirksworth Story: New Life for An Old Town.* Wirksworth: Civic Trust.

Hall, S. (1999) Whose heritage? Unsettling 'the heritage', reimagining the post-nation, *Third Text*, 13(49): 3–13.

Hall Aitken Inc. (2007) *Outer Hebrides Migration Study Final Report*, Comhairle nan Eilean Siar. Glasgow: Western Isles Enterprise and Communities Scotland.

Harvey, D.C. (2015) Heritage and scale: settings, boundaries and relations. *International Journal of Heritage Studies*, 21(6): 577–593.

Ionad Hiort (2017) "Proposal – Ionad Hiort". Available at: www.ionadhiort.org/the-proposal [accessed 6 April 2017].

ICOMOS-UK (2015). *A Cultural Heritage Manifesto*. London. Available at: www.icomos-uk.org/uploads/sidebar/PDF/A%20Cultural%20Heritage%20Manifesto.pdf [accessed 27 September 2017].

Jaramillo, G. (2017) Enabling capabilities: innovation and development in the Outer Hebrides. *M/C Journal*, 20(2). Online. Available at: http://journal.media-culture.org.au/index.php/mcjournal/article/view/1215 [accessed 27 September 2017].

Landorf, C. (2009) Managing for sustainable tourism: a review of six Cultural World Heritage Sites. *Journal of Sustainable Tourism*, 17(1): 53–70.

Lowenthal, D. (1985) *The Past is a Foreign Country*. Cambridge: Cambridge University Press.

Maclean, D. (2010) "Bitter Strife over St Kilda Visitor Centre." *The Caledonian Mercury*. 29 Jan. 2010. Available at: www.caledonianmercury.com/2010/01/29/bitter-strife-over-st-kilda-visitor-centre/001383 [accessed 6 April 2017].

McAra-McWilliam, I. (2007) Impossible things? Negative capability and the creative imagination, in *Creativity or Conformity Conference*. Cardiff, pp. 1–8.

McKenzie, S. (2007) "Opera celebrates St Kilda history." *BBC News*. 23 June. Available at: http://news.bbc.co.uk/1/hi/scotland/highlands_and_islands/6763371.stm [accessed 6 April 2017].

Rebanks, J. (2015) St Kilda Centre – a World Class Idea. Report.

Riley, M. and Harvey, D. (2007) Oral histories, farm practice and uncovering meaning in the countryside, *Social & Cultural Geography*, 8(3): 391–415.

Ronström, O. (2008) A different land: heritage production in the island of Gotland. *Shima: The International Journal of Research into Island Cultures*, 2(2): 1–18.

Smith, L. (2006) *Uses of Heritage*. Oxford: Routledge.

Stornoway Gazette (2016) Refining plan for St Kilda Centre. [Online] Available at: www.stornowaygazette.co.uk/news/refining-plan-for-st-kilda-centre-1-4210361 [accessed 27 June 2017].

Stride, P. (2010) Survival of the fittest: a comparison of medicine and health on Lord Howe Island and St Kilda. *Journal of the Royal College of Physicians Edinburgh*, 40: 368–73.

Tilley, C. (1994) *A Phenomenology of Landscape: Places, Paths, and Monuments*. Oxford: Berg.

UNESCO (2012) *Using remote access technologies: Lessons learnt from the Remote Access to World Heritage Sites – St Kilda to Uluru Conference*. London.

Urry, J. and Larsen, J. (2011) *The Tourist Gaze*. 3rd Edition. London: SAGE Publications Ltd.

14 Made in China

Creating heritage through tourist souvenirs

Penny Grennan

Introduction

This chapter will consider the influence that tourist souvenirs have on cultural stereotyping and cultural seepage, and their role in creating, contesting, and defining heritage and cultural value. In turn, this created heritage is appropriated by tourism and becomes part of touristic practices. The difficulties of locating and understanding heritage and culture are typified by the shifting narrative of souvenirs. This narrative determines their value (Stewart 2007, Miller 2009), as well as contributing to slippery notions of the past. Souvenirs have cultural currency as a result of their origins and associations; however, notions of authenticity and representation are contested through the existence of multiple narratives. Particularly if they are mass produced, souvenirs are often approximations or interpretations of real places and things, but despite their cheapness and ubiquity they carry powerful cultural narratives. The origins of these easily recognisable cultural narratives are complex, particularly as souvenirs are often not made in the places in which they are eventually sold and which they are supposed to represent. Using a Roman soldier pencil sharpener with a moving head bought on Hadrian's Wall and made in China as an example, this chapter will discuss what Lynne Fallwell (2007) calls 'geographic specificity', as well as exploring souvenirs as signifiers (Barthes 1997) and trophies (MacCannell 1999), investigating the fluid narrative content of souvenirs and considering how they contribute to the making of complex personal and public histories. Tourist souvenirs are not expected to be authentic, but conversely, they are expected to represent the truth at some level. This chapter will interrogate notions of created cultural value through an adapted listing schedule from Historic Scotland using intrinsic value, contextual value and associative value as the descriptors. The study aims to illuminate the contradictions between heritage, authenticity and cultural representation in relation to the experience and interpretation of place by visitors, thereby questioning what heritage means to tourists in the twenty-first century.

What is a souvenir?

Morgan and Pritchard (2005: 46) describe souvenirs as 'objects of thresholds set apart from the everyday through the meanings attributed to them by their owners as prisms of remembrance'. Souvenirs have resonance on both physical and emotional levels, with the materiality of the objects playing as important a part in their lure as does their narrative importance. Souvenirs are objects that prompt feelings of loss, longing and nostalgia (Stewart 2007) and are dependent on their narrative for agency. A souvenir may be bought, received as a gift or made, but its key characteristic is its value to the owner and this value is the narrative that has been invested in the object. The role of souvenirs is to fix the past in the present, although the fixed narrative is mutable and always incomplete. Nostalgia is concerned with memory; implicit in this is a longing for another time or place or person, which is in turn blurred by changing contexts over time. The souvenir becomes an aide-memoire through its materiality, which satisfies a need for certainty even if the certainty is contestable, making the past real in the present while provoking feelings of loss and longing.

The question 'What is a souvenir?' addresses both physical and emotional meanings. According to Susan Stewart (2007), a souvenir is an item that is taken, bought and appropriated, which induces feelings of longing and nostalgia in the owner while fixing a narrative in their mind. The nature of the souvenir is defined by ownership and by the intention of the owner. Stewart (ibid.: 136) calls the emotional investment that the owner has in the souvenir (which characterises it and makes it emblematic) the 'narrative of origins'. She asks: 'What is the narrative of origins? It is the narrative of interiority and authenticity. It is not a narrative of the object; it is a narrative of the possessor'. The narrative is the story of the souvenir and its owner, while memory is the means of activating the narrative and making it real. The function of the narrative in the souvenir is so strong that the souvenir does not exist without it. Although the souvenir is material proof of a place and a relationship, the truth lies in the narrative, one that can only be constructed. According to Stewart, the souvenir's 'narrative of origins' has the power to miniaturise monuments, capture cultural emblems and fix the past in the present.

A process of iteration is at work: the object, its fact, our relationship with it and its fictionalisation, the subjective understanding of the truth and therefore the value that we place on it, all feed back into our continuing relationship with the item. As Bourdieu (1979: 91) states, 'the mind is a metaphor of the world of objects which is itself but an endless circle of mutually reflecting metaphors'; objects are vehicles for memory, history, knowledge, change, relationships, beliefs, judgement, value, understanding and progress. Igor Kopytoff (1986: 68) describes the biography of things, each object having a unique personal story as a result of its individual ownership and use: 'We accept that every person has many biographies . . . each of which selects some aspect of the life history and discards others. Biographies of things cannot be but similarly partial'.

The miniature nature of many souvenirs adds to their fantastic quality and further removes them from the realm of the real, which in turn may add to their potency. Interestingly, the purchasing of a miniature Eiffel Tower to remind one of a trip to Paris makes the experience more real once it has passed, although the relationship between the Tower and the souvenir is a fantastic one. The Tower has shrunk and may have been manufactured in the millions somewhere other than Paris, but the purchaser's feelings towards the item are very real since they have invested their individual experience in the souvenir. We all know, however, that souvenirs are an imitation of the experience we have had, a sham. MacCannell (1999: 159) states that, 'to prevent the souvenir from becoming elevated in importance to the point where it breaks its relationship with the attraction, it is always represented as a fallen object, as no substitute for the thing itself'. Stewart (2007: 136) also says that, 'the souvenir must remain impoverished and partial so that it can be supplemented by a narrative discourse, a narrative discourse which articulates the play of desire'.

Making copies of landmarks is, however, fairly straightforward. In terms of promoting identification, it is interesting to look further and consider how a nation or a continent may become, stereotypically, represented by, for example, textiles, sculpture, donkeys, castanets and sombreros. These representations are often as lacking in nuance as the tourist packaged experience that resulted in the purchase of a tourist souvenir may have been in the first place. Nevertheless, as an iterative process of shifting content occurs through the attachment of personal narrative, the souvenir becomes imbued with complexity and personal value; and who knows what epitomised Paris before the Eiffel Tower was built?

It is in the nature of souvenirs to reconcile apparent contradictions between national stereotypes and personal experience; the ubiquity of souvenirs is the very means by which the fiction of other cultures is accessed and made our own. Souvenirs encompass a dual narrative, both personal and cultural; they are shorthand for cultural indicators and a means of buying what is not for sale. The souvenir represents the past in the form of an incomplete symbol of what might be remembered but this, in turn, is fictionalised by the object itself. Although bought at a particular point, the souvenir may become emblematic of a whole trip, a time in a person's life, a relationship, or a country, despite often being mass produced. It becomes an isolated representation of a moment; hence the dichotomy between the individual item, invested with personal and individual feelings and emotions, and the tourist market in mass-produced souvenirs. However, all souvenirs are considered to be unique because of their personal and individual resonance.

All tourist souvenirs have cultural currency. Notions of authenticity and representation are, however, contested because of the influence of the market place and the global economy. It is evident that the manufacturing origins of many souvenirs have nothing to do with what, or where, they represent and this could be regarded as the identifying difference between tourist and so-called 'ethnic' souvenirs; the latter are those which are made where they are bought and which represent some aspect of Indigenous folk or cultural heritage. 'Ethnic' or cultural souvenirs, such as folkloric or craft objects, are often more expensive than mass-produced ones, although they too are often produced on a large scale, as, for example, in government textile and rug shops in India. The same rugs can be bought for a fraction of the price on the internet but the experience for the purchaser is not the same. In the case of a souvenir the key is its *significance* to the owner (Miller 2008). 'Ethnicity' suggests authenticity, but this distinction is often blurred by cultural seepage or the fluid nature of cultural representation. Daniel Miller (1987: 215) argues that authenticity originates within the personal realm:

The authenticity of artifacts as cultural derives, not from their relationship to some historical style or manufacturing process – in other words, there is no truth or falsity immanent in them – but rather from their active participation in a process of social self creation in which they are directly constitutive of our understanding of ourselves and others.

Walter Benjamin (1969: 4) raises questions about value and authenticity in relation to mechanical or mass reproduction, proposing that through reproducing the image its 'aura' is diminished and it becomes distanced in a negative way:

> One might subsume the eliminated element in the term 'aura' and go on to say: that which withers in the age of mechanical reproduction is the aura of the work of art. This is a symptomatic process whose significance points beyond the realm of art. One might generalize by saying: the technique of reproduction detaches the reproduced object from the domain of tradition. By making many reproductions it substitutes a plurality of copies for a unique existence.

Is the aura of a monument, place or event diminished through its replication in the form of a souvenir, and has the way that copies are regarded by Benjamin contributed to current attitudes to authenticity? If this is the case, it could be argued that to regard the aura as immutable, and therefore only capable of being spoiled by reproduction, is to underestimate the value of the new object; the souvenir may be *redeemed* by its narrative, whether personal or cultural, thereby giving it its own authenticity.

Interestingly, the criteria that govern the scheduling of historic buildings and monuments in Scotland resonate with the qualities that need to exist for an object to be a souvenir. The key categories are: intrinsic value, contextual value and associative value. In the following passage, taken from the Scottish Historic Environment Policy (2011), the word *souvenir* has been substituted for *monument*:

> The Cultural significance of any *souvenir*, whether of national importance or more local significance, can be characterised by reference to one or more of the following; the characteristics are in three groups:
>
> **Intrinsic** – those inherent in the *souvenir*;
>
> **Contextual** – those relating to the *souvenir's* place in the landscape or in the body of existing knowledge;
>
> **Associative characteristics** – more subjective assessments of the associations of the *souvenir*, including with current or past aesthetic preferences.

These criteria neatly describe the differing values of souvenirs and are particularly resonant in the case of World Heritage sites and, perhaps ironically, the representations made of them.

The *intrinsic* value of a souvenir may lie in its rarity, beauty, cost or collective cultural narrative value. The *contextual* value of a souvenir may lie in its public narrative; for example, the Elgin Marbles, or the narrative of the place or object of which it is a souvenir. The *associative* value of a souvenir is contained within its personal narrative and this value characterises most souvenirs. However, souvenirs are vehicles for multiple narratives and may contain all three types of characteristic.

It is interesting to consider how attachments are made to such hybridised objects as souvenirs. Konrad Kostlin (2007: 3) states that,

> any stuff can be denominated to be a souvenir. Just let it know its denomination: 'You have to serve me as a souvenir'. It is the authoritative act of the individual, which can convert any stuff into a souvenir, if it is connected with his/her life'.

On this basis, the lack of uniqueness and absence of historical or cultural accuracy is irrelevant to the value of the souvenir; instead, it requires a point of identification that serves as a signifier to be filled with narrative. Barthes describes the Eiffel Tower as a pure signifier to be filled with the dreams of men [sic] in the same way that souvenirs of the tower are. He says:

> The Tower attracts meaning . . . it plays a glamorous part, that of pure signifier i.e. of a form in which men unceasingly put meaning (which they extract at will from their knowledge, their dreams, their history), without this meaning thereby ever being finite and fixed: who can say what the Tower will be for humanity tomorrow? But there can be no doubt it will always be something, and something of humanity itself.
>
> (Barthes 1997: 4)

The often miniature nature of souvenirs contributes to their value as signifiers because, although they are portable versions of monuments and culture, they demand a suspension of disbelief that makes the possibility of personal attachment and narrative compelling. The tourist souvenir has become transformed, both actually and metaphorically, through a process of replication and miniaturisation. A crucial distancing needs to take place to allow the investment of personal narrative to occur. The souvenir is evidence of experience. The distortion of the replica is commonplace, now that the use of fridge magnets and pencil sharpeners to describe and evidence history and place has become normalised. The fridge magnet considered in this research (see Figures 14.1 and 14.2) employs cartoon qualities in its representation of a Roman Centurion, while the pencil sharpener (see Figures 14.3 and 14.4), although rather more realistic, is still a pencil sharpener with a moving head and sword. Where do these designs originate and what relationship do they have to Hadrian's Wall in Northumberland, where they were bought?

Souvenirs, particularly if they are mass produced, are often made from cheap materials like plastic, resin and tin, as this ensures that they are affordable. They are often approximations or interpretations of real places and things, specifically designed for the mass tourist market. Despite their cheapness and ubiquity they carry within them a powerful cultural narrative. The origins of these easily recognisable cultural narratives are complex, particularly as souvenirs are often not

Figure 14.1 Roman souvenir fridge magnet

Figure 14.2 Back of Roman souvenir fridge magnet

Figure 14.3 Roman souvenir pencil sharpener

Figure 14.4 Back of Roman souvenir pencil sharpener

made in the place in which they are eventually sold and which they are supposed to represent. Today many tourist souvenirs are made in China.

Souvenirs are desired, rather than desirable, as they do not embody any collective benefit. However, the manufacture of souvenirs may be deemed desirable as a way of stimulating economies and providing employment through their manufacture and sale. Souvenirs are also a way of disseminating culture and cultural symbols; it is a different question whether or not the particular products are culturally desirable. Souvenirs are bought because they are desired by the purchaser. Value judgements are constantly being exercised in the market place and the trade in souvenirs is no exception to this.

Cultural stereotyping

Geography is part of the defining nature of the tourist souvenir; what Lynne Falwell (2007: 1) calls its 'Geographic Specificity'. She describes a process by which tourism in post-war Germany has resulted in a mediated cultural profile where 'the handiwork and regional crafts of Southern Germany, Bavarian beer steins and Lederhosen, cuckoo clocks from the Black Forest, emerge as typical souvenirs for the country as a whole' (ibid.: 8).

In a similar vein, Adrian Franklin (2010: 196) discusses the way in which the cultural artefacts and images of a marginalised and almost invisible group, the Indigenous people of Australia, have been adopted as symbols of the country that has oppressed them, even though most of the cultural practices that are represented no longer play a central role in Aboriginal life. In this case, it is a combination of a quest for the exoticism of the past, a championing by the white arts community, and guilt, which has resulted in 'at best an extremely confused iconography of nation'. This 'Aboriginal semiotic drenching' (ibid.: 196) has resulted in the appropriation of cultural symbols and practices by predominantly white producers (designers, travel writers, souvenir makers) to serve the market for old, quaint and strange symbols of the nation. Consequently, Aboriginal images and wild life characterise many Australian souvenirs. Since souvenirs are about memory, it is understandable that the design of tourist souvenirs often references the past. The process of cultural fixing is not linear but is often, in the production of souvenirs, mainly driven by the market. Ironically, the very difference and distinctiveness of Aboriginal culture, represented through exotic forms of visual art, make marketing the symbols of Old Australia easy:

> From the early encounters both colonial appropriation and Aboriginal agency played roles in the development of the boomerang as a national symbol. Remarkably soon after the European arrival in Australia Aboriginal groups began manufacturing implements for the purpose of trading with newcomers.
> (Effington in Franklin 2010: 198)

Francisco Fernandez (2007) identifies the hammock as an example of misappropriation of a cultural product as a souvenir. The Merida in Yucatan, Mexico, use hammocks every day for sleeping in and they are rarely used outdoors.

Their homes often have a special alcove built for the purpose of sleeping and resting whereas, among tourists, the hammock is a symbol of outdoor leisure. This is the equivalent of a divan bed becoming a symbol of Western culture, which it may be, but it is not yet a source of souvenir design.

In a world of marketing, logos are the shorthand for identity and authenticity, The Trade Mark symbol ™ signifies uniqueness and originality and that any unauthorised copying is a crime. The fact that the trademark is applied to appropriated items and symbols does not affect its value in the eyes of the manufacturer, the vendor or the purchaser. Cristina Garduno Freeman (2007: 4) says that it is the logo that is considered to be the distinguishing feature of souvenirs sold at the Sydney Opera House in Australia. She quotes from the official website: 'The range of official licensed merchandise has developed into an easily identifiable and highly desirable product, as it is the only product in the market that carries the official Sydney Opera House logo, the mark of authenticity'. Notably, although the Sydney Opera House is intended for musical performances, it is the dominant features of the outside of the building that have become its signifier and which are translated into the logo which is then applied to the commonplace, for example, pencils, tea towels and bowls. In order to be special the souvenir needs to have distinguishing features that are easily recognisable, whether these are particular to a nation, a building, or a place.

Godfrey Evans (1999) charts the rise of Far Eastern producers of souvenirs. Japan was the principal world producer of souvenirs between 1930 and 1965, after which it was superseded by first Taiwan and then China. This migration of primary souvenir manufacture is attributable to global trade and low labour costs. However, lately, there appears to have been a move in British retailing towards supplying high-quality souvenir goods under the logo, Made in Britain, where provenance is the most important aspect of a souvenir's value (ibid.: 95). Themes have developed in the global souvenir market driven by the merchandising strategies and brand promotion of powerful multi-national corporations. The souvenirs bought at Disneyland, for example, carry the narratives of cartoon characters and their films and of mass-produced dreams. These are then supplemented by the narrative of the place where they are bought – Paris or Orlando – and finally by a personal narrative, through their purchase by a tourist.

Narrative investment is not just the province of the typical tourist souvenir. If the narrative defines the souvenir then the souvenir can be any object that has *souvenir qualities*. The cultural exploitation of events and individuals is big business: 'According to one estimate, the total value of "collectable Diana Mementoes" (Princess Diana) in the year from 31 August 1997 exceeded £252 million' (ibid.: 98). These souvenirs were memorial pieces following Princess Diana's death. The pieces will have served the same function as tourist souvenirs except that their narrative is attached to a person instead of a culture. In this case however, the primary cultural resonance is the British royal family and all that they signify, historically and socially, their particular relationship to Diana and the fact that she died in tragic circumstances at a young age. These fixed narratives will then be supplemented by those of the owners – where they were when she died, where they bought the souvenir and what they felt about the circumstances of her death.

Politics, culture and production

During an interview with a man (S), who set up a souvenir manufacturing business in Haiti, the tension between vested interests and the commodification of Haitian culture for a Western market became clear (Grennan 2014). S worked in Haiti in the early 1980s as a development worker with the remit to establish a sustainable Haitian craft business. The scheme was initially funded through the Caribbean Based Initiative, which the then US president, Ronald Reagan, implemented as a means of improving trade between the US and countries in Central American and the Caribbean. The US wanted to forge relationships in the Caribbean in response to the rise in communist insurgents in Nicaragua and this alliance provided import duty breaks and tax incentives to promote trade and political leverage. The prevailing economic and political climate dictated the way that the business was set up and what was made, as well as to whom the goods were sold. Consequently, S had to operate within established US business models, which exploited existing markets. A theme that ran through the interview was the role of foreign intervention, from finance to design and distribution. S described how Haiti was a production annex for the US, its only input into the programme being the supply of cheap labour.

S used his design experience, gained while working for a toy company, when deciding which objects would sell. He cited the design of Fisher-Price play sets, where the toy farms are modelled on those near the company's design centre outside Buffalo in western New York State. This seems to be stating the obvious: that people design what they know, for the markets that already exist, within established cultural and economic frameworks. What became apparent in this interview were the contradictions inherent in producing souvenirs within these frameworks and the ways in which cultural boundaries and origins were blurred. No culture is hermetically sealed, but this case illustrates the way in which the market dictates the design of the product that results in the production of fictive souvenirs and cultural stereotypes. Although he acknowledged that Haitian art is identifiable ('Haitian art was a sort of genre'), he ended up producing souvenirs designed by non-Haitians for the American market. S also commented on how prices for art in Haiti were inflated because of external art markets and the flow of rich tourists, illustrating how external notions of value impact on local economies and result in changes in perceptions of worth.

Despite S's plan to set up sustainable enterprises, the external forces of the market meant that he failed. He noted that, 'We were trying to do some added value so that people could start workshops or start businesses and export and make some money out of it and have some chance of a sustainable business'. But, instead, the business became a production line: 'So this was much more of a mass production sort of thing, so there would be one artist who just did toucans and one guy who just did the background and one guy who just did parrots'.

The manufacturing process calls into question the idea of the *handmade* craft and the role of the hand, or multiple hands, of the artists or makers. The designs were nothing to do with Haiti. However, S still held on to notions of cultural authenticity when he applied the term 'unique' to his mass produced, culturally sanitised souvenirs, describing them as, 'not too unique; these were a little bit more unique at the time'. The idea of relative uniqueness indicates a desire to rationalise the process of pragmatic adaptation that the project had undergone. This interview illustrates how ideas of uniqueness are mediated by politics, economics, and cultural norms. In this case, charitable aims (providing sustainable independent work for Haitians) were matched by external political strategies (the Caribbean Based Initiative), an existing market (in the US) and non-Haitian design considerations (the designers were English, French and Egyptian). At the end of the process the only Haitian input was production line labour and materials. To an external observer, however, it appeared that the souvenir business was a Haitian enterprise and was representative of some aspects of Haitian culture.

Cultural seepage

'Ethnic' souvenirs, as previously mentioned, are often considered to be more authentic than other souvenirs in that they capture cultural practices and designs. Cultural seepage, however, contests notions of authenticity and representation; culture is fluid, as exemplified by the Hot Sun souvenirs from Lamu, Kenya. They did not exist before 1989, but now they are regarded as 'ethnic' souvenirs. The development of the market in *jua kali* (Hot Sun) souvenirs in Lamu is an example of the market determining the design and production of souvenirs. According to Dziedzic (2008), the present coconut carving trade was created in 1989 by a local craftsman, M-urage Ngani Ngatho, in response to the request of an Australian tourist for a copy of a bracelet carved from coconut that she had bought in Mombasa. Before then, most souvenirs had been carved from ebony by the Swahili who originated from Lamu. Coconut shells were considered to be a waste product and were plentiful on the island, whereas ebony was expensive. M-urage Ngani Ngatho copied the bracelet and continued to make bracelets and other items out of coconuts, depending on demand. As a result a new type of 'ethnic' tourist souvenir emerged, although those who bought the items assumed they were representative of Indigenous practices. M-urage and his apprentices do not own souvenir shops and their work is distinctively different from the wood carving of the Swahili. He developed his work and style as an outsider, a Kikuyu (the Kikuyu moved to Lamu as part of a resettlement programme after independence). Any idea of historic cultural representation falters as the makers of Hot Sun souvenirs are considered by others to be immigrants to Lamu. Swahili artisans normally work in wood, and trade through formal channels, whereas the producers of Hot Sun souvenirs mainly sell in an informal way on stalls by the roadside (hence the name). These people are considered to be sub-cultural by the artisanal Swahili, so the Hot Sun souvenirs are produced for outsiders by outsiders, a common trend in the production of souvenirs. However, the Hot Sun souvenirs are handmade and the makers take great pride in the skills that they employ in designing, carving and hand making the tools with which they work. This enterprise began with rubbish – discarded coconut shells – but has become regarded as a specialised craft business. M-urage has become the grand master carver and is now responsible for training all subsequent coconut carvers (who are all non-Swahili in practice and in origin); his apprentices sell his work for him. As Dziedzic (2008: 11) remarks, 'the work of these craftsmen debunks the myth of timelessness, unchanging culture in Lamu, and reveals instead a dynamic, ever-evolving network of cultural exchange and innovation'.

Conclusion

This chapter has considered the critical role that personal narrative plays in the defining of the tourist souvenir, a narrative that is so powerful that it plays a major part in defining the object *as* a souvenir. Notions of authenticity become secondary once the souvenir is imbued with emotional attachment; however, the object has had an existence before it is authenticated through personal attachment and narrative content. The tension between the external characteristics of the object, its origins and purpose, and the internal 'narrative of origins' is constantly at play and memory transforms and obscures as much as the market does. Additionally, the power of cultural stereotyping and cultural seepage in the development and design of souvenirs creates a tension between these influences and notions of authenticity and veracity. Souvenirs created for tourists are expected to represent the truth at some level, to display some notion of heritage. Such are the contradictions of the multiple narratives of the souvenir. The question is where does the truth lie and does it matter if they are made in China, so long as they enable the creation and appropriation of heritage for tourism?

References

Barthes, R. (1997) *The Eiffel Tower and Other Mythologies*. Berkeley, Los Angeles and London: University of California Press.

Benjamin, W. (1969) The work of art in the age of mechanical reproduction, in W. Benjamin *Illuminations: Essays and Reflections*. New York: Schocken Books.

Bourdieu, P. (1979) *Outline of a Theory of Practice*. Cambridge: Cambridge University Press.

Dziedzic, K. (2008) The cleverest of the clever: coconut craftsmen in Lamu, Kenya. *Journal of Modern Craft*, 1(3): 323–343.

Evans, G. (1999) *Souvenirs from Roman Times to the Present*. Edinburgh: NMS Publishing.

Fallwell, L. (2007) Buying a piece of the wall: German cities, American tourists, and the hunt for souvenirs, in Robinson, M. (ed.) *Things that Move: Material World of Tourism and Travel*. Leeds: Leeds Metropolitan University.

Fernandez, F. (2007) Distant Discourses – real proximities: tourism and consumption of souvenirs in Merida, Yucatan, in Robinson, M. (ed.) *Things that Move: Material World of Tourism and Travel*. Leeds: Leeds Metropolitan University.

Franklin, A. (2010) Aboriginalia: souvenir wares and the 'Aboriginalization' of Australian Identity. *Tourist Studies*, 10(3): 195–208.

Garduno Freeman, C. (2007) Souveniring the Sydney Opera House, in Robinson, M. (ed.) *Things that Move: Material World of Tourism and Travel.* Leeds: Leeds Metropolitan University.

Grennan, P. (2014) *Your Trash, My Treasure: An Assessment of the Value of Souvenirs.* PhD thesis. Newcastle upon Tyne: Northumbria University.

Kopytoff, I. (1986) The cultural biography of things: commoditization as process, in A. Appadurai (ed.) *The Social Life of Things: Commodities in Cultural Perspective.* Cambridge: Cambridge University Press, pp. 64–91.

Kostlin, K. (2007) Souvenir: the artefact designs the user, in Robinson, M. (ed.) *Things that Move: Material World of Tourism and Travel.* Leeds: Leeds Metropolitan University.

MacCannell, D. (1999) *The Tourist: A New Theory of the Leisure Class.* Los Angeles. London: University of California Press.

Miller, D. (1987) *Material Culture and Mass Consumption.* Oxford and Cambridge, MA: Basil Blackwell.

Miller, D. (2008) The uses of value. *Geoforum,* 39(3): 1122–1132.

Miller, D. (2009) *The Comfort of Things.* Cambridge: Polity Press.

Morgan, N. and Pritchard, A. (2005) On souvenirs and metonymy: narratives of memory, metaphor and materiality. *Tourist Studies,* 5(1): 29–53.

Scottish Historic Environment Policy Dec Annex 2 (2011). Available at: www.historic-scotland.gov.uk/shep-dec2011 [accessed January 2017].

Stewart, S. (2007) *On Longing: Narratives of the Miniature, the Gigantic, the Souvenir, the Collection.* Durham, N. Carolina: Duke University Press.

15 Creative practices of local entrepreneurs reinventing built heritage

Giovanna Bertella and Maurizio Droli

Introduction

This chapter views creativity as a key element informing the role that built heritage can play as a unique tourist attraction and a meaningful part of the lives of local residents. Adopting a practice-based approach, this study focuses on creative entrepreneurs who reinvent built heritage.

Both cognitive understanding and emotion play an important role in cultural heritage interpretation, conservation, and promotion (Moscardo 1996, Carter 1997). Poria et al. (2003) argue that tourists may be interested in cultural heritage in order to be educated, to have emotional experiences, and to simply 'gaze'. Some studies indicate that the emotional value of cultural heritage may be perceived as particularly meaningful in relation to personal heritage (McIntosh and Prentice 1999, Timothy and Boyd 2006, Staiff 2014). While from the point of view of a tourist this is true mainly for those visiting ancestral homelands and performing genealogy tours, for a site's local community, cultural heritage – especially when actively used for different purposes – may become the expression of a continuity between the everyday life of today and that of the past (Oncescu 2015).

From a business perspective, these considerations may influence tourism entrepreneurship and, more specifically, encourage the development of new ways to use heritage and engage tourists (Richards and Wilson 2006). Therefore this study investigates creative entrepreneurs who reinvent built heritage, focusing on the process through which these reflective practitioners develop tourism products and activities related to local built heritage. In order to help identify the main dimensions relevant to built-heritage reinvention, the research questions are: how do tourism entrepreneurial practices centred on the reinvention of built heritage emerge, and what characterises the entrepreneurs behind such practices? Some hypothetical dimensions, including the key element of creativity, are first identified through a consideration of previous literature and then investigated and discussed on the basis of the study's empirical findings.

The research upon which the chapter is based concerns the emergence of tourism practices related to the use of the local built heritage of the Italian village of Alberobello. This built heritage consists of limestone dwellings (*trulli*) traditionally inhabited by peasant families. The two practices investigated are the use of the *trulli* as accommodation facilities for tourists and as 'canvases' for artistic projections.

Theoretical framework

Creativity, tourism destinations and built heritage

Creativity is the ability to imagine things that do not yet exist and devise possible ways of realising these things (Bascavusoglu-Moreau et al. 2013). Creative production and consumption can lead to changes in a destination's experiential value (Hjalager 2010, Kokkranikala and Morrison 2011). Thus, creativity can be viewed as a key resource for the commodification and diversification of culture, and the transformation of products, services, and destinations into experiences.

For those destinations lacking a rich built heritage, the creative process leading to the facilitation of new experiences often occurs through differentiation strategies based on intangible resources (Richards and Wilson 2007). The case of destinations that have a rich built heritage is different (Yang and Li 2011). The major challenge in this second case is how to conserve such heritage and, at the same time, use it in a way that is meaningful to both tourists and residents – i.e. personally relevant and with distinct elements of novelty, surprise, learning, and engagement (Poulsson and Kale 2004, OECD 2009).

Ideally, the management of heritage should make it work both as a unique tourist attraction and as an important part of the residents' lives (Nuryanti 1996, Tweed and Sutherland 2007). Heritage buildings can be functional while at the same time contributing to the satisfaction of higher needs, such as the achievement of self-identity and realisation, and the establishment of place attachment and solidarity (Gospodini 2004, Tweed and Sutherland 2007).

Creative local entrepreneurs, the reinvention of built cultural heritage, and its use in tourism

This study views entrepreneurship as a set of practices that emerge through the entrepreneur's ongoing reflections and actions and which is relevant to business-related goals as well as to the individual's self-identity and their community's well-being (Cope 2005, Steyaert 2007, Johannisson 2011, Welter 2011). The term 'practice' is here understood in relation to practical wisdom, indicating the individual's engagement in reflective actions as a member of a group and their commitment to the group's well-being (Jamal 2004).

In line with this position, entrepreneurs are viewed as reflective practitioners who are knowledgeable about and embedded in their specific socio-cultural context and who reflect and act in order to cope with the challenges of that context. As suggested by Jamal et al. (2011), tourism actors who act as reflective practitioners tend to critically examine their role and potentials and engage with their community and its relevant societal issues. This may be the case for small entrepreneurs from the tourism and tourism-related sectors who act responsibly as a result of their emotional bond with the local area (Bertella 2014).

In the case of built heritage, entrepreneurs may be viewed as creative business actors who contribute to the development of new products and services that promote innovative ways of perceiving that heritage, characterised by a close interaction with, and a strong sense of attachment to, the specific building, monument, or landscape – and, ultimately, to the destination. Studies suggest that the profile of entrepreneurs who use their creativity for innovative place-making is often that of artists, writers and musicians, ICT (Information Communication Technology) experts and lifestyle entrepreneurs (Giaccardi and Palen 2008, Richards 2011). Moreover, some studies indicate that creative place-making often occurs through projects where various actors engage using both local and non-local resources and contacts (Bærenholdt and Haldrup 2006, Alvarez 2010, Richards 2011).

This study focuses on the case of a destination that has a unique built heritage in the form of traditional rural buildings and asks how the potentials of such heritage are developed through creative practices (Candura et al. 2008, Porto et al. 2012). The literature indicates two developmental paths feasible for this type of destination. The first involves giving tourists the opportunity to experience the destination in a unique and authentic way through products emerging as alternatives to standard products, developed by lifestyle entrepreneurs (Richards 2011). The second developmental path concerns creative spectacles (Paiola 2008, Richards 2011). According to the literature, this second path requires quite a broad spectrum of organising stakeholders and a clear connection between the event and the place (Van Aalst and van Melik 2012).

A conceptual tool for investigating creative entrepreneurs

The entrepreneurs described above may be investigated adopting the Weberian ideal type concept (Soliva 2007, Korsgaard et al. 2015). Ideal types represent 'analytical concepts highlighting and amplifying specific typical aspects of reality and synthesising them into analytical constructs or device in order to make sense of otherwise complex, incoherent and diffuse empirical observations' (Soliva 2015: 8). Ideal types can then be viewed as heuristic devices useful for understanding complex phenomena, analysing and comparing empirical findings.

In this study, the concept of the Weberian ideal type is adapted to the specific context using elements identified in the literature about creativity and entrepreneurship. The following dimensions relating to creative entrepreneurs are identified:

- creativity as imagination and feasibility;
- emotional bond to the place and its specific cultural heritage;
- commitment to the community's well-being.

The empirical investigation aims to understand such dimensions more fully and to uncover other possible dimensions that may contribute to a more complete description of the ideal type of the creative entrepreneur as a re-inventor of their built heritage.

Method

Alberobello, an Italian village located in the region of Puglia, is characterised by the presence of limestone dwellings called *trulli*. In 1926 the *trulli* were declared national monuments. In 1996 Alberobello was included in the UNESCO World Heritage List with the following justification:

> In 1996 Alberobello was included in the UNESCO World Heritage List based on the fact that the village satisfied three out of the ten selection criteria:
>
> **Criterion (iii):** The *Trulli* of Alberobello illustrate the long-term use of dry-stone building, a technique which has a history of many thousands of years in the Mediterranean region.
>
> **Criterion (iv):** The *Trulli* of Alberobello are an outstanding example of a vernacular architectural ensemble that survives within a Historic Urban Landscape context.
>
> **Criterion (v):** The *Trulli* of Alberobello is an outstanding example of human settlement that retains its original form to a remarkable extent.
>
> (UNESCO 2018).

The research undertaken concerns the use of *trulli* as accommodation facilities and as 'canvases' during an event, the Alberobello Light Festival. Data were collected through e-mail communication and interviews, face-to-face, and by Skype. The eight interviewees comprise a representative of a local tourist information agency (Pro Loco Alberobello), the Alberobello Light Festival creators and organisers, and five hotel managers. The festival creators and organisers belong to two organisations: Light Cones, an association of designers, and AGIT, the local association of young tourism entrepreneurs. The five interviewed hotel managers were selected as being inspired by and, in some cases, explicitly adopting the profile of Albergo Diffuso, a hospitality model based on a horizontal structure that aims to contribute to the economic and social life of local communities and to the promotion among tourists of the feeling of being temporary residents (Dall'Ara 2010, Confalonieri 2011). Interviews were conducted with the founders and managers of four of these hotels. In the remaining case, the founder was not available and the interview was performed with the firm's manager in charge of the tour operator services arranged by the hotel.

The interviews were structured around the three identified dimensions of the ideal type: creativity, emotional bond and commitment. Questions were asked about the development and implementation of new products and services, the entrepreneurs' sense of belonging to and embeddedness in the Alberobello community, and their motivation for engaging in new practices.

An online survey was also conducted, targeting the 18 bed and breakfast facilities that the local tourism agency indicated were using the *trulli* as holiday homes. The survey had a low response rate (three respondents). Additional secondary data were collected online through the Airbnb platform to identify the accommodation types for rent in Alberobello.

Findings

The trulli

In the past, the *trulli* were used as houses for peasant families, as stables, and sometimes as a combination of both. As one hotel manager pointed out, during World War II some *trulli* were used to host and sometimes to hide soldiers – from their enemies, and also from their comrades. After the war many families moved to modern houses and numerous *trulli* remained unused for several years.

The findings suggest that the use of the *trulli* in the context of tourism was partly triggered and inspired by their 1996 UNESCO recognition. A hotel manager commented on this, saying that the international recognition contributed to making the local community more aware of the uniqueness of their heritage and, in his case, this had stimulated a commitment towards a high-quality offer:

> We have the beauty of a heritage that is in the UNESCO list, and because of this the hospitality has to offer 'something extra'. They [the tourists] expect something exceptionally beautiful when they come here [. . .]. We started looking around us [. . .] we felt that we had the privilege of living in a marvellous place, with a unique beauty. Why not work on this aspect?

Another hotel manager commented extensively on the development of tourism in Alberobello, highlighting its international aspect. According to him, this can be traced back to the time just after World War II, when former soldiers, mainly from the United States, brought their families to see the place where they had been during the war, sometimes paying visits to the local people who had hosted them. He mentioned that, as a child, he was used to seeing many people from different countries around in the village, and this had made him reflect on the value of the place in terms of attractiveness to tourists. According to him, the UNESCO recognition of 1996 reinforced this belief.

The Alberobello Light Festival director expressed some doubts concerning the extent to which UNESCO recognition really attracted tourists, highlighting instead the benefits that local people had received from it in terms of their awareness of the value of local heritage.

The creativity of the local entrepreneurs

The data suggest that some of the local entrepreneurs are particularly innovative, while others may be described more correctly as imitators. The organisers of the Alberobello Light Festival – engineers and graphic designers grouped in an association called Light Cones – arranged the event for the first time in 2014, inspired by similar festivals held in Italy (Turin) and elsewhere in Europe. They saw the opportunity to use the *trulli* as 'canvases' and tested this idea during a summer jazz festival. The results were satisfying, so the idea was further developed into a summer and a winter light festival. The data from the interview with the Light

Figure 15.1 The *trulli* used as 'canvases' during the Alberobello Light Festival

Cones director suggest that the arrangement of the festival was viewed as a creative challenge for the association's members. Moreover, the members viewed the
festival in relation to its potential to create extraordinary experiences for the tourists as well as business opportunities for the local people. These entrepreneurs'
sense of imagination and their technical skills were crucially important in relation
to the development of the festival. The implementation of the festival was supported by the collaboration with AGIT, the local association of young tourism
entrepreneurs. This collaboration was described by the interviewees as an important element of the festival's practical organisation, in that it helped establish an
open dialogue with the community and gain its support and trust.

    In the case of those *trulli* used as accommodation facilities it is possible to
identify the most innovative entrepreneurs, who established a hotel in line with
the Albergo Diffuso model – a man belonging to a local family of Alberobello
and his wife, who was originally from the US. In 1997, this couple entered the
hospitality sector with limited financial capital, one owned *trullo,* and six rented
ones. Both had working professional experience from other sectors, which, as
they pointed out during the interview, was very useful in the management of the
business. They elaborated a business plan and developed an explicit strategy.
Where the couple felt it necessary, external resources in terms of competence and
skills were brought in; for example, the couple made use of a US tour operator
specialising in upmarket vacation rental properties.

    All the interviewees confirmed that the spread of tourist accommodation into
the *trulli* started after the example set by this first hotel. The manager of another
hotel commented:

We started renting out the *trulli* in 2000. The example of [that hotel] was important . . . I recognised without any doubt that their work had a very important meaning and role for the rest of us who gradually started to restructure the *trulli* for the tourists. We realised that this [renting out *trulli* to the tourists] was actually possible!

Nowadays, accommodation in *trulli* is quite widespread. On the Airbnb platform, among the 20 offers of accommodation possibilities in Alberobello, 15 are in *trulli*. The list provided by the local tourism office includes 20 additional B & Bs that offer accommodation in *trulli*.

The emotional aspect of the reinvention of the trulli

During the interview with the manager of the hotel who began using the *trulli* to host tourists, it appeared quite clear that part of the motivation for entering the tourism business with a new product was intrinsic. Although acting professionally and analysing the situation from a strictly business perspective, several of the expressions that he used to describe the first years of the business indicate a sense of excitement: 'we [he and his wife] started this adventure', 'we were young and had this "lightness" of starting something new', 'we lacked everything [. . .] but we were ready to face everything too!'. The same person highlighted his vision (according to which tourism is about letting the tourists experience the territory) several times, with expressions that indicate a strong sense of attachment to the local area and a sense of pride in showing the local agrarian traditions to tourists and visitors. One example concerns olive harvesting:

I knew about the possibility in France of involving the tourists in picking apples and grapes, and I thought that this could also have been done here. I own land with 800 olive trees [. . .] so I made this package and invited the tourists to join the harvest. And they came! [. . .] The first weekend was fully booked: they lived in my *trulli* [. . .]. The tourists were given all they needed to work in the fields, side by side with us [. . .] and then the final dinner: the long table and the food and the wine [. . .] they loved [. . .] to share the day with us.

A similar pride was observed in the manager of another hotel. He made several passionate comments during his interview about his and his family's strong sense of belonging and attachment to Alberobello, the local area, and more specifically the *trulli*. The latter can be noted in the following comments:

I love to work outside, with my hands [. . .] I work with the *trulli*. I just love the direct physical contact with the *trullo*, the stone [. . .] I work with my father from whom I have learned to restructure the *trulli* [. . .] When we show the *trullo* where the tourists are going to stay, we explain everything, like [. . .] this was the *trullo* that belonged to my aunt's family, and I tell them how it was used, how many people and animals were living there.

The festival director also highlighted the central position that the *trulli* have in the lives of the local people, including himself and his colleagues. Talking about the original idea for the festival, he said:

> We were interested in creating a sort of synergy between the installation and the monument [. . .] in infusing life into these buildings that are old, historical and [. . .] static [. . .] make them more alive [. . .] the *trulli* with their conic shape are perfect [. . .] they belong to our imagination since we were children and are part of our everyday life.

The emotional bond noted in these cases seems to be present also in the cases of the other respondents – both hoteliers and B & B managers. The respondents to the survey recognised that the *trulli* have a strong emotional value due to their being part of local history. For one of them, the *trulli* were also part of their family history. Another survey respondent answered the question about their choice to offer accommodation in *trulli* as follows:

> Having the possibility to meet people from all around the world and therefore open our mind and hearth to different realities, become richer, having the opportunities to inform [people] about the *trullo*, the agrarian culture of our territory, and the immense work of our *maestri trullari* [those who build and restructure the *trulli*] [. . .] it's a way to feel pride and gain respect.

The interview with the representative of the local tourism agency shows that some of those who rent out *trulli* to tourists are not originally from the local area; their motivation might possibly be more financial than emotional.

Commitment to the community's well-being

The hotel manager who was the first to use the *trulli* for accommodation purposes stated that external collaborations were sought when he felt that the desired results could not be reached through collaborations with local actors. He commented on the latter aspect as follows: 'The local community was always involved to the degree and in the modality that better suited the purpose of the business and the potential for our territory'. Commenting on relations with the local community, this hotel owner highlighted that his family has been part of the community for generations, and their reciprocal relationships, business-related or not, were of paramount importance. Such relations were described by almost all the respondents, hotel and B & B managers, as mainly informal and based on personal contacts; in some cases, these were family members, such as elderly people particularly competent in relation to the local culinary traditions.

The contribution of the *trullo* accommodation to the local community was explicitly related by all the hotel managers to the numerous job and business opportunities that the hotels create year-round. One in particular stated that the *trullo* accommodation could potentially give the local people a realistic and interesting way of working and living. He said: 'Instead of moving to other places, other countries [. . .] we can live here and work for ourselves, not for others!' In terms of contribution to the local community through job and business opportunities, the B & B managers professed to contribute only marginally, presumably because of the limited size of these businesses. On the other hand, the accommodation in *trulli* was associated with benefits in terms of the conservation of local cultural heritage. One B & B manager reported that such benefits were more important than the financial benefits of individual businesses.

The festival respondent described their commitment to the local community through their creation of a place-based event that would attract tourists and visitors from nearby villages, and therefore income to local businesses. Recent discussions have focused on the possibility of developing the festival with light installations spread more widely than just the centre of Alberobello, with the aim of involving additional local businesses.

Discussion

Several of the aspects introduced in the theoretical part of this chapter were confirmed by the findings of the study. The cultural heritage investigated seems to be recognised as valuable both in relation to individuals', and the community's, sense of identity and as tourist attraction (Nuryanti 1996, Gospodini 2004, Poulsson and Kale 2004, Tweed and Sutherland 2007). The creative entrepreneurs may effectively be described as competent reflective practitioners, emotionally attached to their socio-cultural context (Jamal 2004, Bertella 2014). Moreover, the presence of certain professions and characteristics among these practitioners has been confirmed, in particular lifestyle entrepreneurs, artists and ICT experts, as commonly found in innovative place-making (Giaccardi and Palen 2008, Richards 2011).

This study's findings also highlight some additional aspects. They suggest that the practices of reinventing the *trulli* were triggered by an external factor, namely the UNESCO recognition of the buildings. This external factor made the local people in general – and those with an entrepreneurial attitude in particular – realise the value that the *trulli* could have in the context of tourism. Such recognition seems to have infused a sense of pride into the local community. Other elements that supported the emergence of such practices can be identified in the local peasant families' tradition of hospitality, and the presence of international visitors in the years following World War II.

The Weberian ideal type has been a useful analytical device and the findings may be discussed in detail in relation to the three dimensions: creativity, emotional bond, and commitment (Soliva 2007, Korsgaard et al. 2015). With regard to the creativity dimension, it may be asserted that two cases clearly qualify as creative entrepreneurs: one hotel manager and the festival organiser. The information gleaned about the hotel manager – more precisely, the couple who first began to offer accommodation in *trulli* – is in line with the ideal type of practitioner, creatively and emotionally active and committed to the responsible development of tourism. A common and distinctive aspect of this case is their openness to external stimuli and outsourcing. Openness to external stimuli also characterises the festival creator, who also reported about the necessity of networking with actors who have different competences – specifically, young local tourism entrepreneurs.

An additional case may be identified as a creative innovator – namely, the hotel manager who followed the example of renting *trulli* out to tourists. This person used his skills, physically to turn the *trullo* from a peasant dwelling into an exclusive place for an authentic Alberobello experience. Thus, the creative dimension here concerns imagination and feasibility, with the latter strictly involved in the implementation process and related technical challenges. This aspect also emerged in the case of the festival association and their technological skills. The evidence suggests that for these three creative entrepreneurs, the reinvention of the *trulli* is viewed as an exciting task, related to their passion for their work and their search for professional challenges. This passion was not observed in the other cases.

The emotional dimension, in the sense of attachment to the local place and heritage, seems to be important for all the entrepreneurs investigated. The reinvention of the *trulli* was described in relation to their willingness to preserve local cultural heritage and, sometimes, family heritage. In most cases, this was also related to the opportunity for local people to work and live in the specific area. The link between these aspects and the third dimension, the entrepreneurs' commitment to their local community's well-being, is clear. In this context, social benefits, in terms of recognising the important role of the older generation and creating job opportunities for the younger generation, were also mentioned.

Based on the findings discussed above, the three dimensions of the Weberian ideal type may be better specified and broadened as follows:

- creativity, as imagination, feasibility evaluation, and implementation, through the application of specialised skills and competence;
- having a strong emotional bond to the place and its specific cultural heritage;
- commitment to the community's well-being;
- passion for job and professional challenges;
- openness to outsourcing and looking to external stimuli for inspiration;
- connection to a local network, mainly through personal contacts.

Conclusion

This study has explored how practices related to the reinvention of built heritage emerge and develop and how the entrepreneurs involved may be described. Based on scholarly contributions concerning a practice-based understanding of entrepreneurship and cultural heritage, and adopting the concept of the Weberian ideal type, this study started by identifying three dimensions relevant to entrepreneurial practices: creativity, emotional attachment and commitment.

In order both to understand the above dimensions more fully, and also to uncover additional dimensions and/or other relevant aspects, an empirical study was conducted. The latter investigated two practices concerning the use of rural limestone dwellings (*trulli*) located in Alberobello, Italy: to accommodate tourists and to show artistic pictures and videos. The findings suggest that the reinvention of the *trulli* has resulted from a combination of creative innovation and imitation, triggered and inspired by some factors external to the local community. External factors may also be important in relation to the outsourcing of resources not locally available.

The three dimensions of ideal type, identified on the basis of the literature, were useful in the analysis of the case study, but the findings highlight the need to specify and broaden the ideal type of creative rural entrepreneurs. One issue concerns the concept of creativity, with the findings relative to the most innovative entrepreneurs studied suggesting that the creativity dimension involves both intellectual aspects (understanding the built heritage, identifying the opportunities and imagining solutions) and more technical aspects (evaluating the feasibility of possible solutions, applying competence and skills). Another attribute that emerged from the findings as characteristic of the most innovative entrepreneurs is their passion and enthusiasm. This can be conceptualised as a new dimension: passion for job and professional challenges. Finally, the entrepreneurs' openness to external stimuli, for inspiration and possible outsourcing, and their local networks through personal contacts are also among the relevant dimensions. The most creative entrepreneurs appear to be particularly rich in terms of resources on these six dimensions, while entrepreneurs who are imitators are characterised by a combination of resources that vary between the different dimensions. Nevertheless, a sense of attachment to local heritage and a commitment to the well-being of the local community have been observed in all the investigated cases.

The findings of the study suggest that built heritage is reinvented for touristic purposes through practices initiated by particularly creative, open-minded and passionate entrepreneurs, and then adopted by a broader group of entrepreneurs, who are embedded in, and emotionally attached and committed to, the local community, the place and the specific cultural heritage.

References

Alvarez, M.D. (2010) Creative cities and cultural spaces: new perspectives for city tourism. *International Journal of Culture, Tourism and Hospitality Research*, 4(3): 171–175.

Bascavusoglu-Moreau, E., Kopera, S. and Wszendybył-Skulska, E. (2013) The role of creativity in development of innovation in tourism. *Journal of Entrepreneurship, Management and Innovation*, 9(1): 5–15.

Bertella, G. (2014) The ethical and local dimensions of sustainable development in relation to small and medium-sized firms participating in tourism relevant projects. *European Journal of Tourism, Hospitality and Recreation*, 5 (Special Issue): 35–53.

Bærenholdt, J.O. and Haldrup, M. (2006) Mobile networks and place making in cultural-tourism staging: Viking ships and rock music in Roskilde. *European Urban and Regional Studies*, 13(3): 209–224.

Candura, A., Dal Sasso, P. and Marinelli, G. (2008) Recovery and reuse of rural buildings: the spread out building case. *Agricultural Engineering International: The CIGR E-Journal*, 10: 1–18.

Carter, J. (1997) *'A Sense of Place': An Interpretive Planning Handbook.* Inverness: Tourism Environment Initiative.

Confalonieri, M. (2011) A typical Italian phenomenon: the 'albergo diffuso'. *Tourism Management*, 32(3): 685–687.

Cope, J. (2005) Toward a dynamic learning perspective of entrepreneurship. *Entrepreneurship Theory and Practice*, 29(4): 373–397.

Dall'Ara, G. (2010) *Manuale dell'Albergo Diffuso. L'idea, la gestione, il marketing dell'ospitalità diffusa.* Milano: Angeli.

Giaccardi, E. and Palen, L. (2008) The social production of heritage through cross-mediainteraction: making place for place-making. *International Journal of Heritage Studies*, 14(3): 281–297.

Gospodini, A. (2004) Urban morphology and place identity in European cities: built heritage and innovative design. *Journal of Urban Design*, 9(2): 225–248.

Hjalager, A.-M. (2010) A review of innovation research in tourism. *Tourism Management*, 31(1): 1–12.

Jamal, T. (2004) Virtue ethics and sustainable tourism pedagogy: phronesis, principles and practice. *Journal of Sustainable Tourism*, 12(6): 530–545.

Jamal, T., Taillon, J. and Dredge, D. (2011) Sustainable tourism pedagogy and academic community collaboration: a progressive service-learning approach. *Tourism and Hospitality Research*, 11(2): 133–147.

Johannisson, B. (2011) Towards a practice theory of entreprenuering. *Small Business Economics*, 36(2): 135–150.

Kokkranikala, J. and Morrison, A. (2011) Community networks and sustainable livelihoods intourism: the role of entrepreneurial innovation. *Tourism Planning & Development*, 8(2): 137–156.

Korsgaard, S., Müller, S. and Wittorff Tanvig, H. (2015) Rural entrepreneurship or entrepreneurship in the rural – between place and space. *International Journal of Entrepreneurial Behavior & Research*, 21(1): 5–26.

McIntosh, A.J., and Prentice, R.C. (1999) Affirming authenticity. consuming cultural heritage. *Annals of Tourism Research*, 26(3): 589–612.

Moscardo, G. (1996) Mindful tourists: heritage and tourism. *Annals of Tourism Research*, 23(2): 376–397.

Nuryanti, W. (1996) Heritage and postmodern tourism. *Annals of Tourism Research*, 23(2):249–260.

OECD (2009) *The Impact of Culture on Tourism.* Paris: OECD.

Oncescu, J. (2015) Rural restructuring and its impact on community recreation opportunities. *Annals of Leisure Research*, 18(1): 83–104.

Paiola, M. (2008) Cultural events as potential drivers of urban regeneration: an empirical illustration. *Industry and Innovation*, 15(5): 513–529.

Porto, S.M.C., Leanza, P.M. and Cascone, G. (2012) Developing interpretation plans to promote traditional rural buildings as built heritage attractions. *International Journal of Tourism Research*, 14(5): 421–436.

Poria, Y., Butler, R. and Airey, D. (2003) The core of heritage tourism. *Annals of Tourism Research*, 30(1): 238–254.

Poulsson, S.H.G. and Kale, S.H. (2004) The experience economy and commercial experiences. *The Marketing Review*, 4(3): 267–277.

Richards, G. (2011) Creativity and tourism: the state of the art. *Annals of Tourism Research*, 38(4): 1225–1253.

Richards, G. and Wilson, J. (2006) Developing creativity in tourist experiences: a solution to the serial reproduction of culture? *Tourism Management*, 27(6): 1209–1223.

Richards, G. and Wilson, J. (2007) *Tourism, Creativity and Development*. London: Routledge.

Soliva, R. (2007) Landscape stories: using ideal type narratives as a heuristic device in rural studies. *Journal of Rural Studies*, 23(1): 62–74.

Staiff, R. (2014) Tilden: beyond resurrection, in R. Staiff (ed.) *Re-imagining Heritage Interpretation: Enchanting the Past-Future*. UK: Ashgate, pp. 29–42.

Steyaert, C. (2007) "Entrepreneuring" as a conceptual attractor? A review of process theories in 20 years of entrepreneurship studies. *Entrepreneurship & Regional Development; An International Journal*, 19(6): 453–477.

Timothy, D.J. and Boyd, S.W. (2006) Heritage tourism in the 21st century: valued traditions and new perspectives. *Journal of Heritage Tourism*, 1(1): 1–16.

Tweed, C. and Sutherland, M. (2007) Built cultural heritage and sustainable urban development. *Landscape and Urban Planning*, 83(1): 62–69.

UNESCO (2018) Available at: whc.unesco.org/en/list/787 [accessed 23rd May 2018].

Van Aalst, I., and van Melik, R. (2012) City festivals and urban development: does place matter? *European Urban and Regional Studies*, 19(2): 195–206.

Welter, F. (2011) Contextualizing entrepreneurship – conceptual challenges and ways forward. *Entrepreneurship Theory and Practice*, 35(1): 165–184.

Yang, C.H. and Lin, H.L. (2011) Is UNESCO recognition effective in fostering tourism? A comment on Yang, Lin and Han: Reply. *Tourism Management*, 32(2): 455–456.

16 Co-creating a heritage hotel for a new identity

Philip Feifan Xie and William Ling Shi

Introduction

Renovated or remodelled historic buildings provide one of the most popular types of tourist accommodation and are increasingly being placed on the heritage tourism map as part of a set of broader initiatives (Timothy and Teye 2009). Heritagisation of a hotel is a process of recontextualisation in which certain aspects of material culture are selected, preserved and reconstructed for commercial purposes. The gentrification process becomes an important part of preservation and tourism promotion in any given destination. Successful examples of heritage hotels include, but are not limited to: the Raffles Hotel in Singapore, showcasing the city's colonial heritage; St. Pancras Renaissance Hotel in London; and the Lion Palace Four Seasons, a restored nineteenth-century palace in St. Petersburg, Russia, all of which have engaged in large-scale restoration and adaptation for the purposes of nostalgia.

Stakeholder cooperation and collaboration are crucial for the survival of these heritage sites. Timothy and Boyd (2003) suggest that such cooperation, collaboration and partnership between private, public and voluntary owners becomes more prominent as they seek to promote the principles and practices of sustainable development. Henderson (2013) argues that heritage hotels should be explored from both theoretical and practical perspectives, as stakeholders play a key role in authenticating the repositories of a destination's heritage and collective memory. Since co-creation offers more flexible and authentic experiences, which can be shared between hosts and guests (Richards 2011), it has increasingly gained attention from tourism and hospitality researchers and plays a vital role in authenticating heritage-themed hotels (Klumbis and Munsters 2005, Roser and Samson 2009).

This chapter attempts to broaden the understanding of co-creation by examining the stakeholders who authenticate the meaning of a heritage hotel. It proposes that a heritage hotel is not only defined in terms of the provenance of material and non-material aspects of a culture, but also by subjective criteria as applied by various stakeholders. Thus, a heritage hotel is characterised by a polyvocality of interpretations, reflective of the array of stakeholders involved. Using the case study of the Hotel Estoril, the first Western-style casino hotel built in the former Portuguese colony of Macau, it shows how government, community organisations and residents endeavour to co-create a new identity for adaptive reuse. The chapter begins with a literature review on the issues of co-creation, authentication and heritage hotels. A brief history of the Hotel Estoril in Macau is introduced and research methods are detailed. An analysis of data is presented, based on content analysis, in-depth interviews and resident surveys, and the chapter ends with a discussion of research implications.

The co-creation and authentication of a heritage hotel

In the tourist industry various perspectives on co-creation have been addressed – from customer experiences with service (Chathoth et al. 2016, Prebensen et al. 2013) to the marketing sector (Gebauer et al. 2010, Chen et al. 2012) and human resources, such as competencies required by frontline employees in order to enhance guest experiences (Bharwani and Jauhari 2013). Most research examines manifestations of co-creation from a consumer perspective (Minkiewicz et al. 2014), although there is increasing interest in shifting the focus of value co-creation research from the consumer to a multi-stakeholder model (Ramaswamy and Gouillart 2010). Key motives for the involvement of multiple stakeholders in co-creation include reputation enhancement, experimentation and relationship building, in order to access an enriched experience. Through innovative resource integration and best practice, a polyphonic process of co-creation emerges that builds upon stakeholders' diverse identities (Ramaswamy and Ozcan 2014).

This chapter proposes a conceptual framework that emphasises the role of *authentication* in the process of co-creation and identity formation. Since authenticity is a negotiated attribute with multiple dimensions, the status of which is evaluated differently by different stakeholders, the process of authentication offers a particularly good vantage point from which to identify specific groups and interests making claims for legitimating their constructions of cultural identity, as symbolised by the heritage hotel. Given the contested nature of authenticity, it is necessary to shift the discussion about authentication to a more traceable dimension. Robinson (1999) suggests that a key issue in authenticating heritage is the inclusion of a wide-ranging set of 'cultural indicators', derived from the various stakeholders involved in tourism development, from the community organisations (as de facto judges of cultural appropriateness) to the governments who exercise control over tourism development. Hitchcock, King and Parnwell (1993) propose that by identifying the main beneficiaries of economic development, one can determine its pattern and pace. Governments often take it upon themselves to act on behalf of the people by facilitating or moderating the development of hospitality facilities within their respective territories, so that a hotel functions primarily for the benefits of the local economy, with its form and dynamics being driven principally by community organisations. Meanwhile, residents may experience a sense of powerlessness and find themselves largely excluded from the decision-making process.

This paper proposes a framework, modelled as a gearbox, in which co-creation, authentication and identity are interconnected (see Figure 16.1). A proposed

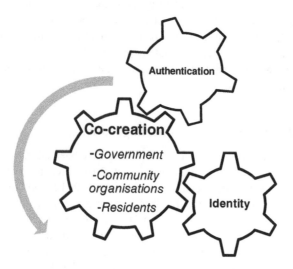

Figure 16.1 Conceptual framework of authentication, co-creation and identity

heritage hotel project sets the issue of authentication in motion, and the cogs of that gear in turn drive the main gear of co-creation. The subjects to be analysed in heritage hotel co-creation should include at least three key stakeholders (others could be included): (a) government, (b) community organisations, and (c) residents. These stakeholders relate to the wider environment of people and entities, which can move, or be moved by, the co-created identity of the heritage hotel. Eventually, a new identity emerges, propelling further co-creation by these selected stakeholders.

Research setting

The Hotel Estoril, opened by Dr. Stanley Ho of STDM (*Sociedade de Turismo e Diversoes de Macau*) was the first casino to provide Western games of chance in Macau (see Figure 16.2). Located near Tap Seac Square, it was hailed as a 'pioneer casino hotel,' featuring a rich cultural ambience at the heart of the city's cultural district. The hotel had initially been a one-story building, used as a public restaurant and dancing venue, when it first opened in 1952. When STDM gained the casino monopoly concession in 1962, the building was expanded by adding three extra stories and was transformed into a casino hotel. A façade with mosaic murals was attached to the front elevation. Additional rooms and gambling spaces were constructed in 1964. However, the Hotel Estoril was abruptly closed in the 1990s and has lain in disrepair ever since. Several repurposing projects have been suggested for the hotel over the years, including hosting the Portuguese School of Macau, but none has been pursued.

Opinions over the fate of the dilapidated Hotel Estoril, known as *Ngoi Dou* ('Love Metropolis') in Cantonese, have become divided in recent years. Some people insist that it represents an important part of Macau's gambling history, while others argue that the hotel structure was altered after new floors were added and that the space is more suitable for adaptive reuse. The building and its façade are viewed as a representative form of 1960s architecture and urbanism, the mosaic fresco being the work of an Italian sculptor, Oseo Acconci, who was part of the Arco-íris artistic movement. At the same time, the exterior of the Hotel Estoril showcases one of the rare manifestations of the Futurism movement in Macau, with a panel featuring a semi-nude woman symbolising the goddess of Fortune. The hotel's patrimonial and historical value is therefore significant, as famous architects designed this iconic building.

The debate about the revitalisation of the building is largely due to its abandonment. The government of Macau Special Administrative Region (SAR) is considering the demolition of the hotel compound and swimming pool complex and the reorientation of the site into a hub for cultural, entertainment and leisure activities for young people. The proposal aims to create an integrated structure to house the Macau Conservatory, providing cultural, arts, educational, sports and other recreational facilities that can be enjoyed by residents. The SAR Government hopes to use this revitalisation plan, centred on the Estoril Hotel, to integrate the building with neighbouring Tap Seac Square and, eventually, to foster community

Figure 16.2 Hotel Estoril in Macau

participation. The primary purpose is to promote an ambience of culture, recreation and leisure in this abandoned hotel complex. It would also serve the goals of enhancing youth sports and transforming Macau to a 'City of Culture and Events'.

Research methods

The research was undertaken in multiple stages. Initially, content analysis was conducted to understand more fully the history of the Hotel Estoril and the perspectives of different governing bodies in Macau. Krippendorf (1980) defines content analysis as a research technique for making replicable and valid interference from data to context. In recent years, content analysis has also been adapted to new media, such as websites and social media, as a method of data mining. This study chose content from newspapers and blogs to represent the personal experiences of people of different demographic groups, cultural backgrounds and walks of life. Cluster analysis was then undertaken to clarify the materials and data through multiple perspectives.

The second stage entailed in-depth interviews with government officials in ministries such as Social Affairs and Culture, the Cultural Affairs Bureau, the Tourism Office, the Education and Youth Affairs Bureau and the Macau Sports Development Board. Participant observation was conducted at public hearings, organised by the government for the future of the Hotel Estoril, in late 2015. Thirteen sessions sponsored by the government entitled 'Revitalization of the Estoril Hotel and Swimming Pool' have been held, involving over 1,800 people, including members from the Cultural Consultative Committee, the Committee for Non-Tertiary Education, *União Geral das Associações dos Moradores de Macau*, residents who live near Tap Seac Square, architects, communities for heritage conservation, and educational associations. These people have actively participated in discussions and exchanged ideas on the renovation of the hotel. In addition, several meetings of urban planning advocacy groups were attended to obtain members' opinions on the revitalisation of the Hotel Estoril.

In the last stage of the research a survey was administered to residents, to assess how the Hotel Estoril is perceived by the local population and to record their broader perceptions of heritage value as applied to the proposed revitalisation plan. The questionnaire comprised three main sections. The first section aimed to investigate residents' perceptions of the Hotel Estoril by asking them to indicate whether it possessed certain attributes for heritage preservation. The second section gauged residents' attitudes towards the redevelopment of the Hotel Estoril, and the last section ascertained residents' views about co-creation. All questions employed a Likert-type scale (1 = strongly disagree to 5 = strongly agree). The data were collected in June and July 2016, in Tap Seac Square and surrounding areas in Macau, by six trained survey administrators using a structured questionnaire between the hours of 6 a.m. and 11 p.m. This method, as opposed to the drop off/pick up method, has the potential to achieve a higher response rate (Czaja and Blair 2005) as well as to minimise possible misunderstandings of the questions. The data collectors provided a brief explanation of the study to each person approached and ensured that resident participation in the survey was voluntary and anonymous, encouraging participants to state their own personal opinions as openly as possible. A total of 602 out of the 1,863 residents approached agreed to participate in the survey (the response rate was therefore about 32 per cent). SPSS 17.0 was used to analyse the questionnaires, summarising respondents' demographic situations and their perceptions of the Hotel Estoril. Cronbach's alpha was employed to test the reliability of measuring perceptions and attitudes towards the rebuilding of the hotel. The alpha values were more than 0.82, showing high internal consistency in this study.

Findings

Government perspectives on authenticating the Hotel Estoril

There is a growing need for the Macau government to establish a sustained, equitable collaboration with all its partners in tourism (McCartney 2006). During the policy address to the Legislative Assembly in April 2015, the Social Affairs and Culture minister announced that Tap Seac Square and its neighbouring areas would be transformed into a cultural hub, and that the ageing Hotel Estoril would be demolished and replaced with a youth centre for arts education. By promoting the development of the area, the proposal planned to transform Macau into a 'City of Culture and Events,' as well as to launch new tourism products (Macau Tourism 2015). Hotel Estoril would be reconstructed to provide for the teaching of arts and culture, including schools of music and dance. In addition to these schools, the government foresaw the transformation of the site into an 'artsy training centre' where students could attend extracurricular activities. The reconstruction of the municipal swimming pool, adjacent to the hotel, was also proposed. Besides training youth, the new complex would host special events and exhibitions, thereby creating a new social and cultural centre in town. Overall, the purpose of this proposed reconstruction was characterised as 'an education about the present of the country, moral and civic awareness of Macau'. The proposed reconstruction of the Hotel Estoril was part of a larger master plan, which encompassed the development of new tourism products such as panoramic buses, street shows, nightlife activities and outdoor terraces, in order to promote economic diversification.

According to Articles 19 and 20 of the Cultural Heritage Law in Macau, local citizens are entitled to provide feedback to the Cultural Bureau about the cultural and heritage value of a property. The Macau government therefore launched a public consultation and ordered a feasibility study of the master plan. A consulting firm was commissioned to conduct a random telephone survey, which reported that more than 70 per cent of interviewees agreed with the government proposal for dismantling the hotel complex and that almost 83 per cent favoured 'rebuilding' the Hotel Estoril. However, the term 'rebuilding' presented in the survey was misleading (it was actually synonymous with 'demolition of the actual premises and construction of new ones') and there was an instant public outcry. Based on the consulting firm's report, the Macau Cultural Heritage Council decided that the building should not be classified for heritage preservation and recommended demolition. The underlying assumption was that the Hotel Estoril did not represent the continuity of gaming history in Macau since it had been renovated several times and forced to close three decades ago. Repurposing of the hotel *in situ* was 'infeasible' and the compound generated little revenue compared to other hotel casinos. Abandoned in Tap Seac Square for many years, the building had become an eyesore for local government.

In March 2016, in the face of opposition by community organisations, the members of the Cultural Heritage Council voted overwhelmingly in favour of the government's decision not to list the Hotel Estoril as a Cultural Heritage Site. The government stood firm against the adaptive reuse of the current building, citing a lack of evidence of architectural or historical value. In addition, the government stressed that the renovation of the Hotel Estoril was 'impractical from an engineering and programming perspective,' as architectural revisions had already caused the loss of heritage characteristics the building once had. The demolition of the hotel is now the most likely course of action and the government has moved forward decisively to convert the site into a space for cultural and educational activities. The President of the Cultural Affairs Bureau argues that all stakeholders should put the past behind them because: (1) the construction has been altered to such an extent that the original hotel structure is lost, (2) the heritage value of the hotel has disappeared, as the interiors have deteriorated beyond the point of any possible conservation, and (3) a new complex will play an important role in promoting art, cultural activities and creative industries, the benefits of which will outweigh the original value of the site. The proposition is that not all revitalisation projects that are proposed relate to a locale's socio-economic history and that, very often, heritage sites should simply be used for other purposes.

The involvement of community organisations in authenticating the Hotel Estoril

Community organisations in Macau comprise mainly non-profit and non-governmental bodies and are considered the third sector in civil society (Salamon and Anker 1999). They are deeply rooted in social life and essential to developing Macau's complex economy (Berlie 2012). Despite the small size of the city, there are about 4,000 community organisations, including various neighbourhood associations and workers' unions. Each plays a critical role in protecting their members' interests (Hao 2011). The government's plan to demolish the Hotel Estoril has drawn opposition from these organisations, especially the associations for conservation and architecture. They argue that the hotel complex is particularly well suited to adaptive reuse, since it contains large and open spaces, and that the historical and emotional significance of the building complex should be taken into consideration. They question the vision of Macau's future held by government (demolition of the hotel and replacing it with a cultural complex) and want to know what versions of authenticity were brought up in debates over the hotel's future. These groups are calling on the government to abandon plans to demolish the hotel building and instead offer a comprehensive reuse scheme that is responsive to the culture, heritage and history represented by the Hotel Estoril. Their primary argument is that the hotel has significant value as a vernacular relic from the 1960s because of its association with casino development in Macau. Most importantly, the hotel was designed and built by prominent architects during the heyday of Macau's economic development.

Alongside this public support for the reconstruction of Hotel Estoril *in situ*, Macau Root Planning, one of the associations of city planners, has launched a petition to re-evaluate the hotel and the adjacent pool. The group claims that the government intentionally ignores the city's 'development concept' in the long run, while the 'development spirit' in the city is missing. The petition cites a local architect, Carlos Marreiros, who demonstrates that the Hotel Estoril was the city's first Western-style casino and is therefore a historical landmark for both public and private enterprises. It goes on to declare that the government accepts 'too much information and documentation', putting too much stress on the council's argument that both the interior and exterior of the hotel have been altered. Despite changes made to the original structure, Root Planning argues that it remains a building of 'great quality' and warrants the title of a heritage hotel. The façade of the building is closely associated with the history of gaming, the largest industry in Macau, and continuously serves (in 'multiple versions') to record the gambling history in Macau. Marreiros comments that 'what remains today is a summation of a building with several hairpieces. In the pristine condition, it was beautiful,' and explains that it should be preserved, as the building forms part of the fabric of a city in constant flux.

At a deeper level, the authenticity of the Hotel Estoril is a question of aesthetic appreciation, as the abandoned complex is increasingly viewed as a form of 'retro chic'. In the popular imagination, authenticity may be bound up with an aesthetic known as 'ruin porn' (Griffioen 2009), where desolate, wrecked and abandoned spaces are presumed to provide the best opportunity for photographs and to represent the most faithful aspects of city culture and heritage. The concept of 'ruin porn', to some extent, reflects shifting views on city identity by the community. Vacant lots enable a reconsideration of land use possibilities, in lieu of new buildings. Several community associations have been bolstered into action after public consultations held by the government introduced the concept of popular organised tours, as offered by several rust belt cities in the US, where tourists visit the sites, snapping photos of sprawling, blighted complexes in order to take a glimpse of the 'nostalgic otherworld'. A new aesthetic identity has thus emerged, based on an experiential learning of gambling history in Macau as a key element in regeneration.

Residents' perceptions of authenticating the Hotel Estoril

The survey of residents was undertaken near Tap Seac Square. Of the 602 respondents, 51.7 per cent (311) were males and 48.3 per cent (291) were females. In terms

Table 16.1 Residents' perceptions of the Hotel Estoril (N = 602)

Perception	M	SD
The new plan should reflect the feedback and comments of the residents	4.13	0.76
The revitalisation plan needs to be communicated better to different stakeholders	4.03	0.731
The idle building is wasteful	4.00	0.963
Youth, parents and teachers should be encouraged to participate in the plan by submitting their ideas	3.95	0.766
The community should be encouraged to participate in the plan by submitting their ideas	3.94	0.742
The government needs to establish better channels for involving more local residents	3.93	0.743
An obstructing effect on the existing world heritage must be restricted in the reuse	3.92	0.945
The revitalisation plan should be transparent and accessible through mass media	3.85	0.762
The historic significance of the hotel must be evaluated by a committee of experts	3.78	0.805
The design should create a new image and identity	3.76	0.889

Note: features were rated on a Likert scale ranging from 1 (completely disagree) to 5 (strongly agree) (Cronbach's $\alpha = 0.821$)

of age, residents aged below 35 years (54.6 per cent) were the largest group in the sample, followed by participants older than 55 years (20.4 per cent). Most of the participants (92.5 per cent) were long-term residents who indicated that they had lived in Macau for at least 7 years. In terms of educational attainment, 67.9 per cent of the participants reported their education level to be between high school and graduate.

Table 16.1 presents the mean ratings of residents' perceptions of the Hotel Estoril redevelopment. On a scale ranging from 1 (completely disagree) to 5 (completely agree), residents were asked to describe various aspects of trust, inclusiveness and openness (Pera et al. 2016), crucial to the process of co-creation. A total of ten characteristics summarised at the end of the interviews seemed to represent attitudes regarding the redevelopment of the Hotel Estoril. Public consultation (4.13) and better communication (4.03) were the two most-liked features, showing that residents were interested in participating in more discussions, particularly about the 'heritage' and 'history' of Macau. Residents agreed that the building being idle was wasteful (4.00) and expressed a preference for re-creating the hotel at its current location. Cultural distinctiveness, preserving Macau's unique heritage, and retaining a connection to the past were all major concerns for further development. The aesthetics and design of the Hotel Estoril appeared to be important determinants in residents' perception of authenticity. Although aesthetic perception was characterised as subjective, it had a marked influence on residents' views of adaptive reuse, as it was seen that a new design must reflect the identity of the hotel's history. In a similar vein, the emphasis on 'historical significance' (3.78) and 'transparency' (3.85) indicated that residents' judgements were shaped by accessible information provided by the mass media.

As far as perceptions of the present Hotel Estoril were concerned, 61 per cent of the residents agreed that the present image of the hotel was negative, while only 39 per cent of the respondents thought the building was still suitable for functioning as a hotel. The mean value of comments on the significant architectural or historical value of the hotel ranged from 3.12 to 3.17, showing that residents generally viewed the hotel as a positive example of Macau's heritage. However, 42.4 per cent of the residents stated that the building had undergone numerous architectural revisions and had now lost its cultural integrity. Meanwhile, 70 per cent of surveyed residents agreed that a brand-new identity could be re-established through the redesign and possible reuse of the hotel. More than 60 per cent believed that a new identity for the hotel would be beneficial for younger generations; among these, 64.8 per cent accepted the proposal of building a youth centre, while 65.5 per cent positively anticipated a recreational centre. Considering the architecture of the building, 40.7 per cent of the respondents expressed the view that the façade should be preserved as part of Macau's history. The majority of respondents suggested that all players should be involved in re-creating the hotel site (80.6 per cent), that an engagement platform should be built (78.2 per cent), that the dissemination of policy ought to be transparent (73.8 per cent) and that dialogue among stakeholders should be open (85.9 per cent). Ostensibly, the resident survey demonstrated that authentication is an important tool to recreate a new identity for the heritage hotel. Co-creation requires more engagement platforms, and transparency is necessary to negotiate and communicate the hotel's fate. It is possible for a new identity to be negotiated with the active involvement of all stakeholders.

Conclusion

Formerly disused or underused heritage hotels have been converted into various new forms, such as residences, restaurants, museums and profitable new businesses. In the case of the Hotel Estoril, government, community organisations and residents exhibit differing views on how best to revitalise the property. The members of the Cultural Heritage Council have voted overwhelmingly in favour of the government's decision not to list the hotel as a Cultural Heritage Site, arguing that dilapidated buildings have very little architectural or historical value and that the hotel has lost its essential cultural characteristics. However, members of Hotel Estoril concern groups argue that the site could be adaptively reused, and that it possesses heritage value that should be carefully preserved. The government has put forward a plan to transform the Hotel Estoril into a youth centre and a space for cultural and educational activities. Local residents support some kinds of re-creation, but believe that the iconic façade of the hotel is an artefact of Macau's gambling history. They agree with the government's perspective that an abandoned building is wasteful, but seek an active role in the decision-making process via the construction of an 'engagement platform'. They hope for greater transparency, better information sharing and a chance to get involved, including more discussions to help residents better understand the master plan.

As proposed in the conceptual framework (Figure 16.1), the distinction between government, community organisations and residents can move forward to form a new identity. Firstly, the authenticity of a heritage hotel has many different meanings, depending on the contexts. Authenticity is often defined in fabricated situations marked by unequal power relations (Smith 1989). In such contexts, what constitutes authentic heritage is hard to pin down objectively and precisely, because the concept is constantly shifting and being transformed. Gardner (2005) points out that the problem of authenticity in the postmodern period is that 'the authentic' has collapsed and been replaced with the 'logic of inauthentic authenticity'. The difficulty with understanding authenticity, according to Yang and Wall (2009: 251), flows from the reality that it embodies 'more than a simple idea underlying the originality of objects, but involves various perspectives, value statements, judgements, stereotypes, and spatial and socio-political influences'. All these dynamics are evident in the case study of the Hotel Estoril in Macau.

Secondly, co-creation is not a fixed entity in tourism study, but a flexible notion to be continuously negotiated and moulded into ad hoc resources, or assets to be spent, in order to achieve common priorities. Fife (2004: 63) coins the term 'semantic slippage', suggesting that an original artefact or sign justifies the authenticity of a 'similar' reproduction. Slippage occurs when what is taken to be the 'original' meaning of an object or event largely turns into the contemporary meaning of an object or enactment. The Hotel Estoril reflects the changing morphology of urban redevelopment. Co-creation needs to be defined by subjective criteria applied by various stakeholders. For example, the enthusiasm for preserving the Hotel Estoril is advocated by community organisations, while the government in Macau diametrically opposes the retention and repurposing of the hotel complex. Consequently, the process of co-creation should be constructed, experienced and managed by a variety of 'cultural mediators' (Ooi 2002), as well as by a menu of choices of various options for configuring products and services (Liechty, Ramaswamy and Cohen 2011). In other words, co-creation is a state of being that can only be judged by stakeholders involved in the process.

In contrast, identity formation should be viewed as a palimpsest, an indigenous process, an overlay of power struggles and conflicts among various stakeholders. It is culturally oriented, being formed through interactions with others in everyday activities. An identity involves emotional bonds and the invention of tradition, emerging from exogenous factors, such as tourism and commercial development. It is suggested that authentication may serve as a process for producing a new identity through public engagement. It is a process not solely exercised by majority groups, but participated in by a wide array of players. Through authentication, a new, traceable and measurable identity emerges, which can be characterised as a means of 'cultural translation' (Bhabha 2004); a product of interplay, for example, between government and community organisations, between government and residents, and between local and national political authorities. Instead of balancing conflicts, or compromising among stakeholders, co-creation is arguably an innovative path for revitalising and sustaining heritage hotels. By authenticating a heritage hotel, co-creation serves as another key in creating a new identity for a society.

References

Berlie, J.A. (2012) *The Chinese of Macao: A Decade After the Handover*. Hong Kong: Proverse Hong Kong.

Bhabha, H. (2004) *The Location of Culture*. New York: Routledge.

Bharwani, S. and Jauhari, V. (2013) An exploratory study of competencies required to co-create memorable customer experiences in the hospitality industry. *International Journal of Contemporary Hospitality Management*, 25(6): 823–843.

Chathoth, P., Ungson, G., Harrington, R. and Chan, E. (2016) Co-creation and higher order customer engagement in hospitality and tourism services. *International Journal of Contemporary Hospitality Management*, 28(2): 222–245.

Chen, L., Mardsen, J.R. and Zhang, Z. (2012) Theory and analysis of company-sponsored value co-creation. *Journal of Management Information Systems*, 29(2): 141–172.

Czaja, R. and Blair, J. (2005) *Designing Surveys: A Guide to Decisions and Procedures*, 2nd Edition. London: Pine Forge Press.

Fife, W. (2004) Semantic slippage as a new aspect of authenticity: Viking tourism on the Northern Peninsula of Newfoundland. *Journal of Folklore Research*, 41(1): 61–84.

Gardner, R. (2005) Tradition and authenticity in popular music. *Symbolic Interaction*, 28(1): 135–144.

Gebauer, H., Johnson, M. and Enquist, B. (2010) Value co-creation as a determinant of success in public transport services: a study of the Swiss Federal Railway operator (SBB). *Management Service Quality*, 20(6): 511–530.

Griffioen, J. (2009) Something, something, something. *VICE Magazine*. Detroit.

Henderson, J. (2013) Selling the past: heritage hotels. *Tourism*, 61(4): 451–454.

Hitchcock, M., King, V. and Parnwell, M. (1993). *Tourism in Southeast Asia*. London: Routledge.

Klumbis, D. F. and Munsters, W. (2005) Culture as a component of the hospitality product, in M. Sigala and D. Leslie (eds.) *International Cultural Tourism: Management, Implications and Cases*. Oxford: Butterworth Heinemann, pp. 26–39.

Krippendorf, K. (1980) *Content Analysis: An Introduction to its Methodology*. Thousand Oaks, CA: Sage.

Liechty, J., Ramaswamy, V. and Cohen, S.H. (2001). Choice menus for mass customization: an experimental approach for analyzing customer demand with an application to a web-based information service. *Journal of Marketing Research*, 38(2): 183–196.

Macau Tourism (2015) 2015 Policy Address: Create a 'City of Culture and Events', available at: http://mtt.macaotourism.gov.mo/201505/en/contents/1/137.html [accessed 29 June 2016].

McCartney, G. J. (2006) Casino gambling in Macao: through legalisation to liberalisation, in C.H.C. Hsu (ed.) *Casino Industry in Asia Pacific: Development, Operation, and Impact*. New York: Haworth Hospitality Press, pp. 37–58.

Minkiewicz, J., Evans, J. and Bridson, K. (2014) How do consumers co-create their experiences? An exploration in the heritage sector. *Journal of Marketing Management*, 30(1–2): 30–59.

Ooi, C. (2002) *Cultural Tourism and Tourism Cultures: The Business of Mediating Experiences in Copenhagen and Singapore*. Copenhagen: Copenhagen Business School Press.

Ramaswamy, V. and Gouillart, F.J. (2010) *The Power of Co-Creation: Build It with Them to Boost Growth, Productivity, and Profits*. New York: Free Press.

Ramaswamy, V. and Ozcan, K. (2014) *The Co-Creation Paradigm*. Redwood, CA: Stanford University Press.

Richards, G. (2011) Creativity and tourism: the state of the art. *Annals of Tourism Research*, 38(4): 1225–1253.

Robinson, M. (1999) Collaboration and cultural consent: refocusing sustainable tourism. *Journal of Sustainable Tourism*, 7(3–4): 379–397.

Roser, T. and Samson, A. (2009) *Co-Creation: New Paths to Value*. London: Promise/ LSE Enterprise.

Salamon, L. M. and Anker, H.K. (1999) *Global Civil Society: Dimensions of the Non-profit Sector*. Baltimore, Maryland: The Johns Hopkins University.

Smith, V. (1989) *Host and Guests: The Anthropology of Tourism*. Philadelphia, PA: University of Pennsylvania Press.

Timothy, D.J. and Boyd, S.W. (2003) *Heritage Tourism*. London: Pearson Education.

Timothy, D. J. and Teye, V. B. (2009) *Tourism and the Lodging Sector*. Oxford: Butterworth Heinemann.

Yang, L. and Wall, G. (2009) Authenticity in ethnic tourism: domestic tourists' perspective. *Current Issues in Tourism*, 12(3): 235–254.

17 Turkish coffee

From intangible cultural heritage to created tourist experience

Ilkay Tas Gursoy

Introduction

Rarely does a drink enjoy such strong social and cultural attributions as coffee does. Tucker (2011) points to cross-cultural commonalities in meanings, attitudes and values assigned to coffee as a special treat, as a sign of civilised society, as a sign of membership to a social class or, on the contrary, as a way of weakening social-class divisions due to its popularity among people from various social backgrounds. Coffee has been a source of inspiration and a tool of expression. Songs or poems have long invited beloved ones for a cup of coffee together. While the miniature opera *Coffee Cantata* (1732) by Johann Sebastian Bach tells a story about the inevitability of coffee in everyday life, the painting *Enjoying Coffee* at the Suna and İnan Kıraç Foundation Pera Museum in İstanbul[1] engages viewers with a young lady who is just about to drink coffee. Even the very substance of coffee can be a material used in artistic interpretations, as in the example of coffee painting where artists infuse their imaginations in coffee.

Coffee is one of only a few beverages that have global popularity while also being a characteristic of local culture and a remarkable part of daily routine (Jolliffe 2010). In 2013, Turkish coffee culture and tradition was inscribed on the representative list of Intangible Cultural Heritage of Humanity by the United Nations Educational, Scientific and Cultural Organisation (UNESCO). Heritage is a politically charged domain, with its links to social identity, agency and history (Franklin, 2003), where actors reshape their environments in line with their own notion of their heritage (Macleod, 2010). This chapter focuses on the (re) creation of Turkish coffee heritage for tourism and as a tourist experience. It is structured into two main parts. Firstly it tells the story of Turkish coffee as intangible cultural heritage by introducing the concept of intangible cultural heritage and then describing the journey of Turkish coffee. The second part demonstrates how Turkish coffee is (re)created for tourism and as a tourist experience through the networked practices of cultural diplomacy, hospitality, performativity, materiality and connectivity. While the first part gives an account of how heritage was created in the past, the second part connects heritage to the present, the living and everyday life.

Turkish coffee as intangible cultural heritage

Intangible cultural heritage

'It is good to learn that UNESCO recognised Turkish coffee, thankfully we were able to protect our own cultural heritage as ours'; these were the words of a salesperson at a souvenir shop in Kızlarağası Hanı, a lively tourist spot in Izmir. He hinted at the argument of Bendix (2009) about power plays at heritage nominations and the dignifying effect of nomination. In fact, the selection of Turkish coffee culture and tradition to be on the representative list of Intangible Cultural Heritage of Humanity by UNESCO was welcomed in the hope both of safeguarding coffee culture at home and also of promoting Turkish cultural tourism abroad. Although it was emphasised by Ahmet Arı, the (then) Director of the Research and Education Unit at The Republic of Turkey Ministry of Culture and Tourism that being on the UNESCO list was not enough for protection (Dünya 2013), newspapers were eager to use the newly acquired international label 'UNESCO' with Turkish coffee. So, the news was released with headlines such as 'Turkish coffee is under UNESCO protection' (Sabah 2013, Hürriyet 2013, Dünya 2013).

Rusalić (2009: 53) describes culture as 'a defining feature of identity of any society, contributing to the way people see themselves and the community they identify with'. Smith (2006) argues that all heritage is intangible, regarding sensing, meaning and knowing aspects of heritage in general. Intangible cultural heritage comprises 'tradition-based creations of a cultural community' which manifest 'its cultural and social identity' (Kirshenblatt-Gimblett 2004: 54). Pratt (2013) underlines that it is the characteristics of cultural transmission and reproduction which differentiate intangible heritage. The UNESCO Convention for the Safeguarding of Intangible Cultural Heritage describes intangible cultural heritage as 'the practices, representations, expressions, knowledge, skills – as well as the instruments, objects, artefacts and cultural spaces associated therewith – that communities, groups and, in some cases, individuals recognise as part of their cultural heritage' (UNESCO 2003).

Tucker (2011: 16) highlights the fact that coffee, in general, is a social-prestige drink based on the level of complexity in preparation. Turkish coffee may certainly be considered as a prestige drink, since it requires patience, a special technique and skill to prepare and present it. Social prestige, nationhood, sense of community and hospitality are some of the associations with coffee. Turkish coffee takes on significance through such associations and becomes an intangible heritage in the network of values assigned to it. As Smith and Akagawa (2009: 6) say, 'Heritage only becomes "heritage" when it becomes recognisable within a particular set of cultural or social values, which are themselves "intangible"'.

Coffee has contributed to the recognition of Turkish culture abroad throughout its history. Currently, its position on the UNESCO list is seen as an opportunity to draw attention to coffee heritage in Turkey at national and international levels, while the international framework provided by UNESCO is welcomed as a basis for further action (The Republic of Turkey Ministry of Culture and Tourism 2017).

Thus, in this case, the UNESCO list is a framework for protection and the UNESCO intangible cultural heritage is a label for internationalisation.

Turkish coffee in the making: a brief history

Coffee's journey to Ottoman lands took place within a network of relations and mobilities. Actually, the coffee plant is indigenous to Ethiopia, but it was cultivated in Yemen and coffee drinking became a habit there in the fifteenth century (Aregay 1988). Coffee entered Ottoman social life in the fifteenth century from Arabia, via Aleppo and Damascus, following Ottoman enlargement into Eygpt (Quataert 2005). The name of coffee in Turkish is 'kahve' which is a modified form of 'qahwah', a word with Arabic origin; interestingly, 'qahwah' meant some kind of wine in Arabic (Reuning 1943). Chase (1991) explains that it was through Sufis in Yemen that coffee became known to the public. Sufis were engaged not only in religious practices but in different parts of economic life, having different professions. Sufis took their habit of coffee drinking with them wherever they went and conveyed coffee culture to whomever they met, for example the students at Cairo's Al-Azar University. Chase (1991) draws attention to the intellectual and spiritual milieu where coffee culture was nurtured.

The penetration of coffee houses into Ottoman social life corresponded with major changes in modes of sociability during the early modern era, according to Kafadar (2014). He notes that changes in the level and forms of urbanisation, the rise of the bourgeoisie, the increasing use of night-time for socialising, and the advent of new types of entertainment or performative arts, all contributed to coffee house culture in Istanbul. The first coffee houses in the city were opened in 1555, soon after tobacco was introduced to Ottoman territories. Tobacco and coffee became artefacts of Ottoman and Middle Eastern culture, as signifiers of hospitality and socialisation (Quataert 2005).

By the first half of the seventeenth century there were several hundred coffee houses in Ottoman lands (Kafadar 2014). Coffee houses were economic businesses, places of (mainly male) sociability, scenes of literary exchanges, the milieu of political discussions and sites of public opinion formation. They provided for relatively secular public space. Coffee houses owned by Janissaries also had policing and lodging functions (Kafadar 2002, Çaksu 2007). Chase (1991: 56) shares the text of a note from Lady Mary Wortley to a fellow Englishwoman in 1717, describing her visit to a hamam: 'in short, it is the women's coffee house, where all the news of the town is told, and scandal invented'. Here coffee appears in association with female sociability.

Coffee's spread through Ottoman territories was, however, not without difficulty. Firstly, coffee was prohibited in 1511, based on the argument that it was unhealthy, while in 1544 social gatherings around coffee were banned. However, these prohibitions did not last long (McCabe 2015) and, as the network of economic, cultural and social relations widened, coffee houses began to spread worldwide. Kırlı (2016) says that coffee as a commodity was transmitted to Europe by Italian merchants, but coffee and coffee house culture were introduced into everyday life by Greek and Armenian entrepreneurs who used to live in Ottoman territories and had become acquainted with coffee culture there. Ellis (2008) notes that coffee houses in seventeenth-century London took coffee houses in the Ottoman Empire as their example.

Quataert (2005: 9) gives a short description of leisure in Europe at this time: 'Ottoman-style coffee houses across Europe became populated with Europeans wearing bright silks, billowing trousers, and upturned "Turkish slippers," smoking "Turkish" pipes and eating "Turkish" sweets'. Ottoman coffee houses were 'one of the most powerful images on the cartography of the European imagination regarding the Orient'. Upon their return home, European travellers used to share their observations and experiences of the lively coffee houses in Ottoman cities (ibid.: 176). McCabe (2015: 124) states that 'the first descriptions of coffee came from travelers with an intellectual interest in the Ottoman Empire or Persia. Many seventeenth-century sources about coffee are Dutch, French and English travel accounts'. Narratives of travellers, artworks, literature and Ottoman artefacts, relating to coffee, nurtured European imaginaries. Coffee, once infused into the everyday life of both Ottomans and Europeans, became a substance for 'the imaginative mill' of travellers (Quataert 2005: 10).

Latour (2005: 72) accepts the 'agency of all sorts of objects', not only human but also non-human. Agents, both human and non-human, can influence some other agent's action; in other words, they can 'modify a state of affairs by making a difference' (Latour 2005: 71). Agents, or actants, can take various forms and, by operating in heterogeneity, they can constitute a network of heritage together (Waterton and Watson 2013). Müller (2015: 30–31), by referring to actor-network theory, argues that 'agency is exclusively a mediated achievement, brought about through forging associations'. Through the lens of actor-network theory (Ren 2010: 201), Turkish coffee may be seen as an agent with the capacity to act, influence and interact by 'deriving power from its surroundings'. The agency of Turkish coffee changes according to the forms it takes, either as a drink, a commodity, a social ritual, a daily habit or an intangible cultural heritage. Thus, its capacity to form associations and then networks changes as well.

The journey of Turkish coffee from a *fincan* (a small ceramic cup designed for Turkish coffee) to the international list of intangible heritage may also be seen through a 'mobilities' perspective. According to mobilities theory, 'to move is to do something' and even 'staying still (insofar as such a thing is possible) is also a notable practical positioning in the face of surrounding mobilities' (Cresswell and Merriman 2011: 5). Turkish coffee either by 'staying still', in the fincan of a craftsman at a traditional bazaar or in the selfie of a tourist enjoying heritage, or by moving to international tourism exhibitions or cultural diplomacy events is doing something; that is, creating 'spaces and stories' via mobilities (ibid.). Mobilities can take various forms, such as physical, imaginative and virtual (Urry and Larsen 2011). Waterton and Watson (2013:553) state that mobilities theory offers a way of looking at heritage as 'the result of dynamic intersections of people, objects and places'. Thus, Turkish coffee heritage is the result of the 'networked mobilities of capital, persons, objects, signs and information' (Urry and Larsen 2011:119).

Coffee is just an excuse: creating tourist experience

The second part of the chapter concentrates on the creation of Turkish coffee heritage for tourism, by and in the dynamic 'network of practices in which it is embedded' (Ren 2011:863); these interrelated practices are identified as cultural diplomacy, hospitality, performativity, materiality and connectivity. Practices of hospitality intersect with those of performativity, as coffee serving is a performance in itself, while practices of performativity connect with materiality, as material objects can perform. Connectivity interacts with performativity and materiality, as making and sharing a coffee selfie involves all three.

Coffee and cultural diplomacy: 'forty years of friendship'

In Turkish, there is a saying that '(enjoying) a cup of coffee (together) commits friendship for forty years'. Cultivating permanent social ties on the international level is one of the aims of states that seek worldwide influence. Soft power 'rests on the ability to shape the preferences of others', not by forcing but by persuading; 'soft power is attractive power. In terms of resources, soft power resources are the assets that produce such attraction' (Nye 2008: 95). Cultural diplomacy, which may be defined as 'not government-to-government communication but . . . communication between governments and foreign people' (Gienow-Hecht and Donfried 2010:13) is one example of soft power. As Palmer (1999: 314) remarks, by 'packaging of selected symbols of identity', tourism helps to encourage identity formation, and this is also the case with cultural diplomacy. Cultural diplomacy and tourism are interrelated due to their role in heritage (re)creation. Macleod (2010: 65) notes the importance of history, identity and economy for heritage (re) creation: 'Given the relevance of history and identity to communities worldwide, as well as the necessity to make money, the production of heritage is a sensitive, serious and valuable activity'.

Winter (2015) notes that heritage becomes international in the networks of capital and the institutionalised practices of governance. It is in this network of relations that Turkish coffee mounts the stage of international politics, as an actor 'performing heritage' in order to create attraction and establish ties with peoples of different nations. Governmental organisations (the Ministry of Culture and Tourism and the Yunus Emre Institute) help to make international space performable for Turkish coffee. The efforts made by the Ministry of Culture and Tourism to get international recognition for Turkish coffee resulted in the acquisition of a UNESCO intangible heritage label (as discussed earlier). To create attraction around coffee, this body organises Turkish coffee workshops in Europe, supports documentary works and integrates Turkish coffee into promotional campaigns and international meetings. As an example, it used the opportunity of the 2015 G20 meeting held in Antalya to create tourist experiences for the participants, organising a cultural space filled with cultural assets representing Turkish heritage, which included a demonstration of coffee preparation and presentation. In the visual materials, coffee was introduced with quite a 'soft power' title: 'love that comes from a tradition'.

A country can be powerful in places where its culture is found attractive (Nye 2008). The Yunus Emre Institute is a governmental body, established to promote Turkish heritage abroad through cultural activities, which has more than 40 cultural centres worldwide, from Austria to Sudan (Yunus Emre Enstitüsü 2017). I contacted officials at the Institutes to learn how they (re)create Turkish coffee heritage for tourism and as an aspect of cultural diplomacy. According to the observations of officers, Turkish coffee, as part of culinary heritage, is indispensable to tourism. Participants in Turkish coffee events become curious about other aspects of cultural heritage, especially gastronomy and customs. Turkish coffee has a power of attraction because of its performative rituals of preparation, serving and tasting, the variety of equipment involved in its preparation, its rich historical background, the colourful stories about it and its unique taste. The official at the Vienna Institute pointed to differentiated (re)creations of coffee heritage according to the historical and cultural backgrounds of the location: 'In Yemen, generally a folk song about coffee is used, while in Vienna, historical links of Vienna with Turkish coffee culture, or in the Balkans and in the Middle East different points can be emphasised'. The Yunus Emre Institute at Khartoum, Sudan, organises a series of meetings entitled 'One (cup of) coffee forty years of friendship'. Coffee is prepared and presented, performing all the traditional stages; for example, it is cooked on the cinder in small cups and presented by people dressed in a traditional way. Skopje Institute, in the Republic of Macedonia, organises art themed activities and introduces Turkish coffee culture alongside these events. As might be expected, in this set of relations, Turkish coffee acts in a traditional way, with the materials (coffee roaster, coffee cups, trays, hand grinders, a special pot called cezve and coffee jug), costumes, and the following of all the sequence of acts (preparation, presentation and degustation), in line with the narratives around it.

Coffee and hospitality: 'The heart desires having a talk, coffee is an excuse'

'The heart desires neither coffee nor coffee house; the heart desires having a talk, coffee is an excuse' is a saying in Turkish. Inviting friends for coffee is an excuse to have a talk; it is the companionship that is desired. Jolliffe (2010: 6) points out that 'coffee is directly connected to hospitality at both intimate and commercial settings'. In order to trace the creation of Turkish coffee culture for tourism in commercial hospitality settings, I observed the settings and interviewed the staff of hotel and coffee houses in Izmir. Turkish coffee is offered on the restaurant menus of both city hotels and holiday resorts. However, Turkish coffee is no longer traditional in city hotels or in most holiday resorts.

One catering manager said: 'At our hotel, there used to be a waiter who served Turkish coffee in traditional clothes but now there isn't. Hotels give up. Because it is costly, you have to engage one person to do only this'. 'Hotels are not the right places to feel locality. Local life is felt better outside the hotel' argued a hotel manager. 'At some special organisations, such as Turkish nights or during Ramadan, we offer Turkish coffee in traditional clothes but generally our service

Figure 17.1 Turkish coffee in a hospitality setting

is standard with Turkish delight and a glass of water' said a general manager of a city hotel. A catering manager of a resort hotel justified their practice: 'We cook it with automatic coffee machines, otherwise we cannot meet the demand, and it is costly in the traditional method of boiling a pot because you have to employ at least one person just doing it all day'. 'We serve Turkish coffee most because it is a coffee house, but in summer cold drinks are the favourite' said a coffee house staff member, while another said: 'Tea is the most popular one and then comes coffee, because tea is cheaper'.

Turkish coffee in a modern hospitality setting (hotel or coffee house) is characterised by the absence of supporting materials (such as coffee roaster or grinder), costumes and rituals (such as cooking on cinder), which were present in the traditional setting. Ren (2011: 864) observes that an 'object is a pattern of not only presences but also absences'. Modern Turkish coffee is presented in an elegant (not necessarily sophisticated) way, accompanied by Turkish delight and a glass of cold water, although it is not fully performed. At hotel restaurants Turkish coffee is offered on the menu, mostly suggested after a good meal, while it is a popular drink in coffee houses. Franklin (2003: 2) argues that 'tourism is infused into the everyday'. Turkish coffee is an everyday routine and the local coffee houses offer a way for tourists to experience 'the local everyday'.

Coffee and Performativity: 'Let what is inside your heart be revealed'

I put the experiencing of Turkish coffee on the itinerary I design. I take them to a special place where coffee is prepared in small cups on cinder. They witness it, the smell, the cinder . . . They try doing it. I know they remember this for a long time.

So said a tour guide I interviewed, pointing to the memory and sensual involvement in the creation of tourist experience. Although traditional Turkish coffee tends to be missing in most city and resort hotels, it reappears at tourist sites as an attraction and a performance, both benefitting from the tourist flow and contributing to it. Antonina travel agency in Istanbul organises tours with the theme of Turkish coffee culture. Their itinerary shows what is seen to be worthy of inclusion in the tourist imaginaries of Istanbul. The tour starts with a seminar on the social life of coffee at the Ottoman Palace. Tourists learn how to interpret what they will encounter during the tour and then move to various spots in the historical heart of Istanbul. Firstly, they visit various madrasahs, which were the places of vivid cultural life during the Ottoman era. Next, to understand the historical roots of coffee culture in the East, they visit Şark Kahvesi (the name can be translated *mot à mot* as Eastern Coffee house), located in Kapalıçarşı, the historical grand bazaar of Istanbul. Then they visit Balkapanı Han, which was an important trade centre for coffee, and the 'nostalgic' coffee shop (as described by the tour organisers) of Kurukahveci Mehmet Efendi. With feelings of nostalgia dipped into coffee, the participants 'witness' the coffee-grinding ritual. At the end of the tour, after having successfully completed all the tasks of being a *good tourist,* the tourists are ready to learn 'the coffee drinking ritual' and drink Turkish coffee (Antonina Turizm 2017). Another milieu where heritage is created through performing is that of 'Turkish nights'. Turkish coffee comes at the end of a Turkish night, after a good meal, and complements the experience.

Turkish coffee provides an affective, interactive and performative experience when coffee reading is included. 'Let what is inside your heart be revealed' are the words used before starting to interpret what is seen through the coffee grounds remaining in the cup. Fortune telling fulfils curiosity about the future. 'Don't believe in fortune-telling but don't be in lack of it' is said at almost every coffee reading ritual (Argan et al. 2015: 28). Coffee reading takes place in both commercial and intimate settings. There are professional coffee readers working at coffee houses (both local and touristic ones). Coffee reading (re)creates coffee heritage for tourists by blending the drinking of coffee with knowing their fortune; in fact, it co-creates, (re)creating a gastronomic experience by adding imagination, curiosity, thinking and excitement.

Coffee and materiality: **In Situ**

Museums may be regarded as sites for practices of materiality involving collections of objects (although, as mentioned above, boundaries are dynamic and museums may be sites of performativity or cultural diplomacy as well). At ethnographic museums, objects relating to Turkish coffee rituals may be exhibited. In June 2015 Topkapı Museum hosted a grand exhibition, entitled 'A drop of pleasure – 500 years of Turkish coffee', dedicated to the (re)creation of coffee heritage in order to attract tourists. Museums can 'perform' various kinds of 'materiality'.

In Situ is the title given by artist duo, AslieMK, to their performance at Pera Museum based on the exhibition Coffee Break: The Adventure of Coffee in

Kütahya Tiles and Ceramics. They took the solid materials (Kütahya tiles and ceramics) and melted them into performance by using the moulding capacity of the space (museum). They (re)created artworks by using techology (a 3D printer and a projector) which enabled the objects to appear behind glass in a way that visitors could touch them. Thus, Kütahya tiles and ceramics used by their owners in the past were touched again in the present. As the name implies, this was a performance. However, regarding its connection with the solid materials and with technology, the performance could be seen as belonging to practices of materiality – perhaps a fluid form of materiality:

> What impressed us here was, first of all, the place itself, the mood of the spatial atmosphere when we entered. Light, general light order, the darkness, the fact that objects in the showcases stood out in the darkness of the whole space . . . The connection between the collection and performance was created to some extent by the place itself . . . Two different foci. Two different times. By transferring data of the objects standing frozen behind the showcases to another focal point, namely to present time, we aimed to create performance. By this way, a visitor can connect with the collection, can touch it and can get into affective communication with it.
>
> (AslieMK, Pera Museum, 2017)

Souvenirs are material objects that function not only as tourist mementos, but also as memory holders (Cave et al. 2013), so they are essential to the tourist experience. Considering the relationship between souvenirs and Turkish coffee culture, it was observed that coffee cups, and sometimes coffee itself, become souvenirs. 'Expats', as well as tourists, use souvenir shops. 'Tourists buy coffee cups. I add a coffee-making pot and Turkish coffee to it, thus I make a set of Turkish coffee' said a salesperson at a souvenir shop in Kızlarağası Hanı, in Izmir, a lively tourist spot where there is a traditional coffee house. 'Expats buy large quantities of coffee as gifts. It is inexpensive and good' added another salesperson. Tour guides were seen to influence the creation of tourist experience directly:

> I do my best to ensure that my guests have tried a good Turkish coffee before they return. But for some of them the taste is strong . . . Well, about souvenirs related to coffee heritage, to be honest, I can't say there is quality and variety in souvenirs. Sometimes, guests try coffee and want to buy some souvenirs, but it is difficult to find a good one

said a tour guide. 'I personally like Turkish coffee, therefore I pay extra attention to take them to enjoy Turkish coffee . . . As a souvenir of coffee heritage . . . I can say that they generally buy small cups with traditional patterns on them' said another tour guide. 'Sometimes a tourist tries and likes Turkish coffee, and wants to buy essential equipment to make it at home', noted another tour guide.

Coffee and connectivity

Wellman (2001: 227) observes that 'a computer network is a social network'. New opportunities of connectivity are provided in the networked practices of connectivity, as such:

> computer-supported interpersonal communication affects the ways in which people connect with each other: greater bandwidth for non-face-to-face communication; wireless portability of computerized communication devices; globalized ease of connecting with others and accessing information; and the personalization of technology and knowledge management.

Turkish coffee is (re)created as tourist experience, personalised and globalised at the same time, by and within the social network supported by computers (smartphones). Ease of connecting with others makes sharing a moment of coffee encounter almost effortless. Social networking sites (Facebook, Twitter, Instagram, Pinterest) hold moments (memories) of people (re)creating coffee experiences in photos, in everyday life. With the ease of accessing and sharing information, one can find where to go for a personalised Turkish coffee experience; traditional, modern, as part of a Turkish night, more touristic, and so on.

Coffee reading benefits from globalised connectivity as well. Coffee reading websites and applications for mobiles take the performance to a global level through the ease of online communication. Interestingly, coffee reading websites in the English language are quite many and detailed. Some of them are commercial, while some just aim to 'share knowledge'. Coffee reading through web-based milieux increases the popularity and commodification of Turkish coffee heritage. Turkish coffee reading websites may be considered as products of 'global social life', (re)creating Turkish coffee heritage in transnational modern life (Franklin 2003:4).

Conclusion

On its way to a place on the UNESCO intangible heritage list, Turkish coffee travelled distances, experienced praise and prohibition, entered homes, palaces, spiritual rites, coffee houses, streets, engagement ceremonies, official meetings, and various arenas of private and public life where people, objects and places intersected. Coffee exercises a power of attraction in intercultural relationships while, as part of cultural heritage, it is inherently connected to tourism. In creating Turkish coffee heritage for tourism, governmental organisations collect materials, performances and narratives selectively. Turkish coffee is created in a traditional way in promotional campaigns and cultural diplomacy. On the other hand, a modernised and standardised version of Turkish coffee is created for hospitality practices. In the network of performativity practices, Turkish coffee becomes more of a play, as in the coffee reading. Materiality practices take objects related to coffee and (re)create them into something else, such as a memory or a performance. Connectivity practices make Turkish coffee part of global social life by recreating Turkish coffee heritage in transnational modern life.

Note

1 The painting *Enjoying Coffee*, from the first half of the eighteenth century by an unknown painter (French School) is in the Orientalist Collection, Suna and İnan Kıraç Foundation, Pera Museum, Istanbul, Turkey. For an animated version of the painting by Pera Museum, see www.youtube.com/watch?v=mN5p5bojZTU.

References

Antonina Turizm (2017) Türk kahvesi üzerine seminer ve kültür turu. [Online] Available at: www.antoninaturizm.com/tur/turk-kahvesi-uzerine-seminer-ve-kultur-turu_8 [accessed 12 October 2017].

Aregay, W. M. (1988) The early history of Ethiopia's coffee trade and the rise of shawa. *Journal of African History*, 29(1): 19–25.

Argan, M., Akyildiz, M., Ozdemir, B., Bas, A. and Akkus, E. (2015) Leisure aspects of Turkish coffee consumption rituals: an exploratory qualitative study. *International Journal of Health and Economic Development*, 1(1): 26–36.

AslieMK, 'In Situ', performance in the program entitled 'Look Again' between March 31 and April 2, 2017 Pera museum. Available at: www.youtube.com/watch?v=C2BN VDbRdBg [accessed 11 March 2017].

Bendix, R. (2009) Heritage between economy and politics: an assessment from the perspective of cultural anthropology, in L. Smith and N. Akagawa (eds.) *Intangible Heritage*. London: Routledge, pp. 253–269.

Cave, J., Baum, T. and Jolliffe, L. (2013) Theorising tourism and souvenirs, glocal perspectives on the margins, in J. Cave, L. Jolliffe and T. Baum (eds.) *Tourism and Souvenirs: Glocal Perspectives from the Margins*. Bristol: Channel View Publications, pp. 1–28.

Chase, H. (1991) The company of qahwa. *Oxford Symposium on Food and Cookery 1991: Public Eating: Proceedings*, Oxford: Prospect Books, pp. 54–60.

Cresswell, T. and Merriman, P. (2011) Introduction: geographies of mobilities-practices, spaces, subjects, in T. Cresswell and P. Merriman (eds.) *Geographies of Mobilities: Practices, Spaces, Subjects*. Surrey: Ashgate, pp. 1–15.

Çaksu, A. (2007) Janissary coffee houses in late eighteenth-century Istanbul, in Sajdi. D. (ed.) *Ottoman Tulips, Ottoman Coffee: Leisure and Lifestyle in the Eighteenth Century*. London: Tauris Academic Studies, pp. 117–132.

Dünya (2013) Türk kahvesi artık UNESCO'nun korumasında, 5 December 2013. [Online] Available at: www.dunya.com/gundem/turk-kahvesi-artik-unesco039nunkorumasinda-haberi-229760 [accessed 14 April 2017].

Ellis, M. (2008) An introduction to the coffee-house: a discursive model. *Language and Communication*, 28(2): 156–164.

Franklin, A. (2003) *Tourism: An Introduction*. London: Sage Publications.

Gienow-Hecht, J. and Donfried, M. (2010). The model of cultural diplomacy power, distance, and the promise of civil society, in J. Gienow-Hecht and M. Donfried (eds.) *Searching for a Cultural Diplomacy*. New York: Berghahn Books, pp. 13–29.

Hürriyet (2013) Türk kahvesi Unesco korumasında, 5 December 2013. [Online] Available at: www.hurriyet.com.tr/turk-kahvesi-unesco-korumasinda-25284675 [accessed 14 April 2017].

Jolliffe, L. (2010) Common grounds of coffee and tourism, in L. Jolliffe (ed.) *Coffee Culture, Destinations and Tourism*, Bristol: Channel View Publication, pp. 3–22.

Kafadar, C. (2002) A history of coffee. *The XIIIth Congress of the International Economic History Association (IEHA)* (pp. 22–26). Available at: https://sites.duke.edu/rethinkingglobalcities/files/2014/09/64Kafadar16-coffeehistory.pdf [accessed 12 March 2017].

Kafadar, C. (2014) How dark is the history of the night, how black the story of coffee, how bitter the tale of love: the changing measure of leisure and pleasure in early modern Istanbul, in A. Öztürkmen and B. Vitz (eds.) *Medieval and Early Modern Performance in the Eastern Mediterranean*. Turnhout: Brepols, pp. 243–269.

Kırlı, C. (2016) Coffeehouses: leisure and sociability in Ottoman Istanbul, in P.N. Borsay and J. H. Furnée (eds.) *Leisure Cultures in Urban Europe, 1700–1870*. Manchester: Manchester University Press, pp. 161–181.

Kirshenblatt-Gimblett, B. (2004) Intangible heritage as metacultural production. *Museum International*, 56(1–2): 52–65.

Latour, B. (2005) *Reassembling the Social: An Introduction to Actor-Network Theory*. Oxford: Oxford University Press.

Macleod, D.V.L. (2010) Power, culture and the production of heritage, in D.V.L. Macleod and J.G. Carrier (eds.) *Tourism, Power and Culture*. Bristol: Channel View Publications, pp. 64–89.

McCabe, I. B. (2015) *A History of Global Consumption 1500–1800*. Oxon: Routledge.

Müller, M. (2015) Assemblages and actor-networks: Rethinking socio-material power, politics and space. *Geography Compass*, 9(1): 27–41.

Nye, J. S. (2008) Public diplomacy and soft power. *Annals of the American Academy of Political and Social Science*, 616(1): 94–109.

Palmer, C. (1999) Tourism and the symbols of identity. *Tourism Management*, 20(3): 313–322.

Pratt, M. L. (2013) Thoughts on intangiblity and transmission, in L. Arizpe and C. Amescua (eds.) *Anthropological Perspectives on Intangible Cultural Heritage*. New York: Springer, pp. 79–82.

Quataert, D. (2015) *The Ottoman Empire, 1700–1922*. Cambridge: Cambridge University Press.

Ren, C. (2010) Assembling the socio-material destination: An actor-network approach to cultural tourism studies, in G. Richards and W. Munsters (eds.) *Cultural Tourism Research Methods*. Oxfordshire: CABI International, pp. 199–208.

Ren, C. (2011) Non-human agency, radical ontology and tourism realities. *Annals of Tourism Research*, 38(3): 858–881.

Reuning, K. (1943) Turkish contributions to western vocabularies. *Monatshefte für Deutschen Unterricht*, 35(3/4): 125–132.

Rusalić, D. (2009) Making the intangible tangible: the new interface of cultural heritage, *Institute of Ethnography Sasa, Special Editions 63*, Available at: www.etnoinstitut.co.rs/lat/monografije/63.php [accessed 11 March 2017].

Sabah (2013) Türk kahvesi UNESCO korumasına giriyor, 2 December 2013. [Online] Available at: www.sabah.com.tr/yasam/2013/12/02/turk-kahvesi-unesco-korumasinagiriyor [accessed 14 April 2017].

Smith, L. (2006). *Uses of Heritage*. London: Routledge.

Smith, L. and Akagawa, N. (2009) Introduction, in L. Smith and N. Akagawa (eds.) *Intangible Heritage*. Oxon: Routledge, pp. 1–9.

The Republic of Turkey Ministry of Culture and Tourism (2017) Turkish coffee culture and tradition. Available at: http://aregem.kulturturizm.gov.tr/TR,132383/turkish-coffee-cultureand-tradition.html [accessed 14 April 2017].

Tucker, C.M. (2011) *Coffee Culture Local Experiences, Global Connections*. New York: Routledge.

UNESCO (2003) Text of the Convention for the Safeguarding of the Intangible Cultural Heritage. Available at: https://ich.unesco.org/en/convention#art2 [accessed 15 May 2017].

Urry, J. and Larsen J. (2011) *The Tourist Gaze*, 3rd Edition. London: Sage Publications.

Waterton, E. and Watson, S. (2013) Framing theory: towards a critical imagination in heritage studies. *International Journal of Heritage Studies*, 19(6): 546–561.

Wellman, B. (2001) Physical place and cyberplace: the rise of personalized networking. *International Journal of Urban and Regional Research*, 25(2): 227–252.

Winter, T. (2015) Heritage diplomacy. *International Journal of Heritage Studies*, 21(10): 997–1015.

Yunus Emre Enstitüsü (2017) Culture and Arts. Available at: www.yee.org.tr/en/culturalarts [accessed 15 May 2017].

18 The reinvention of crab fishing as a local heritage tourism attraction in Northeast Brazil

Claudio Milano

Introduction

The aim of this chapter is to problematise the contemporary trend to create heritage labels in order to strengthen the tourism industry. The heritage in question is linked to the identity of crab fishermen in Northeast Brazil, who are being used to promote event and culinary tourism. The chapter will observe and discuss the relationship between heritage and tourism by focusing on the uça (*Ucides cordatus cordatus*)[1] crab-fishing activity in Parnaíba River Delta, which illustrates the overlap between different dimensions of 'heritagisation of the vernacular past' (Timothy 2014). The research is based on ethnographic fieldwork undertaken over a period of 13 months between 2011 and 2014.

In the Parnaíba River Delta, the role of the crab fisherman has changed as a result of the expansion of tourism. In the past, the figure of the crab fisherman was subject to prejudice and negative stereotyping based on the conditions in which the fishermen were obliged to work, that is, on small sailing or rowing boats, exposed to the sun during the hottest hours of the day, in constant contact with the slimy surface of mangroves and with exposure to humidity and insects. This stereotype is currently being reassessed due to the increased revenue that the activity brings in, through its important role in the tourist image of the region. The collective image of crab fishermen has been reinvented and defined as a locally commoditised form of heritage. In parallel, the uça crab and the crab fishermen have changed from having economic subsistence roles to being emblems of cultural heritage identity. The tourism phenomenon has facilitated this conversion, revaluing the activity and mitigating the negative prejudice experienced by crab fishermen.

Thus, the chapter will focus on the commodification of crab fishermen as an example of the contemporary tendency to heritagise identity emblems in order to attract tourists. In this sense, not only is tourism being created, but also the image of a local and authentic identity based on crab fishing. The Crab Festival, in particular, has played a significant role in commodifying local heritage for regional and international tourism development.

The Parnaíba River Delta in the international tourist market

During the last few decades Brazil has experienced what has been called a tourism revolution. In 2003, during the ABAV Congress (Brazilian Association of

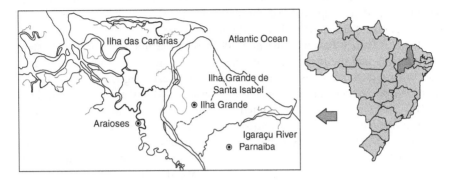

Figure 18.1 Parnaíba River delta
Source: de Andrade et al. 2014

Travel Agencies), former Federal President Lula da Silva asserted that the tourism industry needed to be treated as a 'Miss Brazil'. The region of Northeast Brazil has been part of this 'revolution', experiencing rapid tourism growth (Coriolano and Almedia 2007; Silva and Ferreira 2008, 2011; Cruz 2009, Dantas et al. 2010, Demajorovic et al. 2011, Aledo et al. 2013, Sousa et al. 2016). This tourism development has been driven mainly by public policies and foreign (predominantly European), capital investments in real estate tourism, which have also produced the phenomena of gentrification and rural emigration (Milano 2016).

The Parnaíba River Delta comprises an area of 2,700 km², embracing two Northeast states, Maranhão and Piauí. In the 1990s, the 66–km coastline of the State of Piauí received the initial tourism development and real estate investments. The 2000s saw the first foreign tourist and real estate capital and the establishment of services and tourism infrastructure on the Delta's main island, the 240 km² Ilha Grande of Santa Isabel (population 16,745 in 2012 (Comissão Ilha Ativa 2012)). The island harbour that gives access to the Parnaíba River Delta is the Port of Tatus. The fieldwork for this study has been focused on this island, Ilha Grande of Santa Isabel in Piauí State.

The infrastructural changes and the interest shown by real estate agents have promoted the inclusion of tourism in the political agenda of the region. Several events have marked the tourism development of the Parnaíba River Delta. These developments might be categorised into three stages. The first stage began in 1972 with the construction of the bridge connecting Ilha Grande of Santa Isabel with Parnaíba, the urban centre adjacent to the island. This clearly drove the urbanisation of Ilha Grande of Santa Isabel and established the pre-eminence of the Port of Tatus. After the 1970s, the island became the centre of trade relations, transport and communication between the mainland (Parnaíba urban area) and the other island societies of the Parnaíba River Delta. The urban and structural changes led to a reconfiguration between centre and periphery in economic and symbolic terms. The second stage began with the Federal Government's promotion of the Parnaíba River Delta for tourism, starting in 1990 but gaining intensity in the 2000s. The Port of Tatus in Ilha Grande of Santa Isabel was used as the principal point of access for tourist excursions into the Parnaíba River Delta. Based on its ecological and geographical features, the Federal Government listed the Delta as a tourist hotspot among Brazilian visitor destinations.

The third stage began in the mid-2000s with the initial foreign real estate investments and the purchasing of island land in order to promote residential tourism projects; this has resulted in land rights campaigns, rural gentrification and de-peasantisation (Cañada and Gascón 2016, Gascón 2016, Milano 2016). This stage has also promoted the entrance of new tourism agents that have produced structural and symbolic changes in some economic activities. The island's rural economy is based mainly on family farming, artisanal fishing, uça crab, prawn and other shellfish fisheries, straw, flax, carnauba and clay handicraft production, the construction industry and fruit picking. There are also extensive pastoral areas dedicated to animal husbandry and livestock. Fishing is the principal source of income for the islanders. The rest of this chapter will focus on one of the main activities that characterise the Delta region economy: uça crab fishing.

The evolution of the crab-fishing activity

As part of the tourism revolution experienced by the Northeast region, the uça crab has gone from being a subsistence product related to local demand and consumption to an emblem of identity and a tourist export product, with accompanying growth in collateral businesses like reselling and transport. Where the crab market was looked down upon, it is now considered a point of local pride and an identity symbol. In Northeast Brazilian tourist destinations, the uça crab is one of the attractions of local gastronomy and its commercialisation contributes to the economies of local bars and restaurants. In addition, cities such as Brasilia, Rio de Janeiro, São Paulo, Belem and, more recently, Manaus have also become important consumers of this product (Codevasf 2012). Crab fishing constitutes an important source of income for many island families, as well as embodying local identity.

The character of the fisherman is a stereotype associated with local islanders, the *ilha grandense* and, in the collective imagination, the Parnaíba River Delta is identified as the crab fishermen's land. As well as crab-based food, there are several musical compositions and poems that reveal the significance of the crab fishermen to the self-representation of the island culture. However, in the past, the figure of the crab fisherman implied a person without schooling and with a low social class (Milano 2015a). In part, this pejorative discourse was related to the way in which the activity was performed. Crab fishing in the Parnaíba River Delta is an individual and manual activity that takes place with the help of craft tools (*cambito*). These tools enable the locating of the crab holes, formed in the muddy soil, and the capture of the crabs. The fishermen reach the mangroves in small boats where they make smoky fires to get rid of mosquitoes. They are usually exposed to the sun all day, especially in the hottest hours, and work in direct contact with the muddy mangrove soil, unprotected and exposed to humidity and insect bites. Crab fishing differs from other river fishing activities. Boats tend to leave very early in the morning, depending on the tides, from several small harbour Delta access points. Normally, they return in the afternoon and deliver crabs to intermediaries and resellers. Mostly, the catch arrives at the Port of Tatus, where brokers and buyers load live crabs into trucks and transport them to different regional and urban tourist destinations. The neighbourhood, *Bairro dos Loquinhas* in Ilha Grande of Santa Isabel, ended up being labelled pejoratively 'the crab fisherman's neighbourhood' (Braga 2013). The name *Loquinha* was derived from the Portuguese word *loca*, which means the hole where the crabs live and hide. These factors have led to the low esteem of the fishermen among the local populace.

The average daily production of a Delta crab fisherman is 60 crabs. A unit of four crabs is usually sold for between 1 and 2.50 Brazilian Real. Obviously, these values are subject to market fluctuations and to factors such as size and season; in the high tourist season the price does increase. The crabs are then sold in touristic coastal destinations for between 12 and 20 Brazilian Real, which underlines the economic exploitation of the fishermen (Lustosa 2014). An island inhabitant[2] emphasised the difference from the past by claiming that, in the late 1990s and early 2000s, a fisherman would catch an average of 200 crabs a day while in 2014 the daily average oscillated between 30 and 80, depending on seasonal variables, the usable working hours and temporary regulatory fishing restrictions; however, crab fishing does ensure a steady income for a thousand island families. Another island inhabitant and the current secretary of tourism of the Ilha Grande of Piauí township[3] stated that a fisherman's daily catch was approximately 40 crabs. He also asserted that a unit of four crabs might reach the price of 6 Brazilian Real during the tourist high season (July and August) and that the annual average was between 2 and 3 Brazilian Real.

Despite the prejudice and stereotypes that crab fishermen have suffered over the years, the last decade has seen an increase in uça crab demand in the Northeast region due to the increase in the tourism market. At present, crab fishing is an important resource with a great social value and also a vital generator both of jobs and of the tourist image of the region. The biggest production of crabs comes from the Parnaíba River Delta region that covers the States of Maranhão and Piauí (Silva et al. 2014). It has been estimated that, over the last decade, the catch from there was approximately 21 million uça crabs per year (Legat et al. 2006b). Currently, the crab fisheries, as the principal source of income, absorb most of the manual labour in the Parnaíba River Delta. Around 20 communities in the region survive on the basis of this labour; around 2,500 families are dependent on the fishermen, intermediaries and resellers of Piauí, Maranhão and Ceará States (Lustosa 2014). However, uça crab over-exploitation has increased alongside the rise in tourist demand, particularly in relation to high crab commercialisation in neighbouring tourist markets (for example, in the State of Ceará and its capital Fortaleza). This has led to overfishing and a high crab mortality rate during exportation, threatening the environmental equilibrium and the stability of the productive activity.

Overfishing has been denounced by several Brazilian environmental institutions and organisations (for example, IBAMA, ICMBio and EMBRAPA[4]).
However, the pressure on crab-fishing activity has been intensified by mangrove
degradation and the lack of environmental controls. These have led to the viola-
tion of fishing restrictions during the peak fishing season, which overlaps the
crab breeding season. The annual breeding season occurs between the months of
December and May with a peak in January and February – the warmest months
of the year and a period of increased vulnerability in the life cycle of the crabs
when they leave their holes or *loca* for reproduction and spawning. This phenomenon is known as *andada* or *carnaval* (SEBRAE 2004). The high mortality
rate of crabs during export has been investigated by ecologists and academics
(Legat et al. 2006a, 2006b, 2007, 2009, Mota 2007, Araujo et al. 2011, among
others). According to environmental institutions, this can be approximately 40
to 60 per cent during capture, storage, transportation and commercialisation
(Codevasf 2012).

The State of Ceará, the largest consumer of crabs, has no production capability and is forced to buy from the Parnaíba River Delta. The total increase in crab
production in Brazil is mainly driven by that in Amapá and Maranhão States (and
specifically, the Parnaíba River Delta (MA/PI) and Bragança (PA)), which represent more than 75 per cent of the Brazilian mangrove forests. The States of Pará,
Maranhão and Piauí are the largest uça crab exporters and employ a large number of crab fishermen (Pinheiro and Boos 2016). According to Legat and Legat
(2009), almost all crabs caught in Piauí are consumed in the Piauí coastal municipalities and the capital Teresina, with the rest consumed in Fortaleza (CE) and
other capital states. The uça crab, as previously mentioned, is one of the attractions of the local Northeast gastronomy and regional cuisine and is sold mostly on
the tourism market and locally on a small scale (in hotels and restaurants) in the
big cities and coastal destinations (Legat and Alves 2011); in Teresina (PI) and
Fortaleza (CE), for instance, crabs are usually sold at restaurants and hotels on a
Thursday. The so-called 'Crab Day' is considered an important custom by locals
and tourists, especially in the holiday season (Codevasf 2012). The latter varies
according to tourist profile: July and August, for European tourist flows, and,
for domestic tourists, between December and February (which includes Carnival,
although this might also occur in March), as well as Easter and public holidays
throughout the year. The crab, which is one of the attractions of the local cuisine,
is offered as a much-appreciated appetiser in the tourist areas of the Northeast
region, thus sustaining the economy of bars and restaurants. The city of Fortaleza
is the main consumer market; during some months of the year a restaurant at the
Praia do Futuro in Fortaleza may sell approximately three thousand crabs in a
day (Araujo et al. 2011).

The agents involved in the crab market include, among others, fishermen,
government agents, environmental institutions, intermediaries, buyers and consumers. But it is the latter that imposes the market demand, creating an imbalance
in local ecologies. Over the last decade another set of forces feeding the economic

market and configuring the dynamics of production and consumption has come into play: heritage and symbolic crab consumption.

The heritagisation of crab fishing: the Crab Festival

The role of the crab fisherman has changed over the last decade and acquired new symbolic value in the region's tourist imagery. The celebration of the Crab Festival has played an important part in this scenario, promoting regional and international tourism and attracting many visitors. However, tourism and the Crab Festival, together, have produced a mesh of agents that directly and/or indirectly are involved in resource exploitation.

The Crab Festival, celebrated in Ilha Grande of Santa Isabel, has played a noteworthy role in the promotion of local heritage tourism, attracting many tourists since the first event in 2006. The festival has led to reflection on the relationship between local heritage and its appropriation by the tourism industry. It was not by chance that, for the first Crab Festival in 2006, the *Loquinha* neighbourhood changed its name to São Vicente de Paula neighbourhood, in order to create a new branding image and encourage a wider territorial marketing perspective (Mansilla 2016), so aiding the recovery from earlier prejudice regarding the crab fishermen's neighbourhood. In addition, the crab represents an export product to other destinations and a resource that allows the diversification of the local tourist offering, as well as encompassing the commodification of heritage and the culinary tourism market.

In this scenario tourism is part of postmodern and post-industrial society, within which tourists demand instant fulfilment in heritagescapes shaped by the tourism sector (Burns et al. 2010). The crab may be understood as an artefact with a changing heritage (in that there is not an absolute heritage), a product of historical period, narrators and context (Santana Talavera 2010). Based on texts relating to the European presence in Brazil, the Brazilian anthropologist, Carmen Sílvia de Moraes Rial (2005), identifies the historical importance of food in the country and its link with national identity. However, Jesús Contreras (2005) considers cultural identity and/or heritage as new 'resources' of modernity with a polyvalent use; products now embody and evoke a territory, a landscape, customs and identity. More cases of the interwoven relationship between tourism and heritage in rural contexts are described elsewhere (Gascón and Milano 2017). Within the logic of profitability, heritage is converted into goods, due to their glamour and their characteristics as consumable objects. In this scenario, culinary heritage is strongly related to tourism promotion; for instance, according to Daniel et al. (2008), the importance of lobster culture and fishing heritage events on the Gulf of Maine has been a significant motivation for the promotion of the coastal Maine tourism experience.

The concept of 'gastrodiplomacy' (the use of culinary culture as a means to carry out public diplomacy and raise the awareness of the country brand through foreign policy) is also linked to this phenomenon. Gastrodiplomacy helps to increase soft power, the power of attraction; in other words, it seeks to win hearts and minds through stomachs (Rockower 2012). Although the prevalence of gastrodiplomacy as an instrument of governance is associated mainly with Asian countries, the promotion of national cuisine is also being explored in other regions of the world, particularly Latin America. Peru (Wilson 2011) and Mexico (Pilcher 1998) already view gastronomic culture and food as crucial elements in the representation of collective identity and country brand building. Culinary culture for tourism is offered through gastronomic itineraries, routes and events. In Brazil, a great variety of events organised around local or specific products is held, mainly in the low season, alongside festivals and fairs with the characteristics of 'traditional' holidays (Medeiros and Santos 2009). One example is the Crab Festival in Ilha Grande of Santa Isabel. This festival reflects the trend of converting cultural heritage into one of the pillars of governmental cultural policies and public administration; heritage becomes an industry under development (Contreras 2005). The Crab Festival is promoted by the local municipality in partnership with the Brazilian Micro and Small Business Support Service (SEBRAE). Referring to the political use of heritage, an island inhabitant complained that the festival organisation was carried out by government agencies, while the crab fishermen were excluded from this: 'they don't have a seat at the table' and 'they made fishermen the mascot of the celebration'. In other words, 'they use us to liven up the party'.[5]

The festival usually takes place over a weekend in November and offers a wide range of products, including crab dishes, as well as a schedule of performances of traditional folk dances and theatre productions (*bumba meu boi, pastorinhas* and crab dances). The event is presented as a most important manifestation of gastronomy, local culture and ethnic traditions (Milano 2015b). The menu consists of traditional and regional dishes, many prepared with crab and characterised by tropical, colourful, and diversified ingredients, as well as being highly nutritious and tasty. Some of these dishes are: rice with beans and crab (*baião de três*), desserts based on crab (*doce de caranguejo*), crab pancake (*panqueca de caranguejo*), beans with crab *(feijão tropeiro de caranguejo),* pumpkins and sweet potatoes (*moranga or abóbora*), cracked crabs (*caranguejo toc-toc*), crab claw with sauce (*pata de caranguejo ao molho*), crab couscous and crab cooked in salt water, tomatoes, onions, garlic and coriander (crab *moqueca*). Among the activities scheduled during the festival, there are tourist excursions, music shows, local cultural presentations, culinary competitions, beauty contests, music concerts, and trade, gastronomic and handicraft fairs. According to local government statistics, during the three days of the 2015 Festival approximately 30,000 visitors were registered. Increasing visitor numbers have driven the development and economic growth of the region (Barroco and Barroco 2008). Barring the negative impact of overfishing, the Crab Festival is currently considered a strategic opportunity to hedge against tourism seasonality and drive the island's economy.

Despite the diversity of different tourism-scholarship traditions (Milano 2017), tourism and cultural heritage are closely interrelated. In many cases, the existence of the tourism industry has led to the heritagisation of food and local resources, while food heritagisation may also serve to encourage rural tourism promotion and regional development (Bessière 2013). From a marketing and management perspective, the idea that food identity might lead to the development of new tourism products and promote destination brand identity has been observed by Lin et al. (2011). The value of cultural goods consists, on the one hand, of social practices and, on the other, of interests inherent in the dynamics of the market. Tourism, in its consumerist logic, reinvents cultural heritage (de Almeida 2011). The relationship between heritage and tourism is, of course, not new; heritage has always been the first, or one of the first, reasons to purchase a tour (Prats 1999). The case of the Crab Festival demonstrates how culinary tourism and heritage commodification may merge and reinvent themselves. The festival is part of the processes of adaptation and conversion that affect all destinations which diversify their tourist offerings.

In the Parnaíba River Delta, the temporal coincidence between the first celebration of the Crab Festival in 2006, the advance of public tourism promotion policies (in 2005), and the toponymic change of the crab fisherman's neighbourhood *Loquinha* into São Vicente de Paula, should be noted. There was a clear public interest in cleaning up the image and promoting tourism through culinary and events tourism. In this scenario, cultural heritage was appropriate as an attractive tourist resource and an engine for economic development. The value of cultural heritage, as a new economic dimension, lies in its ability to capture tourist flow (de Almeida 2011). The Crab Festival is an event that responds to the logic of diversification of tourist offerings, based on the rehabilitation and commodification of a local natural resource, the crab.

The symbiotic relationship between tourism and heritage, however, tends to modify the latter and adapt it to the demands of the former. This may lead to the reinterpretation of heritage and the identities related to it (Santana Talavera 2010), as in the case of the crab fisherman's image, which has been modified, adapted, reinterpreted and framed as 'typical' and 'traditional' (Contreras 2005). At the same time, the rise in demand for crabs, and the successful Crab Festival celebrations, have favoured the consolidation of the crab fisherman as an emblem of 'local and island identity', although one islander expressed a doubt in this regard: 'The Crab Festival is directed at contemporary culture and to enhance the value of the crab fishermen. I don't know if they are valued'.[6] The tourist revolution in the Northeast region of Brazil, the increase in demand for uça crabs in neighbouring states, the federal public tourism promotion and the development of the first touristic infrastructures open up new scenarios concerning local heritage use and consumption.

Conclusion

This chapter has focused on the commodification of crab fishermen as an example of the heritagisation of identity emblems in order to attract tourists. Furthermore, the revalorisation of the crab fisherman's stereotype through the rise of tourism and the Crab Festival has been observed. Thus, it is not only tourism that is being created, but also the image of an occupational identity based on crab fishing.

In addition, island vegetable resources such as carnauba and cashew nuts, and animal resources such as crab and shrimp, have become export goods. According to Macleod (2004), the development of locally sourced economic production alongside the rise of tourism has led to an increase in aesthetic value, which is contributing to the emergence of speculative products and leisure areas; for instance, the sea, the Delta landscape and the soil are now objects of new social uses.

It has been assumed by some that economics, planning, impact studies and even anthropology might not influence the tourist industry in late capitalist systems (Burns et al. 2010). However, it is clear that we are now witnessing a heritagisation phenomenon, within which tourism is being reinvented and redesigned for the latest contemporary cultural heritage uses. The crab and the crab fishermen of Northeastern Brazil are examples of the tourism-driven valorisation of identity emblems and cultural heritage. In conclusion, however, the importance of tourism as a 'name of power' (Nogués-Pedregal 2016) over local resources should not be overlooked. Tourism might revalorise local cultural heritage, giving it an aesthetic and economic value, but at the same time apply undue market and socio-environmental pressures on it.

Notes

1 (Linnaeus, 1763) (Crustacea, Brachyura, Ocypodidae).
2 Personal communication with an island-dweller (Ilha Grande 15/03/2014).
3 Telephone interview (Barcelona 15 June 2017).
4 Brazilian environmental institutions: EMBRAPA (Brazilian Agricultural Research Corporation); ICMBio (Chico Mendes Institute for Biodiversity Conservation); IBAMA (Brazilian Institute of the Environment and Renewable Natural Resources).
5 *Na geral eles não opinam, não direcionam as coisas. O catador é colocado dentro para poder puxar a festa* (Interview with an island-dweller, December 2011).
6 *O festival do caranguejo é direcionado muito à cultura de hoje e a questão da valorisação do catador de caranguejo. Mas eu não sei se isso é valorisado* (interview with an island-dweller, December 2011).

References

Aledo, A., Loloum, T., Ortiz, G., and García-Andreu, H. (2013) El turismo residencial internacional en el nordeste de Brasil: un análisis de partes interesadas. *Revista Española de Investigaciones Sociológicas*, 142(1): 3–23.

de Almeida, M. G. (2011) Festas rurais e turismo em territórios emergentes. *Scripta Nova. Revista Bibliográfica de Geografía y Ciencias Sociales*. v. XV, n. 919.

de Andrade, E. B., Leite, J. R. S. A., and de Andrade, G. V. (2014) Anurans from the municipality of Ilha Grande, Parnaíba River Delta, Piauí, Northeastern Brazil. *Herpetology Notes*, 7: 219–226.

Araujo A.J.G., Brandão C.O., Carvalho, F.C.T. and Vieira R.H.S.F. (2011) Qualidade microbiológica do caranguejo-uçá exposto à venda em três pontos na orla da Praia do Futuro, Fortaleza – CE – Brasil. *Boletim do Instituto de Pesca*, 37(4): 409–416.

Barroco, L.M.S. and Barroco, H.E. (2008) A importância da gastronomia como patrimônio cultural, no turismo baiano. *Turydes revista de investigación en turismo y desarrollo local*, 1(2).

Bessière, J. (2013) 'Heritagisation', a challenge for tourism promotion and regional development: an example of food heritage. *Journal of Heritage Tourism*, 8(4): 275–291.

Braga, D.S. (2013) Catadores de caranguejo do Delta do Parnaíba: estereótipos, lutas simbólicas e preconceitos (1960–2010). *Vozes, Pretérito & Devir: Revista de historia da UESPI*, 2(1): 336–342.

Burns, P.M., Palmer, C. and Lester, J.A. (eds.) (2010) *Tourism and Visual Culture: Theories and Concepts* (Vol. 1). London: CABI.

Cañada E, and Gascón, J. (2016) Urbanizar el paisaje: turismo residencial, descampesinización, gentrificación rural. Una introducción, in J. Gascón and E. Cañada (eds.) *Turismo residencial y gentrificación rural*. PASOS, Revista de Turismo y Patrimonio Cultural. Colección PASOS edita, nº16, pp. 5–36.

CIA, Comissão Ilha Ativa. (2012) *Sóciobiodiversidade da Ilha Grande de Santa Isabel: Um olhar da comunidade visando à RESEX do Cajuí*. (ed.1) Ilha Grande/PI. (Cartilha).

Codevasf, Companhia de Desenvolvimento dos Vales do São Francisco e do Parnaíba (2006) *Plano de ação para o desenvolvimento integrado da bacia do Parnaíba: síntese executiva: território da planícielitorânea*. CODEVASF Brasília, DF: TDA Desenho & Arte Ltda.

Contreras, J. (2005) Patrimônio e globalisação: o caso das culturas alimentares, in A.M. Canesqui and R.W.D. Garcia (ed.) *Antropologia e nutrição: um diálogo possível*. Rio de Janeiro: Fiocruz, pp. 129–145.

Coriolano, L.N.M.T. and de Almeida, H.M. (2007) O turismo no nordeste brasileiro: dos resorts aos núcleos de economía solidária. *Scripta Nova. Revista Electrónica de Geografía y Ciencias Sociales*, vol. XI, núm. 245 (57).

Cruz, R. de C.A. (2009) Los nuevos escenarios del turismo residencial en Brasil: un análisis crítico, in T. Mazón, R. Huete and A. Mantecón (eds.) *Turismo, urbanización y estilos de vida: Las nuevas formas de movilidad residencial* (pp. 161–174). Barcelona: Icaria.

Dantas, E.W.C., Ferreira, A.L. and Clementino, M. do L. M. (2010) *Turismo e Imobiliário nas metrópoles*. Rio de Janeiro: Letra Capital.

Daniel, H., Allen, T., Bragg, L., Teisl, M., Bayer, R. and Billings, C. (2008) Valuing lobster for Maine coastal tourism: methodological considerations. *Journal of Food Service*, 19(2): 133–138.

Demajorovic, J., Aledo A. and Landi, B., (2011) Complejos turísticos residenciales: análisis del crecimiento del turismo residencial en el Mediterráneo español y en el litoral nordestino (Brasil) y su impacto socio-ambiental. *Estudios y perspectivas en Turismo*, 20(4): 772–796.

Gascón, J. (2016) Residential tourism and depeasantisation in the Ecuadorian Andes. *The Journal of Peasant Studies*, 43(4): 868–885.

Gascón, J. and Cañada, E. (2016) *Turismo residencial y gentrificación rural*. PASOS, Revista de Turismo y Patrimonio Cultural. Colección PASOS edita, nº16.

Gascón, J. and Milano C. (2017) *El turismo en el mundo rural ¿Ruina o consolidación de las sociedades campesinas e indígenas?* PASOS, Revista de Turismo y Patrimonio Cultural. Colección PASOS edita, nº18.

Legat, J.F.A., Legat, A.P., Pereira, A.M.L., Góes, J.M. and de. Góes, L.C.F. (2006a) *Caranguejo-uçá: métodos para captura, estocagem e transporte*. Teresina: Embrapa Meio-Norte, p. 25. (Embrapa Meio-Norte. Documentos, 139).

Legat, J.F.A., Mota, R.I., Puchnick, A., Bittencourt, C., and Santana, W.S. (2006b) Considerations about Ucides cordatus cordatus fishing in the Parnaíba River Delta region, Brazil. *Journal of Coastal Research*, 39: 1281–1283.

Legat, J.F.A. and Legat, A.P. (2009) Metodologia para o transporte de caranguejo vivo combaixos índices de desperdícios. *Boletim Técnico Científico do CEPENE*, Tamandaré, PE, 17(1): 115–121.

Legat, J.F.A. and Alves, M.C.A. (2011) *Sabores do Delta: Tradições culinárias e espécies capturadas pela pesca artesanal no Delta do Rio Parnaíba*. Teresina: EMPRABA Meio-Norte.

Lin, Y.C., Pearson, T.E. and Cai, L.A. (2011) Food as a form of destination identity: A tourism destination brand perspective. *Tourism and Hospitality Research*, 11(1): 30–48.

Lustosa, A. H. M. (2014) Caracterisação do ambiente natural e cultural dos catadores de caranguejo da RESEX Delta do Parnaíba. *Revista Vox Musei arte e património*, 2(3): 120–130.

Macleod, D.V. (2004) *Tourism, Globalisation, and Cultural Change: An Island Community Perspective*. Bristol: Channel View Publications.

Mansilla, J.A.M. (2016) Urbanismo, privatización y marketing urbano. La Barcelona neoliberal a través de tres ejemplos. *Encrucijadas-Revista Crítica de Ciencias Sociales*, 11, 1102.

Medeiros, M.L. and Santos, E.M. (2009) Festivais Gastronômicos em Belo Horizonte – MG: Considerações sobre os reflexos gerados nos empreendimentos envolvidos. *Revista de Cultura e Turismo*, (2): 81–93.

Milano, C. (2015a) *'Eran bichos de siete cabezas'. Una isla del Delta del Parnaíba (Brasil) en la mira de la promoción turística transnacional*. PhD dissertation. Universidad Autónoma de Barcelona.

Milano, C. (2015b) La movilización de lo étnico en las prácticas turísticas del delta del Parnaíba (Brasil), in I. Verdet and Y. Onghena (eds.) *En tránsito: voces, acciones y reacciones*. CIDOB Barcelona Centre for International Affairs, pp. 177–191.

Milano, C. (2016) Campesinos y pescadores ante la promoción del turismo residencial en el Delta del Parnaíba (Brasil), in Gascón, J. and Cañada E. (eds.) *Turismo residencial y gentrificación rural*. PASOS, Revista de Turismo y Patrimonio Cultural. Colección PASOS edita, nº16, pp. 61–80.

Milano, C. (2017) Otherness Anthropologies: toward Ibero-American Anthropologies of Tourism. *American Anthropologist*, 119(4): 736–741.

Mota, R. I. (2007) Método primitivo de transporte do caranguejo-uçá compromete sustentabilidade do estoque. *Revista Brasileira de Engenharia de Pesca*, 2(1): 76–79.

Nogués-Pedregal, A. M. (2016) Entre el lentisco y la jara. Cinco conclusiones socio antropológicas sobre el turismo. *Quaderns de l'Institut Català d'Antropologia*, (32): 29–50.

Pilcher, J. (1998) *Que vivan los tamales: Food and the making of Mexican identity*. Albuquerque: University of New Mexico Press.

Pinheiro, M. and Boos, H. (2016) *Livro Vermelho dos Crustáceos do Brasil. Avaliação 2010–2014*. Porto Alegre, RS: Sociedade Brasileira de Carcinologia – SBC.

Prats, L. (1997) *Antropología y Patrimonio*. Barcelona: Ariel.

Rial, C.S. de M. (2005) Brasil: primeiros escritos sobre comida e identidade, in Canesqui, A. M., and Garcia, R. W. D. (Ed.) *Antropologia e nutrição: um diálogo possível*. Rio de Janeiro: Fiocruz, pp. 87–100.

Rockower, P.S. (2012) Recipes for gastrodiplomacy. *Place Branding and Public Diplomacy*, 8(3): 235–246.

Santana Talavera, A. (2010) Patrimonio cultural: ¿entre diferenciación y cohesión identitaria? in C. Bataillou (coor.) *Tourismes, Patrimoines, Identités, Territoires*. Presses Universitaires de Perpignan, pp. 23–33.

SEBRAE, Serviço Brasileiro de Apoioàs Micro e Pequenas Empresas (2004) Diagnóstico sócio-econômico e produtivo dos catadores de caranguejo de Araioses-MA. *São Luis,* p. 64.

Silva, T.F.A., dos Santos Fogaça, F.H., Vieira, S.G.A., Ferreira, I.A., dos Santos Filho, L.G.A., Magalhães, J.A. and Legat, J.F.A. (2014) Physicochemical and Sensory Quality Attributes of the Mangrove Crab, *Ucides Cordatus,* from the Parnaíba River's Delta Environmental Protection Area. *Arquivos de Ciências do Mar,* 47(1): 102–109.

Silva, A.F.C. and Ferreira, L.A. (2008) Três momentos da urbanisação turística: estado, mercado e desenvolvimento regional no Nordeste brasileiro, 1997–2007. *Scripta Nova – Revista Electrónica de Geografia y Ciências Sociales.* Vol. XII, núm. 270 (89).

Silva, A.F.C. and Ferreira, L.A. (2011) O imobiliário-turístico e o nordeste brasileiro: dinámicas econômicas e urbanas sobre o litoral. *Revista Geográfica de América Central, Número Especial EGAL,* Costa Rica II Semestre, pp. 1–15.

Sousa, P. G. D., Matias, E. and Selva, V. S. (2016) From residential tourism to tourist real estate complexes: the appropriation of the coastal zone in the Northeast of Brazil by tourist real estate activities. *Ambiente & Sociedade,* 19(3): 177–198.

Timothy, D.J. (2014) Contemporary cultural heritage and tourism: Development issues and emerging trends. *Public Archaeology,* 13(1–3): 30–47.

Wilson, R. (2011) Cocina peruana para el Mundo: Gastrodiplomacy, the culinary nation brand, and the context of national cuisine in Peru. *Exchange: The Journal of Public Diplomacy,* 2(1): 13–20.

19 Creating biocultural heritage for tourism

The case of mycological tourism in Central Mexico

Humberto Thomé-Ortiz

Introduction

Biocultural heritage is a social-historical construction, housing the biological and cultural memory of human groups (Toledo 2012) through a legacy that contains the natural wealth and variety of languages, cultures and products (Toledo and Barrera Bassols 2008), including foods such as wild edible mushrooms. It is a collectively constructed heritage, which is fundamental to peasant economies and is transmitted from generation to generation. The gathering of wild foods is part of the cultural tradition of different social groups around the world (Cunningham 2001), enabling the survival of populations in many different regions (Fernández 2006). At the same time, the practice illustrates the processes of co-evolution between humans and nature, based on a relationship between ecological and cultural factors (Berkes et al. 2000).

Lévi-Strauss (2004) has explored the cultural role of mushrooms, following on from the work of Wasson and Wasson (1957) on social attitudes towards mushrooms. From his study are derived the notions of 'mycophilic' and 'mycophobic' peoples. His main finding is the identification of the fundamental role that mushrooms have played in civilisations. Primitive forms of worship of mushrooms, and the use of hallucinogenic mushrooms, have been identified in almost all mycophilic peoples (Lévi-Strauss 2004). According to Anna Lowenhaupt (2015), mushroom gathering today shows the persistence of pre-capitalist ways of life, alongside the importance of new activities such as tourism and the gourmet food trade. Thus, two forms of economic logic overlap, based on interactions between the global and the local.

The reasons for identifying wild edible mushrooms as an example of biocultural heritage are several, but a key aspect is their contribution to the family economy and the food security of gatherers (Mariaca et al. 2001). In addition, there are other important heritage markers: the traditional ecological knowledge developed around the mushrooms (Pacheco et al. 2015), their presence in traditional cuisines (Santiago et al. 2016) and the reproduction of mushroom gathering practices, through collective and intergenerational learning (Knight 2014).

Mycological tourism is a form of rural tourism in which nature and culture converge, based on collecting, tasting and learning about wild edible mushrooms. In the case of Spain this activity is a tool for rural development and a regulatory mechanism for non-timber forest resources (Thomé-Ortiz 2015). Different case studies of mycological tourism throughout the world (De Castro 2009, De Frutos, Martínez and Esteban 2011, Knight 2014, Thomé-Ortiz 2015, Thomé-Ortiz 2016, Jímenez-Ruiz et al. 2016) reveal a contemporary expression of mycophilic societies, based on the reinterpretation of mushrooms as tourist capital in the context of globalisation (Beck 1998). These examples illustrate how mycological resources are constructed as biocultural heritage and are then commoditised to encourage exchanges of capital through tourism. In order to build a coherent and unified tourism experience, this type of tourism serves as a mechanism for regulating mycological resources. In the same vein as other research (Tzanelli 2013), the present case explores the dominant discourse of capitalism, through the 'cosmopolitan spirit's' view of endogenous resources. The example of mycological tourism illustrates the ability of capital to appropriate the beliefs, knowledge and practices of mushroom gatherer communities and transform them into products that can be reproduced and consumed as objects of cultural consumption.

The aim of this chapter is to identify the social, economic and environmental implications of a link between mycological tourism and biocultural heritage. Mycological tourism illustrates the penetration of capitalist logic into rural areas through the new meanings attached to mushrooms, which were traditionally a common good, a product for self-consumption and a contributor to social cohesion. The identification of mushroom heritage as a tourist product has turned them into capitalisable resources through tourism and new social dynamics have emerged around them. The study of the relationship between traditional ecological knowledge about mushrooms, on the one hand, and tourism, on the other, opens up a new heritage perspective in terms of the creation of a biocultural heritage in response to the logic of the tourist market.

The chapter begins with a discussion of ethnoecology as a framework for mycological tourism. This is followed by a consideration of the development scenarios for this tourism mode and a case study of a Matlatzinca community in central Mexico from the perspective of local mushrooms gatherers. The creation of biocultural heritage for tourism is identified through the analysis of praxis, corpus and cosmos. Finally, conclusions are presented.

Ethnoecology and biocultural heritage: towards a framework for the analysis of mycological tourism in Mexico

Mexico is considered the third country in the world in terms of biocultural wealth (Toledo, et al. 2010). It is the cradle of Mesoamerican civilisation, where 15 per cent of the species that make up the current world food system were domesticated (CONABIO 2008). This represents a historical legacy of more than 9,000 years. In countries like Mexico the use of wild edible mushrooms (even for recreational purposes) occurs within the context of traditional ecological knowledge (Berkes et al. 2000). The latter is the knowledge that a social group develops with respect to specific resources within their environment. Normally, this knowledge is developed around a particular resource, through a linguistic code developed to name and describe aspects such as species, habitats and seasonal appearance (Ruddle 1993). According to Toledo (2001), biocultural heritage is a set of knowledge, practices and beliefs (corpus, praxis and cosmos) that express a civilising process. In the case of mushrooms, the gathering (praxis) is associated with a body of knowledge (corpus) and beliefs (cosmos), in a system where each dimension feeds back to the others (Toledo and Barrera 2008). The theoretical perspective in which the concept of biocultural heritage is framed is ethnoecology, which explores the practices of gathering wild resources within clearly identified socioecological systems (Toledo and Barrera 2008).

Many of the territories where biocultural heritage exists fall into the category of Protected Natural Areas (Boege 2008). The objective of these areas is the preservation and care of natural resources that, despite their protected status, are often linked to tourism projects (Elizondo and Lopez-Merlin 2009). Some heritage conservationists regard biocultural resources as bastions to be preserved. However, there are also debates about the interpretation, commercialisation, planning and appropriation of biocultural heritage as a potential strategy for economic development (Nuryanti 1996). A critical perspective on the reproduction of biocultural heritage as a tourism resource is needed, through the link between heritage and capitalism. This would expose social asymmetries and ambivalences in the processes of appropriation, exploitation and interpretation of biocultural heritage as a tourist resource (Tzanelli 2013).

Since biocultural heritage is dynamic and changing (Voeks and Leony 2004), its appropriation for tourism has become one of the ways in which it has adapted to the economic restructuring of the countryside. Some writers highlight the importance of traditional ecological knowledge for the development of tourism activities in rural areas (Butler and Menzies 2007, Bennett et al. 2012). Biocultural heritage is an element that certainly affects the tourism potential of rural areas (Buhalis 2000). Mycological resources, seen as tourist capital, become attractive as they respond to needs for leisure and recreation, linked to nature and culture. The fact that mushroom gathering is a way of life that is not common to most humans is what increases their interest as a tourist attraction. Productive transformations therefore express the coexistence of prevailing traditions and processes of change within a logic of continuity and rupture (Ochoa and Ladio 2015). In countries like Mexico, where mushrooms have always been linked to gatherers and their culture (Moreno and Garibay 2014), it is necessary to approach their use in tourism from an ethnoecological perspective, since the resources are also a central element in the food security and health of rural communities, particularly in the face of climate change and concomitant economic uncertainty.

Biocultural heritage is therefore a cardinal concept that inextricably merges the biological and cultural components of mycophilic communities. As such, it is an essential element in the design of any heritage tourism proposal (McKercher and Du Cross 2002). It is fundamental to start with the biocultural axiom (Nietschmann 1992), according to which the relationship between biodiversity and culture is expressed as a symbiotic and interdependent conservation process; hence the importance of the use of a resource such as wild edible mushrooms for tourism being compatible with the logic of traditional ecological knowledge.

The recreational use of wild edible mushrooms and local development scenarios

The marginal role of wild edible mushrooms within markets in Mexico is associated with the fact that it is a resource dependent on uncontrollable variables such as climate and inter-species collaboration. The overlapping of two divergent production logics, tourism and mushroom gathering, highlights the interaction between human and nonhuman factors (Lowenhaupt 2015) and the necessity to maintain a balance between the principles of tourism planning and the gathering of an unpredictable wild product. It should, of course, be added that mushroom gathering is not always a pecuniary activity; it is often governed by the logic of exchange and self-consumption within contexts of marginalisation and poverty. This fact justifies the importance of analysing the role that tourism may play in the conservation of biocultural heritage as well as in contributing to an improvement in living conditions for the holders of this heritage (Jolliffe 2003; Jolliffe and Mohamed 2009). The tourist appropriation of the mycological resources of the indigenous peoples of Mexico demands a meticulous analysis of the concept of development on which the heritigisation of these resources, previously used exclusively for food, is built. One of the central purposes in studying the relationship between biocultural heritage and tourism is to identify whether heritage tourism may be a tool for rural development (Butler and Menzies 2007), or whether it simply reflects a process of capitalist appropriation of local resources, previously the exclusive domain of indigenous communities.

Mycological tourism in Mexico illustrates the social construction of biocultural heritage, created (*ex profeso*) and recreated (*ex novo*) to meet the demands of new market niches. In turn, the biocultural meanings of mushrooms show ruptures and continuities between the implications they have for the daily lives of gatherers and the expectations of tourists. The logic of gathering for subsistence overlaps the logic of cultural consumption and entertainment, through the fact that some species of mushrooms have become a 'culturally colorful global commodity' (Lowenhaupt 2015: 40) while, at the same time, a high valuation has been accorded to natural landscapes of exceptional beauty where the mushrooms are collected.

A consideration of the relationship between tourism and mycological culture makes it possible to identify a set of emerging links between capitalist enterprise, agriculture, forestry, anthropology, ethnoecology, and the production of scientific knowledge and, more broadly, between wild edible mushrooms and post-consumer societies (Choy et al. 2009). Thus the study of mycological tourism affords a view of the relationships between culture, natural resources and people, which are central to debates on the use of strategic resources for food and ecological purposes. It also highlights local-global connections, in particular the question of whether it is possible to preserve biocultural heritage within the logic of capitalism (Anderson 2015).

Figure 19.1 Mushroom gathering

An interest in wild foods is not considered to contradict a philosophical and material focus on intensive agriculture (Verinis and Williams 2016), since in situations of crisis (material, spiritual or philosophical) human beings have often returned to gathering as a survival resource (Lowenhaupt 2105). Today, the recreational gathering of wild edible mushrooms has different meanings, but they converge in the pressing need for a reconnection with nature experienced by urban societies. The design of recreational activities related to mycological culture may fulfil several objectives beyond the generation of economic income, such as environmental education or the dissemination of mycological culture. The development of mycological tourism implies that the gatherers develop new knowledge, techniques and ways of organising their work, since the revaluation of wild edible mushrooms and their gatherers constitutes a particular perspective on rural life. The original meanings of gathering mushrooms must be reinterpreted in order to connect rural life and the capitalist world.

Because the use of wild edible mushrooms in Mexico is closely linked to specific ethnic groups and their traditional ecological knowledge, the present work adopts an ethnomethodological perspective, with particular emphasis on ethnomicology. To this end, a qualitative case study was developed (Stake 2000), where the aim was to identify the relationships between biocultural heritage and mycological tourism. The ethnographic method was useful in understanding how biocultural heritage, and its meanings, are transformed through being a structural component of tourism, which is itself a defining practice of contemporary life (Palmer 2009).

The case of mycological tourism in a Matlatzinca community in Central Mexico

San Francisco Oxtotilpan is a community belonging to the municipality of Temascaltepec in the State of Mexico, located at a height of 2,634m above sea level. It has a population of 1,435 inhabitants of which 671 are men and 764 are women (INEGI 2010). In this community live the last descendants of the Matlatzinca ethnic group, whose culture formed the foundation of the civilisation established in the Valley of Toluca (Central Mexico). This ethnic group was evangelised in the seventeenth century by Franciscan missionaries (García 2004). The climate here is temperate subhumid, with rains in summer and an average annual temperature of 15 degrees Celsius. The main ecosystem is *abbies religiosa* forest, which is the type of vegetation with the highest productivity and concentration of wild edible mushrooms in central Mexico (Burrola et al. 2013). The favourable environmental conditions for the production of these mushrooms, combined with an ethnic group that has maintained a continuous occupation of the territory since the twelfth century, have resulted in the establishment of a strong mycological culture in the area (García 2004).

Two types of land tenure predominate in the community: ejido and communal lands. The territory extends to 1,516.14 hectares, distributed among 178 owners. The community lies within the Area of Protection of Flora and Fauna of the Volcano Nevado de Toluca; consequently there are restrictions on forestry and agriculture, including animal husbandry. For this reason tourism has been actively promoted as a local development strategy, compatible with the objectives of conservation. In 2014, the Alternative Tourism Program in Indigenous Areas of the National Commission for the Development of Indigenous Peoples invested in the construction of a complex of cabins and a restaurant to promote the development of tourism in the territory (Thomé-Ortiz 2016). However, this infrastructure

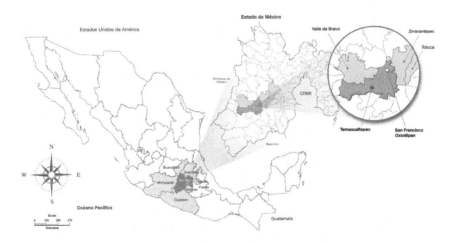

Figure 19.2 Location of San Francisco Oxtotilpan, Central Mexico

has been under-utilised, being limited to the provision of occasional accommodation and food services, due to the lack of a comprehensive tourism strategy. The community has therefore sought alternative product-based strategies, related to endogenous resources. One of the proposed activities, mycological tourism, is a unique enterprise, taking advantage of the tourist market of the Metropolitan Zone of Mexico City, the fourth largest metropolis in the world (Ward 1998).

The case study addressed the perspective of 22 gatherers with extensive knowledge about the identification, gathering and/or preparation of mushrooms. They all belonged to the Matlatzinca ethnic group. The informants were selected using a non-probabilistic snowball technique (Goodman 1961). The saturation criterion was used, so that the number of informants was increased to the point where the incorporation of new data did not provide a significant increase in new knowledge (Eisendhardt and Graebner 2007). The aspects covered during the interviews were the social construction of wild edible mushrooms as a biocultural heritage and the perceptions of the gatherers regarding various uses of these mushrooms, including for tourism.

The praxis, corpus and cosmos of wild edible mushrooms: ruptures and continuities between tourism and biocultural heritage

Praxis

Mushroom gathering is an activity that takes place in Matlatzinca families, particularly those that live in mountain and hillside areas. Many previous studies have investigated both the regulation that mushrooms provide to the ecosystem and the food supply generated by these resources in the rainy season. However, there are few studies that consider the cultural importance of mushrooms (Millenium Ecosystem Assessment Synthesis Report 2005). For the Matlatzinca people, as for others (Knight 2014), mushroom gathering is a recreational practice as well as a source of food. It may take place alongside agricultural, forestry or livestock activities, when the advantage is seized to take some mushrooms home to eat. Alternatively, the people may make long excursions (of up to two days) with the sole purpose of gathering diverse species.

Wild edible mushrooms are part of the food landscape and culinary taste of the Matlatzincas, so the predominant use of them is for food, as evidenced by the 15 typical dishes based on mushrooms that were identified during the research. Due to the seasonal and temporary nature of the resource, it is common practice for the species that are most prized to be dried for storage and used throughout the year. According to Garibay and Ruan (2014), mushrooms make an important economic contribution to the gathering families; in the case of the Matlatzincas, however, this resource is a good of consumption and exchange as there is no sale of mushrooms in the community or in the markets of nearby cities. Recently, small mycological tourism trips have been developed as a new practice to generate income for the gatherers, but insufficient time has passed for the risks and

Figure 19.3 Preparation of mushroom soup in a traditional matlatzinca kitchen

opportunities presented by such tourism to be analysed fully. The incorporation of mycological tourism, however, generates a potential gap between the current and the traditional uses of mushrooms. The initiative lies outside the community, representing one aspect of the global trend for productive restructuring of the countryside (Woods 2007), which serves as the starting point for the commercial and touristic uses of certain species of mushrooms.

One of the reasons for promoting mycological tourism is the lack of ability to generate value around mushroom gathering, which barely reaches minimum subsistence level for the forager families. This lack of economic value also influences the abandonment of the activity by the young, leading to a loss of knowledge associated with mushroom gathering. It is believed that adding value to mushroom gathering through new practices will encourage the preservation of this biocultural heritage (Anderson 2015, Lowenhaupt 2015, Verinis 2016).

Corpus

The Matlatzincas have developed a complex system of knowledge about 25 species of wild edible mushrooms. This includes aspects such as a traditional nomenclature (referring to the morphological characteristics of the species, the ecosystems where mushrooms grow and the plant species within those ecosystems) and the location, uses, identification and abundance of mushrooms (Pacheco et al. 2015). These aspects are fundamental both to traditional gathering practices and to new activities such as tourism. The knowledge is restricted to small local groups, is transmitted from generation to generation, and comprises a form of

Figure 19.4 Morel gathering in the forest

cultural capital (Bourdieu 2001), acquired through the investment of time by gatherers; in no sense should mushroom gathering be considered an easy activity or one suitable for the uninitiated. Practices and knowledge are interdependent. For the continuity of gathering practices it is necessary to have a traditional ecological knowledge base, while this knowledge can only be kept alive to the extent that it is reproduced through the practices. A characteristic of this type of knowledge is that it is dynamic (Ramírez et al. 2014), which allows it to adapt to the demands of globalisation. In this case, the local knowledge can be used to develop species identification guides, to design mycological trails, to promote good gathering practices and to provide guidelines for the interpretation of mycological resources and a mushroom based cuisine.

Cosmos

The set of beliefs built around the mushrooms has a close relationship with the personal identity of the gatherers and the tourists. Many of the collected histories about mushrooms are derived from memories of Matlatzinca gatherers. There is an important relationship between the availability, abundance, distribution and quality of the mushrooms and the ways in which Matlatzincas identify the state of health of the environment; for example, a good harvest means that it was a year of good rains. Mushrooms are perceived as living beings, closely related to the land and the trees, which gives them an important place within the hierarchy of ingredients that make up traditional Matlatzinca cuisine. It is important to emphasise that the perceptions, evaluations and beliefs of the collectors about the land as a supplier of mushrooms and about the value of mushrooms as special foods, their relationship with the health of the environment and their connection with local identity, are fundamental aspects in the maintenance of the traditional practices of gathering as well as in the construction of new cultural and economic uses like tourism.

The persistence of such biocultural memory expresses the validity of the relational worldview that characterises rural communities. Certainly, this belief base should be an important reference point for tourist practices that seek to meet spiritual needs through animistic visions of nature, which may have the potential to bring added meaning to the lives of tourists (Willson et al. 2013, Sharpley and Jepson 2011). On the other hand, mycological tourism collects together those people for whom mushrooms do have a very personal meaning, evoking emotions and memories, with those for whom they are only a food product. The practice of gathering is always viewed through the individual personal experience of tourists, being a postmodern act of mycophilia for people whose only chance of having contact with the mushroom world is through tourism (Knight 2014).

Conclusion

Biocultural heritage, based on biocultural wealth and associated knowledge, may be actively created and recreated for tourism purposes. This paper contributes to the discussion by documenting the ways in which biocultural heritage acts as a substantive input to the productive restructuring of the countryside in the context of cultural globalisation. The case study, investigated here, illustrates both the logic of capitalist appropriation of the endogenous resources of rural spaces and the processes of ambivalent change that variously induce both rupture and continuity in tradition and innovation. The tourist appropriation of the practices, knowledge and beliefs related to mushroom gathering reveals that tourism may lead to a transformation of the traditional practices, but also that the latter remain clearly based on local knowledge and beliefs about the mushrooms. Mycological tourism may therefore represent an opportunity for economic benefits (such as value added, job creation and productive diversification) while also maintaining the ancestral occupation of the gatherers. At the same time it involves risks, such as generating new social tensions around mushrooms, the potential trivialisation of mycological culture and the fragmentation of the forest. Despite this ambivalence, it is important to investigate whether mycological tourism can serve as a resilience strategy to preserve the cultural practices and wisdom needed to cope with the economic and cultural pressures faced by indigenous communities.

In a country like Mexico where there is significant biocultural wealth, the design of conservation and rural development policies requires a careful examination of the deep historical relationship between nature and culture. It is essential that tourism initiatives take into account the importance of the simultaneous preservation of natural resources and the cultural expressions that have given rise to the knowledge and sustainable use of these resources. The present study was limited to considering the perspective of mushroom gatherers concerning the creation of a biocultural heritage focused on tourism. Being limited also to one case study, the possibility of finding connections, perspectives and relationships between categories of analysis was smaller than if multi-sited ethnographic techniques had been developed (Palmer 2005). In future research it would be important to incorporate the vision of other social, institutional and economic actors, who play relevant roles in the co-production of biocultural heritage as a tourist resource, as well as to make comparisons with other cases presenting similar conditions.

References

Anderson, E. (2015) The Mushroom at the End of the World: On the Possibility of Life in Capitalist Ruins. *Ethnobiology Letters*, 6(1): 214–215.

Beck, U. (1998) *¿Qué es la globalización? Falacias del globalismo, respuestas a la globalisación.* Barcelona: Paidós.

Bennett, N., Lemely, R. H., Koster, R., and Budke, I. (2012) A capital assets framework for appraising and building capacity for tourism development in aboriginal protected area gateway communities. *Tourism Management*, 33: 752–766.

Berkes F., Colding J. and Folke C. (2000) Rediscovery of traditional ecological knowledge as adaptive Management. *Ecological Society of America*, 10(5): 1251–1262.

Boege, E. (2008) *El Patrimonio Biocultural de los Pueblos Indígenas de México*. México: Instituto Nacional de Antropología e Historia y Comisión Nacional para el Desarrollo de los Pueblos Indígenas.

Bourdieu, P. (2001) *Poder, derecho y clases sociales*. Bilbao: Desclée de Brouwer.

Buhalis, D. (2000) Marketing the competitive destination of the future. *Tourism Management*, 21(1): 97–116.

Burrola, C., Garibay, R. and Argüelles, A. (2013) Abies religiosa forests harbor the highest species density and sporocarp productivity of wild edible mushrooms among five different vegetation types in a neotropical temperate forest region. *Agroforestry Systems*, 87: 1101–1115.

Butler, C. F. and Menzies, C. R. (2007) Traditional ecological knowledge and indigenous tourism. In R. Butler and T. Hinch (eds.) *Tourism and Indigenous Peoples: Issues and Implications*. Oxford, UK: Butterworth-Heinemann, pp. 15–27.

Choy, T.K., Lieba, F., Hathaway, M.J., Inoue, M., Satsuka, S. and Lowenhaupt, A. (2009) A New Form of Collaboration in Cultural Anthropology: Matsutake Worlds. *American Ethnologist*, 36(2): 380–403.

CONABIO (2008) *Capital Natural de México. Volumen I Conocimiento actual de la biodiversidad, II Estado de conservación y tendencias de cambio y III Políticas y perspectivas de sustentabilidad.* México: Comisión Nacional para el Conocimiento y Uso de la Biodiversidad.

Cunningham AB. (2001) *Applied Ethnobotany: People, Wild Plant Use and Conservation.* London: Earthscan Publications Ltd.

Eisenhardt, K. and Graebner, M. (2007) Theory building from cases: opportunities and chalenges. *Academy of Management Journal*, 50: 25–32.

Elizondo, C. and López-Merlin, D. (2009) *Las Áreas de Conservación Voluntaria en Quintana Roo*. México: El Colegio de la Frontera Sur.

De Castro S. (2009) *Micoturismo: encuadramiento estratégico en áreas protegidas*. Tesis Doctoral. Portugal: Universidad de Técnica de Lisboa.

De Frutos P., Martínez, F. and Esteban, S. (2011) El turismo micológico como fuente de ingresos y empleo en el medio rural. El caso de Castilla y León. *Estudios de Economía Aplicada*, 29(1): 279–307.

Fernández, M.M. (2006) Economía y sistemas de asentamiento aborigen en la cuenca del río Limay. *Memoria Americana*, 14: 37–73.

García, A. (2004) *Matlatzincas*. México: Comisión Nacional para el Desarrollo de los Pueblos Indígenas.

Garibay, O. R. and Ruan, S. F. (2014) Listado de los hongos silvestres consumidos como alimento tradicional en México, in A. Moreno Fuentes and R. Garibay Orijel (eds.) *La Etnomicología en México. Estado del Arte*. México: Red de Etnoecología y Patrimonio Biocultural (CONACYT)-Universidad Autónoma del Estado de Hidalgo-Instituto de Biología (UNAM)-Sociedad Mexicana de Micología-Asociación Etnobiológica Mexicana, A.C.-Grupo Interdisciplinario para el Desarrollo de la Etnomicología en México-Sociedad Latinoamericana de Etnobiología, pp. 91–109.

Goodman, L. (1961) Snowball sampling. *Annals of Mathematical Statistics*, 32: 148–170.

INEGI, (Instituto Nacional de Estadística y Geografía) (2010) Censo de Población y Vivienda 2010. Principales Resultados por Localidad (ITER). *[En línea]*. Available at: www.inegi.org.mx/sistemas/consulta_resultados/iter2010.aspx [accessed 19 May 2017].

Jiménez-Ruiz A., Thomé-Ortiz, H. and Burrola, C. (2016) Patrimonio biocultural, turismo micológico y etnoconocimiento. *El periplo sustentable*, 29(30): 180–205.

Jolliffe, L. (2003) The lure of tea: history, traditions and attractions, in C.M. Hall, L. Sharples, R. Mitchell, N. Macionis, and M. Cambourne (eds.) *Food Tourism Around the World: Development, Management and Markets*. Oxford: Butterworth Heinemann, pp. 121–136.

Jolliffe, L. and Aslam, M. (2009) Tea heritage tourism: evidence from Sri Lanka. *Journal of Heritage Tourism*, 4(3): 331–344.

Knight, D. (2014) Mushrooms, knowledge exchange and polytemporality in Kalloni, Greek Macedonia. *Food, Culture and Society*, 17(2):183–201.

Lévi-Strauss, C. (2004) Los Hongos en la Cultura, in R. G. Wasson (eds) *Antropología Estructural Mito, Sociedad y Humanidades*. México: Siglo XXI Editores, pp. 212–213.

Lowenhaupt, A. (2015) *The Mushroom at the End of the World: On the Possibility of Life in Capitalist Ruins*. Princeton and Oxford: Princeton University Press.

Mariaca, M.R., Silva, P.L. and Castaños, M.C. (2001) Proceso de recolección y comercialización de hongos comestibles silvestres en el Valle de Toluca, México. *Ciencia Ergo-Sum*, 8(1): 30–40.

McKercher, B. and du Cros, H. (2002) *Cultural Tourism: The Partnership Between Tourism and Cultural Heritage Management*. New York: Haworth.

Millennium Ecosystem Assessment Synthesis Report (2005) *Ecosystems and Human Wellbeing: Synthesis*. Washington: Island Press.

Moreno, A. and Garibay, R. (2014) *La etnomicología en México. Estado del Arte*. México: Red de Etnoecología y Patrimonio Biocultural (CONACYT)-Universidad Autónoma del Estado de Hidalgo-Instituto de Biología (UNAM)-Sociedad Mexicana de Micología-Asociación Etnobiológica Mexicana, A.C.-Grupo Interdisciplinario para el Desarrollo de la Etnomicología en México-Sociedad Latinoamericana de Etnobiología, pp. 221–241.

Nietschmann, B. (1992) The interdependence of biological and cultural diversity. *Center for World Indigenous Studies*, 21: 1–8.

Nuryanti, W. (1996). Heritage and postmodern tourism. *Annals of Tourism Research*, 23(2): 249–260.

Ochoa, J. and Ladio, A. (2015) Current use of wild plants with edible underground storage organs in a rural population of Patagonia: between tradition and change. *Journal of Ethnobiology and Ethnomedicine*, 11(70): 1–14.

Pacheco, L., Rosetti, M., Montoya, A. and Hudson, R. (2015) Towards a traditional ecological knowledge-based monitoring scheme: a proposal for the case of edible mushrooms. *Bodivers. Conserv*, 24(5): 1253–1269.

Palmer, C. (2005) An ethnography of Englishness: experiencing identity through tourism. *Annals of Tourism Research*, 32: 7–27.

Palmer, C. (2009) Reflections on the practice of ethnography in heritage tourism, in M-L. S. Sørensen and J. Carman (eds.) *Heritage Studies. Methods and Approaches*. London: Routledge, pp. 123–39.

Ramírez, T. A., Montoya, E. A. and Caballero, N. J. (2014) Una mirada al conocimiento tradicional sobre los hongos tóxicos en México, in A. Moreno Fuentes and R. Garibay Orijel (eds.), *La Etnomicología en México. Estado del Arte*. México: Red de Etnoecología y Patrimonio Biocultural (CONACYT)-Universidad Autónoma del Estado de Hidalgo-Instituto de Biología (UNAM)-Sociedad Mexicana de Micología-Asociación Etnobiológica Mexicana, A.C.-Grupo Interdisciplinario para el Desarrollo de la Etnomicología en México-Sociedad Latinoamericana de Etnobiología, pp. 3–14.

Ruddle, K. (1993) The transmission of traditional ecological knowledge, in J.T. Inglis, (ed.) *Traditional Ecological Knowledge: Concepts and Cases*. Ottawa: International Program on Traditional Ecological Knowledge and International Development Research Centre, pp. 17–31.

Santiago, F., Moreno, J., Cázares, B., Suárez, J., Trejo, E., Montes de Oca, G. and Aguilar, I. (2016) Traditional knowledge and use of wild mushrooms by Mixtecs or Ñuu savi, the people of the rain, from Southeastern Mexico. *J Ethnobiol Ethnomed*, 12(1): 35.

Sharpley, R. and Jepson, D. (2011) Rural tourism: A spiritual experience? *Annals of Tourism Research*, 38(1): 52–71.

Stake, R. (2000) Case studies, in N. Denzin and Y. Lincoln (eds.) *Handbook of Qualitative Research*. London: Sage Publications, pp. 435–454.

Thomé-Ortiz, H. (2015) Turismo micológico: una nueva mirada al bosque. *Ciencia y Desarrollo*, 41: 14–19.

Thomé-Ortiz, H. (2016) Turismo rural y sustentabilidad. El caso del turismo micológico en el Estado de México, in F. Carreño and A. Vásquez (eds.) *Ambiente y patrimonio cultural*. Toluca: Universidad Autónoma del Estado de México, pp. 43–69.

Toledo, V. M. (2001) Biodiversity and indigenous peoples, in S. Levin et al. (eds.) *Encyclopedia of Biodiversity*. New York: Academic Press, pp. 1181–1197.

Toledo, V. (2012) *Red Etnoecología y Patrimonio Biocultural*. México: COANACYT

Toledo, V. and Barrera, N. (2008) *La memoria biocultural La importancia ecológica de las sabidurías tradicionales*. España: Icaria.

Toledo, V. M., Boege, E. and Barrera-Bassols, N. (2010) The biocultural heritage of Mexico: an overview. *Langscape*, 6: 6–10.

Tzanelli, R. (2013) *Heritage in the Digital Era: Cinematic Tourism and Activist Cause*. London: Routledge.

Verinis, P and Williams, R. (2016) The Mushroom at the end of the world: on the possibility of life in capitalist ruins. *Culture, Agriculture, Food and Environment*, 32(2): 131–135.

Voeks, R.A. and Leony, A. (2004) Forgetting the forest: assessing medicinal plant erosion in eastern Brazil. *Econ Bot*, 58: 294–306.

Ward, Peter. (1998) Future livelihoods in Mexico City: A glimpse into the new millennium. *Cities*, 15: 63–74.

Wasson, V. and Wasson, R. (1957) Mushrooms, Russia and history. *Pantheon Books 1 and 2*: 433.

Willson, G., McIntosh, A. and Zahra, A. (2013) Tourism and spirituality: a phenomenological analysis. *Annals of Tourism Research*, 42: 150–168.

Woods, M. (2007) Engaging the global countryside: globalization, hybridity and the reconstitution of rural place. *Progress in Human Geography*, 31(4): 485–507.

20 (Re)creating natural heritage in New Zealand

Biodiversity conservation and tourism development

*Guojie Zhang, James Higham and
Julia Nina Albrecht*

Introduction

It is widely stated that the transition from unrestricted exploitation of natural resources to a focus on sustainable development marks an important milestone in the development history of human civilisation (Pak 2013). In the field of heritage studies, reflections on environmentalism can be traced back to the 1972 UNESCO General Conference at Paris, where the concept of 'natural heritage' was clarified and promoted at the global level. Despite different criteria and guidelines in the production of natural heritage, the definition fundamentally expresses the willingness to cherish and preserve nature. As such, the scale and scope of natural heritage has been extended through new ways of exploring and understanding the natural world. From this starting point, the ongoing interpretation of natural heritage within various socio-cultural contexts is an essential task, one with significant implications for both heritage research and tourism development. With a focus on fenced ecosanctuaries, a group of projects which commit to the conservation and restoration of New Zealand pre-human ecosystems and species (mainly birdlife), this chapter aims critically to investigate how natural heritage is interpreted, protected and (re)created against the background of the global biodiversity crisis, in order to inform the role or roles that tourism may play both in reversing the biodiversity crisis and in (re)creating natural heritage.

The value of New Zealand biodiversity as natural heritage

It is generally accepted that natural heritage represents valuable and unique natural resources that are handed down from the past, conserved at the moment and gifted to the future (Papayannis and Howard 2007). In the twenty-first century in New Zealand, such precious natural resources are embedded in the magnitude and scope of its biodiversity. First officially defined in the 1992 Rio Earth Summit as a concept of resource management, the term 'biodiversity' is defined as 'the variability among living organisms from all sources including, inter alia, terrestrial, marine and other aquatic ecosystems and the ecological complexes of which they are part; this includes diversity within species, between species and of ecosystems' (Convention on Biological Diversity 1992: 3). The value of biodiversity to human well-being has been widely acknowledged and the prosperity of New Zealand should not be encouraged at the expense of its biodiversity status. For instance, a critical link between biodiversity and economic development can be found in New Zealand's nature-driven primary industries (e.g. agricultural and fisheries), which account for more than half of its total export earnings (The Treasury 2016). In addition, nature conservation and biodiversity are key contributors to the success of New Zealand nature-based tourism, in areas such as the World Heritage Areas (WHAs) of Te Wahipounamu and Tongariro National Park. Apart from safeguarding the stable production of food and water, nature conservation and biodiversity also contribute to people's well-being through many essential services, including but not limited to the regulation of ecosystem processes, nutrient recycling, pollination services, cultural and spiritual value and aesthetic experience (Dirzo and Mendoza 2008).

Beyond an anthropocentric assessment of the value of biodiversity, its intrinsic value has been increasingly noted through the lens of ethics and recognised in pieces of environmental legislation such as the Convention on Biological Diversity and the Protocol on Environmental Protection to the Antarctic Treaty (Fosci and West 2016). Thus, the precious nature of New Zealand biodiversity as natural heritage cannot be fully reflected through measures of economic or anthropocentric value. This is particularly so in the case of indigenous species and ecosystems in New Zealand, which, through a unique evolutionary history, make a great contribution to global biodiversity. A high proportion of the indigenous biodiversity in New Zealand is endemic and the disappearance of species means a loss for both New Zealanders and the rest of the world. As the Department of Conservation (2000: 2) observes, 'half a dozen islands in the Hauraki Gulf have a greater level of endemism than the whole of Britain'. Being one of the last places on earth where human beings settled, New Zealand was home to an array of rare biota in the setting of an isolated archipelago with no terrestrial mammalian predators. At least 80 per cent of native plant groups as well as 70 per cent of freshwater fish in New Zealand are found nowhere else in the world (De Freitas and Perry 2012, Goodman et al. 2014). New Zealand's native land mammals include only three types of bats and all of these are endemic (Simberloff 2013). With remarkable features, such as flightlessness, slow reproductive capacity and long-life span, a variety of New Zealand birds add a richness of colour to the ecology of the global avifauna and more than 70 per cent are indigenous (Guild and Dudfield 2009, Martin 2014).

New Zealand as a biodiversity hotspot

A geographical history characterised by the near-total absence of land mammals gave rise to a unique biodiversity in New Zealand. It also made New Zealand's native biodiversity (mainly bird species) highly vulnerable to the invasion of alien species, which resulted largely from human settlement. Within less than 1,000 years from the arrival of the first people, the clearance by fire of New Zealand native vegetation for pasture and farming had been carried out on a large scale on the two main islands (Bowman and Haberle 2010). About three-quarters of indigenous forest cover had been removed, which led to habitat loss and the extensive destruction of New Zealand pre-human biodiversity (Ewers et al. 2006). Worse still, alongside Māori and European colonisation, at least 31 mammal species were deliberately or accidentally introduced to New Zealand. Many of these mammals are notorious predators; they may appear socially or economically desirable but are ecologically devastating (King 1984).

The indigenous birds, lizards and invertebrates of New Zealand are particularly powerless when faced by introduced predatory mammals. Brown et al. (2015) highlight the plight of kakapo (*Strigops habroptilus*, i.e., night parrot) which are vulnerable to attack from ground-based mammalian predators (King 1984). The anti-predator strategy of this bird was effective for avoiding detection and predation from indigenous avifauna such as the Haast's eagle (*Harpagornis moorei*) but counterproductive to coping with the threat of introduced mammals. As well as the predation on native species, alien species also pose a significant threat to indigenous biodiversity through competition for resources, habitat destruction and spread of disease (e.g., bovine tuberculosis). It is estimated that New Zealand has the largest number of introduced mammals of any nation and at least 24,000 introduced plants (Garthwaite 2002). Eight widely distributed pest mammals on the three main islands of New Zealand have been identified by Parkes and Murphy (2003: 341): possums (*Trichosurus vulpecula*), hedgehogs (*Erinaceus europaeus*), Norway rats (*Rattus norvegicus*), ship rats (*Rattus rattus*), feral cats (*Felis catus*), feral sheep (*Ovis aries*) and red deer (*Cervus elaphus*). Given that one prominent feature of New Zealand indigenous wildlife is the rich and diverse birdlife, some of which is the focus of conservation recovery projects, the groups of possums, rats (*Rattus*) and stoats (*Mustela erminea*) are recognised as among the most destructive predatory species due to their devastating effects on New Zealand forest birds (Warburton and Gormley 2015).

Such realities not only put native fauna and flora at risk but also make biological invasion a main threat to the natural heritage of New Zealand. Today, at least 76 of 245 bird species that once existed in New Zealand have vanished, including 41 per cent of endemic species (Innes et al. 2010). Furthermore, many freshwater, terrestrial, and marine species have been facing the risk of extinction since 2005 (Ministry for the Environment and Statistics New Zealand 2015). Based on the New Zealand Threat Classification System 3,540 of 12,223 native species and other taxonomic units in New Zealand have been identified as 'threatened' or 'at risk' (Hitchmough 2013). In order to carry out the United Nations Convention on Biological Diversity (CBD) and review the progress towards meeting the 2020 Aichi Biodiversity Targets against the backdrop of Sustainable Development Goals (SDGs), the status of New Zealand biodiversity crisis has been updated in its Fifth National Report to the CBD. The report (Department of Conservation 2014: 3) acknowledges the conservation progress achieved on offshore islands and mainland protected areas and highlights consistent efforts in halting the decline of New Zealand biodiversity. Nevertheless, it also notes an 'ongoing deterioration in conservation status for many indigenous species'. Clearly, owing to the dependence of human beings on natural resources, the biodiversity crisis, which has resulted from habitat destruction, species invasion and potential climate change, exacerbated by unsustainable patterns in human development, is detrimental to human well-being at a global scale (World Wide Fund for Nature 2012). New Zealand, as a biodiversity hotspot, where a high density of endemic pre-human biodiversity is threatened predominantly by introduced invasive species, presents intriguing and challenging questions when considering which types of nature are defined as 'natural heritage', let alone in determining the conservation practices necessary for the (re)creation of rapidly vanishing nature.

Biodiversity conservation and fenced ecosanctuaries

New Zealand biodiversity, particularly the indigenous fauna and flora, is still in a state of decline. In recent years, progress has been slowly achieved through strategic and tactical shifts in conservation management. Notably, one overarching trend in New Zealand conservation strategy is a transition from a heavy reliance on the DOC to the pursuit of collaboration among various stakeholders (e.g. public–private partnerships), with an ultimate goal of deepening conservation as an essential element of New Zealand national identity (State Services Commission, The Treasury and the Department of the Prime Minister and Cabinet 2014). Such shifts are due, not only to the continuous underfunding of the DOC, but also to awareness that conservation success will not be achieved without wide public knowledge and engagement. Accordingly, a public–private partnership (PPP) approach has been increasingly adopted in the content and forms of conservation practice and more PPP-based conservation programmes are expected to be established in the future (Department of Conservation 2013).

It is estimated that there are at least 500 relatively pristine offshore islands that are less affected by human activities (Mortimer et al. 1996). Since the water surrounded by these islands can act as an efficient barrier to block the (re)invasion of introduced pests (particularly terrestrial mammals), they are considered to be an ideal conservation ark for indigenous fauna and flora. Introduced mammals have been completely removed from at least 100 offshore islands since 1916 (Towns et al. 2013), which has created a solid foundation for success in the species recovery projects of these islands and makes New Zealand stand out in island restoration worldwide (Bellingham et al. 2010). Inspired by this success, attention has now shifted to the conservation of the New Zealand mainland (i.e. North Island and South Island) (Department of Conservation 2016). An emerging conservation concept, mainland island projects, focuses on the restoration of habitats on the New Zealand mainland through creating and utilising 'island effects'. Against this background, one challenging, yet promising, approach to the recreation of natural heritage is the development of fenced ecosanctuaries, where endangered biodiversity is conserved and restored behind a pest-exclusion fence, cemented with community care and efforts.

Fencing for conservation is a common, yet efficient, approach to the protection and restoration of biodiversity resources. Usually, such an approach is committed to moderating conflicts between humans and nature, with a special focus on pre-venting poaching and reducing the negative impacts of alien species (Hayward and Kerley 2009). With respect to New Zealand fenced ecosanctuaries, the use of the fence is more likely to be the latter. Based on the first Sanctuaries of New Zealand workshop (Burns 2007), the common trajectory for New Zealand fenced ecosanctuaries can be summarised as follows: (1) employment and completion of pest-proof fence; (2) aim to achieve zero pest species (alien species) densities within the chosen area (3) reintroduction of missing biotic elements, including rare and endangered species; (4) direct and substantial community participation; (5) experiments to restore indigenous ecosystems; and (6) mitigation of substan-tial and permanent pest (re)invasion risk. Although pest-proof fencing has also been employed to block single pest species in UK and Australia (e.g. fencing for foxes or dingoes), the pest-proof fence in New Zealand ecosanctuaries is normally developed to target multiple pest species and is utilised together with multi-species eradication programmes, such as the aerial drops of 1080 poison (sodium fluoroacetate) (Connolly et al. 2009).

The development of fenced ecosanctuaries on mainland New Zealand can be traced back to the late 1990s; in the last decade the number of such projects has increased (Brooks 2011). Drawing on information from the Sanctuaries of New Zealand website, at least 35 fenced ecosanctuary projects could be identified as of February 2017 (see Tables 20.1 and 20.2). Some of the fenced ecosanctuary projects are located in discrete areas, whereas others are adjacent to each other (e.g. five projects based at Maungatautari). All the projects have completed the construction of fences and achieved, or intended to achieve, near-zero pest den-sities. It is worthy of note that completing the fences is only the first step in a 500-year or more vision to recreate a lost natural inheritance.

The (re)creation of natural heritage in fenced ecosanctuaries

While each fenced ecosanctuary represents a unique experiment to restore threatened nature, the natural heritage that is being recreated may generally be conceived as indigenous ecosystems and threatened species: endemic birds, reptiles, frogs, invertebrates and plants. The term 'ecosystem', first introduced by the British botanist Arthur Tansley (1871–1955), is 'a dynamic complex of plant, animal and micro-organism communities and their non-living environment interacting as a functional unit' (Convention on Biological Diversity 1992: 3). It is widely acknowledged that the emergence of this concept is largely due to a realisation that any conservation effort, either for species or protected areas, is futile without the recognition of this complex interrelatedness as a funda-mental feature of the natural world. In terms of fenced ecosanctuaries, from the coastal forest of Orokonui to the dryland of Mokomoko and from the mountains of Maungatautari to the peat lake complex of Rotopiko, many types of native ecosystem are being restored across New Zealand. Similarly, a desire to restore the ecosystem as closely as possible to its pre-human state is reflected in the vision of some ecosanctuaries. Since an authentic pre-human ecosystem is almost

Table 20.1 The pest-proof fenced ecosanctuary projects in North Island, New Zealand by February 2017

Site (North Island)	Location	Fence enclosed	Size (ha)	Fence length (km)	Visitor centre	Natural heritage highlight
1 ZEALANDIA Ecosanctuary	Wellington	1999	252	8.6	Yes	Indigenous biodiversity of Wellington region
2 Warrenheip Reserve	Waikato	1999	16	2.4	?	Kiwis
3 Rapanui Point	Taranaki	2002	1.0	0.4	?	Grey-faced petrel
4 Lake Waikaremoana	Te Urewera	2003	750	1.3	?	Kiwis
5 Southern Enclosure, Maungatautari	Waikato	2004	65	3.5	Yes	Indigenous biodiversity of Waikato region
6 Northern Enclosure, Maungatautari	Waikato	2004	35	2.8	Yes	Indigenous biodiversity of Waikato region
7 Tawharanui Open Sanctuary	Auckland	2004	530	2.7	?	Indigenous biodiversity of Auckland region
8 Tautari Wetland, Maungatautari	Waikato	2005	3.0	0.8	Yes	Indigenous biodiversity of Waikato region
9 Bushy Park Sanctuary	Manawatu-Wanganui	2005	98	4.7	No	Indigenous biodiversity of a lowland rain forest
10 Nick's Head Predator-Proof Enclosure	Gisborne	2005	35	0.6	No	Black-billed gull
11 Maungatautari Ecological Island	Waikato	2006	3,300	39	Yes	Indigenous biodiversity of Waikato region

No	Name	Region	Year				Description
12	Garland Covenant, Maungatautari	Waikato	2006	16	1.6	Yes	Indigenous biodiversity of Waikato region
13	Motu Kiwi Crèche	Gisborne	2006	1.4	0.5	No	Kiwis
14	Cape Sanctuary	Hawke's Bay	2007	2,200	9.5	?	Indigenous biodiversity of Cape Kidnappers peninsula
15	Opouahi / Panpac Kiwi Crèche	Hawke's Bay	2007	40	3.3	No	Kiwis and pateke (brown teal)
16	Rotokare Scenic Reserve	Taranaki	2007	229	8.4	Yes	Indigenous biodiversity of a natural wetland
17	Driving Creek Wildlife Sanctuary	Coromandel Peninsula	2008	1.6	0.5	Yes	Brown teal and kereru (New Zealand pigeon)
18	Shakespear Open Sanctuary	Auckland	2011	500	1.7	No	Indigenous biodiversity of Whangaparaoa Peninsula
19	Wairakei Golf and Sanctuary	Taupo	2011	150	5.0	?	Kiwis and Takahē (Notornis)
20	Omaha Shorebird Sanctuary	Auckland	2012	3.0	0.4	No	New Zealand dotterel and Variable oystercatcher
21	Lake Serpentine (Rotopiko) Sanctuary	Waikato	2013	10	1.4	No	Indigenous biodiversity of the Waikato peat lakes

Table 20.2 The pest-proof fenced ecosanctuary projects in South Island and other, New Zealand by February 2017

Site (South Island and other)	Location	Fence enclosed	Size (ha)	Fence length (km)	Visitor centre	Natural heritage highlight
1 Caravan Bush (Ellen Elizabeth Preece Conservation Covenant)	Pitt Island	2001	36	3.0	No	Chatham petrel and Chatham snipe
2 Riccarton House and Bush	Christchurch	2004	7.7	1.1	No	Kahikatea trees
3 Macraes Flat 1	Otago	2005	22	1.7	No	Grand skinks and Otago skinks
4 Dancing Star Foundation Preserve	Stewart Island	2005	160	2.1	No	Indigenous biodiversity of Stewart Island
5 Sweetwater Conservation Covenant	Chatham Island	2006	2.4	0.8	No	Chatham Island taiko and Chatham Island petrel
6 Macraes Flat 2	Otago	2007	11	1.3	No	Grand skinks and Otago skinks
7 Orokonui EcoSanctuary	Dunedin	2007	307	9.0	Yes	Indigenous biodiversity of Coastal Otago forest
8 Glenfern Sanctuary	Great Barrier Island	2008	230	2.1	Yes	Indigenous biodiversity of Great Barrier Island
9 Kaipupu Point Sounds Wildlife Sanctuary	Marlborough Sounds	2008	40	0.6	?	Indigenous biodiversity of Queen Charlotte Sound
10 Sooty Shearwater Conservation Project	Stony Bay, Banks Peninsula	2008	0.5	0.3	No	Sooty shearwater
11 Mokomoko Dryland Sanctuary 1	Alexandra	2009	0.3	0.2	No	Otago skinks
12 Hutton's Shearwater colony at Kaikoura Peninsula	Kaikoura Peninsula	2010	1.9	0.5	No	Hutton's Shearwater
13 Mokomoko Dryland Sanctuary 2	Alexandra	2015	14	1.6	No	?
14 Brook Waimarama Sanctuary	Nelson	2016	671	14.5	Yes	Indigenous biodiversity of Nelson region[1]

Note: [1] During June 2017, enquires about the basic information of each fenced ecosanctuary project have been emailed to a total of 29 relevant organizations that drive the sanctuaries. By the end of August 2017, a total of 17 replies had been received and recorded. Based on these replies, previous research of Burns et al. (2012) and Campbell-Hunt and Campbell-Hunt (2013) and existing sanctuary websites, Table 1 and Table 2 have been created to facilitate a better understanding of the natural heritage (re)creation and development of New Zealand fenced ecosanctuaries.

impossible to recreate using existing information and technology, a more likely outcome is the restoration of the degraded ecosystem to a 'healthy functioning state', where the prosperity of all the naturally existing species within could be guaranteed through symbiotic relationships (Innes et al. 2012). Considering the list of species shown in the Tables 20.1 and 20.2, many fenced ecosanctuaries are involved in the conservation and (re)creation of endangered native species, including a high proportion of endemic and iconic species such as kiwi (*Apteryx australis*) and silver fern (*Cyathea dealbata*).

In order to ensure successful (re)creation of natural heritage in the context of the biodiversity crisis, many fenced ecosanctuaries not only focus on the protection of individual species, but also take the approach of ecological restoration (Campbell-Hunt 2008). Being a relatively well-established concept in twenty-first-century conservation management practices, ecological restoration has been widely accepted as 'the process of assisting the recovery of an entire ecosystem that has been degraded, damaged, or destroyed' (Society for Ecological Restoration Science and Policy Working Group 2002: 2). With the enclosure of the fence, ecological restoration at a fenced ecosanctuary often involves intensive control or eradication of pest species and deliberate reintroduction of indigenous species that are missing from the original ecosystem. Although pest-proof fencing is a non-lethal pest-control method, it is often employed together with ordinary lethal control methods, such as trapping, poisoning and shooting. In the case of the ZEALANDIA ecosanctuary (formerly Karori Wildlife Sanctuary), for example, the eradication and monitoring of pest mammals have been undertaken through a combination of pest-control techniques (Campbell-Hunt 2002). As the process of ecological restoration is usually time-consuming, and the fenced ecosanctuary is an emerging concept in conservation science, a thorough understanding of the contribution it makes to the natural heritage still remains unclear. Nevertheless, in reviewing a series of practical research studies on conservation management, Burns et al. (2012) acknowledge the progress already achieved through fenced projects, including the protection of both known and unknown significant species and their territories, the undertaking of species translocation programmes and the facilitation of natural dispersal and population founding events.

In addition to the tangible natural heritage that is being recreated at the level of individual species and of entire ecosystems, the intangible natural heritage of fenced ecosanctuaries also merits attention. Being a relatively new concept, related to that of 'intangible cultural heritage', 'intangible natural heritage' first appeared as the main theme for the 2006 annual conference of the International Committee for Museums and Collections of Natural Heritage (NATHIST) in New Zealand. Although an agreed definition of 'intangible natural heritage' has not been reached, it is interpreted by Dorfman and Carding (2012: 172) as 'the environmental forces that create biological and geological entities, the phenomena that these entities produce, and their interactions with humans and human communities'. Notably, they emphasise that the environmental forces and phenomena only become intangible natural heritage when their relations to human experience are considered. In particular, the elements of intangible natural heritage potentially overlap with many other aspects, such as ecologic food chains, natural sound-scapes and people's perceptions and affections towards natural objects.

The development of fenced ecosanctuaries makes a great contribution to the (re)creation of the intangible natural heritage of New Zealand, especially through education projects relating to biodiversity conservation and the delivery of 'back-to-nature' experiences. Many fenced ecosanctuaries, for example, have education programmes designed for local schools. The Orokonui ecosanctuary in Dunedin is a relatively education-focused sanctuary where the visitor and educational centre was completed immediately following the completion of the fence system. During the 12 months up to March 2016, over 5,000 children and students participated in conservation education programmes at the sanctuary (Otago Natural History Trust 2016). As for 'back-to-nature' experiences, a wide range of bird songs and smells of indigenous plants at fenced ecosanctuaries have been increasingly reported in the newspapers, and online review websites, as significant elements enabling volunteers and visitors to embrace and learn about the natural world (Fox 2009, Meduna 2017).

Tourism development in fenced ecosanctuaries

Alongside ecological restoration as the key objective of fenced ecosanctuaries, successful implementation is dependent upon a sustainable balance of a sanctuary's ecological, economic and social objectives (Campbell-Hunt and Campbell-Hunt, 2013). Among these objectives, financial viability has been recognised as a key challenge. Since the operation of a fenced ecosanctuary involves high costs, from fence construction to ongoing pest monitoring and fence maintenance, financial viability has been identified as a prerequisite for the sustainable operation of a fenced ecosanctuary (Scofield et al. 2011). In order to achieve financial viability, some sanctuaries may receive temporary or ongoing funding support from government, sponsors and business organisations. However, the majority of fenced ecosanctuaries in New Zealand are community-led, non-profit organisations, which usually struggle with the dilemma of fulfilling social objectives with unstable revenue streams, and one-off funding offers only limited help in sustaining the time-consuming process of ecological restoration. Therefore, developing nature-based tourism in fenced ecosanctuaries is considered as an important revenue stream as well as being an opportunity to engage in conservation advocacy.

Many fenced ecosanctuaries are open to the public and some are equipped with a visitor centre (see Tables 20.1 and 20.2). Depending on the differing expectations placed on tourism as a revenue generator, a fenced ecosanctuary may obtain financial benefits from tourism operations through access and service charges, donations from conservation programmes and sales of souvenirs (Campbell-Hunt 2002). According to Campbell-Hunt and Campbell-Hunt (2013), one decisive element in viewing tourism as an important source of income lies in the geographical location of a fenced ecosanctuary. Particularly for those sanctuaries located in city centres or near urban areas (e.g. the ZEALANDIA ecosanctuary), tourism is generally regarded as a major revenue generator, due to the relative ease of nearby visitor markets. Conversely, the rural-based ecosanctuaries (e.g. Maungatautari Ecological Island) may not actively develop tourism to generate income, largely because their relatively hard-to-reach locations and inconvenient transportation have resulted in a comparatively lower tourist base. The four key tourism markets for fenced ecosanctuaries have generally been conceived as: international visitors, non-local visitors from New Zealand, local visitors, and school visits. Currently, domestic visitors have occupied the lion's share of the visitor numbers. Nevertheless, many operators foresee a niche in the international visitor market, providing fenced ecosanctuaries with an opportunity to achieve viable tourism revenue streams.

For fenced ecosanctuaries, dedicated to delivering sound conservation education and visitor experiences while at the same time ensuring the normal running of ecological restoration programmes, interpretation and visitor management are critically important. Little is known about how interpretation programmes should be appropriately framed in fenced ecosanctuaries. However, the time dimension has been suggested as a critical factor in interpretation programme design and delivery (Campbell-Hunt 2002). In particular, since ecological restoration usually takes time to be achieved (e.g. the 500-year vision of the ZEALANDIA ecosanctuary), offering visitors an experience of a healthy restored ecosystem characterised by rich indigenous wildlife is impossible in the early stages of the development of a fenced ecosanctuary. Therefore, interpretation programmes, such as guided tours, pamphlets, displays and websites, need to be carefully planned and delivered in order to meet visitor expectations and enhance the experience of recreation and education. If specific conditions are met, a wide variety of species translocation programmes can be selected and implemented during the development of a fenced ecosanctuary. Thus, despite a common theme of fenced ecosanctuaries approximating pre-human indigenous biodiversity, visitor experiences may be different, both within a fenced ecosanctuary and between different fenced ecosanctuaries, when different time periods and species translocation programmes are taken into account (Campbell-Hunt and Campbell-Hunt 2013). It may, therefore, be necessary for interpretation programmes to be constantly updated, in order to catch up with changes and increase potential visitor numbers and frequency of visits.

Owing to the paradoxical relationship between nature-based tourism and protected areas, a prerequisite for tourism operations at a fenced ecosanctuary is to avoid 'turning a sanctuary into a zoo' (Campbell-Hunt and Campbell-Hunt 2013: 190). Thus, both the management of entry points and the establishment of ecological management zones have been recognised as popular management techniques (Campbell-Hunt 2008). Specifically, due to an increased risk of pest reinvasion associated with tourism operation, visitors are usually asked to check their bags at the gate, while in the case of a sanctuary with vehicle access extra efforts are required to reduce the risk at the entry point. Some ecological management zones act as primary wildlife areas with no access to visitors, whereas others are areas of public use with various well developed walking tracks and facilities. As reported by Campbell-Hunt (2008), the overall tourism development in community-led fenced ecosanctuaries is still at an early stage. Very few fenced ecosanctuaries have achieved intended visitor numbers and forecast tourism revenue. However, by comparing two annual reports of the ZEALANDIA ecosanctuary, which has the longest experience of tourism development, over the span of a decade, it is noted that total visitor numbers have doubled from less than 60,000 (Wellington City Council 2006) to 125,849 (Karori Wildlife Sanctuary 2016). Thus, natural heritage (re)creation at a fenced ecosanctuary may benefit from tourism business. However, further research is required to shed light on the experiences of international visitors to fenced ecosanctuaries.

Conclusion

It has been argued in this chapter that an understanding of the biodiversity crisis is of critical importance to the interpretation, conservation and (re)creation of natural heritage in Aotearoa/New Zealand. Fenced ecosanctuaries, focused on intensive management of critically endangered biodiversity, are a relatively recent development in New Zealand conservation, but they have increased greatly in number over the past decade. In order to recreate lost heritage successfully, both at the level of individual species and that of complex ecosystems, many fenced ecosanctuaries have embarked on the path of ecological restoration. Since ecological restoration usually requires considerable time and effort to be achieved, the New Zealand fenced ecosanctuaries are still at an exploratory stage of a vision that will take 500 years or more to be realised. (Re)creating natural heritage at fenced ecosanctuaries is challenging and there are many questions to be addressed not only in the field of ecology but also in the areas of economics and sociology.

Tourism may be a critical contributor in facilitating the (re)creation of natural heritage at community-led fenced ecosanctuaries. However, to date, little attention has been given to tourist experiences and visitor management, so it is important for academics to address this gap and move the research agenda forward. For example, the (re)creation of natural heritage at fenced ecosanctuaries is shaped by specific interpretations of New Zealand's biodiversity crisis; how that crisis is narrated within a diverse range of socio-ecological contexts will significantly influence the experiences of tourists. Furthermore, since many fenced ecosanctuaries are actively seeking to attract international visitors, is it important to consider the role that international tourism may play in funding these intergenerational conservation programmes and how international visitors may engage with the ecological restoration projects that are already taking place in fenced ecosanctuaries. It is essential for these issues to be thoroughly addressed if the (re)creation of natural heritage at fenced ecosanctuaries is to benefit from the potential symbiosis of interests in conservation and tourism.

References

Bellingham, P. J., Towns, D. R., Cameron, E. K., Davis, J. J., Wardle, D. A., Wilmshurst, J.M *et al.* (2010) New Zealand island restoration: seabirds, predators, and the importance of history. *New Zealand Journal of Ecology*, 34(1): 115–136.

Bowman, D. M. and Haberle, S. G. (2010) Paradise burnt: how colonizing humans transform landscapes with fire. *Proceedings of the National Academy of Sciences*, 107(50): 21234–21235.

Brooks, D. (2011) Both sides of the fence. *Forest & Bird*, 340: 46–50.

Brown, M. A., Stephens, R. T., Peart, R. and Fedder, B. (2015) *Vanishing Nature: Facing New Zealand's Biodiversity Crisis*. Auckland: Environmental Defence Society.

Burns, B. (2007) *Introduction for Sanctuaries of New Zealand Workshop/Hui 2007*. [PowerPoint slides]. Available at: www.sanctuariesnz.org/documents/Burns2007intro. pdf [accessed 15 May 2017].

Burns, B. R., Innes, J. and Day, T. (2012) The use and potential of pest-proof fencing for ecosystem restoration and fauna conservation in New Zealand, in M. J. Somers and M. W. Hayward (eds.) *Fencing for Conservation: Restriction of Evolutionary Potential or a Riposte to Threatening Processes?* New York: Springer, pp. 65–90.

Campbell-Hunt, D. M. (2002) *Developing a Sanctuary: The Karori Experience*. Wellington: Victoria Link Ltd.

Campbell-Hunt, D. M. (2008) Ecotourism and sustainability in community-driven ecological restoration: case studies from New Zealand, in M. F. Schmitz and P. Diaz (eds.) *Tourism as a Challenge*. Southampton: WIT Press, pp. 13–22.

Campbell-Hunt, D. M. and Campbell-Hunt, C. (2013) *Ecosanctuaries: Communities Building a Future for New Zealand's Threatened Ecologies*. Dunedin: Otago University Press.

Connolly, T. A., Day, T. D. and King, C.M. (2009) Estimating the potential for reinvasion of mammalian pests through pest-exclusion fencing. *Wildlife Research*, 36(5): 410–421.

Convention on Biological Diversity (CBD) (1992) *Convention on Biological Diversity*. Secretariat of the Convention on Biological Diversity. United Nations Environmental Programme. Available at: www.cbd.int/doc/legal/cbd-en.pdf [accessed 14 May 2017].

De Freitas, C. and Perry, M. (2012) *New Environmentalism: Managing New Zealand's Environmental Diversity*. Dordrecht: Springer.

Department of Conservation (DOC) (2000) *New Zealand Biodiversity Strategy*. Available at: www.biodiversity.govt.nz/pdfs/picture/nzbs-whole.pdf [accessed 14 May 2017].

Department of Conservation (DOC) (2013) *Statement of Intent 2012–2017*. Available at: www.doc.govt.nz/Documents/about-doc/statement-of-intent-2012-2017/statement-of-intent-2013-2017.pdf [accessed 15 May 2017].

Department of Conservation (DOC) (2014) *New Zealand's Fifth National Report to the United Nations Convention on Biological Diversity: Reporting period: 2009–2013*. Available at: www.cbd.int/doc/world/nz/nz-nr-05-en.pdf [accessed 15 May 2017].

Department of Conservation (DOC). (2016) *Statement of Intent 2016–2020*. Available at: www.doc.govt.nz/about-us/our-role/corporate-publications/statement-of-intent-archive/statement-of-intent-2016–2020/ [accessed 15 May 2017].

Dirzo, R. and Mendoza, E. (2008) Biodiversity, in S. E. Jorgensen and B. Fath (eds.) *Encyclopedia of Ecology*. Oxford: Academic Press, pp. 368–377.

Dorfman, E. and Carding, J. (2012) Towards a unified concept of intangible natural heritage, in E. Dorfman (ed.) *Intangible Natural Heritage: New Perspectives on Natural Objects*. New York: Routledge, pp. 160–179.

Ewers, R. M., Kliskey, A. D., Walker, S., Rutledge, D., Harding, J. S. and Didham, R. K. (2006) Past and future trajectories of forest loss in New Zealand. *Biological Conservation*, 133(3): 312–325.

Fosci, M. and West, T. (2016) In whose interest? Instrumental and intrinsic value in bio-diversity law, in M. Bowman, P. Davies and E. Goodwin (eds.) *Research Handbook on Biodiversity and Law*. Cheltenham: Edward Elgar Publishing, pp. 55–78.

Fox, R. (2009) Orokonui: Eco of the present. *Otago Daily Times* [Online], 2nd November. Available at: www.odt.co.nz/lifestyle/magazine/orokonui-eco-present [accessed 14 May 2017].

Garthwaite, R. (2002) Beyond the vertebrates—what are the threats to forests in the con-servation estate from new organisms? *NZ Journal of Forestry*, 47(2): 10–11.

Goodman, J. M., Dunn, N. R., Ravenscroft, P. J., Allibone, R. M., Boubee, J. A., David, B *et al.* (2014) *New Zealand Threat Classification Series 7, Conservation status of New Zealand freshwater fish 2013*. Wellington: Department of Conservation.

Guild, D. and Dudfield, M. (2009) A history of fire in the forest and rural landscape in New Zealand: Part 1, pre-Maori and pre-European influences. *New Zealand Journal of Forestry*, 54(1): 34–38.

Hayward, M. W. and Kerley, G. H. (2009) Fencing for conservation: Restriction of evo-lutionary potential or a riposte to threatening processes? *Biological Conservation*, 142(1): 1–13.

Hitchmough, R. (2013) *Summary of changes to the conservation status of taxa in the 2008–11 New Zealand Threat Classification System listing cycle*. Available at: www. doc.govt.nz/Documents/science-and-technical/nztcs1entire.pdf [accessed 14 May 2017].

Innes, J., Kelly, D., Overton, J. M. and Gillies, C. (2010) Predation and other factors currently limiting New Zealand forest birds. *New Zealand Journal of Ecology*, 34(1): 86–114.

Innes, J., Lee, W. G., Burns, B., Campbell-Hunt, C., Watts, C., Phipps, H. *et al.* (2012) Role of predator-proof fences in restoring New Zealand's biodiversity: a response to Scofield et al. (2011). *New Zealand Journal of Ecology*, 36(2): 232–238.

Karori Wildlife Sanctuary (2016) *Zealandia Annual Report 2015 / 2016*. Available at: www.visitzealandia.com/Portals/0/Resources/201516%20Annual%20Report.pdf [accessed 11 May 2017].

King, C. M. (1984) *Immigrant Killers: Introduced Predators and the Conservation of Birds in New Zealand*. Auckland: Oxford University Press.

Martin, A. J. (2014) *Dinosaurs Without Bones: Dinosaur Lives Revealed by their Trace Fossils*. Cambridge: Pegasus Elliot MacKenzie Ltd.

Meduna, V. (2017) The great extermination: How New Zealand will end alien species, *New Scientist* [Online], 1 February. Available at: www.newscientist.com/article/mg23331110–600–how-new-zealand-hopes-to-get-rid-of-its-pests/ [accessed 5 May 2017].

Ministry for the Environment and & Statistics New Zealand. (2015) *New Zealand's Environmental Reporting Series: Environment Aotearoa 2015*. Available at: www.mfe. govt.nz/publications/environmental-reporting/environment-aotearoa-2015 [accessed 14 May 2017].

Mortimer, R., Sharp, B. and Craig, J. (1996) Assessing the conservation value of New Zealand's Offshore Islands. *Conservation Biology*, 10(1): 25–29.

Otago Natural History Trust. (2016) Otago *Natural History Trust Annual Report 2015–16*. Available at: https://orokonui.nz/upload/files/Annual%20Report%202016%20AGM. pdf [accessed 11 May 2017].

Pak, M. S. (2013) Environmentalism then and now: from fears to opportunities, 1970–2010. *Environmental Science & Technology*, 45(1): 5–9.

Papayannis, T. and Howard, P. (2007) Editorial: nature as heritage. *International Journal of Heritage Studies*, 13(4–5): 298–307.

Parkes, J. and Murphy, E. (2003) Management of introduced mammals in New Zealand. *New Zealand Journal of Zoology*, 30(4): 335–359.

Sanctuaries of New Zealand (2017) Available at www.sanctuariesnz.org/projects.asp; [accessed 8 February 2017].

Scofield, R. P., Cullen, R. and Wang, M. (2011) Are predator-proof fences the answer to New Zealand's terrestrial faunal biodiversity crisis? *New Zealand Journal of Ecology*, 35(3): 312–317.

Simberloff, D. (2013) *Invasive Species: What Everyone Needs to Know*. New York: Oxford University Press.

Society for Ecological Restoration Science & Policy Working Group (2002) *The SER Primer on Ecological Restoration*. Available at: https://nau.edu/uploadedFiles/Centers-Institutes/ERI/_Forms/Resources/ser-primer.pdf [accessed 15 May 2017].

State Services Commission, the Treasury and the Department of the Prime Minister and Cabinet (2014) *Review of the Department of Conservation (DOC)*. Available at: www. ssc.govt.nz/sites/all/files/pif-review-doc-july14.PDF [accessed 15 May 2017].

The Treasury (2016) *New Zealand Economic and Financial Overview 2016*. Available at: www.treasury.govt.nz/economy/overview/2016/nzefo-16.pdf [accessed 14 May 2017].

Towns, D. R., West, C. J. and Broome, K. G. (2013) Purposes, outcomes and challenges of eradicating invasive mammals from New Zealand islands: an historical perspective. *Wildlife Research*, 40(2): 94–107.

Warburton, B. and Gormley, A. M. (2015) Optimising the Application of Multiple-Capture Traps for Invasive Species Management Using Spatial Simulation. *PLoS ONE*, 10(3): e0120373.

Wellington City Council (2006) Karori *Wildlife Sanctuary Annual Report 2005 / 06 Review*. Available at: http://wellington.govt.nz/~/media/your-council/meetings/subcommittees/council-controlled-organisation-subcommittee/2006/11/08/files/karori_sanctuary_annual_review_2005_06.pdf?la=en [accessed 7 May 2017].

World Wide Fund for Nature (WWF) (2012) *Living Planet Report 2012: Biodiversity Biocapacity and Better Choices*. Gland: WWF.

Index